**Control theory and dynamic
games in economic
policy analysis**

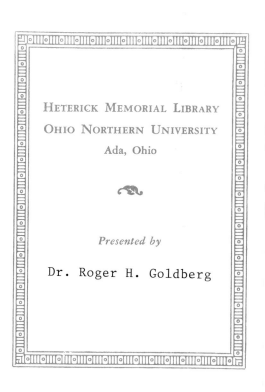

Control theory and dynamic games in economic policy analysis

MARIA LUISA PETIT

University of Rome 'La Sapienza'

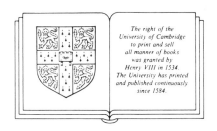

The right of the
University of Cambridge
to print and sell
all manner of books
was granted by
Henry VIII in 1534.
The University has printed
and published continuously
since 1584.

CAMBRIDGE UNIVERSITY PRESS

Cambridge
New York   Port Chester
Melbourne   Sydney

Published by the Press Syndicate of the University of Cambridge
The Pitt Building, Trumpington Street, Cambridge CB2 1RP
40 West 20th Street, New York, NY 10011, USA
10 Stamford Road, Oakleigh, Melbourne 3166, Australia

First published 1990

Photoset and printed by Interprint Ltd, Malta

British Library cataloguing in publication data
Petit, Maria Luisa
    Control theory and dynamic games in economic policy
    analysis.
    1. Economic planning. Mathematical techniques
    I. Title
    338.9′001′51

Library of Congress cataloguing in publication data
Petit, Maria Luisa.
    Control theory and dynamic games in economic policy analysis/
    Maria Luisa Petit.
        p.   cm.
    Includes bibliographical references.
    ISBN 0-521-38523-7
    1. Economic stabilization – Mathematical models. 2. Control
    theory – Mathematical models. 3. Economic policy – Mathematical
    models.   I. Title.
    HB3732.P48   1990
    338.9′001′51 – dc20   89 – 49255
                                            CIP

ISBN   0 521 38523 7
IP

To the memory of my parents

Contents

Figures

Tables

Preface

Economists today make increasing use of sophisticated mathematical methods for both theoretical and applied economic analysis. Though the use of mathematical tools is important for understanding and interpreting the underlying links between the economic variables and for providing rigour and precision to the definition of these economic relations, economists should never forget that they are using mathematics to interpret economics, and not the other way round. In other words, they should always keep in mind the economic meaning and implications of the mathematical methodology used in the analysis.

The task is not always easy. This book is an attempt in this direction. It is concerned with mathematical methods for the stabilization and control of an economic system and it tries to emphasize the links that exist between the 'traditional' theory of economic policy, pioneered by Frisch, Tinbergen and Theil in the fifties and sixties, and the developments of this theory based on advanced mathematical methods. The book aims to provide a unified basis for a *dynamic* theory of economic policy and deals therefore with applications of control theory and dynamic games to economic policy analysis.

It is addressed mainly to economists, rather than to mathematicians, since it aims to fill a gap between very specialized mathematical books, often difficult for economists to approach, and traditional books on economic policy which fail to take full account of the huge and important advances than can be made in economic policy analysis simply by using the appropriate mathematical tools available today.

The most interesting contribution offered by these mathematical methods is that they make it possible to analyse policy problems in a dynamic framework and therefore to extend most of the conclusions of the traditional static theory of policy to a dynamic setting. The importance of this extension can be easily understood if one simply thinks of the inherent dynamic characteristics of all types of economic planning.

The book covers both theoretical and applied policy analysis. It considers deterministic economic models and mathematical methods specified in continuous time. Limitation of space was one of the reasons for these choices. The use of a deterministic framework was also aimed to provide a simpler treatment and a clear view of the problems involved by avoiding the greater complications that necessarily follow the introduction of uncertainty. An important reason for the choice of the continuous-time formulation was the fact that all existing books on applications of control theory to macroeconomic analysis refer mainly to discrete-time models, while a very high number of theoretical, and an increasing number of empirical macroeconomic models are specified in continuous time.

Intellectual debts have obviously been accumulated during the preparation of this book. The most important one is due to Giancarlo Gandolfo, not only for carefully reading the entire manuscript and for his help in improving the text, but also for his invaluable guidance and encouragement during many years of collaboration. I am also very grateful to Mario Amendola, Tamer Basar, Sergio Bruno, Alain Haurie, Andrew Hughes Hallett and Alberto Isidori for their helpful comments and suggestions on different parts of the book. Derrick Plant went through the entire final version to check my English with patience and kindness.

Much of the research reported in this book was supported by grants from the University of Rome, the Ministry of Public Instruction and the Consiglio Nazionale delle Ricerche, for which I am grateful. I am also indebted to the publishers of Annales d'Economie et de Statistique, Economic Notes, Journal of Applied Econometrics and Journal of Economic Dynamics and Control for permission to use materials previously published in these journals.

Finally, to Anna Maria Olivari go my thanks for her expert secretarial work.

1 Introduction

1.1 The origins and evolution of control theory

Although some isolated applications of the feedback principle can be traced to the distant third century B.C. in Greece,[1] it was only in the eighteenth century in Europe that feedback control techniques were used at an industrial level. Some further applications of this type of control in the field of mechanics took place throughout the nineteenth century, followed by the first attempts to give a mathematical formulation to the control problem.

A systematic development of the subject, however, began in the United States around 1930, thanks to the work of mechanical and electronic engineers. The Second World War gave a substantial boost to the research in this field due to the large number of applications of control theory for military problems. It was in fact between the forties and the fifties that the so-called *classical theory* of control developed, a theory formulated in the frequency domain and based on the use of Laplace (or *z*) transforms as a method for analysing the input-output relationship of dynamic systems. A further impulse in the development of control theory took place in the second half of the fifties as shown by the important contributions to the solution of minimum energy problems related to missile launching. *Optimal* control theory started to take shape in this period, as did the first methods based on the state-space representation of dynamic systems.

It was in the second half of the fifties and during the sixties that the state-space approach was definitely consolidated. Kalman introduced the concepts of controllability and observability, which are central in all the subsequent evolution of control theory; Bellman and Pontryagin set down the basis for the development of the theory by introducing new methods for dynamic optimization. All these new advances form the core of the so-called *modern theory of control* and their applications refer not only to the engineering field, but also to economics, biology, medicine and the social sciences. It was also during this period that the most important applications of optimal control in the American space programme took place.

In economics, feedback control systems had already been considered in the fifties, first by Simon (1952) and Tustin (1953) and subsequently by Phillips in 1954 and 1957. These pioneering contributions, however, did not penetrate the main thrust of economic research, and the control theoretical approach was not followed up by economists. Exceptions were Allen (1956, 1967), Culbertson (1968) and Lange (1970). Some explanations as to the failure of these early efforts are discussed in Cochrane and Graham (1976) and Aoki and Leijonhufvud (1976).

It was not until the sixties that optimal control techniques were used in research on optimal growth theory. And we had to wait till the seventies to see the awaking of real interest in *macroeconomic* applications of optimal control methods, in both theoretical and empirical work. In that decade both econometric modelling and optimal control theory reached the necessary degree of maturity, and, at the same time, the software techniques needed to solve the large number of computational problems which arise in econometric applications of optimal control finally became widely available. The evidence of this fact is the great number of contributions on the subject which came to light throughout the seventies (see Kendrick, 1976).

Criticisms of the use of control methods for econometric policy evaluation were raised in the late 1970s by the new classical school and undoubtedly attenuated the initial enthusiasm. Paradoxically, however, dynamic optimization methods – although used in a different context – today constitute the main mathematical tools of the new classical macroeconomics. The use of these methods of analysis makes it possible to take into account the well-known Lucas critique of econometric policy evaluation, as we shall see in chapter 10. Therefore, both in the 'traditional' approach and in the 'new' approach, optimal control methods are still widely applied today in macroeconomic analysis.

1.2 Developments in dynamic game theory

Optimal control theory generally deals with decision processes in which, implicitly or explicitly, the assumption is made that decisions are taken by a single agent. If we abandon this assumption and consider the possibility that the control of a system depends on two or more decision-makers, we immediately enter the realm of dynamic game theory.

It follows that, just as optimal control deals with the intertemporal optimization of a given objective function that represents the preferences of a single economic operator, dynamic games deal with the intertemporal optimization of two or more functions which represent the preferences of two or more economic operators. It is therefore clear that dynamic game theory is more versatile than optimal control theory, since it makes it possible to describe a large number of different assumptions about the behaviour of the decision-makers, usually called 'players'. Thus, for example, a non-cooperative solution is appropriate to describe a decision process when the interests of the players are conflictual and there exists no possibility of agreement, whereas a cooperative mode of play is more appropriate to describe a case in which the possibility of communication and agreement is considered. Further assumptions concerning the behaviour and the information structure of the players can be made, giving rise to different solution concepts.

As stressed by Basar and Olsder (1982, p. 2) *dynamic* game theory can be viewed as the offspring of game theory and optimal control theory. Its history therefore reflects the history of these theories.

The theory of games was born with von Neumann's 1928 and 1937 papers, though some papers by Borel in the early twenties already anticipated its fundamental lines. But it was the celebrated book by von Neumann and Morgenstern (1944) that definitely laid the grounds of game theory and contributed to its diffusion in the context of economic theory. Conflicting situations like those described in a game had already been considered before by economists like Cournot (1838) and subsequently by Amoroso (1921), Bowley (1924), Edgeworth (1925), Frisch (1933) and von Stackelberg (1934), in the framework of duopoly theory. This is an indication of how economic theorists were in search of a rigorous methodological framework for the study of strategic interdependence. The interrelationships between individual decisions and the uncertainty about the decisions of others are essential features of economic problems, and game theory provided the required tools to deal with them. The first applications of this theory were mainly addressed to microeconomics, since game theory made it possible to go beyond the assumption of perfect competition in conventional microeconomic analysis. The following comparison is illuminating: 'In a neoclassical decision problem the outcomes in which the agent is interested (a) depend only on his own choices, and (b) depend on his own choices in a known way. It is as if the only game in the world were Solitaire, and all the cards were face up' (Bacharach, 1976, p. 3).

Economic applications of game theory in the fifties were still related to oligopoly theory, but, in the sixties, as a consequence of Shubik's important paper of 1959, general equilibrium theory became a fertile field of application. Another important source of interest in game theory came in the seventies from social-choice literature, and games were applied to investigating questions of institutional analysis.[2] Although economics is one of the main areas of application of game theory, this theory is increasingly attracting the attention also of other disciplines such as aeronautics, biology, politics and sociology.

Game theory is generally characterized by a set of finite strategies, and the description of the game can be made through two different formulations: the *extensive* (tree) form and the *normal* (matrix) form (see, for example, Luce and Raiffa, 1957; Shubik, 1982). Optimal control theory that, as we have seen, developed independently and in parallel, considers sets of infinite strategies and derives optimal decisions from the maximization (minimization) of intertemporal objective functions in the framework of dynamic models described by difference or differential equations.

Dynamic game theory follows the analytic approach and uses the mathematical tools of optimal control theory in the context of the conflicting behavioural assumptions which characterize the theory of games. The same (cooperative and non-cooperative) solution concepts described in game theory are therefore redefined in the context of dynamic games (see, for example, Starr and Ho, 1969a and b; Simaan and Cruz, 1973a and b). Furthermore, the same kind of problems concerning the introduction of uncertainty in optimal control theory are reformulated in the framework of dynamic games, giving rise to *stochastic games* (see, for example, Basar and Olsder, 1982, chapters 6 and 7).

Nowadays, research in game theory, optimal control theory and dynamic game theory evolves simultaneously and in parallel, in such a way that developments obtained in one of these three fields of research very often contribute to the enrichment and development of the other two.

The use of game theory in *macroeconomic* analysis was very rare in the past,[3] notwithstanding the fact that the problems of decentralized policy decisions and lack of coordination between policy-makers were well known (see Mundell, 1962) and constituted a typical case of conflictuality of decisions, for which game theory was clearly the appropriate mathematical tool.

The situation is very different today; furthermore, dynamic games have made it possible to analyse conflictual situations by making use of *dynamic* macroeconomic models. The first applications of dynamic game theory to economic policy problems belong to the second half of the seventies (Kydland, 1975, 1976; Pindyck, 1976, 1977) and are related to the problem of decentralized policy decisions. Since then, the use of dynamic games in economic policy analysis has had an extensive and rapid development; dynamic game theory has made it possible to analyse not only problems of policy coordination within a single country, but also problems of international policy coordination (see Pohjola, 1986, for a survey). Dynamic games have also made it possible to examine the interrelationships between political institutions and the private sector and to model the policy decision process so as to overcome the Lucas critique (see Lucas, 1987, and chapter 10 of the present volume).

1.3 The theory of economic policy revisited

Without claiming to review the theory of economic policy from its origins, it seems important to make a quick survey of what is usually known as *the* theory of economic policy. Since one of the main aims of this book is to provide a unified basis for a dynamic theory of policy, an overview of the developments of previous static theory is likely to be useful for a better understanding of the progression from statics to dynamics.

The first rigorous contributions to the theory of economic policy are due to Tinbergen (1952, 1954). His theory showed for the first time how policy-makers could utilize their policy instruments efficiently in order to achieve pre-specified policy targets. However, although the well-known target-instrument approach has definitely been attributed to Tinbergen, it must be noted that this classification of variables had already been introduced by Frisch in 1949, in a memorandum submitted to the United Nations. Written in parallel with Tinbergen's work, B. Hansen's 1958 book (Swedish edition, 1955) is also worthy of mention, where a similar classification of variables (called by Hansen 'ends' and 'means') is introduced. As Hansen himself argues (see the postscript to chapter 1), the reason why Tinbergen's work was much more widely known is probably that Tinbergen had the opportunity to apply his theory to empirical models, and therefore to obtain concrete numerical results, while Hansen's contribution was purely theoretical and, inevitably, more abstract.

The mathematical treatment of the policy problem carried out by both authors is very similar and is based on the so-called *fixed target* approach. That is, a static linear model which describes the economic system and the links between targets and instruments is considered, and fixed desired values for the targets are defined. The system is then solved so as to obtain the required values of the policy instruments. A necessary and sufficient condition for a solution is that the number of linearly independent instruments be greater than or equal to the number of linearly independent targets (see section 3.2 for details).

However, the fixed-target approach left many problems unsolved (see Hughes Hallett, 1989). Among these, three important issues concern the problem of policy design when (a) the solution obtained is not politically or administratively feasible, (b) the solution does not exist (for example, when the number of instruments is inferior to the number of targets) and (c) there is more than one solution (for example, when the number of instruments is greater than the number of targets). An answer to these problems came from the so-called *flexible-target* approach which had already been introduced, though not fully developed, in both Hansen's and Tinbergen's work.

The flexible-target approach consists in the optimization of an objective function which represents the preferences of policy-makers under the constraint of a static model that describes the economic system considered. The three above mentioned problems can be solved through this approach, since (a) it is possible to impose constraints on the values of the policy instruments by introducing them explicitly into the objective function, as Theil (1954, 1956) suggested, (b) the policy optimization problem can be solved even when a solution does not exist for the corresponding fixed-target problem (in fact, the optimization problem can be solved even if the number of instruments is inferior to the number of targets), (c) it is possible to select one (optimal) solution from among the infinite number of possible solutions of Tinbergen's problem, once a preference function has been defined for the policy-maker. The price to be paid for following the optimization method is that the policy targets will no longer be achieved exactly, although the economy will get as close to them as possible, given the constraints imposed on the problem.

The development of this approach is mainly due to Frisch (1956, 1957) and Theil (1954, 1956, 1958, 1964), whose contributions complement each other. Frisch highlighted an important problem in the flexible-target approach – the mathematical and numerical specification of the policy-maker's objective function – and proposed useful solutions to overcome it. Theil, on the contrary, was more concerned with the problem of the mathematical solution of the optimization problem and in particular analysed the linear-quadratic case. The Frisch-Theil approach can be seen as a complement to and continuance of Tinbergen's theory, and one which has given greater flexibility and versatility to the theory and practice of policy design. This formulation of the policy problem allowed Theil to consider the problem of uncertainty and to introduce the principle of certainty equivalence (Simon, 1956; Theil, 1957). It also opened the way for the more recent developments in decentralized policy selection by means of game-theory methods.

One limitation of the static theory of policy, which is common to both the fixed and the flexible-target approach, is that it is necessarily based on models: the problems of policy design can only be solved if the economic system is known in detail. This argument had already been pointed out by Theil (1956) and by Hansen (1958):

The ... problem arises when our knowledge of the working of the economy is uncertain, or, to put it in other words, if we are not sure which model is the 'correct' one: if the State acts on the basis of results obtained through deductions from a misleading picture of the economy, policy conducted to achieve a given set of ends will be unsuccessful to a corresponding degree (Hansen, 1958, p. 430).

The flexible-target approach has a further element of arbitrariness: the planners' objective function. Hence the importance of an appropriate choice of model and a correct specification of the criterion function. These two problems of the static theory of policy obviously also extend to the dynamic framework.

The problem of coordination of fiscal and monetary policies was also mentioned in these early works, in particular by Hansen (1958) and Tinbergen (1954). However, decentralized policy design could not be handled systematically at the time and the problem was only touched upon. In fact, game-theory methods were not yet sufficiently developed and any application to macroeconomics was absent.

It can be seen from this brief survey of the static theory of policy that the foundations for a dynamic theory were already laid down. Furthermore, although Tinbergen and Frisch used only static models, Hansen and Theil also considered dynamic ones by following the same approach: they considered economic variables at different dates as different variables (i.e. they worked with stacked-up vectors), so that the dynamic policy problem could be reduced to a static one. This approach is still widely used today in dynamic policy analysis.

What was required for a dynamic theory of policy was simply the introduction of dynamic models and of intertemporal criterion functions into the analysis. However, the solution of the new dynamic problems also required the use of new and more sophisticated mathematical tools. Tinbergen's target-instrument approach was generalized in the framework of dynamic modelling by means of controllability theory. Stability analysis was also used to reconsider Tinbergen's problem from a different point of view. The dynamic setting in which the policy problem was analysed made it possible to consider Tinbergen's theory of policy from new and different perspectives to those available in a static context.

The Frisch-Theil optimization approach required on the other hand the use of optimal control theory, and both Bellman's dynamic programming and Pontryagin's minimum principle have been extensively used in the literature. Finally, although the problem of decentralized policy selection had been examined in a dynamic setting by the use of stability analysis (Mundell's policy-assignment approach), the huge development of dynamic games in recent years has made it possible to reconsider the problem from a new angle and has provided the appropriate tools for a rigorous analysis of the subject.

Since dynamic policy analysis is the topic of this book, we shall not pursue the matter further, as the reader will find sufficient material in the following chapters.

1.4 The continuous-time approach

Dynamic economic models can be specified both in discrete and in continuous time (and also in mixed discrete-continuous time). These mathematical specifications make it possible to describe the evolution over time of the economic variables considered, which are in fact functions of time.

The mathematical difficulties of solving mixed difference-differential equations practically reduce the choice to discrete- *or* continuous-time models. This choice is neither immaterial nor straightforward. In general, if we think that the economic variables under consideration evolve continuously over time and without discontinuous lags, then the continuous-time formalization appears to be more correct. This would be the case for some financial variables (like, for example, the exchange rate), whose behaviour is better described by means of differential equations. On the contrary, if we think that the economic variables considered evolve in a discontinuous way, then the discrete-time specification seems more appropriate. This would be the case for some real variables (like, for example, tax rates) whose evolution over time may be more correctly described by using difference equations. This distinction, however, is not always so clear, and other characteristics of the two types of specification should be considered.

From the analytical point of view, mathematical methods concerning continuous-time systems have, in some cases, reached a degree of sophistication which is not totally shared by discrete-time systems. This asymmetric methodological development might be due to the fact that differential calculus is generally more widespread in other scientific fields, such as physics, biology, engineering,[4] etc. It follows that the economist has a wider choice of mathematical tools when dealing with differential equations.

On the other hand, difference equations have other analytical advantages that differential equations have not. For example, a system of difference equations can be written in stacked-up form (that is by stacking the relevant vectors over time) thus reducing a dynamic system to a static system of greater dimension. This transformation makes it possible to use static (and, therefore, simpler) methods to deal with dynamic systems.[5]

From the theoretical point of view, two points should be mentioned.[6]

(a) A reason for using discrete-time models is that individual decisions are generally taken at discrete-time intervals. However, when the variables considered are the outcomes of a great number of decisions taken by different economic operators – as all aggregate variables are – the discrete-time specification implies the assumption that individual decisions are coordinated in such a way as to be perfectly synchronized, that is taken at the same moment of time. It seems more plausible to assume instead that individual decisions are taken at different points in time, giving rise to a kind of overlapping process. Therefore, a continous-time formulation appears more appropriate for this type of decision process.

(b) When economic phenomena are formalized in discrete time, an important problem arises which is absent in continuous-time specifications: the definition of the unit of time, that is of the time length of the period that characterizes the dynamics of all variables in the model. It is thus necessary to check that no essential result of the analysis performed with a discrete model depends on the specific length of the period, i.e. does not change when the period is, say, doubled or halved.

However, when a discrete-time model is robust with respect to alternative specifications of the period length (therefore also to a period length tending to zero), the same economic phenomenon could also be correctly specified in continuous time.

The two points just considered are very clearly summarized in Goodwin (1948), where, referring to the dynamic multiplier, the author writes:

When one attempts realistically to identify the moments at which these [discrete] steps occur, or the time intervals between them, the concept seems to evaporate. Economic life is extraordinarily continuous, characterized by a getting and spending which does not even cease at night. Furthermore, any reasonable time interval between the steps would have to be so short, that any process would have a rather brief duration. That real discontinuities exist, cannot be denied: the only question is whether or not these are large enough to be significant for macro-dynamic analysis (p. 113).

The arguments just mentioned do not imply that discrete-time specifications should not be considered, but that the choice of one type of specification or another should be based on a prior examination of the economic problem to be analysed. As a matter of fact, the discrete-time specification may be more appropriate to describe some economic phenomena, such as, for example, sequential decision processes, where the focus of the analysis is on the sequential structure of the economic decisions. Expectations referring to specific future moments of time can also be more easily specified by using discrete-time models.

It is obvious that the points just mentioned regarding theoretical specifications in continuous and discrete time also extend to econometric models. Moreover, other specific characteristics of continuous-time *empirical* models should be considered (see Gandolfo, 1981, 1988):

(c) The estimator of continuous-time models is independent of the observation interval. Furthermore, it takes into account the fact that the measure of a flow variable is not an instantaneous value (as is the case of stock variables) but is the result of an aggregation (integral) of instantaneous values over the observation period. This makes an appropriate treatment of stock-flow models possible.

(d) When considering dynamic adjustment processes, the continuous-time formulation makes it possible to obtain the estimates of the adjustment speeds of the relevant variables, even when these speeds are very high and, therefore, when the adjustment is very quick with respect to the observation period. This may not be possible in the discrete-time case if the adjustment takes place in a shorter period than the observation interval.

(e) The use of the continuous-time formulation can make a more satisfactory treatment of distributed lag processes possible. In discrete-time models the assumption of independence of the disturbances in successive observations holds only if the size of the time unit inherent in the model is not too small in relation to the observation period. However, the lags in the system are not always integral multiples of one time unit whose size is compatible with the independence assumption.

(f) Once a continuous-time model is estimated, it is possible to obtain simulation and forecasting results referring to any interval of time. In fact, the paths obtained for the variables concerned are continuous paths and, therefore, provide information about the values of the variables at each point in time and not only at discrete intervals. This point is important, as we shall see in chapters 7 and 9, when optimal control and dynamic game methods are used for policy analysis. Obviously, this advantage of continuous-time econometric models also extends to theoretical ones when numerical simulations are carried out.

We note before concluding this section that the choice of discrete-time econometric models was an obligatory one until not many years ago, as econometric methods were only suitable for estimating these models. Therefore, while theoretical economic models were often specified in continuous time, econometric modelling was restricted to discrete-time formulations, thus causing a gap between theoretical and empirical work. As a consequence of this gap, most of the mathematical methods used in economic analysis were specified in continuous time when theoretical problems were involved, while they were specified in discrete time when empirical problems were considered instead. This asymmetry still exists as regards the applications of control theory and dynamic games to economic problems.

The situation, however, is gradually changing since it is now possible to obtain rigorous estimates of the parameters of a system of stochastic differential equations (see, for example, Bergstrom, 1984, 1988). Econometric techniques for the estimation of continuous-time models and related software are now available and an increasing number of these models are beginning to appear.[7] Thus, applications of control theory and dynamic games to continuous-time econometric models are now also possible (see Gandolfo and Petit, 1987; Hughes Hallett and Petit, 1988a, b and c) Petit, 1989a.

Nevertheless, most applications of these mathematical methods to problems of policy analysis are specified in discrete time in the existing economic literature. The continuous-time approach considered in this book may help to fill this gap.

1.5 Outline of the book

The extension to a dynamic framework of the problems and conclusions which characterized the static theory of policy requires a reconsideration of the two main lines along which the static approach developed.[8] This is why – following a chapter which aims to provide the mathematical background to state-space representations for those readers who are not familiar with these techniques (chapter 2) – the book begins by dealing with the dynamic generalizations of Tinbergen's instrument-target approach (chapters 3 and 4). More specifically, *chapter 3* covers the dynamic generalization of Tinbergen's fixed-target approach by using the methods of controllability analysis. *Chapter 4* provides a different way of generalizing Tinbergen's model, namely what we have called the 'stability approach', a name which covers a huge number of apparently disparate contributions on this topic, all of which share the common aim of seeking policy rules capable of stabilizing the economic system.

The controllability and the stability approaches have one drawback in common: they only provide existence conditions, i.e. they ensure the existence of policies capable of controlling or stabilizing the economic system. Therefore, as we have seen in section 1.3, the problem still remains of choosing one policy out of the many that may exist or, conversely, of choosing the best course of action when the existence conditions are violated. This leads us to the second line of approach, namely to the dynamic generalization of Theil's optimal selection methods (chapters 5 to 9).

Optimal policy selection is considered in the case of both centralized (chapters 5, 6 and 7) and decentralized (chapters 8 and 9) decision-making. More specifically, *chapter 5* introduces the tools of dynamic optimization or optimal control theory (in particular Pontryagin's principle of optimality) and shows how this approach can solve the dynamic policy problem when a single policy-maker is considered. This in turn requires the definition of the policy-maker's objective function, even though the lack of information about the planner's preferences makes it very difficult to give a mathematical and a numerical specification to this function. This problem, the importance of which was already stressed by Frisch in the fifties with reference to the static case, is thoroughly analysed in *chapter 6*. The mathematical methods considered in chapters 5 and 6 are then put to work in *chapter 7*, where we show an application of optimal control methods to optimal policy design in the context of an econometric model of the Italian economy specified and estimated in continuous time.

The optimal control approach to policy analysis is based on the assumption that decisions are centralized. When this assumption is relaxed, optimal control methods are no longer appropriate for dealing with problems of policy selection, and dynamic games should be considered instead. This approach is dealt with in *chapter 8*, where different solution concepts are introduced in order to describe the different assumptions that may characterize the behaviour of policy-makers. Then, in *chapter 9*, an application of this approach to the same econometric model used in chapter 7 is undertaken. The problem of decentralized decision-making is illustrated by considering the case in which the Government and the Central Bank have conflicting objectives; the gains from coordinating fiscal and monetary policies are also examined.

Finally, *chapter 10* deals with the methodological implications of using the mathematical tools described in this book for purposes of econometric policy evaluation and decision. This chapter deals with the difficulties that may arise when the private sector is no longer considered as a passive player in the policy game, and the assumption is made that it forms expectations about future policy. The first problem is that of time inconsistency of optimal policy decisions when the private sector has rational expectations. This problem was already known within the framework of dynamic games, since the global strategy of the leader in a Stackelberg game is indeed time inconsistent. It is shown in this chapter that the optimal control problem in a rational expectations framework is based on the same assumptions that characterize a Stackelberg game.

Another problem which arises from the assumption that the private sector forms expectations about future policy was underlined by Lucas, who criticized the use of econometric models for policy evaluation and decision. In this chapter, a review of the Lucas critique is undertaken and suggestions for overcoming it are discussed. An interesting approach is to describe the interaction between the policy-maker(s) and the private sector as a dynamic game, since it makes it possible for each player to take into account expectations about the future decisions of the other, and to overcome the Lucas critique. The importance of the above-mentioned criticisms of the 'traditional' methods of optimal policy selection are discussed in the conclusion.

2 Mathematical preliminaries: the state space*

2.1 Systems analysis and introduction to the state space

In economics, as in other fields, dynamic models which describe the performance of economic variables are often defined by differential or difference equations of a high order. The opportunity to redefine these equations as a system of first-order dynamic equations in normal form (the state-space form) is a fundamental issue in all applications of the mathematical methods considered in this volume.[1]

It is well known from the theory of dynamic equations that the stability properties of a differential equation (or a system of differential equations) of a higher order than the first can be more easily analysed by first transforming the equation(s) into a system of the first order in normal form, so that each equation involves the derivative of only one function in turn. In this way it is possible to know whether the system (or, equivalently, the higher-order equation(s)) is stable or unstable without the need to explicitly derive the corresponding characteristic equation; there exist specific stability conditions defined on the matrix of the coefficients of first-order (state-space) systems that make it possible (if the conditions are applicable) to check directly the stability (or the instability) of the given system, and, therefore, of the corresponding higher-order equation(s).

Similar arguments can be put forward as far as the controllability properties of higher-order systems are concerned, since the conditions for output controllability (both for point and for path controllability) are stated in terms of the matrices of the coefficients of the corresponding state-space representations. The importance of state-space forms in order

---

*In this chapter some mathematical notions are reviewed that might prove useful in the following chapters. It can therefore be skipped by those who are already familiar with systems theory and with state-space representations in particular. Sections 2.3 and 2.4 can be omitted on a first reading.

to analyse both the controllability and stability properties of dynamic systems of any order will be made clearer in chapters 3 and 4.

Furthermore, as we shall see in chapters 5, 7, 8 and 9, state-space representations are a fundamental prerequisite when both optimal control and dynamic game theory are applied. Since the dynamic optimization method that we consider in those chapters is Pontryagin's minimum principle, the necessary conditions for optimality require the simultaneous verification of the state and costate equations, which in turn obviously require the specification of the dynamic system considered in state-space form.

Another important feature of the state-space approach is that it makes it possible to deal with time-varying systems and with non-linear systems. It therefore represents an important generalization of classical control theory (see below) which is applicable only to linear time-invariant systems.

The modern theory of control, based on the concept of state space, was developed in the engineering literature of the later 1950s, (as we have seen in section 1.1). Before that, the *classical* theory was the standard approach to systems analysis and the system's input-output relationship was analysed by means of a particular function known as *transfer function* (or transfer matrix). This function corresponds to the ratio of the Laplace transform[2] of the output to the Laplace transform of the input, on the assumption that all initial values are zero (see, for example, Aoki 1976a, chapter 2; and section 2.5 of this chapter). Since by means of the Laplace transform it is possible to transform a differential equation of order n into a polinomial equation of degree n, the use of the transfer function makes it possible to define an immediate relation between the input and the output in terms of the parameters of the equation considered. This property of transfer functions explains why they are still used in systems analysis, notwithstanding the increasing utilization of the state-space approach.

As mentioned above, the representation of a dynamic system by means of the *state-space* form makes it possible to transform (a) a differential equation of order n into a differential system of the first order in normal form, and (b) a differential system of a higher order into a system of the first order. The use of *state* variables reduces therefore the complexity of the mathematical relations, transforming the initial dynamic system into a first-order system, which greatly simplifies analytical tractability.

As we shall see in the next sections, state variables are related both to the input and the output variables by specific equations. By making use of state-space methods, the relationship between the input and the output is the result of (a) an input-state relation, according to which the value of the state is, at each time t, a function of the evolution of the input over a given time interval, and (b) a state-output mapping, according to which the output is a function of the state and of the input. The output can be a function of the input, either directly (instantaneous relation) or indirectly, through the state, or both.

Since the state is defined in such a way as to contain all the information concerning the initial conditions of the system, it can also be considered as an auxiliary form of representation of the system itself which meets the requirement of making the input-output relationship unique. The uniqueness of this relation is fundamental in control theory since it makes it possible to determine the behaviour of the output, given a pre-assigned behaviour of the input. This uniqueness is not assured when the dynamic system is represented by the transfer function or transfer matrix (see Ogata, 1970, chapter 14).

As we have already seen, we frequently need to use the concepts of input, output and state. Therefore, we shall briefly define these terms before proceeding to the description of state-space forms.

The *input* of a dynamic system is described by a set of exogenous variables, functions of time, $u_1(t), u_2(t), \ldots, u_r(t)$, called *input* variables. These variables can be either exogenous variables whose time behaviour is exogenously given, or control variables whose behaviour can, on the contrary, be manipulated. These control variables are the instruments of economic policy problems.

The *output* of a dynamic system is described by a set of endogenous variables, functions of time, $y_1(t), y_2(t), \ldots, y_m(t)$, called *output* variables. This set (or a subset) of variables represents policy targets in economic policy problems. The output, in some cases, may, as we shall see later, coincide with the state.

The *state* of a dynamic system is described by a set of endogeneous variables, functions of time, $x_1(t), x_2(t), \ldots, x_n(t)$, called *state* variables. These variables describe completely the behaviour of the dynamic system once the input, for $t \geqslant t_0$, and the initial state, at $t = t_0$, are given. The state variables assume the role of intermediate variables, to be considered in addition to the input and output variables.

The *state space* is the n-dimensional space whose axes consist of the x_1 axis, x_2 axis, $\ldots, x_n$ axis. Any state can be represented by a point in the state space.

The state has to be defined in such a way as to ensure that each input-output pair be deduced from the input-state-output transformation, and vice versa, it should not, therefore, introduce any new input-output pair. Hence the state should be described by the *minimum* set of state variables (see section 3.9).

It is important to point out that a dynamic system admits a state-space representation only if it is a causal system, i.e. if the output at each time t'

depends on the values assumed by the input at time $t \leqslant t'$ and not on the values assumed at time $t > t'$[3].

2.2 State-space representations

We shall see in this section how to compute the state-space representation of a dynamic system, first in the case of a single input and a single output and then in the case of multiple inputs and multiple outputs.

Note that the procedure that we shall use for computing the state-space form is not the only one available. There are other computational techniques which can also be applied, both for continuous- and for discrete-time systems.

The state-space representations obtained by using different techniques may be different, that is, may be characterized by different coefficients. There can be in fact many different state-space representations of the same dynamic system (or equation), as we shall see in section 2.3.

2.2.1 The single-input single-output case

(i) *No derivatives of the input functions*

Let us consider a dynamic system described by the following linear, time-invariant,[4] differential equation of order n

$$\overset{(n)}{y}(t) + a_1 \overset{(n-1)}{y}(t) + \cdots + a_{n-1}\dot{y}(t) + a_n y(t) = b_1 u(t) \tag{2.1}$$

where $y(t)$ is the output variable, $\overset{(n)}{y}(t)$ represents the n-th order derivative of $y(t)$ and $u(t)$ is the input variable; the dot over the variables, as usual, represents the first-order derivative. This equation may represent an economic relationship where derivatives of various orders of the single endogenous (target) variable appear, but only instantaneous values of the single control (policy instrument) variable are considered. In what follows, we shall often omit the term t, for simplicity, taking it for granted that the output, input and state variables are functions of time.

The state-space representation of (2.1) is obtained as follows: first of all define the new variables

$$
\begin{aligned}
x_1 &= y \\
x_2 &= \dot{y} \\
&\cdots \\
x_{n-1} &= \overset{(n-2)}{y} \\
x_n &= \overset{(n-1)}{y}
\end{aligned}
\tag{2.2}
$$

Given this definition, the state equations corresponding to the variables $x_1, x_2, \ldots, x_{n-1}$ can be easily obtained. We have

$$\dot{x}_1 = x_2$$
$$\dot{x}_2 = x_3$$
$$\ldots$$
$$\dot{x}_{n-1} = x_n$$

$$(2.3)$$

In order to obtain the state equation corresponding to the state variable x_n, we have to take into consideration not only the definition of x_n from which we have

$$\dot{x}_n = \overset{(n)}{y}$$

$$(2.4)$$

but also (2.1), from which we obtain

$$\overset{(n)}{y} = -a_n y - a_{n-1} \dot{y} - \cdots - a_2 \overset{(n-2)}{y} - a_1 \overset{(n-1)}{y} + b_1 u$$

$$(2.5)$$

From (2.4) and (2.5), and, considering the definitions given in (2.2), we finally get

$$\dot{x}_n = -a_n x_1 - a_{n-1} x_2 - \cdots - a_2 x_{n-2} - a_1 x_n + b_1 u$$

$$(2.6)$$

The state equations (2.3) and (2.6) can also be written in matrix form as

$$\dot{x} = Ax + Bu$$

$$(2.7)$$

where

$$x = \begin{bmatrix} x_1 \\ x_2 \\ \vdots \\ x_n \end{bmatrix} \quad A = \begin{bmatrix} 0 & 1 & 0 \ldots 0 \\ 0 & 0 & 1 \ldots 0 \\ \cdots\cdots\cdots\cdots\cdots\cdots \\ 0 & 0 & 0 \ldots 1 \\ -a_n & -a_{n-1} & \ldots\ldots -a_1 \end{bmatrix} \quad B = \begin{bmatrix} 0 \\ 0 \\ \vdots \\ 0 \\ b_1 \end{bmatrix}$$

System (2.7) is the state-space representation of (2.1). The variables $x_1, x_2, \ldots, x_n$ are the state variables, and vector x is the state vector. The dimension of the state vector coincides with the order of the differential equation (2.1). As can be seen, system (2.7) describes the relationship between the state and the input. The relationship between the state and the output is given by the output equation, that is

$$y = x_1 \tag{2.8}$$

which can be written in matrix form as

$$y = Cx \tag{2.9}$$

where

$$C = [1 \quad 0 \ldots 0]$$

Recalling what was said in section 2.1, we can now see that system (2.7) contains all the information concerning the behaviour of the dynamic system considered, once the initial values of the state variables and the behaviour of the input are given.

(ii) *Derivatives of the input functions*
Consider the equation

$$\overset{(n)}{y} + a_1 \overset{(n-1)}{y} + a_2 \overset{(n-2)}{y} + \cdots + a_{n-1} \dot{y} + a_n y = b_0 \overset{(n)}{u}$$

$$+ b_1 \overset{(n-1)}{u} + \cdots + b_{n-1} \dot{u} + b_n u \tag{2.10}$$

where some of the coefficients b_i can be zero. In other words, the order of derivation of input u can be lower than, or equal to, that of output y. Therefore, the possibility of introducing also the time variation (i.e. derivatives of various orders) of the control (policy instrument) variable is considered in this case.

Following the same procedure as in (i) the following state system would be obtained

$$\dot{x}_1 = x_2$$
$$\dot{x}_2 = x_3$$
$$\ldots$$
$$\dot{x}_n = -a_n x_1 - a_{n-1} x_2 - \cdots - a_1 x_n + b_0 \overset{(n)}{u} + b_1 \overset{(n-1)}{u} + \cdots + b_n u$$

It can be seen that the r.h.s. of the n-th equation still involves terms with derivatives of various orders of the input variable. We therefore need to redefine the state variables in such a way as to eliminate these derivatives. This can be done by defining the following state variables (see Ogata, 1970, chapter 14)

$$
\begin{aligned}
x_1 &= y - \beta_0 u \\
x_2 &= \dot{y} - \beta_0 \dot{u} - \beta_1 u = \dot{x}_1 - \beta_1 u \\
x_3 &= \overset{(2)}{y} - \beta_0 \overset{(2)}{u} - \beta_1 \dot{u} - \beta_2 u = \dot{x}_2 - \beta_2 u
\end{aligned}
$$

$$\cdots\cdots\cdots\cdots\cdots\cdots\cdots\cdots\cdots\cdots\cdots\cdots \tag{2.11}$$

$$
\begin{aligned}
x_{n-1} &= \overset{(n-2)}{y} - \beta_0 \overset{(n-2)}{u} - \beta_1 \overset{(n-3)}{u} - \cdots - \beta_{n-3}\dot{u} - \beta_{n-2}u \\
&= \dot{x}_{n-2} - \beta_{n-2}u \\
x_n &= \overset{(n-1)}{y} - \beta_0 \overset{(n-1)}{u} - \beta_1 \overset{(n-2)}{u} - \cdots - \beta_{n-3}\overset{(2)}{u} - \beta_{n-2}\dot{u} - \beta_{n-1}u \\
&= \dot{x}_{n-1} - \beta_{n-1}u
\end{aligned}
$$

where

$$
\begin{aligned}
\beta_0 &= b_0 \\
\beta_1 &= b_1 - a_1 \beta_0 \\
\beta_2 &= b_2 - a_1 \beta_1 - a_2 \beta_0 \\
\beta_3 &= b_3 - a_1 \beta_2 - a_2 \beta_1 - a_3 \beta_0 \\
&\cdots\cdots\cdots\cdots\cdots\cdots\cdots\cdots \\
\beta_n &= b_n - a_1 \beta_{n-1} - \cdots - a_{n-1}\beta_1 - a_n \beta_0
\end{aligned} \tag{2.12}
$$

The state equations corresponding to the variables $x_1, x_2, \ldots, x_{n-1}$ are easily obtained from (2.11). We have

$$
\begin{aligned}
\dot{x}_1 &= x_2 + \beta_1 u \\
\dot{x}_2 &= x_3 + \beta_2 u \\
&\cdots\cdots\cdots \\
\dot{x}_{n-1} &= x_n + \beta_{n-1}u
\end{aligned} \tag{2.13}
$$

In order to obtain the state equation corresponding to the state variable x_n we have to follow the same procedure as in (i):
(a) differentiate the last equation of system (2.11), that is

$$
\dot{x}_n = \overset{(n)}{y} - \beta_0 \overset{(n)}{u} - \beta_1 \overset{(n-1)}{u} - \cdots - \beta_{n-2}\overset{(2)}{u} - \beta_{n-1}\dot{u} \tag{2.14}
$$

b) substitute the term $\overset{(n)}{y}$ by the expression obtained from (2.10), that is

$$\dot{x}_n = -a_n y - a_{n-1}\dot{y} - \cdots - a_2 \overset{(n-2)}{y} - a_1 \overset{(n-1)}{y} + b_0 \overset{(n)}{u}$$

$$+ b_1 \overset{(n-1)}{u} + \cdots + b_{n-1}\dot{u}$$

$$+ b_n u - \beta_0 \overset{(n)}{u} - \beta_1 \overset{(n-1)}{u} - \cdots - \beta_{n-2} \overset{(2)}{u} - \beta_{n-1}\dot{u} \tag{2.15}$$

(c) substitute $\overset{(n-1)}{y}, \ldots, \dot{y}, y$ by the expressions obtained from the definitions (2.11), that is

$$\dot{x}_n = -a_n(x_1 + \beta_0 u) - a_{n-1}(x_2 + \beta_0 \dot{u} + \beta_1 u)$$

$$- \cdots - a_2(x_{n-1} + \beta_0 \overset{(n-2)}{u}$$

$$+ \beta_1 \overset{(n-3)}{u} + \cdots + \beta_{n-2}u) - a_1 (x_n + \beta_0 \overset{(n-1)}{u}$$

$$+ \beta_1 \overset{(n-2)}{u} + \cdots + \beta_{n-2}\dot{u}$$

$$+ \beta_{n-1}u) + b_0 \overset{(n)}{u} + b_1 \overset{(n-1)}{u} + \cdots + b_{n-1}\dot{u}$$

$$+ b_n u - \beta_0 \overset{(n)}{u} - \beta_1 \overset{(n-1)}{u}$$

$$- \beta_2 \overset{(n-2)}{u} - \cdots - \beta_{n-2} \overset{(2)}{u} - \beta_{n-1}\dot{u} \tag{2.16}$$

Notwithstanding the apparent complexity, (2.16) can be reduced, after simple manipulations and taking into account the definitions (2.12), to the following equation

$$\dot{x}_n = -a_n x_1 - a_{n-1}x_2 - \cdots - a_2 x_{n-1} - a_1 x_n + \beta_n u \tag{2.17}$$

which is the n-th state equation we were looking for.

From the first definition of (2.11) we can now obtain the output equation

$$y = x_1 + \beta_0 u \tag{2.18}$$

Equations (2.13), (2.17) and (2.18) can be described in matrix form as

$$\dot{x} = Ax + Bu \tag{2.19}$$

$$y = Cx + Du \tag{2.20}$$

where

$$
x = \begin{bmatrix} x_1 \\ x_2 \\ \vdots \\ x_{n-1} \\ x_n \end{bmatrix} \qquad
A = \begin{bmatrix} 0 & 1 & 0 & \cdots & 0 \\ 0 & 0 & 1 & \cdots & 0 \\ \cdots & \cdots & \cdots & \cdots & \cdots \\ 0 & 0 & 0 & \cdots & 1 \\ -a_n & -a_{n-1} & -a_{n-2} & \cdots & -a_1 \end{bmatrix} \qquad
B = \begin{bmatrix} \beta_1 \\ \beta_2 \\ \vdots \\ \beta_{n-1} \\ \beta_n \end{bmatrix}
$$

$$
C = [1 \quad 0 \quad \cdots \quad 0] \qquad D = \beta_0 = b_0
$$

2.2.2 The multiple-input multiple-output case

(i) No derivatives of the input functions

Before considering the multiequation case in a general framework, it may be worthwhile to examine the following example concerning a differential equation system of a higher order than the first, with two inputs and two outputs

$$
\begin{aligned}
&\overset{(3)}{y}_1 + a_{11}^1 \overset{(2)}{y}_1 + a_{12}^1 \overset{(2)}{y}_2 + a_{11}^2 \dot{y}_1 + a_{12}^2 \dot{y}_2 + a_{11}^3 y_1 + a_{12}^3 y_2 \\
&= b_{11} u_1 + b_{12} u_2
\end{aligned}
$$

$$
\begin{aligned}
&\overset{(3)}{y}_2 + a_{21}^1 \overset{(2)}{y}_1 + a_{22}^1 \overset{(2)}{y}_2 + a_{21}^2 \dot{y}_1 + a_{22}^2 \dot{y}_2 + a_{21}^3 y_1 + a_{22}^3 y_2 \\
&= b_{21} u_1 + b_{22} u_2
\end{aligned}
\tag{2.21}
$$

where the assumption is made that only the instantaneous values of the control variables influence the endogenous (target) variables. This assumption will be dropped in (ii).

In order to obtain the state-space representation of this system, we define the following state variables

$$
\begin{aligned}
x_1^1 &= y_1 \\
x_1^2 &= y_2
\end{aligned}
\qquad \text{or, in vector form, } x_1 = y
$$

$$
\begin{aligned}
x_2^1 &= \dot{y}_1 \\
x_2^2 &= \dot{y}_2
\end{aligned}
\qquad \text{or, in vector form, } x_2 = \dot{y}
$$

$$
\begin{aligned}
x_3^1 &= \overset{(2)}{y}_1 \\
x_3^2 &= \overset{(2)}{y}_2
\end{aligned}
\qquad \text{or, in vector form, } x_3 = \overset{(2)}{y}
$$

Recalling that from (2.21)

$$\overset{(3)}{y_1} = -a^3{}_{11}y_1 - a^3{}_{12}y_2 - a^2{}_{11}\dot{y}_1 - a^2{}_{12}\dot{y}_2 - a^1{}_{11}\overset{(2)}{y_1}$$
$$- a^1{}_{12}\overset{(2)}{y_2} + b_{11}u_1 + b_{12}u_2$$

$$\overset{(3)}{y_2} = -a^3{}_{21}y_1 - a^3{}_{22}y_2 - a^2{}_{21}\dot{y}_1 - a^2_{22}\dot{y}_2 - a^1{}_{21}\overset{(2)}{y_1}$$
$$- a^1{}_{22}\overset{(2)}{y_2} + b_{21}u_1 + b_{22}u_2$$

the state equations are given by

$$\dot{x}_1 = x_2$$
$$\dot{x}_2 = x_3 \tag{2.22}$$
$$\dot{x}_3 = \overset{(3)}{y} = -A_3 x_1 - A_2 x_2 - A_1 x_3 + Vu$$

where

$$A_1 = \begin{bmatrix} a^1_{11} & a^1_{12} \\ a^1_{21} & a^1_{22} \end{bmatrix} \quad A_2 = \begin{bmatrix} a^2_{11} & a^2_{12} \\ a^2_{21} & a^2_{22} \end{bmatrix} \quad A_3 = \begin{bmatrix} a^3_{11} & a^3_{12} \\ a^3_{21} & a^3_{22} \end{bmatrix}$$

$$V = \begin{bmatrix} b_{11} & b_{12} \\ b_{21} & b_{22} \end{bmatrix} \quad u = \begin{bmatrix} u_1 \\ u_2 \end{bmatrix}$$

or, in matrix form

$$\dot{x} = Ax + Bu \tag{2.23}$$

where

$$x = \begin{bmatrix} x_2 \\ x_2 \\ x_3 \end{bmatrix} \quad A = \begin{bmatrix} 0 & I & 0 \\ 0 & 0 & I \\ -A_3 & -A_2 & -A_1 \end{bmatrix} \quad B = \begin{bmatrix} 0 \\ 0 \\ V \end{bmatrix}$$

The output equations are given by

$$y_1 = x_1^1$$
$$y_2 = x_1^2 \tag{2.24}$$

or, in matrix form

$$y = Cx \tag{2.25}$$

where

$$C = [I \quad 0]$$

From this example, the generalization to the multiequation system, with r inputs and m outputs, is straightforward. This system can be described, in matrix form, by the following equation

$$\overset{(n)}{y} + A_1 \overset{(n-1)}{y} + \cdots + A_{n-1} \dot{y} + A_n y = Vu \tag{2.26}$$

where

$$y = \begin{bmatrix} y_1 \\ y_2 \\ \vdots \\ y_m \end{bmatrix} \quad A_i = \begin{bmatrix} a_{11}^i & a_{12}^i & \cdots & a_{1m}^i \\ a_{21}^i & a_{22}^i & \cdots & a_{2m}^i \\ \cdots\cdots\cdots\cdots\cdots \\ a_{m1}^i & a_{m2}^i & & a_{mm}^i \end{bmatrix} \quad i = 1, 2, \ldots, n$$

$$V = \begin{bmatrix} b_{11} & b_{12} & \cdots & b_{1r} \\ b_{21} & b_{22} & \cdots & b_{2r} \\ \cdots\cdots\cdots\cdots\cdots \\ b_{m1} & b_{m2} & \cdots & b_{mr} \end{bmatrix} \quad u = \begin{bmatrix} u_1 \\ u_2 \\ \vdots \\ u_r \end{bmatrix}$$

Defining the state in the form of m-dimensional vectors, we have

$$x_1 = y$$
$$x_2 = \dot{y}$$
$$\cdots$$
$$x_n = \overset{(n-1)}{y}$$

where $x_i' = [x_i^1, x_i^2, \ldots, x_i^m], i = 1, 2, \ldots, n$. As usual the prime indicates transposition.

The state-space representation of (2.26) is given by

$$\dot{x}_1 = x_2$$
$$\dot{x}_2 = x_3$$
$$\cdots \tag{2.27}$$
$$\dot{x}_{n-1} = x_n$$
$$\dot{x}_n = -A_n x_1 - A_{n-1} x_2 - \cdots - A_1 x_n + Vu$$

or by

$$\dot{x} = Ax + Bu \qquad (2.28)$$

where

$$x = \begin{bmatrix} x_1 \\ x_2 \\ \vdots \\ x_n \end{bmatrix} \qquad A = \begin{bmatrix} 0 & I & 0 & \cdots & 0 \\ 0 & 0 & I & \cdots & 0 \\ \cdots\cdots\cdots\cdots\cdots\cdots\cdots\cdots\cdots \\ 0 & 0 & 0 & \cdots & I \\ -A_n & -A_{n-1} & -A_{n-2} & \cdots & -A_1 \end{bmatrix} \qquad B = \begin{bmatrix} 0 \\ 0 \\ \vdots \\ V \end{bmatrix}$$

The output equation is given by

$$y = Cx \qquad (2.29)$$

where

$$C = [I \quad 0 \quad \cdots \quad 0]$$

(ii) *Derivatives of the input functions*

Consider the following n-th order differential system in matrix form with r inputs and m outputs

$$\overset{(n)}{y} + A_1 \overset{(n-1)}{y} + \cdots + A_{n-1}\dot{y} + A_n y = B_0 \overset{(n)}{u}$$
$$+ B_1 \overset{(n-1)}{u} + \cdots + B_{n-1}\dot{u} + B_n u \qquad (2.30)$$

where

$$y = \begin{bmatrix} y_1 \\ y_2 \\ \vdots \\ y_m \end{bmatrix} \qquad A_i = \begin{bmatrix} a_{11}^i & a_{12}^i & \cdots & a_{1m}^i \\ a_{21}^i & a_{22}^i & \cdots & a_{2m}^i \\ \cdots\cdots\cdots\cdots\cdots\cdots \\ a_{m1}^i & a_{m2}^i & \cdots & a_{mm}^i \end{bmatrix} \qquad B_i = \begin{bmatrix} b_{11}^i & b_{12}^i & \cdots & b_{1r}^i \\ b_{21}^i & b_{22}^i & \cdots & b_{2r}^i \\ \cdots\cdots\cdots\cdots\cdots\cdots \\ b_{m1}^i & b_{m2}^i & \cdots & b_{mr}^i \end{bmatrix}$$

$$i = 1, 2, \ldots, n$$

$$u = \begin{bmatrix} u_1 \\ u_2 \\ \vdots \\ u_r \end{bmatrix}$$

Define the following state variables (see (2.11))

$$x_1 = y - \Lambda_0 u$$
$$x_2 = \dot{y} - \Lambda_0 \dot{u} - \Lambda_1 u = \dot{x}_1 - \Lambda_1 u$$
$$x_3 = \overset{(2)}{y} - \Lambda_0 \overset{(2)}{u} - \Lambda_1 \dot{u} - \Lambda_2 u = \dot{x}_2 - \Lambda_2 u$$

$$\dots\dots\dots\dots\dots\dots\dots\dots\dots\dots\dots\dots\dots \tag{2.31}$$

$$x_{n-1} = \overset{(n-2)}{y} - \Lambda_0 \overset{(n-2)}{u} - \Lambda_1 \overset{(n-3)}{u} - \cdots - \Lambda_{n-3}\dot{u} - \Lambda_{n-2}u$$
$$= \dot{x}_{n-2} - \Lambda_{n-2}u$$

$$x_n = \overset{(n-1)}{y} - \Lambda_0 \overset{(n-1)}{u} - \Lambda_1 \overset{(n-2)}{u} - \cdots - \Lambda_{n-2}\dot{u} - \Lambda_{n-1}u$$
$$= \dot{x}_{n-1} - \Lambda_{n-1}u$$

where

$$x_i' = [x_i^1, x_i^2, \ldots, x_i^m], \qquad i = 1, 2, \ldots, n$$
$$\Lambda_0 = B_0$$
$$\Lambda_1 = B_1 - A_1\Lambda_0$$
$$\Lambda_2 = B_2 - A_1\Lambda_1 - A_2\Lambda_0$$
$$\Lambda_3 = B_3 - A_1\Lambda_2 - A_2\Lambda_1 - A_3\Lambda_0$$
$$\dots\dots\dots\dots\dots\dots\dots\dots\dots\dots\dots\dots$$
$$\Lambda_{n-1} = B_{n-1} - A_1\Lambda_{n-2} - A_2\Lambda_{n-3} - \cdots - A_{n-1}\Lambda_0$$
$$\Lambda_n = B_n - A_1\Lambda_{n-1} - A_2\Lambda_{n-2} - \cdots - A_n\Lambda_0$$

A state-space representation of system (2.30) is given by (see (2.13) and (2.17))

$$\dot{x}_1 = x_2 + \Lambda_1 u$$
$$\dot{x}_2 = x_3 + \Lambda_2 u$$
$$\dots\dots\dots\dots\dots \tag{2.32}$$
$$\dot{x}_{n-1} = x_n + \Lambda_{n-1}u$$
$$\dot{x}_n = -A_n x_1 - A_{n-1}x_2 - \cdots - A_2 x_{n-1} - A_1 x_n + \Lambda_n u$$

while, from (2.31), the output equation is

$$y = x_1 + \Lambda_0 u \tag{2.33}$$

Equations (2.32) and (2.33) can be described in matrix form as

$$\dot{x} = Ax + Bu \tag{2.34}$$
$$y = Cx + Du \tag{2.35}$$

where

$$
x = \begin{bmatrix} x_1 \\ x_2 \\ \vdots \\ x_n \end{bmatrix}
\quad
A = \begin{bmatrix}
0 & I & 0 & \cdots & 0 \\
0 & 0 & I & \cdots & 0 \\
\multicolumn{5}{c}{\cdots\cdots\cdots\cdots\cdots\cdots\cdots\cdots} \\
0 & 0 & 0 & \cdots & I \\
-A_n & -A_{n-1} & -A_{n-2} & \cdots & -A_1
\end{bmatrix}
\quad
B = \begin{bmatrix} \Lambda_1 \\ \Lambda_2 \\ \vdots \\ \Lambda_{n-1} \\ \Lambda_n \end{bmatrix}
$$

$$
C = [I \quad 0 \quad \cdots \quad 0] \qquad D = \Lambda_0 = B_0
$$

Note that in this state-space representation the matrices $A_i (i = 1, \ldots, n)$ that appear in (2.34) are respectively the same matrices that appear in (2.28). This means that the presence of derivatives of the input variables alters only the elements of the B matrix.

2.3 Non-uniqueness of the state space

The state-space representations described in the previous section are not the only possible ones. In fact, the state-space representation of a given dynamic system is not unique. Let us consider the state variables $x_1, x_2, \ldots, x_n$; any other set of variables $z_1, z_2, \ldots, z_n$ such that

$$
z_1 = f_1(x_1, x_2, \ldots, x_n)
$$
$$
z_2 = f_2(x_1, x_2, \ldots, x_n)
$$
$$
\cdots\cdots\cdots\cdots\cdots
$$
$$
z_n = f_n(x_1, x_2, \ldots, x_n)
$$

may represent an alternative set of state variables capable of describing the same dynamic system, provided that a one-to-one correspondence between the two sets exists.

For example, a vector z defined as

$$
z = Tx \tag{2.36}
$$

is an alternative state vector, if T is a non-singular matrix.

Let

$$
\dot{x} = Ax + Bu \tag{2.37}
$$

be a state-space representation of a given dynamic system

$$
\overset{(n)}{y} + \sum_{i=1}^{n} A_i \overset{(n-i)}{y} = \sum_{i=0}^{n} B_i \overset{(n-i)}{u} \tag{2.38}
$$

and let

$$y = Cx + Du \tag{2.39}$$

be the output equation of the same system. From definition (2.36)

$$x = T^{-1}z \tag{2.40}$$

and, substituting (2.40) into (2.37)

$$T^{-1}\dot{z} = AT^{-1}z + Bu \tag{2.41}$$

Pre-multiplying both sides of (2.41) by T, we get

$$\dot{z} = TAT^{-1}z + TBu \tag{2.42}$$

which is another state-space representation of system (2.38).
The output equation is, in this case, given by

$$y = CT^{-1}z + Du \tag{2.43}$$

Different state-space representations of a given dynamic system therefore provide the same information about its dynamic behaviour.

2.4 The relationship between the transfer function and the state space

As we have seen in section 2.1, a dynamic system can be represented both by a transfer function (or transfer matrix) and by a state-space form. The relationship between the two types of representation, the frequency domain and the time domain representations, can be examined by considering the following dynamic equation

$$\overset{(n)}{y} + a_1 \overset{(n-1)}{y} + \cdots + a_n y = b_0 \overset{(n)}{u} + b_1 \overset{(n-1)}{u} + \cdots + b_n u \tag{2.44}$$

with given initial values $y(0), \ldots, \overset{(n-1)}{y}(0), u(0), \ldots, \overset{(n-1)}{u}(0)$, for $t = 0$.

Taking the Laplace transform of both sides of (2.44) – on the assumption that such a transform exists for the same complex variable s – and indicating the Laplace transforms of $y(t)$ and $u(t)$ by $Y(s)$ and $U(s)$ respectively, we get

$$\begin{aligned}(s^n + a_1 s^{n-1} + \cdots + a_n) Y(s) &= (b_0 s^n + b_1 s^{n-1} \\ &+ b_{n-1} s + b_n) U(s) + W(s)\end{aligned} \tag{2.45}$$

where

$$\begin{aligned}W(s) = s^{n-1}[y(0) - b_0 u(0)] + s^{n-2}[\dot{y}(0) - b_0 \dot{u}(0) - a_1 y(0) - b_1 u(0)] \\ + \cdots + [\overset{(n-1)}{y}(0) - b_0 \overset{(n-1)}{u}(0) - \cdots - a_{n-1} y(0) - b_{n-1} u(0)]\end{aligned}$$

The transfer function $H(s)$ of a given dynamic system is defined as the relationship between the Laplace transform of the input and the Laplace transform of the output on the assumption that all initial values are zero. It can therefore be written as

$$H(s) := \frac{Y(s)}{U(s)} = \frac{b_0 s^n + b_1 s^{n-1} + \cdots + b_{n-1} s + b_n}{s^n + a_1 s^{n-1} + \cdots + a_{n-1} s + a_n} \tag{2.46}$$

where, as can be seen, the terms containing the initial values have vanished.

The transfer function makes it possible to represent the dynamics of a linear system by means of an algebraic equation in s. It describes in fact the input-output relationship in terms of the parameters of the system considered. This type of representation (known as the explicit approach or as the input-output approach), however, provides no information on the system's structure: the same transfer function can represent different dynamic systems (see Ogata, 1970, chapter 2).

As we have just seen, system (2.44) can also be represented, by means of the state and output equations which, in matrix form, are given by

$$\dot{x} = Ax + Bu \tag{2.47}$$

$$y = Cx + Du \tag{2.48}$$

Taking the Laplace transforms of both sides of (2.47) and (2.48), we have

$$sX(s) - x(0) = AX(s) + BU(s) \tag{2.49}$$

$$Y(s) = CX(s) + DU(s) \tag{2.50}$$

From (2.49) we get

$$(sI - A)X(s) = x(0) + BU(s) \tag{2.51}$$

and, by pre-multiplying both sides by $(sI - A)^{-1}$ – on the assumption that s is not an eigenvalue of A, so that $(sI - A)$ is non-singular – we obtain

$$X(s) = (sI - A)^{-1}x(0) + (sI - A)^{-1}BU(s) \tag{2.52}$$

By substituting now (2.52) into (2.50) we get

$$Y(s) = C\{(sI - A)^{-1}[x(0) + BU(s)]\} + DU(s) \tag{2.53}$$

Since the transfer function $H(s)$ is given by the ratio between $Y(s)$ and $U(s)$, given the assumption that all initial values are zero $[x(0) = 0]$, we have, from (2.53)

$$H(s) = Y(s)/U(s) = C(sI - A)^{-1}B + D \tag{2.54}$$

Equation (2.54) therefore describes the transfer function in terms of the matrices which appear in the state-space form. As (2.46) and (2.54) are equal, we finally obtain the following relationship

$$C(sI - A)^{-1}B + D = \frac{b_0 s^n + b_1 s^{n-1} + \cdots + b_{n-1} s + b_n}{s^n + a_1 s^{n-1} + \cdots + a_{n-1} s + a_n} \qquad (2.55)$$

In the case of a multiequational system with r inputs and m outputs, the relationship between the Laplace transform of the input and the Laplace transform of the output is given by an $m \times r$ matrix called the *transfer function matrix*, that is

$$Y(s) = G(s)U(s) \qquad (2.56)$$

where

$$Y(s) = \begin{bmatrix} Y_1(s) \\ Y_2(s) \\ \vdots \\ Y_m(s) \end{bmatrix} \quad G(s) = \begin{bmatrix} G_{11}(s) & G_{12}(s) & \ldots & G_{1r}(s) \\ G_{21}(s) & G_{22}(s) & \ldots & G_{2r}(s) \\ & & & \\ G_{m1}(s) & G_{m2}(s) & \ldots & G_{mr}(s) \end{bmatrix} \quad U(s) = \begin{bmatrix} U_1(s) \\ U_2(s) \\ \vdots \\ U_r(s) \end{bmatrix}$$

The element $G_{ij}(s)$ of $G(s)$ is the transfer function corresponding to the i-th output and the j-th input.

The relationship between a state-space representation of a given multiequational system and the corresponding transfer matrix can be obtained in the same way as for the single input–single output case examined above; therefore, if we consider system (2.34)–(2.35), this relationship is given by

$$G(s) = C(sI - A)^{-1}B + D \qquad (2.57)$$

where the matrices C, A and D are defined as above.

Representations of dynamic control systems by means of transfer functions have seldom been used in economic applications. Two exceptions which are worth mentioning are Vines, Maciejowski and Meade (1983) and Christodoulakis and Van der Ploeg (1987), where classical theory of control is applied to macroeconomic policy analysis and the relationship between targets and instruments is described by means of transfer functions.

3 Static and dynamic controllability

3.1 The properties of dynamic systems

When a dynamic macroeconomic model is used for policy analysis, it is important first to examine the dynamic properties which are specific to the system of equations that describe the model itself. The most important properties of dynamic systems are *controllability*, *observability* and *stability*. The absence of one or more of these properties can be an indication of possible limitations of the dynamic model involved.

In this chapter we shall deal in particular with controllability and observability, given that stability has already been extensively treated in the economic literature. However, the approach to economic policy analysis based on the stability of dynamic models will also be discussed in the next chapter.

If a dynamic model has the controllability property, then policy-makers can know in advance whether the economic system considered can be taken to any desired position in a given time interval by the use of the available policy instruments (or control variables). It is important, however, to distinguish between state controllability (ability of the system to reach a given point in the state space) and output controllability (ability of the system to reach a given point in the output space). Another important distinction is that between point and path controllability or controllability of a time trajectory of the output. We shall discuss these different controllability concepts in the next sections.

The controllability conditions are conditions for the *existence* of a set of policy instruments, functions of time, capable of moving the target (or the state) vector into some desired position in a given finite time interval. Since the well-known Tinbergen condition (Tinbergen, 1952, 1966) is also a condition for the existence of a set of policy instruments, such that the target vector assumes some given desired value, Tinbergen's condition has often been called, in the recent literature, the *static controllability condition* (Preston, 1974). Dynamic controllability has therefore been considered as the dynamic generalization of Tinbergen's approach to the theory of economic policy. This point, however, has given rise to contradictory opinions that we shall discuss in sections 3.7 and 3.8.

Observability, on the other hand, is a property of dynamic systems which makes it possible to identify the initial state of the system through the observation of the behaviour of the input and output at future moments; it therefore allows us to examine the links between the output and the state. Observability is a dual of the controllability property as we shall see in section 3.9.

Before concluding this section, we wish to point out that, in this chapter, we shall always refer to *fixed targets*, that is targets whose values are fixed in advance (for example, a given level of income or a given rate of inflation). Targets can also be flexible, if, for example, they are defined by some optimal position. In this case the value of the optimal point is not known in advance (for example, the higher possible level of income or the lower possible rate of inflation).

3.2 Tinbergen's approach to the theory of economic policy and static controllability

Tinbergen's contributions to the formulation of a rational approach to the theory of economic policy have been of extreme importance. His pioneering work has portrayed the formulation of economic policy decisions as the problem of obtaining pre-assigned target values with the use of the available policy instruments, given an econometric model which describes the economic system considered. We refer in particular to Tinbergen's definition of *quantitative economic policy* aimed at facing temporary disequilibrium situations without trying to alter the system's structure (Tinbergen, 1952, chapter 1). Quantitative economic policy must be distinguished from *qualitative*, which instead is aimed at modifying the structure of the economic system.

The targets of quantitative economic policy can be obtained by modifying the value of the policy instruments considered in the model. Even though Tinbergen's quantitative economic policy concerns both fixed and flexible objectives, we shall here refer only to the case of fixed objectives, as already mentioned in the preceeding section.

The relations which describe Tinbergen's model can be summarized by the following linear system

$$\hat{A}y = \hat{B}u \tag{3.1}$$

where $y \in R^m$ is the target vector, $u \in R^r$ is the vector of policy instruments and $\hat{A}$, $\hat{B}$ are constant matrices of appropriate dimensions. We assume, for simplicity's sake, that all endogenous variables are target variables and that all exogenous variables are policy instruments (see footnote 2). It is also assumed that the m targets are linearly independent and that the r instruments are also linearly independent. As generally accepted, we mean that the instruments (or the targets) are *linearly independent* when the corresponding matrix is of full rank,[1] that is rank $[\hat{A}] = m$ and rank $[\hat{B}] = r$. The economic meaning of this property has been clearly illustrated by Mundell:

Consistency also requires that targets and instruments be mutually *independent*. For example, full employment and maximum output could not be considered targets if there is a unique functional relationship between the level of employment and of output, just as an adjustment of the exchange rate and certain applications of tariffs and export subsidies could produce equivalent effects on output and on the balance of payments (1968, pp. 201–2).

System (3.1) is said to be *statically controllable* if there exists a vector u^* such as to make the target vector y assume any given pre-assigned value y^*. A vector u^* exists if and only if the rank of the matrix $\hat{B}$ is equal to m, that is[2]

$$\text{rank } [\hat{B}] = m \qquad\qquad (3.2)$$

Condition (3.2) is known as *Tinbergen's condition*, or as the *static controllability condition*. Given the dimension of matrix $\hat{B}$, this means that a vector u^* exists if and only if *the number of linearly independent instruments is greater than or equal to the number of linearly independent targets*. As the targets are linearly independent by assumption, the requirement that the number of linearly independent instruments must be greater than or equal to the number of linearly independent targets means that the matrix $\hat{B}$ must contain at least m linearly independent columns, or, what amounts to the same thing, that its rank must equal m.[3]

It follows from condition (3.2) that a necessary condition for static controllability of system (3.1) is

$$r \geqslant m \qquad\qquad (3.3)$$

i.e., the number of instruments must be greater than or equal to the number of targets. This condition is known as Tinbergen's 'counting rule'. When (3.2) is satisfied and $r = m$ the vector u^* is unique.

A simple example of Tinbergen's problem is given by the well-known internal-external equilibrium model under fixed exchange rates described in Mundell (1962); the targets are full-employment $(Y = Y^F)$ and balance-of-payments equilibrium $(B = 0)$, while the instruments are Government expenditure (or budget surplus), G, and the rate of interest, i. A diagrammatic representation of this model is given in figure 3.1 (see Mundell, 1962, p. 72),

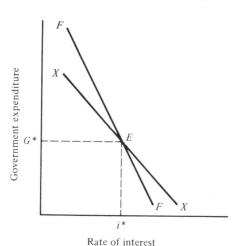

Figure 3.1   Internal and external equilibrium

where the FF line represents the locus of all pairs of interest rates and Government expenditure along which the balance of payments is in equilibrium, while the XX line is the locus of all pairs of interest rates and Government expenditures which give rise to full-employment equilibrium in the real market. Tinbergen's problem would be that of verifying the *existence* of a vector of instruments $u^* = [G^*, i^*]$ which satisfies the given static model (3.1) for the equilibrium values of the target variables, that is

$$\hat{A}\begin{bmatrix} Y^F \\ 0 \end{bmatrix} = \hat{B}\begin{bmatrix} G^* \\ i^* \end{bmatrix}$$

This vector is given by point E in figure 3.1.

Since the target vectors considered by Tinbergen are static equilibrium vectors (see, for example, Culbertson, 1968, chapter 18) a dynamic generalization of Tinbergen's problem should therefore be seen as the problem of reaching a given equilibrium target vector *over time* (see section 3.7).

3.3 Dynamic controllability

3.3.1 State controllability

Consider now the dynamic system

$$\dot{x}(t) = Ax(t) + Bu(t) \tag{3.4}$$

where $x(t) \in R^n$ is a state vector, $u(t) \in R^r$ is the control vector and A, B are matrices of appropriate dimensions which are assumed constant for simplicity; $x(t)$ can represent either the output of a first-order differential system or the state-space representation of a higher-order differential system (see chapter 2).

A state x is said to be *controllable* at $t = t_0$ if there exists a piecewise continuous and unconstrained control vector $u(t)$, defined on the interval $[t_0, t_f]$, capable of transferring the state from any initial point x_0 at time t_0 to any final point x_{t_f} at some finite time $t_f \geqslant t_0$.[4] If every state $x(t)$ is controllable, then the dynamic *system* is said to be (completely) *controllable*. From now on we will use the term 'dynamic controllability' or simply 'controllability' to indicate the complete controllability of the system. When the dynamic system (3.4) is completely controllable we also say that A, B is a controllable pair.

Since the solution of system (3.4) at time t_f is given by

$$x(t_f) = e^{A(t_f - t_0)} x(t_0) + \int_{t_0}^{t_f} e^{A(t_f - \tau)} Bu(\tau) \, d\tau \qquad (3.5)$$

the problem of the complete controllability of the state can be seen as the problem of the existence of a control vector $u(\tau)$ such that (3.5) is satisfied for any given vector $x(t_f)$ in the state space, given $x(t_0)$.

A *necessary and sufficient condition* for dynamic state controllability is

$$\text{rank}[P] = n \qquad (3.6)$$

where P is the $n \times nr$ matrix

$$P = [B \ AB \ A^2 B \dots A^{n-1} B] \qquad (3.7)$$

This matrix is called the controllability matrix.

Before showing the necessity and sufficiency of condition (3.6), we shall demonstrate that the problem of guiding the system from the initial state x_0 at time t_0 to any given final position x_{t_f} at time t_f is equivalent to guiding the system from the initial state x_0 at time t_0 to the origin of the state space at time t_f. If we pre-multiply the l.h.s. of (3.5) by $e^{A(t_f - t_0)} \cdot e^{A(t_0 - t_f)}$ (which is the identity matrix), we obtain, after simple manipulations,

$$0 = e^{A(t_f - t_0)} [x(t_0) - e^{A(t_0 - t_f)} x(t_f)] + \int_{t_0}^{t_f} e^{A(t_f - t_0)} Bu(\tau) \, d\tau \qquad (3.8)$$

Given the arbitrariness of $x(t_0)$, the term in square brackets can be considered as a new initial position of the system. It follows that system (3.4) is state controllable if there exists a vector $u(\tau)$ capable of taking the system from the initial position $(x(t_0) - e^{A(t_0 - t_f)} x(t_f))$ to the origin $(x(t_f) = 0)$ in the time interval $[t_0, t_f]$.

In order to show now the *necessity* of the controllability condition (3.6), we must demonstrate that, if the system is controllable, condition (3.6) is always satisfied. To that purpose we assume, without loss of generality, that the initial time t_0 is zero and that there exists a vector $u^*(\tau)\,(0 \leqslant \tau \leqslant t_f)$ capable of guiding the system from any arbitrary initial position $x(0)$ to the origin of the state space in the time interval $[0, t_f]$. We can thus write (3.5) as

$$0 = e^{At_f} x(0) + \int_0^{t_f} e^{A(t_f - t)} Bu^*(\tau)\,d\tau \tag{3.9}$$

whence, remembering that e^{At_f} is a non-singular matrix, we have

$$x(0) = -e^{-At_f} \int_0^{t_f} e^{A(t_f - t)} Bu^*(\tau)\,d\tau = -\int_0^{t_f} e^{-A\tau} Bu^*(\tau)\,d\tau \tag{3.10}$$

Since (see, Apostol, 1969, vol. 3, chapter 3)

$$e^{-A\tau} = \sum_{k=0}^{n-1} q_k(\tau) A^k \tag{3.11}$$

where q_k is a scalar function of τ, $\tau \in [0, t_f]$, equation (3.10) can be written

$$x(0) = -\sum_{k=0}^{n-1} \int_0^{t_f} q_k(\tau) A^k Bu^*(\tau)\,d\tau \tag{3.12}$$

On the other hand, the control vector $u^*(\tau)$ can be written

$$u^*(\tau) = \sum_{j=1}^{r} u_j^*(\tau) e_j \tag{3.13}$$

where e_j $(j = 1 \ldots r)$ are the elements of the natural basis of R^r (see, for example, Athans and Falb, 1966, chapter 2).

By substituting (3.13) into (3.12) and remembering that the matrices $A^k B$ are constant and can therefore be taken out of the integral, we obtain

$$x(0) = -\sum_{k=0}^{n-1} \sum_{j=1}^{r} \left[\int_0^{t_f} q_k(\tau) u_j^*(\tau)\,d\tau \right] A^k b_j \tag{3.14}$$

where b_j is the j-th column of the matrix B.

By then defining

$$\alpha_{kj} = \int_0^{t_f} q_k(\tau) u_j^*(\tau) \, d\tau \tag{3.15}$$

equation (3.14) becomes

$$x(0) = -\sum_{k=0}^{n-1} \sum_{j=1}^{r} \alpha_{kj} A^k b_j \tag{3.16}$$

From (3.16) we deduce that, if the state is completely controllable, then, given any initial state $x(0)$, (3.16) must be satisfied. This means that the initial state $x(0)$ can be expressed as a linear combination of the vectors $b_j, Ab_j, \ldots, A^{n-1} b_j$ $(j = 1, 2, \ldots, r)$. Therefore, since $x(0)$ is an n-dimensional vector, there should be, among the vectors $b_j, Ab_j, \ldots, A^{n-1} b_j$ $(j = 1, 2, \ldots, r)$, at least n linearly independent ones, so as to span the n-dimensional space; and this means that condition (3.6) must be satisfied. This proves the necessity of (3.6).

In order to prove now the *sufficiency*, let us assume that (3.6) is satisfied, i.e. that P is a matrix whose rank is n. Since, by an appropriate choice of the control vector $u(t)$, it is always possible to obtain scalars α_{kj} (defined as in (3.15)) such that the r.h.s. of (3.16) equals any given vector $x(0)$ in the space spanned by the linearly independent columns of P, and since, by assumption, the columns of P span the n-dimensional space, it follows that any given terminal state can be reached or, what amounts to the same thing, that the state is completely controllable.

From what has been said above, it seems clear that the state will be completely controllable if and only if any given initial vector $x(0)$ in the n-dimensional space can be expressed as a linear combination of the column vectors of the P matrix. If the number of the linearly independent columns of P is inferior to n, only a sub-space of the state space will be controllable: the sub-space spanned by the linearly independent vectors of P. In this case, the state space will be partitioned into two sub-spaces: a controllable and an uncontrollable sub-space.

It is also important to observe that if there is only one control variable – i.e. if the control vector $u(t)$ contains only one element – the dimension of the P matrix will be $n \times n$ (the B matrix becomes an n-dimensional vector) and the controllability condition will therefore be given by the non-singularity of P.

These results are of great importance in dynamic economic policy analysis. In fact, in all those economic models in which the output (target) vector and the state vector coincide (first-order dynamics), it can easily be

shown that Tinbergen's static controllability condition is no longer
a necessary condition for dynamic controllability (Preston, 1974; this result
still holds for dynamic systems of higher order). Any given target vector can
be reached even if the number of policy instruments is inferior to the
number of targets, provided condition (3.6) is satisfied. As a limiting case, as
we have just seen, it may be possible to control n targets completely with
only one instrument, if the P matrix is non-singular. In a dynamic
framework the controllability conditions do not depend only on the rank of
B (matrix of the coefficients of the control variables) as happens, on the
contrary, in the static case (a point to which we shall return in sections 3.3.2
and 3.5).

The condition for dynamic controllability of a given system can also be
stated in terms of the transfer function (or transfer matrix) of that system. In
this case, a *necessary and sufficient condition* is that *no cancellation occurs in
the transfer function (or transfer matrix)*.

Consider, for example, a given dynamic equation which can be represented
by the following transfer function

$$H(s) = \frac{b_0 s^2 + b_1 s + b_2}{s^3 + a_1 s^2 + a_2 s + a_3} \tag{3.17}$$

that is

$$H(s) = \frac{(s - z_1)(s - z_2)}{(s - p_1)(s - p_2)(s - p_3)} \tag{3.18}$$

where z_1 and z_2 are the zeros of the transfer function and p_1, p_2 and p_3 are
the poles.[5]

Whenever one (or more) pole(s) of the function happen to be on the same
point of the complex plane as one (or more) zero(s), the cancellation
problem occurs. If we have, for example, $z_1 = p_1$, the function (3.18) reduces
to

$$H(s) = \frac{s - z_2}{(s - p_2)(s - p_3)} \tag{3.19}$$

and the state of this system is not completely controllable.

Finally, we wish to underline that the dynamic controllability condition
is independent of the time interval considered; therefore, if the controllability condition is satisfied, the time required to transfer the state from one
position to another can be made as small as desired. But, since the control
vector is not constrained, it can, in principle, assume values which are
unrealistic from an economic point of view, or undergo variations which are
too great or too sudden. For this reason a tradeoff between the number of

policy instruments and the length of the programming horizon might arise, even when the system is controllable. It may be useful in some cases in which the time horizon is given, to make use of a larger number of policy instruments, since a greater number of instruments means less intensive use of each (Preston, 1974; see also Kalman, Ho and Narendra, 1962). Alternatively, if the number of policy instruments is given, it might be advisable to consider a larger programming horizon so as to obtain smoother paths for the control variables considered.

3.3.2 Static and dynamic controllability conditions

Since the static equilibrium solution of system (3.4) is

$$-Ax = Bu \qquad (3.20)$$

it is possible to consider Tinbergen's static system (3.1) as the equilibrium position of the dynamic system (3.4), such that[6] $\hat{A} = -A$ and $\hat{B} = B$. This specifies a relation between Tinbergen's static model and the dynamic model (3.4) and makes it possible to analyse the relationship between static and dynamic controllability conditions.

Although Tinbergen's rank condition is, obviously, sufficient for dynamic state controllability, it is not a necessary condition. It is possible to have rank $[P] = m$ even when rank $[B] < m$. In a dynamic framework it is therefore possible to reach any point in the state space with a number of linearly independent instruments inferior to the number of linearly independent targets (Preston, 1974).

In addition, since condition (3.6) may be satisfied even if $r < m$, it is possible to have state controllability even if the number of instruments is (numerically) inferior to the number of targets. That is, not even Tinbergen's 'counting rule' (3.3) is necessary for dynamic state controllability.

Therefore, when first-order dynamics is considered, any given target vector x can be reached even if the number of instruments is inferior to the number of targets. This result still holds for dynamic systems of a higher order, as we shall see in section 3.5.

3.4 Minimal set of instruments for dynamic controllability

As we have seen in the previous section a dynamic system may be controllable even when the number of targets is greater than the number of instruments. An obvious question therefore arises: if a dynamic system is controllable with the use of r instruments, would it still be controllable with the use of $r-1, r-2, \ldots$ or even with only one instrument? Since the use of policy instruments in economics has a cost, it is important to find the minimum number of control variables needed for the dynamic controllability condition to be satisfied.

To this purpose, consider again the dynamic system

$$\dot{x}(t) = Ax(t) + Bu(t) \tag{3.21}$$

and assume – following the line suggested by Preston (1974) – that matrix A possesses n distinct eigenvalues[7] $(\lambda_1, \ldots, \lambda_n; \lambda_i \neq \lambda_j)$. It is then possible to find a non-singular matrix Λ such that

$$\Lambda^{-1} A \Lambda = \begin{bmatrix} \lambda_1 & 0 & \ldots & 0 \\ 0 & \lambda_2 & \ldots & 0 \\ \multicolumn{4}{c}{\cdots\cdots\cdots\cdots\cdots} \\ 0 & 0 & \ldots & \lambda_n \end{bmatrix} \tag{3.22}$$

where λ_i $(i = 1, 2, \ldots, n)$ are the eigenvalues of matrix A, and Λ is the eigenvector matrix: each column of the Λ matrix is an eigenvector of A associated with the corresponding λ_i. We recall that, if the eigenvalues of A are distinct, the eigenvectors of A are also distinct, while the converse is not true.

Then by defining a new state vector $w(t)$ such that

$$x(t) = \Lambda w(t) \tag{3.23}$$

it is possible to write (3.21) as

$$\Lambda \dot{w}(t) = A \Lambda w(t) + Bu(t) \tag{3.24}$$

whence

$$\dot{w}(t) = \Lambda^{-1} A \Lambda w(t) + \Lambda^{-1} Bu(t) \tag{3.25}$$

Now by defining an $n \times r$-dimensional matrix

$$F = \Lambda^{-1} B = [f_{ij}] \tag{3.26}$$

we can rewrite (3.25) as

$$\begin{aligned} \dot{w}_1 &= \lambda_1 w_1 + f_{11} u_1 + f_{12} u_2 + \cdots + f_{1r} u_r \\ \dot{w}_2 &= \lambda_2 w_2 + f_{21} u_1 + f_{22} u_2 + \cdots + f_{2r} u_r \\ &\;\;\cdots\cdots\cdots\cdots\cdots\cdots\cdots\cdots\cdots\cdots\cdots\cdots \\ \dot{w}_n &= \lambda_n w_n + f_{n1} u_1 + f_{n2} u_2 + \cdots + f_{nr} u_r \end{aligned} \tag{3.27}$$

which is the *canonical*[8] representation of (3.21). It can easily be seen that in this kind of representation each state variable is independent of the others: there is a *decoupling* between the components of the state vector due to the fact that the new axes of the state space have the same direction as the eigenvectors.

From (3.27) it is possible to observe that, if the elements of any one row of matrix F are all zero, the corresponding state variable cannot be controlled by any of the r control variables u_i. Let the equation considered be the i-th equation; it then becomes

$$\dot{w}_i(t) = \lambda_i w_i(t) \tag{3.28}$$

the solution of which is

$$w_i(t) = e^{\lambda_i t} w_i(0) \tag{3.29}$$

The behaviour of $w_i(t)$ is clearly non-controllable. Therefore, the condition for state controllability of system (3.21) can also be stated as follows: *system (3.21) is completely controllable if and only if matrix F has no zero rows.*

This alternative controllability condition – also known as the *coupling criterion* (Preston, 1974) – is the starting point of the search for the minimum set of instruments required for dynamic controllability. In general, there may exist many combinations of the control variables (i.e. many combinations of the columns of F) which satisfy the coupling criterion (controllability condition) and, therefore, we have to find the minimum number of such columns. As a first step let us consider one single instrument, the i-th instrument u_i. In order to find out if the system is controllable with this single instrument we have to consider the following sub-system

$$\dot{x}(t) = Ax(t) + b_i u_i(t) \tag{3.30}$$

where b_i is the i-th column of matrix B, and verify if the controllability condition is satisfied.

System (3.30) – and, therefore, system (3.21) – will be controllable with the i-th instrument alone if and only if the column vector $f_i = \Lambda^{-1} b_i$ has no zero elements. In that case, (3.27) will be given by

$$\begin{aligned}
\dot{w}_1 &= \lambda_1 w_1 + f_{1i} u_i \\
\dot{w}_2 &= \lambda_2 w_2 + f_{2i} u_i \\
&\cdots\cdots\cdots\cdots\cdots \\
\dot{w}_n &= \lambda_n w_n + f_{ni} u_i
\end{aligned} \tag{3.31}$$

It is then evident that (3.31) will not be completely controllable when any one element of f_i is zero.

Since there are r similar sub-systems to (3.31) corresponding to each of the r control variables, if the coupling criterion is satisfied for at least one of the r vectors f_i, the minimum number of instruments required for the controllability of system (3.21) will be *one* (which is not necessarily unique). If, on the contrary, there is no vector f_i $(i = 1, 2, \ldots, r)$ which satisfies the coupling criterion, we have to carry on the search for any one $n \times 2$ matrix, formed by the combination of two vectors $f_i f_j$ $(i, j = 1, 2, \ldots, r, i \neq j)$, which eventually satisfies this criterion. As many matrices of this type will exist as there are combinations of the r columns taken two by two.

If we fail to find a matrix with no zero rows even in this way, we must still continue the construction of all possible $n \times 3, n \times 4, \ldots, n \times r$ matrices until we find the matrix which satisfies the non-zero row condition or coupling criterion.

In general, if we represent the $\binom{r}{j}$ possible combinations of the r column vectors $(j = 1, \ldots, r)$ by the $n \times j$ matrix $F_j(i)$, $i = 1, \ldots, \binom{r}{j}$, the minimum number of instruments $\hat{r}$ required for the dynamic controllability of system (3.21) is given by the number of columns of the smaller matrix $F_{\hat{r}}(i)$ which satisfies the coupling criterion. This set of instruments will be unique if and only if, among the $\binom{r}{\hat{r}}$ matrices, there is only one matrix which satisfies the coupling criterion.

Before concluding this section we wish to stress that, once the minimal set of instruments has been singled out, the problem of the tradeoff between the number of instruments and the length of the programming horizon mentioned above (section 3.3) should also be taken into consideration.

3.5 Output controllability

When the dynamic system considered is of a higher order than the first (i.e. the state vector does not coincide with the system's output) it becomes important to single out the conditions for complete output controllability. In economics as in other fields, the problem to be solved is usually the control of the *output* of a dynamic system so as to ensure that a given set of policy targets can be reached in some finite period of time.

In order to derive the output controllability conditions, consider the following time-invariant linear differential system

$$
\overset{(n)}{y} + A_1 \overset{(n-1)}{y} + \cdots + A_{n-1} \dot{y} + A_n y = B_0 \overset{(n)}{u}
$$
$$
+ B_1 \overset{(n-1)}{u} + \cdots + B_{n-1} \dot{u} + B_n u \tag{3.32}
$$

where $y(t) \in R^m$ is the target vector (output of the system), $u(t) \in R^r$ is the control vector (input of the system) and A_i, B_i $(i = 0, 1, \ldots, n)$ are constant matrices of the required dimensions (some of the B_i matrices might be the null matrix). The superscript in brackets indicates the order of the derivative (the first derivative is indicated, as usual, by a dot over the variable).

As above, we assume that all endogenous variables are target variables and that all exogenous variables are control variables. If policy-makers are interested only in a subset of the m output variables it may be useful to reduce, if possible, the dimension of the output vector. The control of a lower number of targets, given the available instruments, is of course easier (see Hughes Hallett and Rees, 1983, chapter 6).

An output y is said to be *controllable* at $t = t_0$ if there exists a piecewise continuous and unconstrained control vector $u(t)$, defined on the interval $[t_0, t_f]$, capable of transferring the output vector from any initial point y_0 at time t_0 to any final position y_{t_f} at some finite time $t_f \geqslant t_0$. If every point $y(t)$ in the output space is controllable, then the system is said to be (completely) *output controllable*.

As we have seen in chapter 2, the dynamic system (3.32) can be represented by the following state-space system

$$\dot{x}(t) = Ax(t) + Bu(t) \tag{3.33}$$

$$y(t) = Cx(t) + Du(t) \tag{3.34}$$

where $x \in R^n$ is the state vector and A, B, C, D are constant matrices of appropriate dimensions; $y(t)$ and $u(t)$ are the vectors defined in (3.32).

A *necessary and sufficient condition* for the complete output controllability of system (3.32) is

$$\text{rank}[M] = m \tag{3.35}$$

where M is the $m \times (n+1)r$ matrix

$$M = [CB \vdots CAB \vdots \ldots \vdots CA^{n-1}B \vdots D] \tag{3.36}$$

In order to show the *necessity* of condition (3.35) we shall follow the same line as in section 3.1.1. Assume, therefore, that the output is completely controllable; i.e. there exists a vector $u^*(\tau)$ $(0 \leqslant \tau \leqslant t_f)$ capable of taking any arbitrary initial vector $y(0)$ to the origin of the target space in the time interval $[0, t_f]$. Then, from (3.34), we have, at time t_f

$$0 = y(t_f) = Cx(t_f) + Du^*(t_f) \tag{3.37}$$

Since the solution of (3.33) at time t_f is given by

$$x(t_f) = e^{At_f} \left[x(0) + \int_0^{t_f} e^{-A\tau} Bu^*(\tau) \, d\tau \right] \tag{3.38}$$

we have, after substituting (3.38) into (3.37)

$$0 = Ce^{At_f} \left[x(0) + \int_0^{t_f} e^{-A\tau} Bu^*(\tau) \, d\tau \right] + Du^*(t_f) \tag{3.39}$$

from which

$$Ce^{At_f}x(0) = -\left[C\int_0^{t_f} e^{A(t_f-\tau)}Bu^*(\tau)\,d\tau + Du^*(t_f)\right] \tag{3.40}$$

where $Ce^{At_f}x(0)$ is a vector of the same dimension (m) as the y vector.
   Since (see (3.11))

$$e^{A(t_f-\tau)} = \sum_{k=0}^{n-1} q_k(t_f-\tau)A^k \tag{3.41}$$

$$Ce^{At_f}x(0) = -\left[C\sum_{k=0}^{n-1}\int_0^{t_f} q_k(t_f-\tau)A^kBu^*(\tau)d\tau + Du^*(t_f)\right] \tag{3.42}$$

The control vector $u^*(\tau)$ can be written (see (3.13))

$$u^*(\tau) = \sum_{j=1}^{r} u_j^*(\tau)e_j \tag{3.43}$$

and, therefore, we can rewrite (3.42) as

$$Ce^{At_f}x(0) = -\left\{C\sum_{k=0}^{n-1}\sum_{j=1}^{r}\left[\int_0^{t_f} q_k(t_f-\tau)u_j^*(\tau)\,d\tau\right]A^kb_j + \sum_{j=1}^{r} u_j^*(t_f)d_j\right\} \tag{3.44}$$

where b_j and d_j are the j-th columns of the matrices B and D respectively.
   Then by defining a scalar α_{kj} as

$$\alpha_{kj} = \int_0^{t_f} q_k(t_f-\tau)u^*(\tau)\,d\tau \tag{3.45}$$

we have, after substituting it into (3.44)

$$Ce^{At_f}x(0) = -\left[\sum_{k=0}^{n-1}\sum_{j=1}^{r}\alpha_{kj}CA^kb_j + \sum_{j=1}^{r} u_j^*(t_f)d_j\right] \tag{3.46}$$

   From (3.46) we can easily observe that, when the output of a dynamic system is completely controllable, any given vector $Ce^{At_f}x(0)$ can be expressed as a linear combination of the vectors Cb_j, CAb_j, $CA^2b_j, \ldots,$ $CA^{n-1}b_j, d_j\,(j=1, 2, \ldots, r)$. And, since $Ce^{At_f}x(0)$ is an m-dimensional vector, the vectors $Cb_j, CAb_j, \ldots, CA^{n-1}b_j, d_j\,(j=1, 2, \ldots, r)$ must be such as to span an m-dimensional space; and this means that condition (3.35) has to be satisfied.

The *sufficiency* of condition (3.35) can be proved in the same way that the sufficiency of the state controllability condition (3.6) was proved in section 3.3.1. We therefore refer the reader to that section.

Finally, the output controllability condition (3.35) confirms what was said in section 3.3.2, i.e. that in a dynamic framework it is possible to reach a given target position even if the number of policy instruments is inferior to the number of targets. We can show in fact that Tinbergen's condition is not a necessary condition for complete output controllability.

As in section 3.3.1 we consider Tinbergen's static system (3.1) as the equilibrium position of the dynamic system (3.32), which is given by

$$A_n y = B_n u \tag{3.47}$$

so that $\hat{A} = A_n$ and $\hat{B} = B_n$. It is quite clear that it is possible to have rank $[M] = m$ even when rank $[B_n] < m$. This means that in a dynamic framework it is possible to reach a point in the target space even if the number of the linearly independent instruments is inferior to the number of linearly independent targets.

In addition, since (3.35) can clearly be satisfied even if $r < m$, it is possible to have output controllability even if the number of instruments is (numerically) inferior to the number of targets. That is, not even Tinbergen's 'counting rule' (3.3) is necessary for dynamic output controllability.

3.6 Path controllability

Path controllability no longer refers to the controllability of a point – as was the case in the controllability concepts introduced in the previous sections – but to the controllability of a time trajectory. Path controllability is indeed very important in economics since the aim of economic policy interventions is not only to reach a given target point at a given moment of time, but also to keep the target at the position reached (or to impose a given dynamic behaviour on that target) *throughout* some finite period of time.

As we have just seen, the controllability concepts introduced above ensure only that the system will 'hit' a given target position at a given moment of time, but they do not say anything about the behaviour of the system *after* that moment. In fact, if the target position is not an equilibrium of the system, or if it is not a stable equilibrium, the system will tend to move away from it. Hitting a target might be a satisfactory result in engineering problems where, for example, it may be necessary for a spacecraft to reach a given point at a given moment. In economics, on the contrary, it is not sufficient to reach some desired position if it is not possible to remain there. To give an example, it is not only sufficient to bring employment to a given desired level at a given moment, it is just as important to keep it at that level subsequently.

Path controllability ensures that the system will remain in the position reached for a given period of time, or that it will follow, during this period, any pre-assigned trajectory. The concept of path controllability has been introduced into the theory of economic policy by Aoki (1975), though it was already known previously in control theory (Brockett and Mesarovic, 1965; Sain and Massey, 1969; Basile and Marro, 1971). Path controllability is also known as *functional reproducibility* or as *perfect controllability*. In order to distinguish path controllability from the controllability concepts (state and output controllability) introduced in the previous sections, we shall refer to those concepts as *point controllability*.

Let us now examine first the definition of path controllability and then, in section 3.5.1, the conditions for path controllability. To this purpose consider again the differential system

$$\overset{(n)}{y} + A_1 \overset{(n-1)}{y} + \cdots + A_{n-1} \dot{y} + A_n y = B_0 \overset{(n)}{u}$$
$$+ B_1 \overset{(n-1)}{u} + \cdots + B_{n-1} \dot{u} + B_n u \tag{3.48}$$

and the corresponding state-space representation

$$\dot{x}(t) = Ax(t) + Bu(t) \tag{3.49}$$

$$y(t) = Cx(t) \tag{3.50}$$

where we have assumed, for simplicity, that the term $B_0 \overset{(n)}{u}(t) = 0$.[9]

The dynamic system described by (3.48) (or by (3.49) and (3.50)) is said to be *path controllable* on the interval $[t_0 \, t_f]$ if there exists a piecewise continuous and unconstrained control vector $u(t) \, (t_0 \leqslant t \leqslant t_f)$ capable of moving any initial vector of target variables at time t_0 along any pre-assigned *trajectory* $y^*(t) \, (t_0 \leqslant t \leqslant t_f)$. The pre-assigned trajectory (that we represent by $y^*_{[t_0, t_f]}$) can be either a vector which moves in time or a vector whose value remains constant during the given time interval. It can easily be seen that the concept of path controllability is very restrictive since it requires that the system follows *exactly* (and not just as closely as possible) any given trajectory (therefore, also disequilibrium trajectories) during a given interval of time.

3.6.1 Path controllability conditions

In order to introduce path controllability conditions we shall follow the approach presented in Sain and Massey (1969), which is based on the relation between path controllability and invertibility of dynamic systems.

Let $X(s)$, $U(s)$ and $Y(s)$ indicate the Laplace transforms of $x(t)$, $u(t)$ and $y(t)$ respectively. Then, taking the Laplace transforms of both members of (3.49) and (3.50), we have

$$sX(s) - x(0) = AX(s) + BU(s) \tag{3.51}$$

$$Y(s) = CX(s) \tag{3.52}$$

Assuming that[10] $x(0) = 0$, from (3.51) we get

$$X(s) = (sI - A)^{-1} BU(s) \tag{3.53}$$

and, by substituting (3.53) into (3.52), we obtain

$$Y(s) = G(s)U(s) \tag{3.54}$$

where $G(s)$ is an $m \times r$ rational matrix in s and is the transfer function matrix of system (3.48) defined by

$$G(s) = C(sI - A)^{-1} B \tag{3.55}$$

Equation (3.54) describes the relationship between the Laplace transform of the control vector $U(s)$ and the Laplace transform of the target vector $Y(s)$. We now recall some definitions of invertibility and of path controllability of dynamic systems in the *frequency* domain.

The dynamic system described by (3.48) is said to be left *invertible* if the transfer matrix $G(s)$ has a left inverse, while it is said to be *right invertible*[11] if the transfer matrix $G(s)$ has a right inverse. If the system is right invertible there always exists a vector $U(s)$, so that (3.54) is satisfied for any given arbitrary vector $Y(s)$.

The dynamic system (3.48) is said to be *path controllable* if, given any arbitrary vector $Y(s)$, there always exists a vector $U(s)$ so that (3.54) is satisfied. It therefore follows that path controllability and right invertibility are *equivalent* properties of system (3.48). If matrix $G(s)$ has a right inverse, it is always possible to solve (3.54) for $U(s)$, given $Y(s)$. But to say that system (3.48) is right invertible is the same as saying that the dual (see section 3.10) of system (3.48) is left invertible, since the transfer matrix of the dual system is defined as

$$G_D(s) = G'(s) \tag{3.56}$$

that is

$$G_D(s) = B'(sI - A')^{-1} C' \tag{3.57}$$

Therefore, the conditions for path controllability of system (3.48) are the same as the conditions for right invertibility of the same system, i.e. are the same as the conditions for left invertibility of the dual of system (3.48).

Considering therefore the conditions for left invertibility (we refer the reader to Sain and Massey for a demonstration of these conditions), we can now state the conditions for path controllability:

(a) the system described by (3.48) is path controllable (i.e., the dual of system (3.48) is left invertible) *if and only if*

$$\text{rank}[G_D(s)] = m \tag{3.58}$$

over the field of rational functions in s. This condition is the same as condition (b) in Brockett and Mesarovic (1965, p. 559).

(b) The system described by (3.48) is path controllable (i.e., the dual of system (3.48) is left invertible) *if and only if*

$$\text{rank}[N] = (n+1)m \tag{3.59}$$

where N is the $(n+1)m \times 2nr$ matrix

$$N = \begin{bmatrix} CB & CAB\ldots\ldots & CA^{2n-1}B \\ 0 & CB & CAB\ldots & CA^{2n-2}B \\ \ldots\ldots\ldots\ldots\ldots\ldots\ldots\ldots\ldots\ldots \\ 0 & 0\ldots & CB\ldots & CA^{n-1}B \end{bmatrix} \tag{3.60}$$

This condition is the same as condition (17) in Brockett and Mesarovic (1965, p. 556).[12]

It is worth underlining that, when $G_D(s)$ is a *square* invertible matrix (rank$[G_D(s)] = r = m$), the vector $U(s)$ which satisfies (3.54) is unique so that (3.48) possesses a unique solution for $u(t)$, which is obtained by taking the inverse of the Laplace transform. Note also that as $G_D(s)$ is an $r \times m$ matrix, an immediate consequence of (3.58) is the following condition:

(c) the dynamic system (3.48) is path controllable (i.e. the dual of system (3.48) is left invertible) *only if*

$$r \geqslant m \tag{3.61}$$

that is, only if the number of control variables is greater than or equal to the number of target variables. This condition is also stated in Aoki (1975, corollary 2).

Given the form of the matrix N another necessary condition for path controllability can be derived from condition (3.59), i.e.

$$m \leqslant \frac{2n}{n+1}r \tag{3.62}$$

But, since condition (3.61) is more restrictive than condition (3.62), condition (3.62) is irrelevant when (3.61) is satisfied.

3.6.2 Static and path controllability conditions

Following Aoki's (1975) paper in which the concept of and the conditions for path controllability were introduced, a number of papers[13] have been published which discuss the relation between Tinbergen's conditions and path controllability conditions, and which have given rise to a debate on this issue.

The confusion which had initially characterized the debate has had its uses in encouraging clarification of the issue. In this section, following the line suggested in an earlier paper (Petit, 1987), we will show that, although Tinbergen's 'counting rule' (3.3) (i.e., number of instruments $\geqslant$ number of targets) is a necessary condition for path controllability of continuous-time systems, Tinbergen's rank condition (3.2) (i.e., number of linearly independent instruments $\geqslant$ number of linearly independent targets) is not a necessary condition for path controllability of differential systems of a *higher order* than the first.

Consider again Tinbergen's system (3.1) as the static equilibrium solution of the dynamic system (3.48), so that $A_n = \hat{A}$ and $B_n = \hat{B}$.

Let us now assume that Tinbergen's rank condition (3.2) is *not* satisfied (i.e. rank $[B_n] < m$). It can be shown that the path controllability condition (3.58) and consequently condition (3.59) can be satisfied even if condition (3.2) is not. It is possible to have rank $[C(sI - A)^{-1}B] = m$ even if rank $[B_n] < m$; since rank $[(sI - A)^{-1}] = n$, and, since we can have rank $[C] = m$ and also rank $[B] = m$ even when rank $[B_n] < m$, it is possible to have rank $[G(s)] = m$.[14]

The same conclusion holds as far as condition (3.59) is concerned: it is possible to have rank $[N] = (n + 1)m$ even when rank $[B_n] < m$. As we have just seen, we can have rank $[B] = m$ even when rank $[B_n] < m$; so we can also have rank $[CB] = m$ even when rank $[B_n] < m$. Given the form of matrix N this would be sufficient to have rank $N = (n + 1)m$.

An example will help to clarify what has just been said. Consider the following differential system

$$\overset{(2)}{y} + 2\dot{y}_1 + \dot{y}_2 + 2y_2 = \dot{u}_1 + 3\dot{u}_2 + u_1 + 2u_2$$

$$\overset{(2)}{y} + \dot{y}_1 + 2y_1 + y_2 = \dot{u}_1 + \dot{u}_2 + u_1 + 2u_2$$

$$\tag{3.63}$$

which can be written in matrix form

$$\overset{(2)}{y} + A_1\dot{y} + A_2 y = B_1\dot{u} + B_2 u \tag{3.64}$$

or

$$\begin{bmatrix} \overset{(2)}{y_1} \\ \overset{(2)}{y_2} \end{bmatrix} + \begin{bmatrix} 2 & 1 \\ 1 & 0 \end{bmatrix} \begin{bmatrix} \dot{y}_1 \\ \dot{y}_2 \end{bmatrix} + \begin{bmatrix} 0 & 2 \\ 2 & 1 \end{bmatrix} \begin{bmatrix} y_1 \\ y_2 \end{bmatrix} = \begin{bmatrix} 1 & 3 \\ 1 & 1 \end{bmatrix} \begin{bmatrix} \dot{u}_1 \\ \dot{u}_2 \end{bmatrix} + \begin{bmatrix} 1 & 2 \\ 1 & 2 \end{bmatrix} \begin{bmatrix} u_1 \\ u_2 \end{bmatrix} \quad (3.65)$$

The static equilibrium solution of system (3.63) is

$$A_2 y = B_2 u \quad (3.66)$$

Although the counting rule is satisfied $(r = m)$, system (3.63) is not statically controllable: Tinbergen's condition is not satisfied since rank $[B_2] = 1$. Nevertheless, system (3.63) is dynamically path controllable. A state-space representation of this system is

$$\dot{x}(t) = A x(t) + B u(t)$$

$$y(t) = C x(t)$$

where

$$A = \begin{bmatrix} 0 & 0 & 1 & 0 \\ 0 & 0 & 0 & 1 \\ 0 & -2 & -2 & -1 \\ -2 & -1 & -1 & 0 \end{bmatrix} \quad B = \begin{bmatrix} B_1 \\ B_2 - A_1 B_1 \end{bmatrix} = \begin{bmatrix} 1 & 3 \\ 1 & 1 \\ -2 & -5 \\ 0 & -1 \end{bmatrix} \quad (3.67)$$

$$C = \begin{bmatrix} 1 & 0 & 0 & 0 \\ 0 & 1 & 0 & 0 \end{bmatrix}$$

Since rank $[C] = 2$, rank $[B] = 2$ and $(sI - A)^{-1}$ is a non-singular 4×4 square matrix, it follows that

$$\text{rank}[C(sI - A)^{-1}B] \leqslant 2 \quad (3.68)$$

In order to be sure that the equality prevails in (3.68), we have to check whether the rank of N is 10 (i.e., $m(n+1)$), where

$$N = \begin{bmatrix} CB & CAB & CA^2B & CA^3B & CA^4B & CA^5B & CA^6B & CA^7B \\ 0 & CB & CAB & CA^2B & CA^3B & CA^4B & CA^5B & CA^6B \\ 0 & 0 & CB & CAB & CA^2B & CA^3B & CA^4B & CA^5B \\ 0 & 0 & 0 & CB & CAB & CA^2B & CA^3B & CA^4B \\ 0 & 0 & 0 & 0 & CB & CAB & CA^2B & CA^3B \end{bmatrix} \quad (3.69)$$

Since $CB = B_1$ and since rank $[B_1] = 2$, it follows also that rank $[CB] = 2$.

Given the upper triangular form of the matrix N, this is sufficient to assert that rank $[N] = 10$.

Therefore, though Tinbergen's 'counting rule' is necessary for path controllability, Tinbergen's rank condition is not. The 'counting rule' (3.3) says nothing about the linear dependence or independence between the instruments; thus, while a static economic system might not be controllable because of the linear dependence between the policy instruments – even if there are as many of them as there are targets – in a dynamic framework a path objective might instead be controllable in spite of the linear dependence between the instruments. The dynamics of the system allows the control variables to move in time so that not only their levels (instant values) influence the targets but also their time variations. It is this dynamic effect of the instruments on the targets that 'cancels' the necessity of linear independence between the instruments, which, on the contrary, is essential in a static framework.

Before concluding, we note that, when no derivatives of the control variables are considered (i.e., $B_i = 0(i = 0, 1, \ldots, n-1)$, $B_n \neq 0$ in (3.48)), Tinbergen's rank condition *is* a necessary condition for path controllability. (The reader can easily check this result.) A particular case is the dynamic system with state target variables. Note however that when $n = 1$ in (3.48) (with $A_i = 0$, $B_i = 0$, $i = 2, \ldots, n$), that is when the dynamics of the target vector is of the first order but there is at least one first-order derivative of one of the control variables, Tinbergen's rank condition (3.2) is no longer necessary for path controllability.

We can therefore conclude that, when *general* dynamic economic models are considered, the condition of linear independence between the instruments is not necessary for path controllability, provided that there are as many instruments as there are targets. The economic implications of this result are immediate if one thinks how frequently dynamic economic models are described by systems of equations of a higher order than the first and how often they include derivatives of policy instruments, such as, for instance, the rate of growth of the money stock.

3.6.3 Sufficient conditions for path controllability

The necessary and sufficient conditions for path controllability stated above have an obvious drawback: they are rather complicated and difficult to compute, especially when systems of many equations and/or of high-order differential equations are considered.

A list of sufficient conditions for path controllability of differential systems was proposed by Aoki and Canzoneri (1979) which are much easier to check and are, therefore, very important in economic applications where large econometric models are frequently used (see Wohltmann and Krömer, 1984, for the discrete-time case).

We here simply state these conditions and refer the reader to Aoki and Canzoneri (1979) for the relevant demonstrations.

Considering the state-space system

$$\dot{x}(t) = Ax(t) + Bu(t) \tag{3.70}$$

$$y(t) = Cx(t) + Du(t) \tag{3.71}$$

each of the following conditions is sufficient for path controllability:

(a) $\det [D] \neq 0$,
(b) $D = 0$ and $\det [CB] \neq 0$,
(c) $\det [D - CA^{-1}B] \neq 0$,
(d) rank $[D] = p < m$; there exists a non-singular matrix S such that $[SC \; SD] = \begin{bmatrix} C_1 D_2 \\ C_2 0 \end{bmatrix}$ where D_2 is $p \times m$ and $\begin{bmatrix} D_2 \\ C_2 B \end{bmatrix}$ has rank m.

3.7 An economic example of controllability

It is important at this point to apply the controllability analysis described in the previous sections to a dynamic economic model. We shall therefore consider a very simple model, the Phillips' (1954) model, that was explicitly introduced for purposes of economic policy analysis.

Phillips considers a dynamic model based on the multiplier accelerator mechanism, with one target variable (output) and one control variable (public expenditure). Using alternative feedback control functions, he then examines the stability of the system so as to compare its dynamic behaviour under the different control assumptions.

In this exercise we intend to examine the dynamic controllability properties of Phillips' model, and in particular to check whether this model satisfies the state, output and path controllability conditions. To that purpose we shall follow the general lines of Gandolfo's exposition (1980, chapter 5) of the Phillips' model, where a dynamic mechanism of the multiplier type is considered.

The first assumption is that output adjusts to excess demand as follows

$$\dot{Y} = \alpha(D - Y), \quad \alpha > 0 \tag{3.72}$$

where Y is domestic output, D is aggregate demand and α is the speed of adjustment of output to the discrepancy between aggregate demand and current output.

Since Phillips considers a closed economy, aggregate (private and public) demand is defined as

$$D = (1 - \omega)Y + G, \quad 0 < \omega < 1 \tag{3.73}$$

where $(1 - \omega)$ is the marginal propensity to spend.

Phillips assumes further that actual public expenditure G is different from its theoretical or potential value $\hat{G}$, since time is required to adjust current expenditure to the theoretical value. This adjustment is described by

$$\dot{G} = \beta(\hat{G} - G), \quad \beta > 0 \tag{3.74}$$

where β is the speed of response to a discrepancy between the theoretical and the current value of public expenditure.

By manipulating the model, the three equations (3.72), (3.73) and (3.74) can be reduced to one. By differentiating (3.73) we have

$$\dot{D} = (1 - \omega)\dot{Y} + \dot{G} \tag{3.75}$$

Multiplying both members of (3.73) by β and adding the result to (3.75) we obtain

$$\dot{D} + \beta D = (1 - \omega)\dot{Y} + \beta(1 - \omega)Y + \dot{G} + \beta G \tag{3.76}$$

whence, from (3.74),

$$\dot{D} + \beta D = (1 - \omega)\dot{Y} + \beta(1 - \omega)Y + \beta\hat{G} \tag{3.77}$$

From (3.72) we have

$$D = \frac{\dot{Y} + \alpha Y}{\alpha} \tag{3.78}$$

and, by differentiating both members

$$\dot{D} = \frac{\overset{(2)}{Y} + \alpha\dot{Y}}{\alpha} \tag{3.79}$$

Now, by multiplying both members of (3.78) by β and adding the result to (3.79), we obtain

$$\dot{D} + \beta D = \frac{\overset{(2)}{Y} + (\alpha + \beta)\dot{Y} + \alpha\beta Y}{\alpha} \tag{3.80}$$

Equating the r.h.s. of (3.80) and (3.77), we get

$$\frac{\overset{(2)}{Y} + (\alpha + \beta)\dot{Y} + \alpha\beta Y}{\alpha} = (1 - \omega)\dot{Y} + \beta(1 - \omega)Y + \beta\hat{G} \tag{3.81}$$

hence, after simple manipulations

$$\overset{(2)}{Y} + (\alpha\omega + \beta)\dot{Y} + \alpha\beta\omega Y = \alpha\beta\hat{G} \tag{3.82}$$

Phillips' model is thus described by the second-order differential equation (3.82), where Y is the target variable and $\hat{G}$ the control variable. In order to analyse the controllability properties of this model, we first reduce it to state-space form. We therefore define the following state variables

$$\begin{aligned} x_1 &= Y \\ x_2 &= \dot{Y} \\ x_3 &= \overset{(2)}{Y} \end{aligned} \tag{3.83}$$

whence, using (3.82)

$$\begin{aligned} \dot{x}_1 &= x_2 \\ \dot{x}_2 &= -(\alpha\omega + \beta)\dot{Y} - \alpha\beta\omega Y + \alpha\beta\hat{G} \end{aligned} \tag{3.84}$$

that is

$$\begin{aligned} \dot{x}_1 &= x_2 \\ \dot{x}_2 &= -\alpha\beta\,\omega x_1 - (\alpha\omega + \beta)x_2 + \alpha\beta\hat{G} \end{aligned} \tag{3.85}$$

which is a state-space representation of (3.82).

The output equation is

$$Y = x_1 \tag{3.86}$$

Considering the matrix form, we have

$$\begin{aligned} \dot{x}(t) &= Ax(t) + Bu(t) \\ y(t) &= Cx(t) \end{aligned} \tag{3.87}$$

where

$$x' = [x_1, x_2], \quad u = \hat{G}, \quad y = Y$$

$$A = \begin{bmatrix} 0 & 1 \\ -\alpha\beta\omega & -(\alpha\omega + \beta) \end{bmatrix} \quad B = \begin{bmatrix} 0 \\ \alpha\beta \end{bmatrix}$$

$$C = [1, 0]$$

We can now check if the state, output and path controllability conditions are satisfied.

The dynamic system (3.87) is state controllable if and only if (see (3.6))

$$\text{rank } [B \vdots AB] = 2 \tag{3.88}$$

where

$$[B \vdots AB] = \begin{bmatrix} 0 & \alpha\beta \\ \alpha\beta & -\alpha\beta(\alpha\omega + \beta) \end{bmatrix}$$

Since det $[B \vdots AB] = -\alpha^2\beta^2$, rank $[B \vdots AB] = 2$, and therefore the state controllability condition is satisfied.

The necessary and sufficient output controllability condition is also satisfied. This condition is (see (3.35))

$$\text{rank } [CB \vdots CAB] = 1 \qquad (3.89)$$

where

$$[CB \vdots CAB] = [0 \quad \alpha\beta]$$

which is clearly of rank 1.

Finally, the dynamic system (3.87) is path controllable if and only if (see (3.59))

$$\text{rank}[N] = \text{rank} \begin{bmatrix} CB & CAB & CA^2B & CA^3B \\ 0 & CB & CAB & CA^2B \\ 0 & 0 & CB & CAB \end{bmatrix} = 3 \qquad (3.90)$$

where

$$N = \begin{bmatrix} 0 & \alpha\beta & -\alpha\beta(\alpha\omega + \beta) & \alpha^2\beta^2\omega + \alpha\beta(\alpha^2\omega^2 + \beta^2) \\ 0 & 0 & \alpha\beta & -\alpha\beta(\alpha\omega + \beta) \\ 0 & 0 & 0 & \alpha\beta \end{bmatrix}$$

It can easily be seen that the determinant of the matrix formed by the last three columns of N is $-\alpha^3\beta^3$. The rank of the matrix N is therefore 3.[15]

Phillips' model satisfies the three controllability conditions. It is therefore both point and path controllable for any value of the parameters, provided that α and β are different from zero. This means that by manipulating public expenditure over time it is possible not only to obtain the desired level of output at a given finite time, but also to keep this desired level thereafter. Moreover, since the model is path controllable, it is possible, by adequately using public expenditure, to move the output along any desired trajectory.

This can easily be seen in our case since – given that the number of instruments (one) is equal to the number of targets (one) – it is possible to obtain a *unique* control solution for each pre-assigned target path.

Assume for example that the desired time trajectory for output is given by

$$Y^D(t) = Y_0 e^{\delta t} \qquad (3.91)$$

where Y_0 is the initial value at $t = t_0$ and δ represents the desired rate of growth. The problem to be solved consists therefore in finding the time path for $\hat{G}(t)$ which satisfies (3.82) over a given time interval $[t_0, t_f]$, when $Y(t)$ is defined by (3.91).

If we set

$$\hat{G}(t) = \hat{G}_0 \, e^{\rho t} \tag{3.92}$$

the problem is reduced to finding the values of $\hat{G}_0$ and ρ. Thus, considering (3.82), (3.91) and (3.92), we have, after collecting terms

$$Y_0 \, e^{\delta t} [\delta^2 + \alpha \omega (\delta + \beta) + \delta \beta] = \alpha \beta \hat{G}_0 \, e^{\rho t} \tag{3.93}$$

Taking logs and differentiating with respect to time, we get

$$\rho = \delta \tag{3.94}$$

The initial value $\hat{G}_0$ can now be obtained from (3.93), i.e.

$$\hat{G}_0 = \{ [\delta^2 + \alpha \omega (\delta + \beta) + \delta \beta] / \alpha \beta \} Y_0 \tag{3.95}$$

The time trajectory of the control variable $\hat{G}(t)$ is therefore given by

$$\hat{G}(t) = \{ [\delta^2 + \alpha \omega (\delta + \beta) + \delta \beta] / \alpha \beta \} Y_0 \, e^{\delta t}, \quad t \in [t_0, t_f] \tag{3.96}$$

Obviously the time trajectory of actual public expenditure $G(t)$ can also be obtained simply by substituting (3.96) into (3.74) and by solving the resulting differential equation.

This means that the output oscillations, which are a typical feature of the Phillips model (Phillips, 1954; Gandolfo, 1980, chapters 5 and 7) when feedback control rules are applied, can, therefore, in theory, be completely eliminated. We say 'in theory' to take account of the fact that 'in practice' the values of public expenditure required to guide the output along the desired path might be unrealistic from an economic point of view or administratively unfeasible, and therefore, not implementable. This possibility should always be kept in mind when controllability analysis is applied in economics.

3.8 Issues in the dynamic generalization of Tinbergen's theory

As we have seen in section 3.3, the dynamic (*point*) controllability concept was introduced into the theory of economic policy as the dynamic generalization of Tinbergen's theory (Preston, 1974). Tinbergen's approach was based on static economic models (see section 3.2) but, after Phillips' pioneering articles (1954, 1957), a considerable amount of research on the dynamic theory of economic policy came out in the sixties, also following the growing literature on dynamic econometric modelling. An extension of

Tinbergen's approach in a dynamic context was therefore needed and dynamic controllability appeared to be the natural extension.

Nevertheless, the introduction in 1975 of the *path* controllability concept into the theory of economic policy (Aoki, 1975), gave rise to conflicting opinions, since it was then maintained that path controllability, and not point controllability, was the natural generalization of Tinbergen's theory (Aoki, 1975, 1976a, chapter 3; see also Nyberg and Viotti, 1978 and, for different views on the problem, Buiter and Gersovitz, 1981; Preston and Pagan, 1982, chapter 7). The argument against the point controllability approach in economic applications centred on the fact that, as we have seen above, point controllability ensures only that the system will hit the target point at a given moment in time, but says nothing about the behaviour of the system thereafter.

In section 3.6 we have already stressed the importance of path controllability in economic applications. We believe, however, that the importance of one concept does not exclude that of the other, and that both path and point controllability can be considered as dynamic extensions of Tinbergen's static controllability. It is the *dynamic* framework in which the economic problem is analysed that makes it possible to use different concepts of controllability, and the choice of one or the other depends exclusively on the purpose of the analysis.

As already mentioned in section 3.2, the target vectors considered by Tinbergen were static equilibrium vectors, and, therefore, a natural generalization of Tinbergen's problem could be seen as the problem of moving the system from a disequilibrium situation to an equilibrium position in a given period of time; that is, as the problem of reaching a given equilibrium target vector *over time*. This means that, given a dynamic system in disequilibrium (like the differential system (3.48)), described by target variables and control variables which are functions of time, the dynamic extension of Tinbergen's theory should be stated as the problem of the existence of a control vector $u^*(t)$ capable of moving an initial disequilibrium target vector $y_0(t_0)$ to any given equilibrium point $y^*(t_f)$, in the time interval $[t_0, t_f]$.

But this is exactly what dynamic (point) controllability ensures: the existence of this vector $u^*(t)$. Point controllability is therefore important in all the economic problems in which the policy-maker wants to guide the system to a (stable) *equilibrium* position[16] (Buiter and Gersovitz, 1981; Preston and Pagan, 1982). In these cases, the problem of what happens to the system *after* target $y^*(t_f)$ has been reached is no longer important. In fact, as the target point is a stable equilibrium, the spontaneous forces of the economy will subsequently keep the system at the equilibrium position reached. Once this equilibrium position has been attained, the control vector will assume the value which is consistent with the equilibrium values of the targets. This means that the action of the control variables must stop if the equilibrium target is a stock value, or else the control variables must be kept at a constant value if the equilibrium target is a flow.

For example, let us assume that the equilibrium target is the full-employment level of output, a flow variable, which should be reached by manipulating public expenditure. Assuming that the target is attained at t_f with a corresponding level of public expenditure equal to $G^*(t_f)$, this level of public expenditure has to be kept constant for $t_f \leqslant t \leqslant t_f + \delta$ ($\delta > 0$) since otherwise the level of output will drop again below the full-employment level after t_f.

If the equilibrium target is a stock value, the control action has to stop once the target has been reached. Assume, for example, that the target consists of a given endowment of infrastructures to be obtained at a given time t_f, by managing public investment in fixed capital. Once the target at time t_f has been reached, the investment (control action) has to stop and return to its initial level, otherwise the infrastructures endowment, after t_f, will exceed the desired amount.

It might however be objected that, when the target vector considered is an equilibrium of the system and the dynamic system considered is stable, it will tend to return spontaneously to the equilibrium position without the need of specific policy actions. Although this is undoubtedly true, it should be noted that the stability property ensures no more than a tendency towards equilibrium (for $t \to + \infty$), while the point controllability property ensures the existence of at least one control vector capable of guiding the system *exactly* to the equilibrium position in a *given* and *finite* interval of time (see section 4.7).

Point controllability therefore assumes great relevance as far as Tinbergen's dynamic generalization is concerned, since it ensures that targets, which–as in Tinbergen's theory – are equilibrium points, can be reached in a given time and automatically maintained until a new perturbation appears.

When the target position which the policy-maker wishes to reach and hold is an unstable equilibrium or is not an equilibrium position, then – if we want to analyse the Tinbergen problem in a dynamic framework – we must instead turn our attention to the property of *path* controllability of dynamic systems.

It thus follows that we cannot speak of a single dynamic generalization of Tinbergen's theory. The choice of one type of objective or another – and of the corresponding dynamic controllability analysis (point or path controllability) – depends each time on the goals pursued by policy-makers and on the intrinsic nature of the model representing the underlying economy.

3.9 Observability

Observability is a property of dynamic systems which guarantees the determination of the state at a given moment through the observation of the output at future moments.

Though not as important as controllability – as far as the possibility of applications to the theory of economic policy is concerned – observability is a useful property of dynamic systems in those cases in which the state variables are not measurable or are subject to measurement errors. If the observability conditions are satisfied, it is then possible *uniquely* to determine the state at a given time from the observation of the output dynamics after that time. Furthermore, observability, together with controllability, ensure the *minimality* of the system's state space.

Before providing a definition of observability, an example will help to clarify its meaning.

Consider the following *non-observable* system (Preston and Pagan, 1982, chapter 6)

$$\begin{bmatrix} x_1(t) \\ x_2(t) \end{bmatrix} = \begin{bmatrix} a_{11} & 0 \\ a_{21} & a_{22} \end{bmatrix} \begin{bmatrix} x_1(t) \\ x_2(t) \end{bmatrix} + \begin{bmatrix} b_1 \\ b_2 \end{bmatrix} u(t)$$

$$y(t) = \begin{bmatrix} c_1 & 0 \end{bmatrix} \begin{bmatrix} x_1(t) \\ x_2(t) \end{bmatrix} + du(t)$$

where, as can easily be seen, the output $y(t)$ does not depend on the state variable $x_2(t)$, either directly ($c_2 = 0$), or indirectly ($a_{12} = 0$). Therefore, given $u(t)$, any initial value $x_2(t_0)$ which gives rise to a given behaviour $x_2(t)$ of the state variable, will have no influence on $y(t)$. It follows that a given behaviour of $y(t)$ ($t_0 \leqslant t \leqslant t_f$) is compatible with an infinite number of trajectories of the state variable $x_2(t)$ ($t_0 \leqslant t \leqslant t_f$). In this case, the state $[x_1(t), x_2(t)]$ is not completely observable, and the non-observable variable $x_2(t)$ is redundant, i.e. the dimension of the state space is not minimal. Observability therefore guarantees a given behaviour of the target vector $y(t)$ to be determined through a *unique* path of the state $x(t)$.

Consider now the dynamic system

$$\dot{x}(t) = Ax(t) + Bu(t) \tag{3.97}$$

$$y(t) = Cx(t) + Du(t) \tag{3.98}$$

whose solution is

$$y(t) = Ce^{A(t-t_0)} x(t_0) + C \int_{t_0}^{t} e^{A(t-\tau)} Bu(\tau) \, d\tau + Du(t) \tag{3.99}$$

Since the matrices A, B and D are given, as is the control vector $u(t)$, the two last terms on the r.h.s. of (3.99) are known. They can therefore be subtracted from the l.h.s. so that

$$\tilde{y}(t) = C e^{A(t-t_0)} x(t_0) \tag{3.100}$$

where $\tilde{y}(t) = y(t) - [C \int_{t_0}^{t} e^{A(t-\tau)} Bu(\tau)\, d\tau + Du(t)]$

The behaviour of $y(t)$ can immediately be obtained from that of $\tilde{y}(t)$. It thus makes no difference which is considered.

We can now provide a definition of the observability property and obtain the observability condition. Let

$$y(t) = C e^{A(t-t_0)} x_0 \tag{3.101}$$

be the response of $y(t)$ to the initial state $x(t_0) = x_0$. The system described by (3.97)–(3.98) is *completely observable*, if, for every t_0, there exists a t_f $(t_f < \infty)$ such that

$$C e^{A(t-t_0)} x_0 = C e^{A(t-t_0)} x'_0, \quad t_0 \leqslant t \leqslant t_f \tag{3.102}$$

implies

$$x_0 = x'_0 \tag{3.103}$$

The fact that the same output response corresponds to two different initial values of the state implies the uniqueness of the state.

From this definition of observability it follows that system (3.97)–(3.98) is completely observable if, for every t_0, there exists a t_f $(t_f < \infty)$ such that

$$C e^{A(t-t_0)} x_0 = 0, \quad t_0 \leqslant t \leqslant t_f \tag{3.104}$$

implies

$$x_0 = 0 \tag{3.105}$$

If we recall then that (see (3.11))

$$e^{A(t-t_0)} = \sum_{k=0}^{n-1} A^k q_k(t) \tag{3.106}$$

where $q_k(t)$ is a scalar function, (3.104) can be written as

$$C \sum_{k=0}^{n-1} A^k q_k(t) x_0 = 0 \tag{3.107}$$

or else

$$[C q_0(t) + CA q_1(t) + CA^2 q_2(t) + \cdots + CA^{n-1} q_{n-1}(t)] x_0 = 0 \tag{3.108}$$

Therefore, since (3.108) is no more than a different way of writing (3.104), we can say that, if the system is completely observable, (3.108) implies $x_0 = 0$. This result can be used to obtain the following observability condition:

A *necessary and sufficient condition* for complete observability of system (3.97)–(3.98) is

$$\text{rank}[L] = n \qquad (3.109)$$

where L is the $nm \times n$ matrix

$$L = \begin{bmatrix} C \\ CA \\ CA^2 \\ \vdots \\ CA^{n-1} \end{bmatrix} \qquad (3.110)$$

This matrix is called the *observability matrix*.

To show the *necessity* of condition (3.109), assume the rank of the L matrix to be inferior to n. There exists therefore a vector $x_0 \neq 0$ such that

$$Lx_0 = 0 \qquad (3.111)$$

that is

$$Cx_0 = 0, \quad CAx_0 = 0, \quad CA^2x_0 = 0, \ldots, CA^{n-1}x_0 = 0 \qquad (3.112)$$

This shows that the vector $x_0 \neq 0$ verifies (3.108) and, therefore, that (3.104) does not imply (3.105): the system is not completely observable.

To show the *sufficiency* of condition (3.109), assume it to be satisfied, i.e. assume the rank of L to be n. Assume furthermore that

$$y(t) = Ce^{A(t-t_0)}x_0 = 0 \quad (t_0 \leqslant t \leqslant t_f) \qquad (3.113)$$

By evaluating $y(t)$ and its first- and higher-order derivatives at t_0 we get from (3.113)

$$y(t_0) = Cx_0 = 0$$
$$\dot{y}(t_0) = CAx_0 = 0$$
$$\overset{(2)}{y}(t_0) = CA^2x_0 = 0 \qquad (3.114)$$
$$\ldots\ldots\ldots\ldots\ldots\ldots$$
$$\overset{(n-1)}{y}(t_0) = CA^{n-1}x_0 = 0$$

and therefore

$$Lx_0 = 0 \qquad (3.115)$$

Since rank $[L] = n$ by assumption, (3.115) is verified only if $x_0 = 0$. Therefore (3.113) implies, in this case, $x_0 = 0$ and, consequently, the system is completely observable.

Very often the observability condition is written as

$$\text{rank } [L'] = n \qquad (3.116)$$

where

$$L' = [C' \vdots A'C' \vdots (A')^2 C' \vdots \cdots \vdots (A')^{n-1} C'] \qquad (3.117)$$

3.10 The duality principle[17]

The obvious symmetry between the controllability and observability properties examined in the previous sections can be made explicit by introducing the concept of *duality* due to Kalman (1960).

Consider the system[18]

$$\dot{x}(t) = Ax(t) + Bu(t) \qquad (3.118)$$

$$y(t) = Cx(t) \qquad (3.119)$$

where, we recall, $x(t) \in R^n$, $y(t) \in R^m$ and $u(t) \in R^r$.

The *dual* of system (3.118)–(3.119) is the following system

$$\dot{x}^D(t) = A'x^D(t) + C'u^D(t) \qquad (3.120)$$

$$y^D(t) = B'x^D(t) \qquad (3.121)$$

where $x^D(t) \in R^n$, $y^D(t) \in R^r$ and $u^D(t) \in R^m$.

The dual of system (3.120)–(3.121) is the original system (3.118)–(3.119).

The relation between the controllability and observability properties of a system and its dual is given by the *duality principle*:

System (3.118)–(3.119) *is completely controllable (observable) if and only if its dual is completely observable (controllable)*.

In fact, the observability matrix L^D of system (3.120)–(3.121) is equal to the transpose of the controllability matrix P of system (3.118)–(3.119), that is

$$L^D = \begin{bmatrix} B' \\ B'A' \\ B'(A')^2 \\ B'(A')^{n-1} \end{bmatrix} = P' \qquad (3.122)$$

On the other hand, the controllability matrix P^D of system (3.120)–(3.121) is equal to the transpose of the observability matrix L of system (3.118)–(3.119), that is

$$P^D = [C' \vdots A'C' \vdots \cdots \vdots (A')^{n-1}C'] = L' \tag{3.123}$$

Since the rank of a matrix is equal to the rank of its transpose, the duality principle follows. The study of the controllability and observability properties of a dynamic system can therefore be reduced to the study of a single one of these properties, by considering the dual of the given system. The duality principle is also important for the derivation of path controllability conditions, as we have seen in section 3.6.1.

3.11 Phase-variable canonical forms

When the dynamic system considered has only one input variable[19] it can be useful, in order to analyse the dynamic properties of the system, to describe it by means of two particular state-space representations: the *phase-variable canonical form* and the *dual phase-variable canonical form*.

The *phase-variable canonical form* of a single input time-invariant linear system is the following

$$\dot{z}(t) = \tilde{A}z(t) + \tilde{B}u(t) \tag{3.124}$$

$$y(t) = \tilde{C}z(t) \tag{3.125}$$

where

$$\tilde{A} = \begin{bmatrix} 0 & 1 & 0\ldots\ldots\ldots\ldots 0 \\ 0 & 0 & 1\ 0\ldots\ldots\ldots 0 \\ \cdots\cdots\cdots\cdots\cdots\cdots\cdots\cdots\cdots \\ 0 & 0 & 0\ldots\ldots\ldots 0\ 1 \\ -\alpha_0 & -\alpha_1\cdots\cdots\cdots\cdots\cdots -\alpha_{n-1} \end{bmatrix} \quad \tilde{B} = \begin{bmatrix} 0 \\ 0 \\ \vdots \\ 0 \\ 1 \end{bmatrix}$$

and where α_i are the coefficients of the characteristic equation $\det [A - \lambda I] = 0 (\alpha_n = 1)$; matrix $\tilde{C}$ can have any form. The system (3.124)–(3.125) is always completely state controllable.

Any single-input completely controllable system can be transformed into the phase-variable canonical form, since non-singular transformations preserve the state controllability.

Consider the single-input differential system

$$\dot{x}(t) = Ax(t) + Bu(t) \tag{3.126}$$

$$y(t) = Cx(t) \tag{3.127}$$

To obtain the phase-variable canonical form (3.124)–(3.125) define the following transformation

$$x = Tz \qquad (3.128)$$

so that $\tilde{A} = T^{-1}AT$, $\tilde{B} = T^{-1}B$ and $\tilde{C} = CT$. T is the non-singular transformation matrix

$$T = PQ \qquad (3.129)$$

where P is the controllability matrix

$$P = [B \vdots AB \vdots A^2 B \vdots \cdots \vdots A^{n-1}B] \qquad (3.130)$$

which, in this case, is an $n \times n$ square matrix, as B is a column vector. Since the system is completely controllable by assumption the matrix P is non-singular. The matrix Q is the following $n \times n$ matrix

$$Q = \begin{bmatrix} \alpha_1 & \alpha_2 \ldots \ldots \ldots \ldots \ldots .\alpha_n \\ \alpha_2 & \alpha_3 \ldots \ldots \ldots \ldots .\alpha_n \quad 0 \\ \ldots \ldots \ldots \ldots \ldots \ldots \ldots \ldots \ldots \\ \alpha_{n-1} & \alpha_n \quad 0 \ldots \ldots \ldots \ldots .0 \\ \alpha_n & 0 \quad 0 \ldots \ldots \ldots \ldots .0 \end{bmatrix} \qquad (3.131)$$

and is also non-singular: since $\alpha_n = 1$, it can easily be checked that $\det[Q] = 1$. T is therefore a non-singular matrix.

In a similar way it is possible to transform an observable dynamic system into the *dual phase-variable canonical form*

$$\dot{w}(t) = \bar{A}w(t) + \bar{B}u(t) \qquad (3.132)$$

$$y(t) = \bar{C}w(t) \qquad (3.133)$$

where

$$\bar{A} = \begin{bmatrix} 0 & 0 & \ldots & 0 & -\alpha_0 \\ 1 & 0 & \ldots & 0 & -\alpha_1 \\ 0 & 1 & 0 \ldots \ldots & -\alpha_2 \\ \ldots \ldots \ldots \ldots \ldots \ldots \\ 0 & 0 & \ldots .1 & -\alpha_{n-1} \end{bmatrix} \qquad \bar{C} = [0 \quad 0 \ldots 0 \quad 1]$$

and $\bar{B}$ can have any form. The system (3.132)–(3.133) is always completely observable.

Any single-output completely observable system can be transformed into the dual phase-variable canonical form since non-singular transformations preserve the state observability.

To obtain the dual phase-variable canonical form we define the following state transformation

$$x = Sw \tag{3.134}$$

where S is the non-singular matrix

$$S = QL \tag{3.135}$$

Q is defined as in (3.131) and L is the observability matrix

$$L = \begin{bmatrix} C \\ CA \\ CA^2 \\ \vdots \\ CA^{n-1} \end{bmatrix} \tag{3.136}$$

Phase-variable canonical forms are important, among other things, to prove the existence of asymptotically stable control rules capable of stabilizing the economic system (see section 4.3).

4 Different approaches to dynamic policy analysis

4.1 The stability approach

In the preceding chapter we have seen how, in the seventies, Tinbergen's theory of economic policy was generalized in a dynamic framework by using the concepts of dynamic controllability. The controllability approach appears to be the most natural generalization of Tinbergen's theory, although it is not the only attempt made in this direction. The target-instrument approach that Tinbergen introduced in 1952 had already been analysed in a dynamic context during the sixties, making use of another property of dynamic systems: the stability property (Mundell, 1960, 1962, 1968; McFadden, 1969; Patrick, 1968, 1973).

We can therefore say that the theory of economic policy, in particular the theory of fixed policy targets, can be extended to a dynamic framework following two different approaches, which we shall call, for simplicity, 'the controllability approach' and 'the stability approach'. In this chapter we shall focus in particular on the methodology which underlies the stability approach and we shall then compare this with the controllability approach already examined in chapter 3. In order to provide a homogeneous formalization of the models analysed in this chapter, we shall only consider differential equations of the first order; on the other hand, as we have seen in chapter 2, any differential system of a higher order can be reduced to a first-order system, and the stability of the former can be analysed by studying the stability properties of the latter.

The stability approach to the theory of economic policy goes back to the pioneering work of Tustin (1953) on the possibility of stabilizing unstable economic systems by applying the same methods used in physics.[1] His book emphasizes 'the remarkable analogy that exists between economic systems and certain physical systems' (p. V), and argues that 'it is relevant therefore to ask what analogous means exist in the world of economics of modifying the operation of the system so as to replace instability by stability' (p. 73).

For a better understanding of the stability approach and of the methodology which underlies it, it will be useful to examine separately, as we shall do in the following sections, the main features of the following contributions:

(1) The articles by Phillips (1954, 1957) on the possibility of stabilizing the economic system through economic policy interventions.
(2) The works based on the concept of stabilizability (see, for example, Kwakernaak and Sivan, 1972; Aoki, 1976a), which originates from systems theory and has been recently used within the framework of the theory of economic policy (Aoki, 1976a, 1981; Buiter and Gersovitz, 1981).
(3) The articles of Mundell (1960, 1962, 1968), McFadden (1969) and Patrick (1968, 1973) mentioned above, and the works by Aoki (1976a and b) which deal in particular with the assignment problem, that is with the problem of the assignment of the instruments to the targets.

A common feature of all the contributions just mentioned is the assumption of a *feedback* control law which, when applied in the economic model considered, makes it possible to stabilize the behaviour of the endogenous variables. A *feedback* control law defines control actions which are functions of the controlled variables. Therefore, unlike the control actions considered in the previous chapter which – given the initial values of the endogenous variables – were only functions of time (*open-loop* controls), feedback control is the result of an interaction between the input and the output of a given system. A stabilizing feedback control is therefore a control that either renders the behaviour of the system stable, if it was unstable, or renders this behaviour 'more stable' if it was already stable.

Loosely speaking, by 'more stable' we mean a better dynamic performance of the model, such as a larger margin for stability or a lower margin for oscillations. When dealing with models whose coefficients are known numerical values (either estimated or assumed), so that the time trajectories of the endogenous variables can also be known, a 'more stable' behaviour can be interpreted as a path for those variables such that the convergence to equilibrium takes place by keeping this path closer to the equilibrium path (or equilibrium value) than it was before the feedback control law was applied. Therefore, if (damped) oscillations were present, a 'more stable' behaviour would mean a behaviour without, or with more damped, oscillations (see, for example, Phillips, 1954, 1957; Allen, 1956, chapter 3); whereas, if the behaviour was already monotonically convergent, a 'more stable' behaviour would mean a quicker convergence.[2]

Since the models which we shall examine in this chapter are linear ones, we can consider their stability properties as global asymptotic stability; otherwise, if we assume the linear models to be linearized versions of non-linear ones, the stability properties of the former will have the meaning of local asymptotic stability.

For expositionary purposes we shall try to put all the models considered into a common framework, in order to emphasize the methodological features which characterize the different approaches. Many details will therefore be left out of consideration.

In the following sections (4.2, 4.3 and 4.4), target variables will be defined as deviations from corresponding desired values. Therefore, the stability of the system will ensure the asymptotic convergence of the system itself towards a desired position.

4.2 Phillips' stabilization policies

Although Simon (1952) and Tustin (1953, chapter 8) first suggested the use of feedback policy rules to stabilize an economic system, Phillips, in a seminal paper (1954), effectively applied the principle of servomechanisms to the theory of economic policy (see also Phillips, 1957). He considered first a dynamic economic model based on the multiplier principle, and subsequently introduced the accelerator effect in order to analyse also the multiplier-accelerator dynamics (see section 3.7 for a description of the multiplier model). Both models were characterized by a target variable (output) and a control variable (public expenditure). Three different feedback control functions were considered, and Phillips' problem was to find which of the three functions (or which combination of these) improved the time behaviour of output.

In general terms, Phillips' approach can be summarized as follows.[3] Consider the dynamic equation which describes the behaviour of the endogenous (target) variable $x(t)$

$$\dot{x}(t) = ax(t) + bu(t) \tag{4.1}$$

where $u(t)$ is the policy instrument (control variable), and assume p different feedback control laws of the type

$$u(t) = f_i[x(t)], \quad i = 1, 2, \ldots, p \tag{4.2}$$

It should be remembered that the control laws considered by Phillips (1954, 1957) are: the proportional stabilization policy ($u(t) = -k_p x(t)$), the derivative stabilization policy ($u(t) = -k_d \dot{x}(t)$) and the integral stabilization policy ($u(t) = -k_I \int_0^t x(t)\, \mathrm{d}t$), where k_p, k_d and k_I are positive constants. The f_i operator in (4.2) should therefore be interpreted in a broad sense, so as to include the instruction to take the derivative or the integral of $x(t)$.

Now, substituting each of the p control laws (4.2) (or a combination of them) into (4.1), p differential equations in $x(t)$ are obtained, that is

$$\dot{x}(t) = ax(t) + bf_i[x(t)], \quad i = 1, 2, \ldots, p \tag{4.3}$$

An analysis of the dynamic behaviour of the model for each i, by comparing the corresponding stability conditions, makes it possible to choose the control law (or the combination of these) that renders the equilibrium of the model stable in the sense mentioned above. In particular, since Phillips assigns hypothetical values to the parameters, he can obtain the hypothetical time paths of the endogenous variable corresponding to each of the control laws. Thus, in the case of an oscillatory behaviour of output (as can be the case in Phillips' model), the economic policy action should help to dampen these oscillations or even to eliminate them.

4.3 The stabilizability of dynamic systems

As we have seen in the previous section, Phillips recognized the importance of stabilizing an economic system by choosing appropriate feedback rules for the instruments of economic policy. Today, questions related to the stabilization of national and international economies are the core of most of the research on economic policy analysis. Again, tools from the engineering literature come to the rescue of the economist in investigating the stabilization problem. In fact, another property of dynamic systems, *stabilizability* (Galperin and Krasovskii, 1963; Wonham, 1967, 1974), enables us to reconsider the approach suggested by Phillips. The concept of stabilizability – defined in the framework of systems theory with reference to the stabilization of physical systems – provides an appropriate analytical basis for the problem of the stabilization of economic systems.[4]

In this section, we first state the definition of and the conditions for stabilizability, and then derive the conditions for the existence of feedback control actions capable of improving the stability of the system or of stabilizing it, if it is initially unstable.

In order to introduce the concept of stabilizability we need to recall the definitions of controllable and uncontrollable sub-spaces and of stable and unstable sub-spaces. Consider the first-order time-invariant linear system

$$\dot{x}(t) = Ax(t) + Bu(t) \tag{4.4}$$

where $x(t) \in R^n$ is a vector of target variables, $u(t) \in R^r$ is a vector of control variables and A and B are constant matrices of the corresponding dimensions.

We have seen in section 3.3.1 that, when a linear differential system fails to satisfy the controllability conditions (i.e. rank $P = q < n$; see (3.6)), the state space can be partitioned into two sub-spaces: a controllable sub-space, which is the sub-space spanned by the q linearly independent columns of the controllability matrix P, and an uncontrollable sub-space, which is the sub-space spanned by the remaining $n - q$ columns of P.

In the same way, the state space of a linear differential system can be partitioned into a stable and an unstable sub-space. If we consider the free system corresponding to system (4.4), i.e.

$$\dot{x}(t) = Ax(t) \tag{4.5}$$

and we assume that A has n distinct eigenvalues, a stable sub-space can be defined as the sub-space spanned by the eigenvectors of A that correspond to those eigenvalues which have strictly negative real parts; while an unstable sub-space can be defined as that which is spanned by the eigenvectors of A which correspond to those eigenvalues that have non-negative real parts.

We can now define the property of *stabilizability*: *a linear differential system is stabilizable if its unstable sub-space is contained in its controllable sub-space.* In other words, a system is stabilizable if any state vector in the unstable sub-space is also in the controllable sub-space. It follows that any asymptotically stable differential system is stabilizable, and that any completely controllable system is stabilizable.

The property of stabilizability might be more easily understood if we consider the following non-singular transformation of system[5] (4.4)

$$\dot{z}(t) = \begin{bmatrix} \tilde{A}_{11} & \tilde{A}_{12} \\ 0 & \tilde{A}_{22} \end{bmatrix} z(t) + \begin{bmatrix} \tilde{B}_1 \\ 0 \end{bmatrix} u(t) \tag{4.6}$$

where $z'(t) = [z'_1(t), z'_2(t)]$, $z_1(t) \in R^q$ (controllable sub-space) and $z_2(t) \in R^{n-q}$ (uncontrollable sub-space); the pair $\tilde{A}_{11} \tilde{B}_1$ is a completely controllable pair (see section 3.3.1). The state-space form (4.6) is also known as the *controllability canonical form*.

System (4.6) is stabilizable *if and only if* the matrix $\tilde{A}_{22}$ is asymptotically stable. The demonstration of this theorem is straightforward: assume $\tilde{A}_{22}$ to be stable; then, any vector in the unstable sub-space must be in the controllable sub-space (as $\tilde{A}_{11} \tilde{B}_1$ is a controllable pair) and the system is therefore stabilizable. For the 'only if' part of the theorem, suppose that the system is stabilizable and that $\tilde{A}_{22}$ is not stable. Then, there is a vector in the unstable sub-space which is not in the controllable sub-space and this contradicts the assumption of stabilizability (see Kwakernaak and Sivan, 1972, chapter 1).

Let us now analyse the problem of the *existence* of some feedback control law capable of stabilizing a given dynamic system and derive the conditions for the existence of this law. A *linear feedback control law*

$$u(t) = -Fx(t) + v(t) \tag{4.7}$$

is a stabilizing (asymptotically stable) *control law* for system (4.4), if the system obtained by substituting (4.7) in (4.4), i.e.

$$\dot{x}(t) = (A - BF)x(t) + Bv(t) \tag{4.8}$$

is *asymptotically stable* (see, for example, Aoki, 1976a). The r-vector $v(t)$ is the new control vector of the resulting system (4.8) and F is a constant matrix. The control law (4.7) contains a feedback element $Fx(t)$, which describes the dependence of the control on the endogenous vector $x(t)$, and an exogenous element $v(t)$.

It is quite clear that the stability of (4.8) depends on the eigenvalues of the matrix $(A - BF)$. Therefore, if the original system (4.4) is unstable, the stabilizability problem consists in finding a matrix F such that all the eigenvalues of $(A - BF)$ have negative real parts. Therefore, since target variables are defined as deviations from desired values, a stabilizing control law will move the system towards this desired position for $t \to +\infty$. If, on the contrary, the original system is stable, the stabilizability problem is limited to finding a matrix F which improves the behaviour of the system.

At this point the similarity between stabilizability and the Phillips approach to the economic policy problem seems clear. In both cases the problem consists in finding a feedback policy rule which stabilizes the original dynamic model. One difference is that, following the stabilizability approach, we consider only linear feedback rules, while Phillips considered policy rules not only of the proportional type (which could be compared with the linear stabilizing rule (4.7)), but also more complicated ones like the derivative and the integral rules (see section 4.2). Therefore, the policy rules considered by Phillips could differ both in the coefficients and in the functional form, while the rules considered in the stabilizability approach can differ only in the coefficients, that is in the elements of matrix F and of vector v.

However, the assumption of linearity of the feedback rules makes it possible to derive the conditions under which a stabilizing control law exists. These conditions, also known in systems theory as *pole assignment conditions*, are the following (see, for example, Kwakernaak and Sivan, 1972; Aoki, 1976a):

(i) an asymptotically stabilizing control rule exists for the dynamic system (4.4), *if* this system is completely controllable. We report only the proof for the single-input case, referring the reader to Heymann (1968) and Aoki (1976a) for the general case. Considering a single-input system, (4.4) becomes

$$\dot{x}(t) = Ax(t) + b\mu(t) \tag{4.9}$$

where $\mu(t)$ is a control variable and b a column vector.

Assume (4.9) to be completely controllable. Then there exists a nonsingular transformation matrix which transforms the system into its phase-variable canonical form (see section 3.11), that is

$$\dot{z}(t) = \begin{bmatrix} 0 & 1 & 0.........0 \\ 0 & 0 & 1 & 0......0 \\ .... \\ 0 & 0.........0 & 1 \\ -\alpha_0 & -\alpha_1......... & -\alpha_{n-1} \end{bmatrix} z(t) + \begin{bmatrix} 0 \\ 0 \\ \vdots \\ 0 \\ 1 \end{bmatrix} \mu(t) \quad (4.10)$$

or, more compactly

$$\dot{z}(t) = \tilde{A}z(t) + \tilde{b}\mu(t) \tag{4.11}$$

Let

$$\mu(t) = -fz(t) + \omega(t) \tag{4.12}$$

be a feedback control law, where f is the row vector $f = [\theta_1, \theta_2, \ldots, \theta_n]$.
By substituting (4.12) into (4.11), we obtain

$$\dot{z}(t) = (\tilde{A} - \tilde{b}f)z(t) + \tilde{b}\omega(t) \tag{4.13}$$

where

$$\tilde{A} - \tilde{b}f = \begin{bmatrix} 0 & 1 & 0...............0 \\ 0 & 0 & 1 & 0............0 \\ .... \\ 0 & 0 & ....0 & 1 \\ -\alpha_0 - \theta_1 & -\alpha_1 - \theta_2................ & -\alpha_{n-1} - \theta_n \end{bmatrix}$$

The coefficients of the characteristic polynomial of the matrix $\tilde{A} - \tilde{b}f$ are $(-\alpha_i - \theta_{i+1})$, $i = 0, 1, \ldots, n-1$. Therefore, by a suitable choice of the θ_i, these coefficients can be given any desired value, that is: any set of eigenvalues can be generated.

(ii) An asymptotically stabilizing control rule exists for the dynamic system (4.4) *if and only if* this system is stabilizable. In order to prove this condition, consider again the controllability canonical form of system (4.4), that is

$$\dot{z}(t) = \begin{bmatrix} \tilde{A}_{11} & \tilde{A}_{12} \\ 0 & \tilde{A}_{22} \end{bmatrix} z(t) + \begin{bmatrix} \tilde{B}_1 \\ 0 \end{bmatrix} u(t) \tag{4.14}$$

where $\tilde{A}_{11} \tilde{B}_1$ is a completely controllable pair.

Consider the feedback control law

$$u(t) = -[F_1, F_2]z(t) + v(t) \tag{4.15}$$

By substituting (4.15) into (4.14) we obtain

$$\dot{z}(t) = \begin{bmatrix} \tilde{A}_{11} - \tilde{B}_1 F_1 & \tilde{A}_{12} - \tilde{B}_1 F_2 \\ 0 & \tilde{A}_{22} \end{bmatrix} z(t) + \begin{bmatrix} \tilde{B}_1 \\ 0 \end{bmatrix} v(t) \tag{4.16}$$

The eigenvalues of the first matrix in (4.16) are the eigenvalues of $\tilde{A}_{11} - \tilde{B}_1 F_1$ and those of $\tilde{A}_{22}$. Since the pair $\tilde{A}_{11}\tilde{B}_1$ is completely controllable, it is possible to find a matrix F_1 such that $\tilde{A}_{11} - \tilde{B}_1 F_1$ is stable (see condition (i)). To prove the sufficiency of condition (ii), assume that system (4.4) is stabilizable. Therefore $\tilde{A}_{22}$ is asymptotically stable, and, since $\tilde{A}_{11} - \tilde{B}_1 F_1$ is also stable, system (4.16) is stable. To prove the necessity assume that a feedback law exists that stabilizes the system. For this law to exist, the matrix $\tilde{A}_{22}$ must be asymptotically stable and therefore the system (4.4) is stabilizable.

From what has been said above we can conclude that, if the policy problem is that of stabilizing the economic system, the first things to check are the controllability and/or the stabilizability of the system considered.

The results stated here are entirely intuitive. In fact, if a linear system is completely controllable, it is always possible to find a feedback control rule which modifies its eigenvalues, and hence the behaviour of the system. When this is not the case, that is when the system is not completely controllable, only a part of the eigenvalues can be affected by the control actions. Hence, for the new system to be stable, the remaining eigenvalues must (initially) have strictly negative real parts, i.e. the system must be stabilizable.

It is important to observe that the problem of economic stabilization is still not solved when we know that the system is stabilizable. The property of stabilizability does not throw any light on the criteria of choice from among the many control laws which might stabilize the system, but tells us only that these laws exist. At this point, optimal control theory should appear on the scene, guiding the policy-maker in the choice of a policy rule, as we shall see in the next chapter (see also section 4.7).

It is also important to mention a further problem that arises when the economic system is stabilizable but the model which describes it is not known with certainty. In this case the control rule should respect a further requirement: that of maintaining the stability of the system even in the face of system uncertainty. This requirement is known in the control literature as *stability robustness* (see, for example, Petkovski, 1987, 1989). Testing for this type of robustness requires the specification of a finite region about the nominal path. This makes it possible to check the stability of the (controlled) system when the latter is perturbed within the bounds of the region specified.

Robustness methods make it possible to compare different control rules in relation to their effects on the performance of the system in the presence of modelling errors and/or perturbations. This approach can also be applied for testing other properties of the economic model considered, under uncertainty, like, for example, controllability and observability, and also performance properties (i.e., variations of the optimized performance index) of the controlled system (see section 5.16).

4.4 The assignment problem

The problem of the assignment of instruments to targets was first studied by Mundell (1960, 1962) and subsequently developed by Mundell himself (1968), by MacFadden (1969), Patrick (1968, 1973) and Aoki (1976a and b), among others. The aim of this approach is to assign each given instrument (control variable) to the achievement of one single target in the most effective way, where the 'measure' of this effectiveness is provided by the stability properties of the system considered. In fact, Mundell's principle, also known as the *principle of effective market classification*, states that 'policies should be paired with the objectives on which they have the most influence. If this principle is not followed, there will develop a tendency either for a cyclical approach to equilibrium or for instability' (Mundell, 1962, p. 76).

Although the stabilization problem had already been analysed in a dynamic framework by Phillips in the fifties (as we saw in section 4.2), Mundell's contributions develop a new line of research starting from Tinbergen's formulation of the target-instrument approach (see section 3.2);

Tinbergen's Principle is concerned with the existence and location of a solution to the system. It does not assert that any given set of policy responses will in fact lead to that solution. To assert this, it is necessary to investigate the *stability properties* of a *dynamic* system. In this respect, the Principle of Effective Market Classification is a necessary companion to Tinbergen's Principle. (Mundell, 1962, p. 77; emphasis added).

The assignment problem can arise mainly:
(i) Whenever the policy instruments are in the hands of distinct authorities which act simultaneously and independently of each other: each political institution can manipulate only one or a few of the given policy instruments. It is therefore important, in this case, to know which

instrument should be assigned to which objective, so as to give the political institutions concerned with planning indications as to the targets on which each of them should concentrate. The same kind of problem might arise in the context of an international economic system, formed by interdependent economies (Patrick, 1968, 1973; Aoki, 1976a, b).

(ii) Whenever the policy authorities have incomplete information as to the parameters of the economic model that describes the relations between the instruments and the targets. In this case, the policy-maker must try to approach the targets by way of successive approximations, hence the importance of knowing on the basis of which indicators to manipulate the given policy instruments (see, e.g., Cooper, 1969b).

The assignment problem consists therefore in pairing off instruments with objectives so as to render the system stable or to improve its behaviour. Evidently, assigning a given instrument to a given target may facilitate policy decision-making, but does not prevent the given instrument from producing undesired effects on the other targets to which it is not principally assigned. Cooper (1969a) maintains that these undesired spill-over effects increase with the degree of dependence between targets, and shows that coordination may increase stability. However, when a given assignment produces, as we shall see, a stable asymptotic behaviour of the economic system, this means that the undesirable side effects of instruments on targets fade as time goes by and that they, therefore, tend to disappear. In any case, it seems clear that the lack of coordination is inefficient and the price to be paid for it will be reflected in the greater size of the intervention needed to achieve the policy targets and in the lower speed of convergence of the system (see Hughes Hallett, 1989; see also Gandolfo, 1974, 1986, and section 9.6 of the present volume).

In this section we shall briefly examine the main features of the following models: (a) Mundell (1962, 1968) and Patrick (1968, 1973); (b) McFadden (1969); (c) Aoki (1976a, chapter 6, 1976b). The approaches to the assignment problem described in these models present some different characteristics to which it is worth drawing attention.

(a) The Mundell and Patrick models can be described, in a general form, by two systems of equations (see Patrick, 1973): a reduced form static system which describes the instantaneous relationship between an n-dimensional target vector $x(t)$ and an n-dimensional control vector $u(t)$, i.e.

$$x(t) = Bu(t) \tag{4.17}$$

and a dynamic system which describes the time behaviour of the control variables, each as a function of only one target, i.e.

$$\dot{u}_1(t) = k_{11} x_1(t)$$

$$\dot{u}_2(t) = k_{22} x_2(t)$$

$$\dots\dots\dots\dots$$

$$\dot{u}_n(t) = k_{nn} x_n(t)$$

(4.18)

or, in matrix form

$$\dot{u}(t) = K x(t)$$

(4.19)

where, as we have said, $x(t)$ is defined in terms of deviations from a desired target vector. The matrix K is an $n \times n$ constant diagonal matrix representing speeds of adjustment or reaction coefficients.

By substituting (4.17) into (4.19) we get

$$\dot{u}(t) = K B u(t)$$

(4.20)

which is the system that describes the dynamic performance of the policy instruments.

The particular assignment described in (4.18) – that is: instrument 1 to target 1, instrument 2 to target 2, and so on – can obviously be modified, giving rise to different assignments. This can be done by altering the order of the elements of the target vector $x(t)$ in (4.19) or the order of the rows of matrix B in (4.20). Moreover, since each new assignment can also be characterized by different values of the diagonal elements of K, a different matrix K may be considered in each case, provided that its elements respect the economic constraints implied by each assignment. For example, if the interest rate is assigned to the achievement of full employment, it cannot be assumed that it should rise when output is below the full-employment level; this imposes a constraint on the sign of the corresponding diagonal element of K. The signs of the elements of K are determinant in the analysis of the stability conditions.

We can therefore obtain $n!$ possible alternative assignments and the corresponding $n!$ alternative differential systems. In symbols

$$\dot{u}(t) = K^i x^i(t) \quad i = 1, 2, \dots, n!$$

(4.21)

and

$$\dot{u}(t) = K^i B^i u(t) \quad i = 1, 2, \dots, n!$$

(4.22)

The stability analysis of each of the $n!$ systems described by (4.22) will provide the required information on the stability of each particular assignment.

It should be remembered at this point that Mundell considers two objectives (full-employment and balance-of-payments equilibrium) and two policy instruments (Government budget deficit and interest rate); there are therefore two possible assignments. The use of this simple model makes it possible to single out the economic mechanisms at work and thus to specify a priori the most effective assignment of the instruments to the targets. Mundell argues that, *ceteris paribus*, the rate of interest has a relatively greater effect than the Government budget deficit on external equilibrium, since it acts, not only on current transactions (through imports) but also on capital movements. This consideration allows Mundell to apply his 'principle of effective market classification' by assigning monetary policy to the external target and fiscal policy to the internal target (Mundell, 1962). The demonstration that the opposite assignment gives rise to instability is used by the author simply to show the correctness of his argument.

However, Mundell's model has been subsequently extended by Patrick (1973) to the more general case of n targets and n instruments that we have just considered, and, in this case, the stability properties of each (or at least of some) of the $n!$ differential systems should be analysed.

Since the stability conditions depend on the form of the matrices $K^i B^i$ ($i = 1, 2, \ldots, n!$), it is possible to apply the Fisher and Fuller (1958) theorems; these describe the conditions that a matrix B must fulfill for a diagonal matrix K to exist capable of rendering the product matrix KB stable. We refer the reader to Fisher and Fuller (1958, pp. 418–19) for the demonstration of the theorems and to Patrick (1973) for an interesting discussion about them, and confine ourselves here simply to stating the results that most closely concern our own problem.

(i) Let B be a square constant matrix. If B has at least a nested sequence of non-zero principal minors M_j of every order, $j = 1, 2, \ldots, n$, a real diagonal matrix K exists, such that the product matrix KB is stable. A sequence of principal minors is nested if M_{j-1} is itself a principal minor of the determinant of order j (M_j) in the sequence.

Condition (i) clearly implies matrix B to be non-singular, which implies, in turn, the number of linearly independent instruments to be equal to the number of linearly independent targets.

A necessary condition is the following:

(ii) Let B be a square constant matrix. A real diagonal matrix K exists such that matrix KB is stable only if B has at least one non-zero principal minor of every order.[6]

The diagonal matrix K may further be chosen so that the matrix KB has strictly negative *real* eigenvalues. It follows that, if B is unstable but satisfies the required conditions, it may be possible to find a matrix K that not only stabilizes the system but also eliminates possible oscillations.

It may happen, however, that some of the possible $n!$ assignments are unrealistic from an economic point of view, and only a subset of them can be taken into consideration: our treatment refers, of course, to a general case. We may therefore conclude that, if the stability of different assignments is to be tested, this can be done by obtaining the corresponding permutations of the rows of B together with the corresponding matrix K, given the constraints on the economic significance of this matrix. It is possible in this way to choose the 'best' assignment, i.e., the one which renders the dynamic system stable. When more than one assignment happens to be stable a criterion for choice can be that of selecting the assignment that requires the least restrictive stability conditions (see Gandolfo, 1970, for an application of this criterion).

(b) McFadden (1969) considers the assignment problem by assuming decentralized policy decisions and analyses it in a way very similar to that of Mundell and Patrick examined in (a) above. His model can be described by the following system of equations

$$\dot{x}(t) = Bu(t) \tag{4.23}$$

$$u(t) = Kx(t) \tag{4.24}$$

where K is, as above, a constant diagonal matrix; $x(t), u(t) \in R^n$ are vectors of targets and control variables respectively. As can be seen from (4.23), it is now the target variables which adjust in time under the action of the control variables, while (4.24) simply describes a given assignment of the instruments to the targets. In this case, the elements of the main diagonal of K cannot be interpreted as speeds of adjustment, since an instantaneous adjustment of the instruments to the targets is implicitly assumed.

Inserting (4.24) into (4.23) yields

$$\dot{x}(t) = BKx(t) \tag{4.25}$$

which is the dynamic model whose stability is to be analysed.

As (a) above, the initial assignment can be modified by altering the order of the elements of the target vector $x(t)$ in (4.24) and in (4.25), obtaining $n!$ possible alternative assignments

$$u(t) = K^i x^i(t), \quad i = 1, 2, \ldots, n! \tag{4.26}$$

and $n!$ differential systems

$$\dot{x}(t) = BK^i x^i(t), \quad i = 1, 2, \ldots, n! \tag{4.27}$$

or else

$$\dot{x}(t) = B^i K^i x(t), \quad i = 1, 2, \ldots, n! \tag{4.28}$$

As in (4.21), the elements of the matrix K^i can be modified in each assignment, provided that they respect the required economic constraints. As for matrix B^i, only the order of its columns is changed for each i.

Since the stability of the $n!$ differential systems (4.28) depends on the form of the product matrices $B^i K^i$ ($i = 1, 2, \ldots, n!$), it is possible again to apply the Fisher and Fuller conditions to matrix B^i (see (a) above; see also McFadden, 1969, theorems 1 and 4). The stability analysis of the $n!$ dynamic systems (4.27) will then tell us which is the stable (or the 'most stable') assignment.

(c) More recently, the assignment problem has been reconsidered by Aoki (1976a and b), with reference to decentralized decision-making in the context of an international economic system. Aoki proposes a more general model in which a dynamic behaviour both of the targets and of the instruments is considered. Aoki's model is therefore a summing-up of Mundell's and McFadden's models examined above and can be summarized by the following system

$$\dot{x}(t) = Ax(t) + Bu(t) \tag{4.29}$$

$$\dot{u}(t) = Kx(t) + Lu(t) \tag{4.30}$$

where A, B, K and L are constant $n \times n$ matrices; K is, as usual, a diagonal matrix that represents the particular instrument-target assignment. L is also assumed to be diagonal, meaning that the dynamics of each instrument does not directly depend on the other instruments (but only indirectly through $x(t)$). K and L can be chosen by policy-makers, subject, as usual, to the constraints on the economic significance of their elements.

System (4.29)–(4.30) can also be written

$$\begin{bmatrix} \dot{x}(t) \\ \dot{u}(t) \end{bmatrix} = G \begin{bmatrix} x(t) \\ u(t) \end{bmatrix} \tag{4.31}$$

where

$$G = \begin{bmatrix} A & B \\ K & L \end{bmatrix} \tag{4.32}$$

The same analysis that was carried out above ((a) and (b)) can still be applied to this model. The alternative $n!$ assignments can be described by

$$\dot{u}(t) = K^i x^i(t) + Lu(t), \quad i = 1, 2, \ldots, n! \tag{4.33}$$

or else

$$\dot{u}(t) = \tilde{K}^i x(t) + Lu(t), \quad i = 1, 2, \ldots, n! \tag{4.34}$$

which is another way of writing (4.33), simply by changing the order of the rows[7] of K^i. The problem, as in the two cases considered above, becomes that of finding the assignment which stabilizes system (4.29)–(4.30).

Aoki's problem is however more general, since the focus is now on the research for a dynamic control rule (4.33) capable of stabilizing the given initial system. It is thus possible, in this case, to manipulate not only matrix K but also matrix L. And, since the stability properties of system (4.31) depend on the form of matrix G, it is necessary to find the conditions to be fulfilled by matrices A and B, so that two matrices K and L exist and render G stable. These conditions are derived in Aoki (1976b), where some particular cases are also analysed. Here we state only the main result.

Consider the system (4.29)–(4.30), and assume $n = 2$ and A to have one asymptotically stable eigenvalue; a matrix $K = \text{diag}(k_{11}, k_{22})$ and a matrix $L = \text{diag}(-l_{11}, -l_{22})$ exist such that G is asymptotically stable if $b_{11}b_{22} = 0$ and if $\text{tr}(L^{-1}A^{-1}B_2) > 0$. Two such choices are: $l_{ii} - a_{ii} > 0$, $i = 1, 2$, such that $\text{tr}(L^{-1}A^{-1}B^2) > 0$, and $\text{sgn}(k_{ii}) = -\text{sgn}(b_{ii})$, $i = 1, 2$.

In the case in which A is initially stable (i.e. has two asymptotically stable eigenvalues) but G is not, G can be made asymptotically stable by choosing an L such that its eigenvalues are sufficiently negative real numbers (Aoki, 1976b, pp. 147–8).

The analysis carried out in this section was based on the assumption that K is a diagonal square matrix, which implies in turn the assumption that there are as many instruments as targets, and that the assignments are made in such a way that the same instrument cannot correspond to two different objectives and that two different instruments cannot be assigned to the same objective. The target-instrument assignments considered were one to one. However, it is possible to consider the case in which the decentralization of policy decisions is not such as to imply this restrictive hypothesis, assuming instead that each decision-maker manages a set of instruments to be assigned to a set of targets, and/or that the number of instruments is inferior to the number of targets. In this case K will be a block-diagonal matrix.

4.5 The assignment of instruments to targets: an example

A typical policy assignment problem in economics is to find out whether fiscal policy should be assigned to the internal (employment) target and monetary policy to the external (balance-of-payments) target, or vice versa. This problem was first examined by Mundell (1960, 1962), as we have seen in section 4.4 (a).

In this section we shall consider the problem posed by Mundell, but we shall examine it by means of a more general model, which belongs to the class of models described in point (c) of the previous section. As we saw in that section, this type of models takes into consideration the dynamic adjustment of both target and control variables.

We first consider the case in which monetary policy, in particular the interest rate, is assigned to external equilibrium (i.e. balance-of-payments equilibrium) whereas fiscal policy, in particular, Government expenditure, is assigned to internal equilibrium (i.e. full-employment equilibrium). We also assume that income adjusts in time in response to excess demand in the real market. Prices are assumed to be constant, as well as the exchange rate.

The equations which characterize this model are therefore the following (see Gandolfo, 1986, chapter 15)

$$\dot{Y} = v_1[d(Y, r) + x_0 + G - Y], \quad v_1 > 0$$

$$\dot{r} = v_2[m(y, r) - x_0 - K(r)], \quad v_2 > 0 \tag{4.35}$$

$$\dot{G} = v_3(Y_F - Y), \quad v_3 > 0$$

The first equation describes income adjustment: income (Y) increases (decreases) if there is a positive (negative) excess demand in the real market. The two last equations are dynamic control rules of the type described by (4.30); the dynamic adjustment of the two policy instruments takes place as follows: Government expenditure (G) increases (decreases) if income is lower (higher) than the full-employment level Y_F, and the interest rate (r) increases (decreases) if there is a deficit (surplus) in the balance of payments. Function d represents internal demand, m represents the import function, K represents capital moments and x_0 represents exports which are taken as exogenous. The constants v_1, v_2 and v_3 represent the adjustment speeds.

Linearizing system (4.35) at the point of equilibrium we have

$$\begin{bmatrix} \dot{\bar{x}}(t) \\ \dot{\bar{u}}(t) \end{bmatrix} = G \begin{bmatrix} \bar{x}(t) \\ \bar{u}(t) \end{bmatrix} \tag{4.36}$$

where the bar over the variables indicates deviations from equilibrium, and

$$G = \begin{bmatrix} v_1(d_y - 1) & v_1 d_r & v_1 \\ v_2 m_y & v_2(m_r - K_r) & 0 \\ -v_3 & 0 & 0 \end{bmatrix} \tag{4.37}$$

where

$$d_Y = \frac{\partial d}{\partial y} > 0, \quad d_r = \frac{\partial d}{\partial r} < 0 \quad m_Y = \frac{\partial m}{\partial Y} > 0 \quad m_r = \frac{\partial m}{\partial r} < 0 \quad K_r = \frac{dK}{dr} > 0$$

Indicating the eigenvalues of the system by λ, the characteristic equation is given by

$$\lambda^3 + [v_2(K_r - m_r) + v_1(1 - d_Y)]\lambda^2 + [v_2 v_1(K_r - m_r)(1 - d_y)$$
$$- v_2 v_1 m_Y d_r + v_1 v_3]\lambda + v_1 v_2 v_3(K_r - m_r) = 0 \qquad (4.38)$$

The necessary and sufficient conditions for stability are (see Gandolfo, 1980, chapter 6)

$$v_2(K_r - m_r) + v_1(1 - d_Y) > 0$$
$$v_1 v_2(K_r - m_r)(1 - d_Y) - v_1 v_2 m_Y d_r + v_1 v_3 > 0$$
$$v_1 v_2 v_3(K_r - m_r) > 0$$
$$[v_2(K_r - m_r) + v_1(1 - d_Y)][v_1 v_2(K_r - m_r)(1 - d_Y) \qquad (4.39)$$
$$- v_1 v_2 m_Y d_r + v_1 v_3] - v_1 v_2 v_3(K_r - m_r)$$
$$= [v_2(K_r - m_r) + v_1(1 - d_y)][v_1 v_2(K_r - m_r)(1 - d_y)$$
$$- v_1 v_2 m_Y d_r] + v_1 v_3(1 - d_Y) > 0$$

It can easily be seen that, given the signs of the various derivatives and assuming $d_Y < 1$, all the conditions are satisfied.

Let us now consider the opposite assignment, that is monetary policy is assigned to internal equilibrium and fiscal policy to external equilibrium. The dynamic model is now given by

$$\dot{Y} = k_1[d(Y, r) + x_0 + G - Y] \qquad k_1 > 0$$
$$\dot{r} = k_2[Y - Y_F] \qquad k_2 > 0 \qquad (4.40)$$
$$\dot{G} = k_3[x_0 - m(Y, r) + K(r)] \qquad k_3 > 0$$

As already mentioned in the previous section, when considering the new assignment the values of the adjustment speeds and their signs need to be modified in order to respect the underlying economic assumptions. In this case, it is assumed that the interest rate increases (decreases) if income is higher (lower) than the full-employment level and that Government expenditure increases (decreases) if there is a surplus (deficit) in the balance of payments (note that the signs of the expressions in square brackets have now changed). As above, by linearizing we obtain

$$\begin{bmatrix} \dot{\bar{x}}(t) \\ \dot{\bar{u}}(t) \end{bmatrix} = G' \begin{bmatrix} \bar{x}(t) \\ \bar{u}(t) \end{bmatrix} \qquad (4.41)$$

where

$$G' = \begin{bmatrix} k_1(d_Y - 1) & k_1 d_r & k_1 \\ k_2 & 0 & 0 \\ -k_3 m_Y & k_3(K_r - m_r) & 0 \end{bmatrix} \qquad (4.42)$$

The characteristic equation is given by

$$\lambda^3 + k_1(1 - d_Y)\lambda^2 + (k_1 k_3 m_Y + k_1 k_2 d_r)\lambda - k_1 k_2 k_3(K_r - m_r) = 0 \quad (4.43)$$

Since, as we have seen above, $K_r > 0$ and $m_r < 0$, the constant term is negative. Therefore one of the stability conditions is violated.

It follows that the only efficient policy assignment consists in pairing fiscal policy with the internal target and monetary policy with the external target, since the opposite assignment would take the system away from the equilibrium values of the targets. By using the correct assignment, the system will asymptotically approach (as $t \to \infty$) full-employment and balance-of-payments equilibrium.

Comparing the simple problem just examined with the general problem of section 4.4 (c), we can see that the change in assignment has implied, in this case, a modification of the two sub-matrices K and L corresponding to (4.32). The simplicity of the problem considered has allowed us to compute the stability conditions concerning each of the two assignments directly. When more complex problems are considered, this computation may not be possible or may require very cumbersome calculations. That is why it is important to be able to verify the existence conditions stated in the previous section, in order to be sure in advance that at least one stable assignment exists.

4.6 The 'controllability approach' and the problem of decoupling

The controllability approach to economic policy-making has been extensively analysed in chapter 3. Both point and path controllability have been examined, as well as the economic implications of these two concepts. In this section we intend to focus on the same kind of problem examined in the previous section – the assignment problem – but by analysing it by means of the controllability approach.

The assignment problem, therefore, has to be seen in a different perspective. We are no longer dealing with the problem of singling out that assignment which renders the dynamic system stable (or more stable), but with the problem of showing the *existence* of a feedback control rule able to transform a given dynamic system in which each instrument influences all the targets into a system in which each instrument influences *only one* different target: that is, a decoupled system.

The decoupling problem, like the assignment problem, might arise in the case of decentralized policy decisions, when each political institution can manipulate only one or a few of the given policy instruments.

The choice of a particular path for a given instrument by a given policy-maker might give rise to undesired effects on other target variables for which the policy-maker is not directly responsible. Even in the case in which one instrument is managed as a function of only one target, the control action usually affects the other targets. The undesired spillovers which might take place between instruments and targets should be offset by means of appropriate policy rules, and this can be done if the dynamic system is *decouplable.* 'When two target variables are such that one of them can be modified by suitable change of instruments while the other is not affected by the instrument change, we say that these two target variables can be controlled or modified in a decoupled or non-interactive manner' (Aoki, 1974, p. 261).

Decoupling or *non-interacting control* (Falb and Wolovich, 1967; Aoki, 1974), can be described by again considering the following system

$$\dot{x}(t) = Ax(t) + Bu(t) \tag{4.44}$$

where $x(t)$, $u(t) \in R^n$, and A, B are constant square matrices. Define a feedback control rule

$$u(t) = Fx(t) + Rv(t) \tag{4.45}$$

where $v(t) \in R^n$ and F, R are constant square matrices, and insert (4.45) into (4.44), i.e.

$$\dot{x}(t) = (A + BF)x(t) + BRv(t) \tag{4.46}$$

$v(t)$ is therefore the control vector of the new system (4.46).

System (4.44) is said to be *decouplable* (Aoki and Canzoneri, 1979) if two matrices F and R exist such that the feedback control rule (4.45) reduces the system to a set of n independent equations of the form

$$f_1[\dot{x}_1(t), x_1(t), v_1(t)] = 0$$
$$f_2[\dot{x}_2(t), x_2(t), v_2(t)] = 0$$
$$\dots\dots\dots\dots\dots\dots\dots \tag{4.47}$$
$$f_n[\dot{x}_n(t), x_n(t), v_n(t)] = 0$$

which represents a *decoupled* system. In fact, as can be seen, the behaviour of each target variable $x_i(t)$ depends, as a consequence of the decoupling, only on the corresponding new control variable $v_i(t)$. It may be said, therefore, that the instrument $v_i(t)$ is assigned to the target $x_i(t)$, and that $v_i(t)$ has no influence on the other targets $x_j(t)$ $(j \neq i)$.

System (4.44) can, for example, represent an economic model that describes the interactions between instruments and targets; then, in order to carry out the decoupling, a control law like (4.45) is needed that cancels out the undesired interactions. Each control variable can be seen as divided into two components: one which describes the direct effects of the control action on the corresponding target variable (depending on the assignment); and another that is used, through an automatic feedback mechanism, to cancel undesired effects of control actions on target variables.

A deeper insight into the definition of decoupling can be attained by considering the Laplace transform of system (4.44) (Aoki, 1976a, chapter 8), obtaining

$$X(s) = (sI - A)^{-1} BU(s) \tag{4.48}$$

where $(sI - A)^{-1} B$ is the transfer matrix $G(s)$ of system (4.44) (see section 2.4). This system is said to be decoupled if $G(s)$ is non-singular (except for those values of s which are equal to the eigenvalues of A) and diagonal. If $G(s)$ is non-singular, system (4.44) is path controllable (see section 3.6.1); moreover, if $G(s)$ is diagonal, $x_i(s)$ depends only on the corresponding $u_i(s)$, for each $i = 1, 2, \ldots, n$.

Conversely if system (4.44) is not decoupled, it can be decoupled through a feedback control law like (4.45). By taking the Laplace transform of system (4.46), we obtain

$$X(s) = (sI - A - BF)^{-1} BRV(s) \tag{4.49}$$

which is a decoupled system if the new transfer matrix $(sI - A - BF)^{-1} BR$ is non-singular and diagonal. If (4.46) is a decoupled system, $v(t)$ affects $x(t)$ non-interactively.

It is important, at this stage, to examine the conditions for decoupling; that is, the conditions for the existence of a linear feedback control law which makes the decoupling of a non-decoupled system possible.

A set of sufficient conditions is given in Aoki and Canzoneri (1979), and these are the same as the sufficient conditions for path controllability derived by the same authors and stated in section 3.6.3, to which we refer the reader. Notice that, since we are considering a first-order system, $D = 0$ and $C = 1$ (see section 3.6.3). Condition (b), for example, reduces therefore to the non-singularity of B.

With the aid of a simple example, we shall show how system (4.44) is decouplable if B is non-singular. Define the following control law

$$u(t) = -B^{-1} Ax(t) + B^{-1} v(t) \tag{4.50}$$

that is, set $F = -B^{-1} A$ and $R = B^{-1}$. Then by inserting (4.50) into (4.44), we obtain

$$\dot{x}(t) = v(t) \tag{4.51}$$

since $A + BF = 0$ and BR is the identity matrix (see (4.46)). Equation (4.51) is obviously a decoupled system, since each element of $\dot{x}(t)$ depends only on the corresponding element of $v(t)$. Equation (4.50) is therefore a feedback control law through which system (4.44) can be decoupled, provided that B is non-singular.

Once a control rule that decouples the system has been found, policy actions can be applied in a decentralized manner on the economic system considered, by assigning one single instrument to each single target. It should however be emphasized that no policy-maker is free to manage the 'whole' instrument at his disposal, since a part of it is employed in offsetting undesired economic interactions. It should also be noted that, even if we have considered the one-to-one assignment in this section, the decoupling criterion can also be extended to the case in which a given set of instruments is assigned to a given set of targets and the assignment has to be made in a non-interacting way.

4.7 Concluding remarks

As we have seen, the stability and the controllability approaches are two different ways of analysing the economic policy problem in a dynamic context. It is therefore difficult, if not impossible, to draw any conclusion as to the superiority of one approach over the other.

From what has been said in this and in the previous chapter we can, however, make the following observations:

(a) It is not possible, by following the stability approach, to ensure that the desired equilibrium targets will actually be reached, even if the stability conditions are satisfied. This follows from the concept of stability itself, which, even in its strongest form, is an asymptotic concept. On the other hand, if the controllability conditions are satisfied, it is possible to assert that there exists at least one path for the control vector really capable of taking the system to the desired position in a finite interval of time; and this is, of course, an important issue in policy-making.

It should be noticed, however, that this distinction, which is clear in theory, is by no means so clear in practice. It is true that stability does not ensure the 100 per cent achievement of the desired targets in a finite interval of time, but it is equally true that this approach makes it possible to ensure in some cases that, if the stability conditions are satisfied, the targets will be 'almost' (for example, 99 per cent) reached in finite time. Clearly, the time and the percentage of convergence can be known only if we have available the numerical values of all the parameters of the model. The choice of one approach or the other can, therefore, be made according to the type of problem which is to be analysed (see Petit, 1984).

(b) The stability approach requires policy rules in feedback form, since only rules of this type can modify the stability properties of the economic system considered. This is not required when the controllability approach is followed, since controllability implies the existence of (open-loop) control trajectories capable of taking the system to the desired position or along the desired path.

The two approaches have, however, a common drawback: the conditions for stabilizability and the conditions for controllability are just *existence* conditions: they ensure the existence of feedback (open-loop) policy rules capable of stabilizing (controlling) the given dynamic system, but they provide no information on the specific policy rule that should be chosen in each given case. Furthermore, there can be and usually is, more than one policy rule which stabilizes a given system, just as there is more than one control path capable of controlling it. As we have seen in section 3.6, the solution for the control trajectory is unique only in the case of path controllability, if the transfer matrix of the dynamic system considered is non-singular. But, even in this case, the control solution might be unrealistic from an economic point of view, since no constraints are imposed on the control vector.

Because of the huge number of policy rules that are candidates for stabilizing or for controlling the system a criterion of choice is required; as we shall see in the next chapter, optimal control is the appropriate method to aid the planner in making this choice. The dynamic optimization of a given objective function which represents the preferences of policy-makers will definitely help in the choice of a policy rule which not only meets the policy-maker's objectives, but also satisfies both the mathematical and the economic requirements.

If we consider the case of decentralized policy decisions, the same type of criticism can be made to the assignment and to the decoupling approaches: they provide no information about the specific policy rules that should be chosen in each case. Indeed, when dealing with the problem of decentralized decisions, the selection of policy rules should be made by the optimization of the objective function of each policy-maker and by explicitly taking into account the interdependence between them. This can be done by using the tools of game theory, as we shall see in chapters 8 and 9.

5 Optimal control*

5.1 From controllability to optimal control

The solution of a policy problem with fixed objectives examined in chapters 3 and 4 has not the character of optimality; in fact, once the desired targets have been attained, the situation so determined is a 'satisfactory', but not an optimal, one. By *optimal* we mean the *best* situation that can be reached, given collective preferences and the constraints described by the structure of the economic system considered.

As Theil explains when considering Tinbergen's approach:

> the choice criterion of target values is not optimal or 'best'; it has the character of 'good enough'. This does not mean that it has to be rejected. On the contrary, there is sufficient reason to believe that the criterion is realistic for many actual policy decisions. But its suboptimal character is sufficient to justify a further exploration (Theil, 1956, p. 362).

Theil's opinion of Tinbergen's approach can of course be extended to the controllability and the stability approaches examined in the preceding chapters. In order to find the *optimal* solution of a problem of economic policy, we need to specify a social welfare function, and to optimize it under the constraint given by the macroeconomic model which describes the working of the economy.

The optimization approach to economic policy analysis had been explicitly proposed by Frisch and by Theil in the 1950s.[1] They both considered, as we shall see in the next chapter, an objective function reflecting the preferences of policy-makers, so as to obtain the 'best' policy choices from the optimization of that function. The Frisch–Theil approach is also known in the literature as the *flexible-target* approach, as opposed to the *fixed-target* approach that characterizes Tinbergen's theory. As we

---

*An important source of the mathematical methods used in the present chapter is Athans and Falb (1966).

have seen in chapter 3, Tinbergen's problem was to make the set of policy objectives take on given *pre-specified* values; whereas, in the Frisch–Theil approach, the values that the target variables will assume is not known a priori, as they are the result of the optimization problem.

The flexible-target approach to policy selection was extended by Theil to a dynamic framework by considering discrete-time models and stacked-up vectors (see section 6.8), so that the optimization problem could be solved simply by using the tools of static optimization (Theil, 1958, 1964). Today, the adoption of modern control theory in economic analysis has had a considerable impact on the treatment of policy problems in a dynamic context, and optimal control methods are widely used.

The search for optimal solutions is not, however, the only reason for choosing the optimal control approach; other important features distinguish it from the controllability approach. Assume that the policy problem consists of driving the economic system to a pre-assigned point in the state space in a given interval of time. The controllability approach tells us whether this is possible or not, but it does not enable us to find a *unique* control path: as we have seen in chapter 3, if the system is point controllable the trajectories of the control variables capable of taking the system to the desired position can be, and usually are, more than one.

The need to choose among the many possible control solutions is therefore another reason for using optimal control in solving economic policy problems, since optimal control will give an answer to the following question: which is the *best* among all the possible control trajectories capable of taking the system to the given target position? It seems clear, however, that, in order to give an answer to this question, we have first to define a *criterion of choice* which will be represented by a particular performance criterion.

The problem of non-uniqueness of the control solution is less likely to arise in the static case. As we have seen in section 3.2, the solution of Tinbergen's problem is unique whenever the system is statically controllable and the number of linearly independent instruments is not greater than the number of linearly independent targets. A unique control trajectory can also be found in the dynamic case when path controllability is considered; in particular, when the system is path controllable with a number of control variables equal to the number of target variables (see section 3.6).

Another case in which the optimal control approach is important is when the economic system that has to be taken to a given target position is not point controllable, that is when no control trajectory exists which takes the system to the desired position in a finite time interval. In this case, though optimal control does not make it possible to reach the desired position exactly, it does enable us to take the system as close as possible to this position. Similarly, when the policy problem is to take the system along a pre-assigned path and the system is not path controllable (for example, because the number of instruments is insufficient), optimal control makes it possible to guide the system along the path closest to the desired one.

Finally, even when the controllability approach enables us to find a unique path for the control variables (as, for example, in the case of path controllability mentioned above), it might happen that the values that the control variables have to assume over time are unrealistic from an economic point of view. In fact, since control vectors considered in controllability problems are unconstrained, they can in principle assume any value. By using optimal control methods this problem can be avoided both because it is possible in this case to impose constraints on the control trajectories and also because it is not necessary for the desired path to be followed exactly. This makes possible a tradeoff between greater (lesser) proximity to the desired path and lesser (greater) economic acceptability of the values of policy instruments.

However these are not new problems. Similar ones can arise in the static case considered by Tinbergen: if the system is not statically controllable, i.e. Tinbergen's conditions are not satisfied, there is no solution for the policy instruments which give rise to the desired values of the targets. If, on the other hand, Tinbergen's conditions are satisfied, the values of the policy instruments which are the solutions of Tinbergen's problem may be unrealistic from an economic point of view. In both cases the (static) optimization approach makes it possible to obtain target values which are the closest to the desired ones, while keeping the economic acceptability of the required values of the instruments.

5.2 Optimal control: a general view

In order to solve a problem of economic planning by using optimal control methods the following elements have to be considered:

(i) a macroeconomic model described by a system of dynamic equations,

(ii) a performance or cost functional which reflects the preferences of policy-makers and measures the degree of effectiveness of each control action.

In what follows, this functional will be referred to as the *objective function*,

(iii) an infinite set U of admissible controls,

(iv) a given planning horizon $[t_0, t_f]$ during which the control action takes place.

The macroeconomic model describes the relationship between the control variables (input of the system) and the target variables (output of the system). It represents the economic system which has to be controlled and sets up a constraint to the optimization problem. The relation between targets and instruments over time is 'constrained' by the dynamic equations which describe the behaviour of the economic system considered.

An objective function must also be specified so as to aid the policy-maker in his choice of the 'best' control path. The definition of the objective function is however a very subjective matter, both as regards the variables to be taken into consideration and the functional (and numerical) form to be given to this function. Problems concerning the construction of an objective function need therefore a more complete treatment and will constitute the subject of the next chapter.

Policy-makers may also wish the values of the control variables not to exceed certain given thresholds. In this case, a set of admissible controls will be defined and the behaviour of the control variables will be bounded within this set.

Finally, since problems of economic planning usually refer to finite time intervals, a planning horizon has to be defined.

Frequently, a given final objective that the policy-maker wishes the system to attain is also defined in the control problem.[2] This can be described either by a given target vector or by a given target set to which the target vector must belong at the end of the planning horizon (see section 5.3). Policy-makers may also wish to control the system in such a way as to keep the output as close as possible to a given 'ideal' trajectory during the whole planning horizon. This is a particular optimal control problem – known as the 'tracking' problem in the engineering literature – which is very important in economic applications (see sections 5.4 and 5.13).

In general, an optimal control problem consists in determining an admissible control trajectory $u^*(t)$ which minimizes (maximizes) a given objective function $J(u)$; the solution of this problem, when it exists, is called an *optimal control*. Assuming that the optimization problem is one of minimization, the optimal control solution can be obtained by minimizing the objective function

$$J(u) = \int_{t_0}^{t_f} I[x(t), u(t), t] \, dt \tag{5.1}$$

subject to

$$\dot{x}(t) = f[x(t), u(t), t] \tag{5.2}$$

$$x(t_0) = x_0$$

$$x(t_f) \in S$$

where (5.2) describes the dynamic behaviour of the economy, $S \subseteq R^n$ is the final target set, $x(t) \in R^n$, and $u(t) \in U_t$. It is assumed that for each t of the planning interval $[t_0, t_f]$ there is a given set $U_t \subseteq R^r$ called the constraint set at time t. The set of all U_t is given by

$$\Omega = \{U_t : t \in [t_0, t_f]\}$$

where Ω is usually called *the constraint*. The control vector, at each t, $u(t)$, must therefore belong to Ω, that is $u(t) \in \Omega$, $t \in [t_0, t_f]$. On the other hand, if we represent $u_{[t_0, t_f]}$ – that is the control function along the whole interval $[t_0, t_f]$ – by u – then the set U is the set of all admissible *trajectories* u such that their values at each t satisfy the constraint Ω. Therefore, each element u of U is called an *admissible* control.

Constraints on the control variables make it possible to keep the values of these variables within an admissible interval. These constraints, however, often give rise to optimal controls that are piecewise constant (bang-bang) functions of time.[3]

Variable t included in the functions I and f may represent either the fact that I and/or f are time-varying functions or the presence of other exogenous (non-control) variables, which are known functions of time.

System (5.2) has been written in state-space form for the sake of simplicity. For the same reason, the objective function (5.1) contains state variables $(x(t))$ and not output variables $(y(t))$. However, a problem of optimal control of the system's output can easily be transformed into the optimal control problem defined by (5.1) and (5.2).

Let us consider the following optimal control problem: find the control that minimizes the cost functional

$$J(u) = \int_{t_0}^{t_f} I[y(t), u(t), t] \, dt \tag{5.3}$$

under the constraint of a macroeconomic model described by a system of differential equations of a higher order than the first

$$\phi(\overset{(n)}{y}, \overset{(n-1)}{y}, \ldots, \overset{(2)}{y}, \dot{y}, y) = \Psi(\overset{(m)}{u}, \overset{(m-1)}{u}, \ldots, \overset{(2)}{u}, \dot{u}, u, t) \tag{5.4}$$

given $y(t_0)$.

Since (5.4) can be written in state-space form, that is

$$\dot{x}(t) = f(x(t), u(t), t) \tag{5.5}$$

$$y(t) = g(x(t), u(t), t) \tag{5.6}$$

then, if the system is observable (see section 3.9), the optimal control problem just described can be transformed, by substituting (5.6) into (5.3), into a problem of minimizing

$$J(u) := \int_{t_0}^{t_f} I[g(x(t), u(t), t), u(t), t] \, dt \tag{5.7}$$

under the constraint of system (5.5), given $x(t_0)$, which is the form described by (5.1) and (5.2) (see section 5.12 where this transformation is performed for the linear-quadratic case).

5.3 The final target set

The general problem of optimal control described in the previous section may assume different specific forms according to the definition of the final target set. In this section we shall examine the most important of these forms, with frequent reference to the engineering literature. The transposition from the engineering to the economic field, on the other hand, will be useful in order to understand why some specific forms of control and not others are most often used in economic applications.

For the sake of simplicity we shall consider only quadratic objective functions throughout this section (and most of this chapter), and shall refer the reader to the next chapter for a discussion of different functional forms. Let us now examine the following cases:

(i) *The target set is a point in the state space*
Consider the system

$$\dot{x}(t) = f[x(t), u(t), t]$$
$$x(t_0) = x_0 \tag{5.8}$$

In this case, the optimal control problem is to take the state from the initial position x_0 to a final position x_f in a given interval of time[4] $[t_0, t_f]$ so as to optimize a given objective function.

A classical example is the *minimum energy problem* which consists in forcing a system from x_0 to x_f in a given time so as to minimize the cost (energy) of the control action. Assuming r control variables $u_i(t)$, the optimal control problem consists in finding a vector $u^*(t)$ which minimizes, for example, the following (cost) functional

$$J(u) = \int_{t_0}^{t_f} \sum_{j=1}^{r} r_j u_j^2(t) \, dt = \int_{t_0}^{t_f} u'(t) R u(t) \, dt \tag{5.9}$$

where R is a positive definite diagonal matrix (see section 6.3), which, for simplicity, is assumed to be constant.

This is therefore a case of *fixed* objectives,[5] known in the engineering literature as the 'fixed-end point, fixed-time problem'. If we generally call S the target set, this will be defined, in the case of fixed objectives now considered, by

$$S = \{x_f\} \cdot \{t_f\} \tag{5.10}$$

(ii) *The target set is an hypersurface in the state space*

In this case the control problem consists in taking system (5.8) from its initial position x_0 at time t_0 to a terminal hypersurface S_f at time t_f so as to optimize a given objective function.

The final position reached by the system (x_f) must therefore belong to a well-defined hypersurface S_f, that is

$$x_f \in S_f, \qquad t = t_f \tag{5.11}$$

This hypersurface may be defined by the following set of equations

$$g_1(x) = 0, \qquad g_2(x) = 0, \ldots, g_{n-k}(x) = 0, \quad 1 \leqslant k \leqslant n - 1 \tag{5.12}$$

i.e.

$$S_f = \{x : g_i(x) = 0; i = 1, 2, \ldots, n - k\} \tag{5.13}$$

If the problem is, as in case (i), that of minimizing energy, the objective function can also be defined by (5.9). In this case, however, the system must not be taken to a given point, as in case (i), but to a given *hypersurface S_f*.

The control problem therefore becomes a problem of flexible objectives, since the point of arrival of the state $x(t_f)$ can be any point which satisfies (5.12), that is, which belongs to S_f.

The target set S will be defined in this case by

$$S = \{S_f\} \cdot \{t_f\} \tag{5.14}$$

(iii) *The target set is the whole space R^n; a terminal*
cost is considered

In this case the final position of the system is *free*: there is no final condition on the state. This means that the point of arrival of the system is not of particular importance. In general, in this case, the problem is defined as that of taking the system *as close as possible* to a given 'desired' position $x^D(t_f)$. This 'desired' position is defined by a pre-assigned value of the state vector at time t_f, and the condition imposed on the control problem is usually called 'terminal cost', 'terminal condition', and also, in economic applications, 'salvage value'.

The optimal control problem is thus the following: take system (5.8) from a given initial position x_0 at time t_0 to a point in the state space R^n which is as close as possible to a given 'desired' point defined by the vector $x^D(t_f)$, so as to minimize a given objective function.

If we consider a quadratic function as before, this must be of the type

$$J(u) = [x(t_f) - x^D(t_f)]'F[x(t_f) - x^D(t_f)] + \int_{t_0}^{t_f} [u'(t)Ru(t)]\, dt \qquad (5.15)$$

where F is a constant diagonal matrix positive semidefinite. The term $u'(t)Ru(t)$ may represent, as before, the cost of energy employed to transfer the system from the initial to the final position.

Since in this case the point of arrival of the system at time t_f can be any point in R^n, the target set will be defined by

$$S = \{R^n\} \cdot \{t_f\} \qquad (5.16)$$

This therefore is also a case of flexible objectives, since the final point is not fixed in advance.

A terminal cost can also be considered in case (ii), in which the target set is an hypersurface. This means that the final point $x(t_f)$ must belong to the hypersurface S_f and must also be as close as possible to a given desired position $x^D(t_f) \in S_f$. In this case, the objective function to be minimized can also be described by (5.15).

5.4 Optimal control problems with a conditioned state trajectory

The three cases examined in section 5.3 refer to the problem of taking a dynamic system from a given initial position at time t_0 to a given target set S at time t_f, where S is defined by a given final position x_f, by a given final hypersurface S_f or by the whole state space R^n. In this kind of problem the time trajectory that the system will follow when moving from the initial position $x(t_0)$ to the final position $x(t_f)$ is not important, provided that this movement takes place with, for example, the minimum use of energy.

However, since the time trajectory followed by the system may be an important feature of the control problem, it is possible to take it into consideration by introducing the state variables into the objective function, that is, by conditioning the state trajectory. The optimal control problem then assumes the following forms:

(i) *The target set is a point in the state space*

As in case (i) of the previous section, the problem consists in taking system (5.8) from the initial position x_0 at time t_0 to a given final position x_f

at time t_f, but in so doing the trajectory followed by the state variables must remain as close as possible to a given 'desired' trajectory $x^D(t)$, $t \in [t_0, t_f]$, $x^D(t_f) = x_f$.

Considering a quadratic objective function as before, the control problem consists in the minimization of

$$J(u) = \int_{t_0}^{t_f} \{ [x(t) - x^D(t)]Q[x(t) - x^D(t)] + u'(t)Ru(t) \} \, dt \tag{5.17}$$

where Q is a constant diagonal matrix, positive semidefinite.

This is also a fix-end point problem since the final objective is fixed, that is

$$S = \{x_f\} \cdot \{t_f\} \tag{5.18}$$

(ii) *The target set is an hypersurface in the state space*

As in case (ii) of the previous section, the problem consists in taking the system from the initial position x_0 at time t_0 to the terminal hypersurface S_f at time t_f, but in such a way as to keep the state as close as possible to the desired trajectory $x^D(t)$, $t \in [t_0, t_f]$. The objective function can as well be described by (5.17), as in case (i).

The final objective is therefore flexible since

$$S = \{S_f\} \cdot \{t_f\} \tag{5.19}$$

(iii) *The target set is the whole space R^n; a terminal*
cost is considered

As in case (iii) of the previous section the problem is to drive system (5.8) from an initial position x_0 at time t_0 to some point in the state space R^n as close as possible to a given pre-assigned point $x^D(t_f)$; furthermore, in so doing, the trajectory of the state must be kept as close as possible to a given desired trajectory $x^D(t)$, $t \in [t_0, t_f]$. The objective function therefore takes the form

$$J(u) = [x(t_f) - x^D(t_f)]'F[x(t_f) - x^D(t_f)]$$

$$+ \int_{t_0}^{t_f} \{ [x(t) - x^D(t)]'Q[x(t) - x^D(t)] + u'(t)Ru(t) \} \, dt \tag{5.20}$$

Since the deviation of the state at time t_f from its desired position (term $x(t_f) - x^D(t_f)$ in 5.20) is also included under the integral, the presence of the term $[x(t_f) - x^D(t_f)]'F[x(t_f) - x^D(t_f)]$ serves to emphasize the greater importance of this (final) deviation.

If, on the contrary, the deviation concerning the last moment of the time horizon has no particular significance, the terminal condition can be dropped and the objective function becomes

$$J(u) = \int_{t_0}^{t_f} \{ [x(t) - x^D(t)]'Q[x(t) - x^D(t)] + u'(t)Ru(t) \} \, dt \qquad (5.21)$$

On the other hand, if we wish to assign greater or lesser importance to deviations corresponding to different moments of time, it is possible to do it simply by considering a matrix $Q(t)$ whose elements are functions of time (see section 6.6). When the problem consists in keeping the state near zero, i.e. $x^D(t) = 0, t \in [t_0, t_f]$, the optimal control problem now described is called a 'state regulator problem' (see section 5.9).

As in case (iii) of the previous section the target set, also in this case, is the whole state space, that is

$$S = \{R^n\} \cdot \{t_f\} \qquad (5.22)$$

Finally, we observe that, as we have seen in section 5.3 (iii), a terminal cost can also be considered when the target set is a hypersurface. Therefore, when the final deviation is of particular significance, an objective function like (5.20) should be considered so that $x(t_f)$, besides belonging to S_f, is the closest point to $x^D(t_f) \in S_f$.

5.5 The target set of macroeconomic policy

In sections 5.3 and 5.4 we have examined the different control problems that arise when different target sets are considered and/or when the state vector is conditioned to be 'near' a desired trajectory.

In applications of optimal control theory to macroeconomic problems the case most often considered is (iii) of section 5.4, that is the case in which the state trajectory must be kept as close as possible to a given desired trajectory $x^D(t)$ along the planning horizon $[t_0, t_f]$, and therefore deviations of the state variables from their corresponding ideal values are penalized. However, the objective functions defined in that sub-section usually have to be modified where economic applications are concerned. Since, when we deal with problems of economic policy, the control variables are the policy instruments, there is little sense in minimizing the values of these instruments (term $u'(t)Ru(t)$ in 5.20 and 5.21), that is, deviations from zero. Therefore, a desired trajectory is usually also defined for the control variables, and the deviations of these variables from their corresponding ideal values are minimized. The objective functions (5.20) and (5.21) thus become, respectively

$$J(u) = [x(t_f) - x^D(t_f)]'F[x(t_f) - x^D(t_f)]$$

$$+ \int_{t_0}^{t_f} \{[x(t) - x^D(t)]'Q[x(t) - x^D(t)]$$

$$+ [u(t) - u^D(t)]'R[u(t) - u^D(t)]\} \, dt \qquad (5.23)$$

when a terminal condition is considered, and

$$J(u) = \int_{t_0}^{t_f} \{[x(t) - x^D(t)]'Q[x(t) - x^D(t)]$$

$$+ [u(t) - u^D(t)]'R[u(t) - u^D(t)]\} \, dt \qquad (5.24)$$

in the opposite case.

Furthermore, when the control vector is unconstrained, the inclusion of the term $[u(t) - u^D(t)]'R[u(t) - u^D(t)]$ in the objective function makes it possible to keep the values of the policy instruments close to the corresponding ideal ones and so prevent these instruments from taking on values that might be unrealistic from an economic point of view (see section 6.5).

Since the elements of matrices F, Q and R in (5.23)–(5.24) represent the weights (penalties) that the policy-maker attributes to deviations of targets and instruments from their corresponding desired values, it is possible to assign different weights to deviations at different moments of time simply by defining Q and R as time-varying matrices. If F, Q and R are not diagonal, cross products of these deviations can also be penalized, as we shall see in section 6.6.

The reasons why objective functions like (5.23) or (5.24) are mostly used in macroeconomic applications are easy to understand. While in engineering problems, the aim of the control action can be simply that of hitting a given target at a given moment, and the trajectory followed by the system from the initial to the final position may be unimportant; in economics, on the contrary, the position of the economic system *at each moment of time* is important. Policy-makers cannot impose an economically 'wrong' behaviour on a system simply because they wish to reach a given policy target at a given moment of time. What principally concerns policy problems is therefore the *path* that the system follows from the initial to the final time. This explains why deviations of the state variables from given desired values must be considered in the objective function.

As for the target set, the aim of most economic policy problems is to take the system as *close as possible* to a given desired position, and therefore the whole state space R^n is the final target set usually considered. However, the case in which, for example, for electoral purposes, policy-makers wish to reach a well-defined point in the state space at a given moment of time is not to be excluded. In fact, it may be important for the policy authorities to obtain a given rate of inflation in a given year, or month, in which elections have to take place. In this particular case we obviously have to consider a fixed target point in the state space.

Finally, it might also be the case – though it is to be considered less common in economic applications – that policy-makers wish to reach a given hypersurface in the state space, defined by the possible (desired) combinations of some given objectives. For example, such a surface could be represented by an 'ideal' Phillips curve, and the aim of policy-makers might be to take the state variables (unemployment and inflation, in this case) to any point along this curve.

5.6 The solution of optimal control problems: the minimum principle of Pontryagin

The two methods most frequently used to solve optimal control problems are the minimum (maximum) principle of Pontryagin – introduced by Pontryagin *et al.* in 1962 (though the first Russian publications go back to 1956–8) – and the dynamic programming method, introduced by Bellman (1957). This last method is more appropriate for dealing with optimal control problems formulated in discrete time and has become the method most often used in macroeconomic applications, since most dynamic macroeconometric models are in fact discrete-time models.[6] Conversely, in engineering problems, where dynamic systems are often formulated in continuous time, Pontryagin's minimum principle is frequently applied.

As we have already stressed, our intention here is to focus on control problems concerning continuous-time macroeconomic models. We shall therefore consider in particular Pontryagin's minimum principle, referring the reader, for example, to Bertsekas (1976, 1978, 1987), Chow (1975, 1981) and Murata (1982), for a clear and complete description of the dynamic programming method and its applications to discrete-time models.

Pontryagin's principle has been widely analysed, both in the engineering and the economic literature.[7] We do not intend therefore to present here a further description of this principle, but simply to discuss some of its features that we consider important for economic applications. In particular, in this section, we shall briefly recall the conditions for optimality, considering the different cases examined in sections 5.3 and 5.4. A general form of the dynamic system and of the objective function will be considered in this section; we shall then deal with the linear-quadratic case in the following sections.

Let us consider again the optimal control problem defined in section 5.2, taking into account that the target set can be defined by (see section 5.3)

(a) $\quad S = \{x_f\} \cdot \{t_f\}$

(b) $\quad S = \{S_f\} \cdot \{t_f\}$ $\qquad\qquad\qquad\qquad\qquad$ (5.25)

(c) $\quad S = \{R_n\} \cdot \{t_f\}$

For the convenience of the reader we rewrite the objective function (5.1)

$$J(u) = \int_{t_0}^{t_f} I[x(t), u(t), t] \, dt \qquad\qquad\qquad (5.26)$$

and the dynamic system (5.2)

$$\dot{x}(t) = f[x(t), u(t), t] \qquad\qquad\qquad (5.27)$$

and assume that I and f satisfy appropriate conditions of continuity and differentiability.

Now, given the initial state x_0 at time t_0, the set of admissible controls U and the target set S, the optimal control problem consists in finding a control u in U which transfers system (5.27) from x_0 to S and minimizes (5.26).

Before stating the minimum principle we still need to define the *Hamiltonian function* (or, simply, the *Hamiltonian*). This function is given by

$$H[x(t), \lambda(t), u(t), t] = I[x(t), u(t), t] + \lambda'(t) f[x(t), u(t), t] \qquad (5.28)$$

where $\lambda(t) \in R^n$ is the vector of *costate variables* (*costate vector*).

5.6.1 The minimum principle when the target set is a point

Consider first the case in which the target set is a given point x_f in the state space (case (a) of 5.25). In order for the control solution $u^*(t)$ to be optimal it is necessary:

(i) that there exists a vector $\lambda(t)$, and a vector $x^*(t)$ corresponding to $u^*(t)$, so that the following equations are satisfied

$$\dot{x}^*(t) = \frac{\partial H[x^*(t), \lambda(t), u^*(t), t]}{\partial \lambda} \qquad\qquad (5.29)$$

$$\dot{\lambda}(t) = -\frac{\partial H[x^*(t), \lambda(t), u^*(t), t]}{\partial x} \qquad\qquad (5.30)$$

with boundary conditions

$$x^*(t_0) = x_0, \qquad x^*(t_f) = x_f$$
$$\lambda(t_f) \text{ free} \tag{5.31}$$

(ii) that $u^*(t)$ minimizes[8] the Hamiltonian $H[x^*(t), \lambda(t), u(t), t]$ for $t \in [t_0, t_f]$, that is

$$\min_{u \in \Omega} H[x^*(t), \lambda(t), u, t] = H[x^*(t), \lambda(t), u^*(t), t], \quad t \in [t_0, t_f] \tag{5.32}$$

If u^* is an interior solution, then condition (5.32) can be substituted by

$$\frac{\partial H[x^*(t), \lambda(t), u^*, t]}{\partial u(t)} = 0 \tag{5.33}$$

and

$$\frac{\partial^2 H[x^*(t), \lambda(t), u^*, t]}{\partial u^2(t)} > 0, \qquad t \in [t_0, t_f] \tag{5.34}$$

i.e., the matrix defined by (5.34) is *positive definite*.

System (5.29) and (5.30) is a *Hamiltonian system* and is formed by $2n$ differential equations called *canonical equations*.

Now we want to see how the necessary conditions just stated change when the target set is not a point but a hypersurface S_f in the state space (case (b) of 5.25), the whole state space R^n (case (c) of 5.25) and when there is a terminal cost in the objective function. We notice that condition (ii) does not change in any of these cases. As for condition (i) only the boundary conditions must be modified in each case, as we shall see in the following sub-sections. These conditions will only be outlined in what follows, and the reader is referred to Athans and Falb, (1966, chapter 5) for the relevant demonstrations.

5.6.2 The minimum principle when the target set is a hypersurface: the transversality condition

In this case, the vector of costate variables at time t_f, $\lambda(t_f)$, must be transversal to the hypersurface S_f at the point in which the optimal state trajectory $x^*(t)$ meets S_f at time t_f. Therefore, assuming that S_f is a smooth[9] hypersurface described by the $n-k$ equations (5.12), the final value of the costate vector must be

$$\lambda(t_f) = \sum_{i=1}^{n-k} \alpha_i \left(\frac{\partial g_i}{\partial x} \right)_{x = x^*(t_f)}, \quad \alpha_i \neq 0, \quad 1 \leqslant k \leqslant n-1 \tag{5.35}$$

where $(\partial g_i / \partial x)_{x = x^*(t_f)}$ is the gradient vector of $g_i(x)$ at $x^*(t_f)$. Since the gradient vector evaluated at $x^*(t_f)$ is transversal to the tangent hyperplane of S_f at $x^*(t_f)$, it follows that for the costate vector to be transversal to S_f at $x^*(t_f)$ it has to be colinear to the gradient vector at the same point; in fact condition (5.35) defines the final value of $\lambda(t)$ as a linear combination of the $n-k$ gradient vectors.

An example in the bi-dimensional case may help to clarify this condition, known as the *transversality condition*. Let us suppose that there are two state variables $(n=2)$. The target set will therefore be defined by only one equation $g_1(x_1, x_2)=0, (k=1)$. Then, as can be seen from figure 5.1, the final

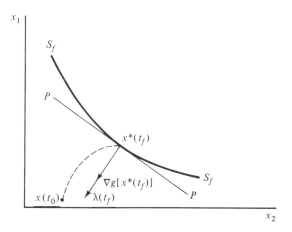

Figure 5.1   Final surface and transversality conditions

hypersurface S_f is a curve in the bi-dimensional space and the tangent hyperplane P in $x^*(t_f)$ is a line. The gradient

$$\nabla g[x^*(t_f)] = \begin{bmatrix} \partial g/\partial x_1 \\ \partial g/\partial x_2 \end{bmatrix}_{x=x^*(t_f)} \tag{5.36}$$

is a vector, normal to the line P. Therefore, for the transversality condition, the vector $\lambda(t_f)$ will be given by

$$\lambda(t_f) = \alpha \begin{bmatrix} \partial g/\partial x_1 \\ \partial g/\partial x_2 \end{bmatrix}_{x=x^*(t_f)} \qquad \alpha \neq 0 \tag{5.37}$$

To summarize, condition (i) is now described by the following canonical equations

$$\dot{x}^*(t) = \frac{\partial H[x^*(t), \lambda(t), u^*(t), t]}{\partial \lambda} \tag{5.38}$$

$$\dot{\lambda}(t) = -\frac{\partial H[x^*(t), \lambda(t), u^*(t), t]}{\partial x} \tag{5.39}$$

with boundary conditions

$$x^*(t_0) = x_0 \qquad \lambda(t_f) = \sum_{i=1}^{n-k} \alpha_i \left(\frac{\partial g_i}{\partial x}\right)_{x = x^*(t_f)}$$

$$x^*(t_f) \in S_f \tag{5.40}$$

5.6.3 The minimum principle when the target set is the whole state space

As in the case examined in the previous section, the necessary conditions (i) and (ii) stated in section 5.6.1 are still the same when the target set is the state space R^n and only the boundary conditions change. In fact, when $S_f = R^n$, the transversality condition becomes

$$\lambda(t_f) = 0 \tag{5.41}$$

and the canonical equations are therefore

$$\dot{x}^*(t) = \frac{\partial H[x^*(t), \lambda(t), u^*(t), t]}{\partial \lambda} \tag{5.42}$$

$$\dot{\lambda}(t) = -\frac{\partial H[x^*(t), \lambda(t), u^*(t), t]}{\partial x} \tag{5.43}$$

$$x^*(t_0) = x_0 \qquad \lambda(t_f) = 0$$

$$x^*(t_f) \text{ free} \tag{5.44}$$

It can be observed from conditions (5.31), (5.40) and (5.44) that the more the state vector is free at the terminal time t_f, the more the costate vector is constrained at that time.

There can also be some mixed cases in which some state variables have a free end point and some are constrained to end at a fixed point or at a hypersurface. Assume, for example, that the first p state variables have a free end point, the following h have a fixed end point and the remaining $n - (p + h)$ are constrained to end at a given hypersurface.

The boundary conditions then become

$$x(t_0) = x_0$$

$$\lambda_j(t_f) = 0 \quad j = 1, \ldots, p$$

$$x_j^*(t_f) = x_f \quad j = p + 1, \ldots, p + h \tag{5.45}$$

$$\lambda_j(t_f) = \sum_{i=1}^{n-k} \alpha_i \left(\frac{\partial g_i}{\partial \tilde{x}} \right)_{\tilde{x} = \tilde{x}^*(t_f)}, \quad j = p + h + 1, \ldots, n$$

$$\alpha_i \neq 0 \quad p + h + 1 \leq k \leq n - 1, \quad \tilde{x}' = [x_{p+h+1}, \ldots, x_n]$$

5.6.4 The minimum principle when a terminal cost is considered

We have just discussed how the boundary conditions change when different target sets are considered. We shall now see how these conditions must be modified when a terminal cost $E[x(t_f)]$ is included in the objective function, that is, when the latter is given by

$$J = E[x(t_f)] + \int_{t_0}^{t_f} I[x(t), u(t), t] \, dt \tag{5.46}$$

where E is a continuously differentiable function. As we have seen in section 5.3, the target set can be given, in this case, either by a hypersurface in the state space S_f or by the whole state space R^n. In the case of a target point there is obviously no need of further terminal conditions.

Since the Hamiltonian function is still given by (5.28), conditions (i) and (ii) of section 5.6.1 also remain unchanged, except for the boundary conditions corresponding to the canonical system.

In fact, if the target set is a hypersurface S_f, it is the vector $[\lambda(t_f) - (\partial E/\partial x)_{x = x^*(t_f)}]$ which has to be transversal[10] to S_f at the point of arrival $x^*(t_f)$. Therefore, the final value of that vector must be (see 5.35)

$$\lambda(t_f) - \left(\frac{\partial E}{\partial x} \right)_{x = x^*(t_f)} = \sum_{i=1}^{n-k} \alpha_i \left(\frac{\partial g_i}{\partial x} \right)_{x = x^*(t_f)}, \quad \alpha_i \neq 0, \quad 1 \leq k \leq n - 1 \tag{5.47}$$

or, equivalently

$$\lambda(t_f) = \sum_{i=1}^{n-k} \alpha_i \left(\frac{\partial g_i}{\partial x} \right)_{x = x^*(t_f)} + \left(\frac{\partial E}{\partial x} \right)_{x = x^*(t_f)}, \quad \alpha_i \neq 0, \quad 1 \leq k \leq n - 1 \tag{5.48}$$

Condition (i) then becomes

$$\dot{x}^*(t) = \frac{\partial H[x^*(t), \lambda(t), u^*(t), t]}{\partial \lambda} \tag{5.49}$$

$$\dot{\lambda}(t) = -\frac{\partial H[x^*(t), \lambda(t), u^*(t), t]}{\partial x} \tag{5.50}$$

$$x^*(t_0) = x_0, \qquad \lambda(t_f) = \sum_{i=1}^{n-k} \alpha_i \left(\frac{\partial g_i}{\partial x}\right)_{x = x^*(t_f)} + \left(\frac{\partial E}{\partial x}\right)_{x = x^*(t_f)} \tag{5.51}$$

$$x(t_f) \in S_f$$

If, on the contrary, $x^*(t_f)$ is free, i.e. the target set is the whole state space R^n, the terminal condition for the costate vector is (see 5.41)

$$\lambda(t_f) - \left(\frac{\partial E}{\partial x}\right)_{x = x^*(t_f)} = 0 \tag{5.52}$$

that is

$$\lambda(t_f) = \left(\frac{\partial E}{\partial x}\right)_{x = x^*(t_f)} \tag{5.53}$$

The canonical equations therefore become

$$\dot{x}^*(t) = \frac{H[x^*(t), \lambda(t), u^*(t), t]}{\partial \lambda} \tag{5.54}$$

$$\dot{\lambda}(t) = -\frac{\partial H[x^*(t), \lambda(t), u^*(t), t]}{\partial x} \tag{5.55}$$

$$x^*(t_0) = x_0, \qquad \lambda(t_f) = \left(\frac{\partial E}{\partial x}\right)_{x = x^*(t_f)} \tag{5.56}$$

$$x^*(t_f) \text{ free}$$

The terminal cost may also refer to only a part of the state variables, giving rise to mixed cases like the ones considered in section 5.6.3.

For the convenience of the reader, the different boundary conditions stated in section 5.6.1 through 5.6.4 are summarized in table 5.1 (mixed cases are not considered).

Table 5.1   Boundary conditions

Target set	Terminal cost	Initial conditions	Final conditions
$S = x_f$	$E = 0$	$x(t_0) = x_0$	$x^*(t_f) = x_f$ $\lambda(t_f)$ free
$S = S_f$	$E = 0$	$x(t_0) = x_0$	$x^*(t_f) \in S_f$ $\lambda(t_f) = \sum_{i=1}^{n-k} \alpha_i \left(\dfrac{\partial g_i}{\partial x} \right)_{x^*(t_f)}$
$S = R^n$	$E = 0$	$x(t_0) = x_0$	$x^*(t_f)$ free $\lambda(t_f) = 0$
$S = S_f$	$E = E[x(t_f)]$	$x(t_0) = x_0$	$x^*(t_f) \in S_f$ $\lambda(t_f) = \sum_{i=1}^{n-k} \alpha_i \left(\dfrac{\partial g_i}{\partial x} \right)_{x^*(t_f)} + \left(\dfrac{\partial E}{\partial x} \right)_{x^*(t_f)}$
$S = R^n$	$E = E[x(t_f)]$	$x(t_0) = x_0$	$x^*(t_f)$ free $\lambda(t_f) = \left(\dfrac{\partial E}{\partial x} \right)_{x^*(t_f)}$

5.7 The linear-quadratic case: description of the problem

We have seen in the previous section that Pontryagin's minimum principle provides *necessary* conditions for optimality. The solution obtained from these conditions will define a minimum of the objective functional, but this might not be an absolute minimum. There can be more than one control solution that satisfy all the necessary conditions. The problem is therefore to find *the optimal* control among the controls which satisfy the necessary conditions provided by the minimum principle.

Two approaches can be followed to solve this problem: either to apply sufficiency conditions for an optimum or to make use of objective functionals with a *unique* minimum: for example, functionals with a convex integrand $I(x, u, t)$ in x, u (see, for example, Kamien and Schwartz 1981, Part II, section 3).

A *sufficient condition* for optimality is the Hamilton-Jacobi equation (Lee (1963)), which defines a condition in the behaviour of the objective function. This condition is however described by a partial differential equation which may present computational difficulties. For this reason the Hamilton-Jacobi equation cannot always be used.

It therefore becomes extremely important to define objective functions with a unique minimum since, in this case, the control derived from Pontryagin's principle will be the (unique) optimal control.[11] This is one of the reasons why quadratic objective functions are so often used in optimal control problems, both in engineering and economic applications. Quadratic functions are not only easy to deal with from a mathematical point of view, but have also the property of being concave (convex) functions. It follows that the necessary conditions for optimality stated in the previous section are also sufficient conditions in the linear-quadratic case (i.e. linear dynamic system and quadratic objective function).

Another important feature of linear-quadratic optimal control problems is that the optimal control solution is a linear function of the state: the optimal feedback system is linear (provided that the control vector is not constrained). We shall deal with this property in section 5.10.

A linear-quadratic optimal control problem, in its most general form, can be described as follows: determine the optimal control $u^*(t)$ which minimizes

$$J(u) = \tfrac{1}{2}[\bar{x}'(t_f)F\bar{x}(t_f)] + \frac{1}{2} \int_{t_0}^{t_f} [\bar{x}'(t)Q(t)\bar{x}(t) + \bar{u}'(t)R(t)\bar{u}(t)]\, dt \qquad (5.57)$$

subject to

$$\dot{x}(t) = Ax(t) + Bu(t)$$
$$x(t_0) = x_0, \qquad x(t_f) \in R^n \qquad\qquad (5.58)$$

where the bar over the variables indicates deviations from the corresponding desired values, that is $\bar{x}(t) = x(t) - x^D(t)$ and $\bar{u}(t) = u(t) - u^D(t)$. The multiplicative factor $1/2$ is introduced only for convenience. We assume that there are no constraints on the control vector, i.e. $\Omega = R^r$.

The optimal control problem consists therefore in guiding the system from x_0 to a point $x(t_f)$ as close as possible to a given desired point $x^D(t_f)$. Furthermore, the trajectories followed by the state variables and by the control variables must remain 'near' the pre-assigned trajectories $x^D(t)$ and $u^D(t)$, respectively, $t \in [t_0, t_f]$. Since the control vector is unconstrained it could assume any value and therefore even extremely unrealistic values. In order to avoid such situations the term $\bar{u}'(t)R\bar{u}(t)$ is introduced, since it serves to keep the control trajectory as close as possible to a desired (acceptable) trajectory, as has been already pointed out in section 5.5.

The term $\bar{x}'(t_f)F\bar{x}(t_f)$ is introduced to emphasize the particular importance of deviations of the state at the final time. However, since these deviations are already included in the integrand, it is often assumed that $F = 0$ in most macroeconomic policy problems.

We also assume that the matrices $Q(t)$ and $R(t)$ are functions of time. The elements of these matrices represent, as we have seen in section 5.5 (see also section 6.6), the weights assigned to deviations of the state and control variables from their corresponding desired values. It therefore seems reasonable to consider the possibility of assigning different weights to these deviations at different moments of time. Indeed, it might be more important to take the system 'near' the policy targets in the first years of the planning horizon and, conversely, to attribute less importance to results concerning later years or vice versa. F, on the contrary, is a constant matrix since it refers to a given moment of time.

Since policy authorities are not necessarily interested in the behaviour of *all* the state variables – i.e. each state variable might not be a policy target – some of the rows and/or columns of $Q(t)$ and F might be zero. This means that $Q(t)$ and F can be positive semidefinite matrices. $R(t)$, on the contrary, must be positive definite as we shall see in the following section. The matrices F, $Q(t)$ and $R(t)$ are symmetric (see section 6.3), though not necessarily diagonal.

Finally, for simplicity, (5.58) is assumed to be a time-invariant system. The substance of the analysis does not change if the dynamic system is time varying. It can also be observed that the target set, in this case, is the whole state space R^n.

In the next section we shall first assume that $F = 0$ and then consider the case in which $F \neq 0$. The optimal control problems that we shall examine therefore correspond to those described in sections 5.6.3 and 5.6.4.

5.8 The minimum principle in the linear-quadratic case

We shall now apply Pontryagin's minimum principle to the linear-quadratic control problem described in the previous section, considering first the case in which $F = 0$.

Define the Hamiltonian

$$H = \tfrac{1}{2}[\bar{x}'(t)Q(t)\bar{x}(t) + \bar{u}'(t)R(t)\bar{u}(t)] + \lambda'(t)\,[Ax(t) + Bu(t)] \tag{5.59}$$

From condition (i) of section 5.6, we obtain the canonical equations

$$\dot{x}(t) = \frac{\partial H}{\partial \lambda} = Ax(t) + Bu(t) \tag{5.60}$$

$$\dot{\lambda}(t) = -\frac{\partial H}{\partial x} = -Q(t)\bar{x}(t) - A'\lambda(t) \tag{5.61}$$

Considering condition (ii) of section 5.6, we have

$$\frac{\partial H}{\partial u(t)} = R(t)\bar{u}(t) + B'\lambda(t) = 0 \tag{5.62}$$

$$\frac{\partial^2 H}{\partial u^2(t)} = R(t) > 0 \tag{5.63}$$

Therefore, the matrix $R(t)$ must be positive definite, so that the control vector $u(t)$ obtained from (5.62) *minimizes* the Hamiltonian function. The positive definiteness of $R(t)$ also makes it possible to obtain $u(t)$ from (5.62), since it implies the non-singularity of $R(t)$, that is

$$\bar{u}(t) = -R^{-1}(t)B'\lambda(t) \tag{5.64}$$

Since $\bar{u}(t) = u(t) - u^D(t)$, we get from (5.64)

$$u(t) = -R^{-1}(t)B'\lambda(t) + u^D(t) \tag{5.65}$$

Then, by substituting (5.65) into (5.60) and taking into account that $x(t) = x(t) - x^D(t)$, we obtain the linear time-varying differential system

$$\dot{x}(t) = Ax(t) - BR^{-1}(t)B'\lambda(t) + Bu^D(t) \tag{5.66}$$

$$\dot{\lambda}(t) = -Q(t)x(t) - A'\lambda(t) + Q(t)x^D(t) \tag{5.67}$$

Since $u^D(t)$ and $x^D(t)$ are known functions of time, system (5.66)–(5.67) – which is a time-varying differential system of $2n$ equations – can be solved, once the boundary conditions are defined. These are given by n initial conditions on the state variables

$$x(t_0) = x_0 \tag{5.68}$$

and n final conditions on the costate variables[12] (see (5.44) and table 5.1)

$$\lambda(t_f) = 0 \tag{5.69}$$

The solution of system (5.66)–(5.67), given the boundary conditions (5.68)–(5.69), provides the optimal trajectories of the state and costate vectors $x^*(t)$ and $\lambda^*(t)$. Then, by substituting $\lambda^*(t)$ into (5.65), we obtain the *optimal (open-loop) control solution* $u^*(t)$ (see chapter 7 for an application of this method to a macroeconometric model).

If we now consider the case in which a terminal cost is present ($F \neq 0$), then, as we have seen in section 5.6.4, the boundary conditions need to be modified. In fact, the final condition on the costate vector becomes

$$\lambda(t_f) = \frac{\partial \frac{1}{2}[\bar{x}'(t_f)F\bar{x}(t_f)]}{\partial x(t_f)} = F\bar{x}(t_f) \tag{5.70}$$

5.9 The matrix Riccati equation

We shall now see how the optimal control solution can be derived through the matrix Riccati differential equation. This procedure makes it possible to obtain the optimal *feedback* control rule, as we shall see in section 5.10. In order to simplify the mathematical treatment we shall first consider the case in which $\bar{x}(t) = x(t)$ and $\bar{u}(t) = u(t)$, that is, a state-regulator problem since

$x(t) = 0$ (we shall drop these simplifying assumptions in section 5.13). The problem therefore consists in determining the optimal control $u^*(t)$ which minimizes

$$J(u) = \tfrac{1}{2}[x'(t_f)Fx(t_f)] + \frac{1}{2}\int_{t_0}^{t_f}[x'(t)Q(t)x(t) + u'(t)R(t)u(t)]\,dt \qquad (5.71)$$

subject to

$$\dot{x}(t) = Ax(t) + Bu(t) \qquad (5.72)$$

$$x(t_0) = x_0 \qquad x(t_f) \in R^n, \qquad \Omega = R^r$$

From condition (i) we obtain the canonical equations (see (5.60)–(5.61))

$$\dot{x}(t) = Ax(t) + Bu(t) \qquad (5.73)$$

$$\dot{\lambda}(t) = -Qx(t) - A'\lambda(t) \qquad (5.74)$$

and from condition (ii) we get (see (5.65))

$$u(t) = -R^{-1}(t)B'\lambda(t) \qquad (5.75)$$

By substituting (5.75) into (5.73) we then have (see (5.66)–(5.67))

$$\dot{x}(t) = Ax(t) - BR^{-1}(t)B'\lambda(t) \qquad (5.76)$$

$$\dot{\lambda}(t) = -Q(t)x(t) - A'\lambda(t) \qquad (5.77)$$

given the boundary conditions (see (5.68)–(5.70))

$$x(t_0) = x_0, \qquad \lambda(t_f) = Fx(t_f) \qquad (5.78)$$

By considering system (5.76)–(5.77), we shall show that there is a linear interdependence between the costate and the state vectors and therefore that the former can be written as a linear function of the latter, that is

$$\lambda(t) = K(t)x(t) \qquad t \in [t_0, t_f] \qquad (5.79)$$

In fact, let $\Lambda(t; t_0)$ be the transition matrix of the homogeneous system (5.76)–(5.77), given t_0. We thus have

$$\begin{bmatrix} x(t) \\ \lambda(t) \end{bmatrix} = \Lambda(t; t_0)\begin{bmatrix} x(t_0) \\ \lambda(t_0) \end{bmatrix} \qquad (5.80)$$

and, setting $t = t_f$ and $t_0 = t$, we get

$$\begin{bmatrix} x(t_f) \\ \lambda(t_f) \end{bmatrix} = \Lambda(t_f; t)\begin{bmatrix} x(t) \\ \lambda(t) \end{bmatrix} \qquad (5.81)$$

If we now partition the transition matrix Λ into four sub-matrices we can write (5.81) as

$$x(t_f) = \Lambda_{11}(t_f; t)x(t) + \Lambda_{12}(t_f; t)\lambda(t) \tag{5.82}$$

$$\lambda(t_f) = \Lambda_{21}(t_f; t)x(t) + \Lambda_{22}(t_f; t)\lambda(t) \tag{5.83}$$

Since for the transversality conditions (see (5.78))

$$\lambda(t_f) = Fx(t_f) \tag{5.84}$$

we obtain, by substituting (5.82) into (5.84)

$$\lambda(t_f) = F[\Lambda_{11}(t_f; t)x(t) + \Lambda_{12}(t_f; t)\lambda(t)] \tag{5.85}$$

Now, by equating (5.83) and (5.85), we get

$$\Lambda_{21}(t_f; t)x(t) + \Lambda_{22}(t_f; t)\lambda(t) = F\Lambda_{11}(t_f; t)x(t) + F\Lambda_{12}(t_f; t)\lambda(t) \tag{5.86}$$

hence (assuming that the indicated inverse exists; see Kalman, 1960)

$$\lambda(t) = [\Lambda_{22}(t_f; t) - F\Lambda_{12}(t_f; t)]^{-1}[F\Lambda_{11}(t_f; t) - \Lambda_{21}(t_f; t)]x(t) \tag{5.87}$$

This confirms (5.79) and shows that matrix $K(t)$ is given by

$$K(t) = [\Lambda_{22}(t_f; t) - F\Lambda_{12}(t_f; t)]^{-1}[F\Lambda_{11}(t_f; t) - \Lambda_{21}(t_f; t)] \tag{5.88}$$

We can observe from (5.88) that $K(t)$ is a time-varying matrix, even when R and Q are constant matrices, since the transition matrix is always a function of time.

Once we obtain matrix $K(t)$, the optimal control $u^*(t)$ can be derived as a function of $x(t)$ (feedback control) simply by substituting (5.79) into (5.75), and also as a function of time (open-loop control) by then solving (5.72), given x_0, together with the equation defining the feedback control (see section 5.10). However the computation of $K(t)$ from (5.88) is extremely complicated for large n (which is usually the case in macroeconomic applications) and sometimes even impossible. Therefore $K(t)$ is usually obtained by solving a matrix differential equation of the Riccati type known as *matrix Riccati equation* or, simply, *Riccati equation*. $K(t)$ is often called the *Riccati matrix* or the *gain matrix*.

We now show how to derive this equation. Consider again relation (5.79) and differentiate both sides with respect to time, that is

$$\dot{\lambda}(t) = \dot{K}(t)x(t) + K(t)\dot{x}(t) \tag{5.89}$$

By substituting (5.79) into (5.76) and (5.77) we obtain

$$\dot{x}(t) = Ax(t) - BR^{-1}(t)B'K(t)x(t) \tag{5.90}$$

$$\dot{\lambda}(t) = -Q(t)x(t) - A'K(t)x(t) \tag{5.91}$$

and by substituting (5.90) into (5.89) we get

$$\dot{\lambda}(t) = [\dot{K}(t) + K(t)A - K(t)BR^{-1}(t)B'K(t)]x(t) \tag{5.92}$$

Then, by equating (5.91) and (5.92), after simple manipulations we obtain

$$[\dot{K}(t) + K(t)A - K(t)BR^{-1}(t)B'K(t) + A'K(t) + Q(t)]x(t) = 0 \tag{5.93}$$

Since (5.93) must hold for any value of $x(t)$, $K(t)$ must satisfy the matrix differential equation

$$\dot{K}(t) + K(t)A - K(t)BR^{-1}(t)B'K(t) + A'K(t) + Q(t) = 0 \tag{5.94}$$

which can be written as

$$\dot{K}(t) = -K(t)A - A'K(t) + K(t)BR^{-1}(t)B'K(t) - Q(t) \tag{5.95}$$

Equation (5.95) is the *matrix Riccati equation*.

In order to solve (5.95) we need to define the boundary conditions. From (5.79) we have that, at $t = t_f$

$$\lambda(t_f) = K(t_f)x(t_f) \tag{5.96}$$

Furthermore, from the transversality condition (5.78)

$$\lambda(t_f) = Fx(t_f) \tag{5.97}$$

From (5.96) and (5.97) we conclude that

$$K(t_f) = F \tag{5.98}$$

which is the terminal condition required.

From the matrix Riccati equation (5.95), given (5.98), we obtain the solution $K(t)$, which exists and is unique (Kalman, 1960). Since $K(t)$ is an $n \times n$ *symmetric* matrix (see Athans and Falb, 1966, Lemma 9.5), equation (5.95) describes a system of $n(n+1)/2$ first-order non-linear time-varying differential equations (and not of n^2 differential equations). It goes without saying that when $F = 0$ (no terminal cost considered), $K(t_f) = 0$ in (5.98).

It should also be observed from (5.95) and (5.98) that $K(t)$ depends exclusively on the coefficients of the dynamic system and on those of the objective function. It can therefore be computed once these coefficients are known and, once computed, we can obtain the optimal control solution, as we shall see in the following section.

5.10 Optimal feedback control

As we have already mentioned, an important feature of linear-quadratic optimal control problems is that the optimal control solution can be expressed as a linear function of the state variables; this means that the control vector can be described by a feedback rule

$$u(t) = G(t)x(t) \tag{5.99}$$

where $G(t)$ is an $r \times n$ time-varying matrix. Feedback rules show how current decisions depend on past decisions, whose effects are incorporated in the current value of the state vector $x(t)$.

In contrast with open-loop optimal control which is a function of time only and is completely specified at time t_0, feedback control makes it possible to modify the control action at each t, according to the new information on the state variables accruing at each moment of time.

Therefore, if, for example, the state variables represent the inflation rate, the balance of payments and the level of output, and the control variables represent public expenditure and the rate of interest, (5.99) describes the optimal relation, at each moment of time, between each instrument and the three target variables. This relation indicates therefore how the two policy instruments must be manipulated through time, according to the values assumed by the target variables considered.

The possibility of defining the optimal control solution as a feedback rule is particularly important in the framework of stochastic control. In the deterministic case it is possible to determine exactly, at time t_0, the time behaviour of all the endogenous variables between t_0 and t_f, once the initial values, the dynamic system and the feedback controls are given. It therefore makes no difference whether we consider the feedback rule (5.99) or the optimal open-loop control $u^*(t)$. Conversely, in the stochastic case, it is not possible to know the exact behaviour of the endogenous variables between t_0 and t_f in advance and it thus becomes important to be able to modify the control actions according to the values assumed by those variables at each moment of time. This enables us to take into account possible exogenous shocks and therefore to obtain a lower value of the objective function.

We shall now see how to obtain the optimal feedback control and also how to compute from it the optimal open-loop control. As mentioned in the previous section (equation (5.75)), the control rule obtained from condition (ii) is given by

$$u(t) = - R^{-1}(t)B'\lambda(t) \tag{5.100}$$

Therefore, we only need to substitute (5.79) into (5.100) to obtain

$$u(t) = - R^{-1}(t)B'K(t)x(t) \tag{5.101}$$

where $K(t)$ is the solution of the matrix Riccati equation (5.95). Since $R(t)$ and B are given matrices and $K(t)$ is the unique solution of the Riccati equation, the control $u(t)$ given by (5.101) is also unique and is the *optimal feedback control*.

Matrix $G(t)$ of (5.99) is thus defined by

$$G(t) = -R^{-1}(t)B'K(t) \qquad (5.102)$$

Since $K(t)$ is a time-varying matrix, as long as the planning horizon $[t_0, t_f]$ is finite, the optimal feedback rule is *always a time-varying rule*, even when the dynamic system and the objective function are time invariant. Matrix $K(t)$ is a constant matrix and the feedback rule is a constant rule only in the case of an infinite time horizon (see, for example, Carlson and Haurie, 1987, chapter 1).

As mentioned before, the optimal open-loop control can be easily obtained from the optimal feedback control in the deterministic case. Indeed, if we substitute (5.101) into (5.72), we obtain

$$x(t) = [A - BR^{-1}(t)B'K(t)]x(t) \qquad (5.103)$$

which is a first-order homogeneous equation that can be solved for $x(t)$, given x_0. The solution of (5.103) gives the optimal state trajectory $x^*(t)$, $t \in [t_0, t_f]$ which can be substituted into the feedback rule (5.101) yielding the optimal open-loop control

$$u^*(t) = -R^{-1}(t)B'K(t)x^*(t) \qquad (5.104)$$

In the deterministic case, therefore, the optimal feedback control and the optimal open-loop control coincide. It is sometimes simpler to compute the open-loop control directly from the canonical equations, as we have seen in section 5.8 (see also chapter 7). However, it is not always easy to obtain this solution, for example in the case in which a terminal cost is considered. Alternatively, the Riccati matrix $K(t)$ can be obtained with adequate computer programs but, in this case too, its computation may not always be very simple, specially in the framework of macroeconomic analysis where the economic models considered are usually large. The computation of $K(t)$ requires, as we have seen, the solution of $n(n+1)/2$ non-linear differential equations (where, we recall, n is the number of equations of the dynamic system).

We have already underlined the importance of feedback rules when the problem considered is stochastic. Another advantage of obtaining the feedback rule is the possibility of checking the stability conditions of the 'controlled' system (5.103) in order to investigate whether the optimal control rule *stabilizes* the dynamic model considered (see chapter 4).

We note however that the stability of the (optimally) controlled system can also be checked, even when the feedback rule is not explicitly calculated but the optimal open-loop control is directly derived from the optimality conditions of the minimum principle. Indeed, the dynamic system (5.66)–(5.67), with boundary conditions (5.68)–(5.69) (section 5.8) is, as we have seen, a Hamiltonian system whose equilibrium solution is a saddle point, either a saddle-saddle or a saddle-focus. When the Hamiltonian system is linear – as in the linear-quadratic case considered here – it is possible to obtain the eigenvalues which characterize the dynamic behaviour of the controlled system and therefore analyse its stability properties. This is the procedure which has been followed in the economic applications of chapter 7, to which we refer the reader.

5.11 An example of feedback control

A simple example with a single control variable may help the reader to understand how to compute the optimal feedback control through the Riccati matrix. Consider the optimal control problem (with planning horizon $t_0 = 0$, $t_f = 4$)

$$\min_u J(u) = \tfrac{1}{2}[x_1^2(4) + 2x_2^2(4)] + \frac{1}{2}\int_0^4 [2x_1^2(t) + 4x_2^2(t) + \tfrac{1}{2}u^2(t)]\, dt \qquad (5.105)$$

subject to

$$\begin{aligned}\dot{x}_1(t) &= x_1(t) + 2x_2(t)\\ \dot{x}_2(t) &= x_2(t) + u(t)\end{aligned} \qquad (5.106)$$

The matrices which characterize this problem are

$$F = \begin{bmatrix} 1 & 0 \\ 0 & 2 \end{bmatrix} \quad Q = \begin{bmatrix} 2 & 0 \\ 0 & 4 \end{bmatrix} \quad R = \tfrac{1}{2}$$

$$A = \begin{bmatrix} 1 & 2 \\ 0 & 1 \end{bmatrix} \quad B = \begin{bmatrix} 0 \\ 1 \end{bmatrix}$$

Let the Riccati matrix $K(t)$ be

$$K(t) = \begin{bmatrix} k_{11}(t) & k_{12}(t) \\ k_{21}(t) & k_{22}(t) \end{bmatrix} \qquad (5.107)$$

Since the Riccati equation is (see equation (5.95))

$$\dot{K}(t) = -K(t)A - A'K(t) + K(t)BR^{-1}B'K(t) - Q, \qquad (5.108)$$

then (omitting t for simplicity) we have

$$\begin{bmatrix} \dot{k}_{11} & \dot{k}_{12} \\ \dot{k}_{21} & \dot{k}_{22} \end{bmatrix} = -\begin{bmatrix} k_{11} & k_{12} \\ k_{21} & k_{22} \end{bmatrix}\begin{bmatrix} 1 & 2 \\ 0 & 1 \end{bmatrix} - \begin{bmatrix} 1 & 0 \\ 2 & 1 \end{bmatrix}\begin{bmatrix} k_{11} & k_{12} \\ k_{21} & k_{22} \end{bmatrix}$$

$$+ \begin{bmatrix} k_{11} & k_{12} \\ k_{21} & k_{22} \end{bmatrix}\begin{bmatrix} 0 \\ 1 \end{bmatrix}\, 2\, [0 \quad 1]\begin{bmatrix} k_{11} & k_{12} \\ k_{21} & k_{22} \end{bmatrix} - \begin{bmatrix} 2 & 0 \\ 0 & 4 \end{bmatrix} \qquad (5.109)$$

Then by performing the matrix operations indicated, we get

$$\dot{k}_{11} = -2k_{11} + 2k_{12}^2 - 2$$
$$\dot{k}_{12} = -2k_{11} - 2k_{12} + 2k_{12}k_{22}$$
$$\dot{k}_{21} = -2k_{11} - 2k_{21} + 2k_{21}k_{22}$$ (5.110)
$$\dot{k}_{22} = -2k_{22} - 2k_{21} - 2k_{12} + 2k_{22}^2 - 4$$

Since $K(t)$ is symmetric, $k_{21} = k_{12}$ and therefore the third equation can be eliminated (it is in fact equal to the second one). The differential equations to be solved are thus three $[n(n+1)/2 = (2 \cdot 3/2)]$

$$\dot{k}_{11} = -2k_{11} + 2k_{12}^2 - 2$$
$$\dot{k}_{12} = -2k_{11} - 2k_{12} + 2k_{12}k_{22}$$ (5.111)
$$\dot{k}_{22} = -2k_{22} - 4k_{12} + 2k_{22}^2 - 4$$

with boundary conditions $(K(t_f) = F)$

$$k_{11}(4) = 1$$
$$k_{12}(4) = 0$$ (5.112)
$$k_{22}(4) = 2$$

The solution of system (5.111), given (5.112), makes it possible to find the optimal feedback control which, as we have seen, is given by

$$u(t) = -R^{-1}B'K(t)x(t)$$ (5.113)

By substituting the corresponding matrices into (5.113) we get

$$u(t) = -2[0 \quad 1] \begin{bmatrix} k_{11}(t) & k_{12}(t) \\ k_{21}(t) & k_{22}(t) \end{bmatrix} \begin{bmatrix} x_1(t) \\ x_2(t) \end{bmatrix}$$ (5.114)

that is

$$u(t) = -2k_{12}(t)x_1(t) - 2k_{22}(t)x_2(t)$$ (5.115)

We observe that the linear feedback rule (5.115) is time varying, notwithstanding that both the dynamic system (5.106) and the objective functional (5.105) have constant coefficients.

5.12 Optimal control of the system output

In the previous section we considered a dynamic system of the first order: the state variables were target variables and the optimal control problem was a state-regulator problem. As mentioned in section 5.2, the methods for the solution of linear-quadratic optimal control problems described above

:an easily be extended to deal with higher-order systems, that is with the optimal control of the system output.

Consider the differential system

$$\overset{(n)}{y} + A_1 \overset{(n-1)}{y} + \cdots + A_{n-1} \dot{y} + A_n y = B_0 \overset{(m)}{u} + B_1 \overset{(m-1)}{u} + \cdots + B_m u \quad (m < n)$$

(5.116)

and rewrite it in state-space form

$$\dot{x}(t) = Ax(t) + Bu(t)$$ (5.117)

$$y(t) = Cx(t)$$ (5.118)

The optimal control problem is to minimize the cost functional

$$J(u) = \frac{1}{2} \int_{t_0}^{t_f} [\bar{y}'(t)Q(t)\bar{y}(t) + \bar{u}'(t)R(t)\bar{u}(t)] \, dt$$ (5.119)

subject to (5.117)–(5.118), where $Q(t) \geqslant 0$ and $R(t) > 0$. We also assume, for simplicity, that $\bar{y}(t) = y(t)$ and $\bar{u}(t) = u(t)$. In the next section this last assumption will be dropped.

If the dynamic system (5.117)–(5.118) is observable, it is possible to reduce the problem of optimal control of the output to a problem of optimal control of the state. Indeed, by substituting (5.118) into (5.119), we can write the objective function (5.119) as a function of the state variables, that is[13]

$$J(u) = \frac{1}{2} \int_{t_0}^{t_f} [x'(t)C'Q(t)Cx(t) + u'(t)R(t)u(t)] \, dt$$ (5.120)

The Hamiltonian function is therefore given by

$$H = \tfrac{1}{2}[x'(t)C'Q(t)Cx(t) + u'(t)R(t)u(t)] + \lambda'[Ax(t) + Bu(t)]$$ (5.121)

From condition (ii) of section 5.6, we have

$$\frac{\partial H}{\partial u(t)} = R(t)u(t) + B'\lambda(t) = 0$$ (5.122)

$$\frac{\partial^2 H}{\partial u^2(t)} = R(t) > 0$$ (5.123)

and therefore

$$u(t) = -R^{-1}(t)B'\lambda(t)$$ (5.124)

Now considering condition (i) of section 5.6 and equation (5.124) we obtain the canonical equations

$$\dot{x}(t) = \frac{\partial H}{\partial \lambda} = Ax(t) - BR^{-1}(t)B'\lambda(t) \qquad (5.125)$$

$$\dot{\lambda}(t) = -\frac{\partial H}{\partial x} = -C'Q(t)Cx(t) - A'\lambda(t) \qquad (5.126)$$

which can be solved given the boundary conditions

$$x(t_0) = x_0 \qquad \lambda(t_f) = 0 \qquad (5.127)$$

The solution of system (5.125)–(5.126), given the boundary conditions (5.127), provides the optimal trajectories of the state and costate vectors $x^*(t)$ and $\lambda^*(t)$. Then, by substituting $x^*(t)$ into (5.118), we get the optimal trajectory of the output vector $y^*(t)$ and, by substituting $\lambda^*(t)$ into (5.124), we can then obtain the optimal control solution $u^*(t)$.

In the same way, the procedure followed in section 5.10 can also be followed in this case in order to obtain the optimal feedback control. If we examine the case in which a terminal cost is considered, the optimal control problem is to minimize

$$J(u) = \tfrac{1}{2}[y'(t_f)Fy(t_f)] + \frac{1}{2}\int_{t_0}^{t_f} [y'(t)Q(t)y(t) + u'(t)R(t)u(t)]\,dt \qquad (5.128)$$

subject to (5.117)–(5.118) where $F \geqslant 0$, $Q(t) \geqslant 0$ and $R(t) > 0$.

If we substitute (5.118) into (5.128) we have

$$J(u) = \tfrac{1}{2}[x'(t_f)C'FCx(t_f)] + \frac{1}{2}\int_{t_0}^{t_f} [x'(t)C'Q(t)Cx(t)$$

$$+ u'(t)R(t)u(t)]\,dt \qquad (5.129)$$

which is the cost functional to be minimized subject to (5.117), where $C'FC$ and $C'Q(t)C$ are positive semidefinite matrices (see footnote 13).

The matrix Riccati equation is thus given by

$$\dot{K}(t) = -K(t)A - A'K(t) + K(t)BR^{-1}(t)B'K(t) - C'Q(t)C \qquad (5.130)$$

with boundary condition

$$K(t_f) = C'FC \qquad (5.131)$$

Since the Hamiltonian is again given by (5.121), the optimal feedback control is, as before, obtained from (5.124), that is

$$u(t) = -R^{-1}(t)B'K(t)x(t) \tag{5.132}$$

where $K(t)$ is the solution of (5.130)–(5.131).

The optimal trajectory of the state vector $x^*(t)$ can be obtained by substituting (5.132) into (5.117), that is, by solving

$$\dot{x}(t) = [A - BR^{-1}(t)B'K(t)]x(t) \tag{5.133}$$

given $x(t_0)$.

From the output equation (5.118), the optimal trajectory of the output $y^*(t)$ can finally be obtained simply by substituting $x^*(t)$ into (5.118).

5.13 Deviations from desired values

In the previous sections we have considered the case in which deviations of the target and control variables from zero were penalized. We shall now examine an optimal control problem often found in macroeconomic applications, that is the problem in which deviations from given *desired trajectories* of those variables are penalized; this problem is known as the 'tracking' problem in the engineering literature. We shall also assume a terminal cost in order to cover the more general case.

Consider again the linear differential system

$$\dot{x}(t) = Ax(t) + Bu(t) \tag{5.134}$$

The optimal control problem thus consists in minimizing

$$J(u) = \tfrac{1}{2}[\bar{x}'(t_f)F\bar{x}(t_f)] + \frac{1}{2}\int_{t_0}^{t_f}[\bar{x}'(t)Q(t)\bar{x}(t) + \bar{u}'(t)R(t)\bar{u}(t)]\,\mathrm{d}t \tag{5.135}$$

where, as above, $\bar{x}(t) = x(t) - x^D(t)$ and $\bar{u}(t) = u(t) - u^D(t)$; $x^D(t)$ and $u^D(t)$, $t \in [t_0, t_f]$, are the desired trajectories of the state (target) variables and of the control variables (policy instruments) respectively.

The Hamiltonian of this problem is given by

$$H = \tfrac{1}{2}[\bar{x}'(t)Q(t)\bar{x}(t) + \bar{u}'(t)R(t)\bar{u}(t)] + \lambda'(t)[Ax(t) + Bu(t)] \tag{5.136}$$

The canonical equations are given by (5.60)–(5.61) which we rewrite here for completeness

$$\dot{x}(t) = Ax(t) + Bu(t) \tag{5.137}$$

$$\dot{\lambda}(t) = -Q(t)\bar{x}(t) - A'\lambda(t) \tag{5.138}$$

From condition (ii) of section 5.6, we have

$$\frac{\partial H}{\partial u} = R(t)\bar{u}(t) + B'\lambda(t) = 0$$

from which (see (5.65))

$$u(t) = -R^{-1}(t)B'\lambda(t) + u^D(t) \tag{5.139}$$

The control (5.139) minimizes the Hamiltonian, since $R(t)$ is positive definite by assumption, that is

$$\frac{\partial^2 H}{\partial u^2(t)} = R(t) > 0 \tag{5.140}$$

If we now substitute (5.139) into (5.137) we obtain

$$\dot{x}(t) = Ax(t) - BR^{-1}(t)B'\lambda(t) + Bu^D(t) \tag{5.141}$$

$$\dot{\lambda}(t) = -Q(t)x(t) - A'\lambda(t) + Q(t)x^D(t) \tag{5.142}$$

which is a system of $2n$ differential equations with n boundary conditions on the initial state

$$x(t_0) = x_0 \tag{5.143}$$

and n boundary conditions on the costate, provided by the transversality conditions

$$\lambda(t_f) = F[x(t_f) - x^D(t_f)] \tag{5.144}$$

Since the solution of the differential system (5.141)–(5.142), with boundary conditions (5.143)–(5.144), is not computationally simple, we follow the same procedure as in section 5.9. Also in this case it is possible to show (see Athans and Falb,1966, chapter 9) that the costate $\lambda(t)$ is linearly related to the state $x(t)$ by

$$\lambda(t) = K(t)x(t) - k(t) \tag{5.145}$$

where $K(t)$ is the $n \times n$ Riccati matrix and $k(t)$ is an n-dimensional vector. Once we obtain $K(t)$ and $k(t)$ the optimal feedback control can be derived simply by substituting (5.145) into (5.139).

In order to get the solution for $K(t)$ and $k(t)$, we first have to differentiate both sides of (5.145) with respect to time, that is

$$\dot{\lambda}(t) = \dot{K}(t)x(t) + K(t)\dot{x}(t) - \dot{k}(t) \tag{5.146}$$

Then by substituting (5.145) into (5.141) we obtain

$$\dot{x}(t) = [A - BR^{-1}(t)B'K(t)]x(t) + BR^{-1}(t)B'k(t) + Bu^D(t) \tag{5.147}$$

and by substituting (5.147) into (5.146) we have

$$\dot{\lambda}(t) = [\dot{K}(t) + K(t)A - K(t)BR^{-1}(t)B'K(t)]x(t)$$
$$+ K(t)BR^{-1}(t)B'k(t) + K(t)Bu^D(t) - \dot{k}(t) \qquad (5.148)$$

Consider now (5.142) and substitute (5.145) into it, that is

$$\dot{\lambda}(t) = [-Q(t) - A'K(t)]x(t) + A'k(t) + Q(t)x^D(t) \qquad (5.149)$$

Then by equating (5.148) and (5.149), after simple manipulations, we finally get

$$[\dot{K}(t) + K(t)A - K(t)BR^{-1}(t)B'K(t) + A'K(t) + Q(t)]x(t)$$
$$+ [K(t)BR^{-1}(t)B' - A']k(t) - \dot{k}(t) + K(t)Bu^D(t) - Q(t)x^D(t) = 0$$
$$(5.150)$$

Equation (5.150) must hold for all $x(t)$, $x^D(t)$ and $u^D(t)$. Therefore $K(t)$ must satisfy the matrix differential equation

$$\dot{K}(t) = -K(t)A - A'K(t) + K(t)BR^{-1}(t)B'K(t) - Q(t) \qquad (5.151)$$

which is the Riccati equation. For the same reason, the vector $k(t)$ must satisfy the vector differential equation

$$\dot{k}(t) = [K(t)BR^{-1}(t)B' - A']k(t) + K(t)Bu^D(t) - Q(t)x^D(t) \qquad (5.152)$$

Now, in order to derive the boundary conditions, consider again (5.145) at $t = t_f$, that is

$$\lambda(t_f) = K(t_f)x(t_f) - k(t_f) \qquad (5.153)$$

On the other hand, from (5.144) we have

$$\lambda(t_f) = Fx(t_f) - Fx^D(t_f) \qquad (5.154)$$

and therefore

$$K(t_f) = F \quad \text{and} \quad k(t_f) = Fx^D(t_f) \qquad (5.155)$$

The differential equations (5.151) and (5.152) can now be solved for $K(t)$ and $k(t)$, given the boundary conditions (5.155). Since, as we have seen, $K(t)$ is symmetric, the number of equations to be solved is $n(n+1)/2 + n$.

Once $K(t)$ and $k(t)$ have been obtained, we can compute the optimal feedback control simply by substituting (5.145) into (5.139), that is

$$u(t) = -R^{-1}(t)B'K(t)x(t) + R^{-1}(t)B'k(t) + u^D(t) \qquad (5.156)$$

The optimal trajectory of the state can also be easily obtained by solving (5.147) given x_0. This solution can then be substituted into (5.156) to yield the optimal open-loop control. Of course, when $F = 0$ (no terminal cost), $K(t_f) = 0$ and $k(t_f) = 0$ in (5.155) and the optimal control obtained through the matrix Riccati equation will coincide with that obtained in section 5.8, simply by solving the canonical equations.

We notice that, in the linear-quadratic case just considered in which deviations from desired (non-zero) values of the targets and instruments are penalized, the optimal feedback control is of the form

$$u(t) = G(t)x(t) + g(t) \tag{5.157}$$

where $G(t)$ is a time-varying matrix

$$G(t) = -R^{-1}(t)B'K(t) \tag{5.158}$$

and $g(t)$ is a time-varying vector

$$g(t) = R^{-1}(t)B'k(t) + u^D(t) \tag{5.159}$$

It can be observed from (5.102) and (5.158) that $G(t)$ is the same both when deviations from zero and when deviations from non-zero values are penalized. In fact, (5.95) and (5.151) and the corresponding boundary conditions are the same and the Riccati matrix is independent of the desired values of instruments and targets. This means that the eigenvalues (and therefore the stability properties) of the controlled system are the same in both cases.

Conversely, the vector $g(t)$ depends on the desired values of the state and control variables, both directly and through $k(t)$. This has important implications in economic policy analysis, since it underlines the dependence of the optimal path of the policy instruments on the desired values of the targets and of the instruments themselves.

Furthermore, the optimal control solution at each time t depends not only on the present desired values of targets and instruments, but also on their *future* desired values. We can observe that the desired values $u^D(t)$ and $x^D(t)$, $t \in [t_0, t_f]$, in (5.152) appear as elements of the forcing vector $[K(t)Bu^D(t) - Q(t)x^D(t)]$. Therefore, letting $\Lambda(t; t_0)$ be the transition matrix for the system (5.152), we have

$$k(t_f) = \Lambda(t_f; t)k(t) + \int_t^{t_f} \Lambda^{-1}(\tau; t)[K(\tau)Bu^D(\tau) - Q(\tau)x^D(\tau)] \, d\tau \tag{5.160}$$

and hence

$$k(t) = \Lambda^{-1}(t_f; t)k(t_f) - \int_t^{t_f} \Lambda^{-1}(\tau; t)[K(\tau)Bu^D(\tau) - Q(\tau)x^D(\tau)] \, d\tau \tag{5.161}$$

From (5.161), we can now observe that the present value of $k(t)$ depends on the future desired values of the state and control variables, $x^D(\tau)$ and $u^D(\tau)$, for all $\tau \in [t, t_f]$. And, since the optimal control $u^*(t)$ depends in turn on $k(t)$ (see (5.156)), we can conclude that the value of the optimal control at each t of the planning horizon depends upon the future desired values of state and control variables. Today an optimal policy action must be such as to minimize also future variations in the relevant variables. And, since future deviations depend also on future desired values of those variables, the policy-maker, when defining the desired paths of target variables and policy instruments, must be aware that optimal decisions today also depend on the path he wishes these variables to follow in the future.

Moreover, since optimal decisions today also depend on current and future penalties assigned to deviations of the relevant variables (matrices $Q(\tau)$ and $R(\tau)$, $\tau \in [t, t_f]$), it is important to keep in mind how the choice of ideal paths and weighting matrices might influence current optimal decisions.

We also wish to note that, when time-varying dynamic systems are considered, optimal control decisions at each time t will also depend on values of the system coefficients evaluated at t and later, given the dependence of $K(t)$ on the A and B matrices through (5.151). Equation (5.161) serves therefore to emphasize the dependence of current optimal decisions on those current and future elements that characterize both the dynamic system and the objective function considered.

In this section we have examined a problem of optimal control of the state. However, the analysis carried out here can easily be extended to cover the problem of optimal control of the output, by following the same procedure described in section 5.12. We leave this as an exercise for the reader.

5.14 Optimal control in macroeconomics

We shall now examine some economic implications of the use of the optimal control methods described in the previous sections. This will help towards an understanding of the main problems and shortcomings of using optimal control theory in macroeconomic analysis.

5.14.1 Open-loop or feedback control?

An important point to consider in macroeconomic applications is the choice between open-loop and feedback rules. As we have seen in section 5.10, in the deterministic case, open-loop and feedback control coincide, since the exact evolution of the state variables can be known at the initial time. It is therefore indifferent, in this case, to compute one form of control or the other. When stochastic models are considered instead, the paths for the control variables may be different if the control is in the feedback or in the open-loop form. Indeed, in a stochastic framework it is not possible to know the exact performance of the endogenous (controlled) variables in advance, and it thus becomes important to modify the control actions according to the values taken by those variables over time. This possibility renders feedback control superior to open-loop control, at least in theory. We say 'in theory' because, in practice, feedback control presents a number of computational and practical problems.

From the computational point of view feedback control can be obtained by solving the matrix Riccati equation, as we have seen in section 5.9. However, in the case of a finite time horizon and when a big model (as econometric models usually are) is considered, obtaining the numerical solution of this non-linear differential equation can be a very cumbersome process.[14] On the other hand, even if the feedback solution could easily be obtained, its practical implementation may be complicated. The reason for this further difficulty is that feedback rules are usually rather complex. First, because in these rules the policy instruments generally depend on all the state variables of the model. Secondly, because, in the finite horizon case, feedback rules are time varying (see section 5.10) and, therefore, rather difficult for the policy-maker to apply. The complexity of feedback rules is particularly important in a world where expectations matter. A complex rule is clearly difficult for the private sector to understand and this may create a situation of uncertainty about future policy actions with all the negative consequences that can derive from this – as already emphasized by Friedman, 1953, and Kydland and Prescott, 1977.

A possible solution to this second problem is to consider an infinite time horizon. This assumption simplifies the computation of the solution of the Riccati equation (which becomes a static equation) and provides constant (time-invariant) feedback rules. Of course the price to be paid for greater simplicity is the assumption that policy-makers have an infinite planning horizon, which is rather unrealistic.

In view of these problems, the recent literature suggests the advisability of computing *simple macropolicy rules*, characterized by the dependence of policy instruments on *only a subset* of the state variables of the model and by *constant* coefficients. It is claimed that simple policy rules are not only more easily understood by the private sector, but also more *robust*, in the sense that they are less sensitive to uncertain shocks acting upon the system. The argument is that optimal complex rules provide a better performance of the system because they exploit all the information about its dynamic characteristics. But these characteristics may be precisely the uncertain features of the system, that is, those features about which the policy-maker has least information. The optimal complex rules may thus perform badly in the face of changes in those features. Therefore, even if *optimal* complex rules are superior, since their use makes it possible to take the system closer to the ideal path, simple rules can be considered superior in terms of robustness.

The (constant) coefficients of the simple policy rules can be optimally obtained by using minimization procedures.[15] The choice of the subset of target variables that are considered in the feedback rule is instead arbitrary. This subset of variables may also contain *intermediate targets* or *indicators*; the use of these variables is due to the quicker availability of observations – in comparison with the usual ultimate targets – and to the information they contain about these ultimate targets.[16]

However, one limitation on simple rules is the arbitrariness of the choice of the subset of endogenous variables on which each control variable depends. In fact, a new type of assignment problem arises which has to be solved on arbitrary grounds. Furthermore, as mentioned in section 4.4, the use of a given instrument on the basis of the performance of a pre-specified target (or targets), may produce undesirable side effects on the other targets to which the instrument is not principally assigned. This may give rise to losses in efficiency which can result in a more intensive use of policy instruments or in a longer period of time to achieve the policy targets.

The shortcomings of feedback policy rules suggest that open-loop control should not be discarded. Open-loop control is computationally simpler, depends only on time and is therefore more easily understood both by policy-makers and by the private sector. Of course, the impossibility of taking exogenous shocks on the state of the system explicitly into consideration is a serious drawback when a stochastic framework is considered, but the problem can be partly solved by successive reoptimizations, that is, by recomputing the optimal (open-loop) path at each new t, and by using all the new information available at that time (see Hughes Hallett and Rees, 1983, chapter 7).

5.14.2 Certainty versus uncertainty

An important characteristic of optimal control in policy decision-making is the implicit assumption that policy-makers know *the* model which describes the economic system to be controlled. Of course, knowledge of the economic model is not a specific requirement of optimal control: any qualitative or quantitative method used for policy analysis, such as stability or controllability analysis, simulations, forecasting, etc., requires this knowledge. However, it is the literature on optimal control that has been mainly concerned with the implications of this assumption.

Model uncertainty is a well-known problem, not only in economics, but also in physics and in other sciences. Indeed, a model is, by definition, an abstraction: even the most sophisticated economic model will provide only an approximate description of reality. A discrepancy, therefore, will always exist between the mathematical relations used to describe the economic system considered and the economic system itself.

Modelling inaccuracies are mainly the result of two different types of misspecifications:

(a) Misspecification of the equations from a *mathematical* point of view, which can be due to ignoring the influence of some variables, to the absence of some dynamic effects, to the neglecting of non-linearities, etc. A model cannot be mathematically too complex because this would imply great difficulties from a computational point of view. Therefore when choosing between simpler or more complex mathematical specifications, the tradeoff is between modelling accuracy and computational convenience, and some degree of modelling accuracy is generally sacrificed for computational convenience.

(b) Misspecifications of the equations of the model from an *empirical* point of view, due to uncertainty in the parameters, to measurement errors, to unexpected exogenous shocks, etc. When this type of uncertainty can be explicitly considered in the model (because estimated distributions of the model's parameters and residuals can be defined), it is then possible to use probabilistic methods – in particular, *stochastic optimal control* – which have already a long history in the control literature. The use of these methods will be discussed in the next section.

Otherwise, when uncertainty about the economy cannot be explicitly modelled, a way to deal with this problem is the *robustness* approach that will be considered in more detail in section 5.16.

A proof of the fact that a given model cannot be considered as an exact description of the economy is the existence of different models all describing the same economy, where the differences can be both theoretical and empirical. Therefore, when problems of policy design are considered, policy-makers (and policy-advisers) must be aware that different models will provide different policy rules. This problem, known as *model rivalry*, has been receiving increasing attention in recent literature,[17] where, as we shall see in section 5.16, the problem is overcome by designing policies which are robust with respect to the choice of the econometric model.

A further assumption implicit in policy optimization problems is the knowledge of *the* objective function that represents the preferences of policy-makers. This assumption has important consequences in policy design, since optimal policies obtained from different objective functions will differ. Also, in this case, the recent literature focusses on the search for policies which are robust to changes in the specification of the function. This type of robustness is important when the relative priorities of policy-makers over target variables are uncertain, as is often the case. The difficulties of providing an accurate specification of the objective function will be discussed in detail in chapter 6, to which the reader is referred.

5.15 Stochastic control and decision under risk

As mentioned in the previous section, when uncertainty can be explicitly introduced into the model, stochastic control methods can be used to obtain optimal policies. In this section a brief introduction to stochastic control is provided and some references for further reading are suggested.

The simplest way to deal with a stochastic control problem is to assume that uncertainty in the system is only of the *additive* type. In this case, if the econometric model considered is linear and the objective function is quadratic, it is possible to apply the principle of *certainty equivalence* or *separation principle*. According to this principle, demonstrated by Simon (1956) and Theil (1957) (see Chow 1975, chapter 8; Bertsekas 1987, chapter 2, for the multiperiod case), the optimal feedback control rule obtained from the optimization of a quadratic function under the constraint of a linear-stochastic model is also the solution of the corresponding deterministic problem.[18] The solution of the stochastic optimal control problem is obtained by maximizing (minimizing) the mathematical expectation of the objective function under the constraint of the stochastic model, given the information available at the initial time.

However, even if the feedback control law is the same in both the stochastic and the deterministic case, the optimal time trajectory of the control variables is different. When a stochastic problem is considered, it is not possible to know the time path of the state variables in advance, and it is on these variables that the control variables depend. Therefore, unlike the deterministic case, feedback and open-loop control do not coincide in the stochastic case.

The meaning of the 'separation principle' is that, for the class of problems just mentioned, it is possible to separate the process of estimating the model from its use in optimal control. This separation is no longer possible when other types of uncertainty are considered, such as, for example, multiplicative uncertainty. Stochastic control becomes a more complex problem in the case of *multiplicative* uncertainty, i.e., when uncertainty in the parameters is assumed (or when measurement errors are considered; see Kendrick 1981, chapter 12; Bertsekas 1987, chapter 3). The certainty-equivalence principle no longer holds in this case and optimal control decisions are functions of the distributions of the parameters, in particular of the mean vector and of the covariance matrix.

In the case of uncertainty in the parameters, two cases can be considered when solving optimal control problems: (i) passive learning and (ii) active learning. Both refer mainly to numerical problems since analytical solutions generally cannot be obtained (see Aoki 1967; Kendrick 1980).

(i) When *passive learning* is considered, the fact that the distribution of the estimates of the parameters may change over time is taken into account. The optimal control law corresponding to a given time interval $[t_0, t_f]$ can be computed at time t_0 by taking the mathematical expectation of the parameter distribution, given the information available at t_0. Moreover, most stochastic control algorithms make it possible to take into account the possibility of learning, i.e., of improving the knowledge of the estimates of the parameters through the new information accruing at future moments. These algorithms make use of new data for updating the parameter estimates at each t, before computing the corresponding control action.

(ii) When we consider not only that the knowledge of the parameter estimates can improve through time, but also that it is the choice itself of the optimal control actions at each time t that affects this learning process, then *active learning* has to be introduced. This type of stochastic control is more commonly known as *dual* control or as *adaptive* control.[19]

The main assumption underlying *dual* control is that the learning process on the parameters of the econometric model takes place as a consequence of the control actions themselves. These actions have therefore a double role (hence the name *dual*): they have to be chosen not only so as to steer the system towards the desired path, but also to reduce the uncertainty about the system's response. The optimization problem must thus include a tradeoff between performance and learning: a given control action at time t, which causes a worse current performance of the system, but which is useful to provide more accurate information about the parameters of the model, might be taken as a preferable control action when the whole planning horizon is taken into consideration (Kendrick 1981, chapter 8 and ff.; Bertsekas, 1987, chapter 4).

Dual control thus makes it possible to obtain control rules that give rise to satisfactory results even when the dynamic characteristics of the system under control are modified during the planning horizon considered. These modifications, for example, can be the result of wide variations in the parameters or of strong exogenous disturbances. When the expected modifications of the external conditions are too intense, a control system of the traditional type can be inadequate or even unstable, giving rise to a movement away from, instead of towards, the given desired trajectory. The control system must therefore have the ability to adapt, that is to self-adjust to unpredictable changes. The parameters of dual control rules are therefore changed through time, as a function of some particular signals capable of evaluating the behaviour of the controlled system instant by instant. These parameters are modified in such a way as to keep the system along the optimal path notwithstanding the modifications in the external conditions. A typical example of adaptive control in engineering applications is spacecraft control systems where changes in mass and atmospheric conditions take place.

Dual control should be used when the parameter estimates have very large confidence intervals at the initial time or when it is predicted that important structural modifications of the controlled system will take place (for example, in economics, when radical technological innovations are expected). However, dual control is computationally complicated and expensive, particularly if applied to large macroeconometric models. Its use in applied macroeconometrics is in fact uncommon (for an example, see Kendrick, 1981, chapter 12).

As far as optimal policy design is concerned, the principle of certainty equivalence is the approach generally considered, although its use implies several important limitations like a very simple specification of the model (linear), a very particular form of the objective function (quadratic), and very restrictive assumptions about the type of uncertainty present in the model (additive). Furthermore, the certainty equivalence procedure for optimal policy selection has another important shortcoming: it produces control rules that are invariant to risk, i.e., are *risk neutral*. Indeed, the optimal control rule obtained from the minimization (maximization) of the expected value of a quadratic objective function under the constraint of a linear-stochastic model depends only on the first moment of the distribution of the stochastic variables.

It has been pointed out by several authors (see, for example, Johansen, 1978; Mitchell, 1979) that optimal decisions obtained under certainty equivalence are independent of the usual measures of risk aversion. The suggestion that these authors make, in order to introduce some measure of risk into the stochastic optimization problem is to consider moments of higher order of the (stochastic) objective function. To this purpose, two different lines can be followed:

(a) That of abandoning the quadratic specification of the objective function and, instead, of adopting functional forms whose mathematical expectation also includes moments of a higher order than the first (see, for example, Whittle, 1983). The most common form of this type used in the economic literature is the exponential function (see Waud, 1976; Johansen, 1980; see also section 6.11.2).

(b) That of retaining the quadratic objective function, but of introducing into the quadratic specification those higher moments of the distribution that the certainty equivalence procedure neglects. This is the line mainly followed in the recent literature, in particular the so-called *mean-variance* approach.

This approach, as its name indicates, consists in the minimization of a linear combination of the mathematical expectation and the conditional variance of a given quadratic function. The minimization of this type of function can be carried out with no loss of tractability with respect to the traditional certainty equivalence approach, and the optimal policies obtained are preferable to risk neutral ones: the same expected outcomes for the target variables can now be obtained with less risk, as measured by the variance of the expected outcomes. Some degree of flexibility can also be introduced simply by considering different weights on the first and on the second moments: a relatively higher weight on the variance reflects a more risk sensitive choice, while the opposite reflects stronger risk neutrality. Certainty equivalence can therefore be considered as a particular case of this specification of preferences, which results when a zero weight is assigned to the variance term (see, for example, Hughes Hallett, 1984b).

An important property of the mean-variance approach is that, in the linear-quadratic-gaussian framework,[20] it produces policy rules that are also robust to exogenous shocks: the minimization of the mean and variance combination implies, in this case, the minimization of the specific objective function that ensures the derivation of robust policies (see Rustem, 1989; see also the next section).

5.16 Robust control

A way to approach the problem of uncertainty is to look for results that are *robust* with respect to variations in the economic environment. This approach, which is well known in the control literature (see, for example, Patel *et al.* 1977; Frank, 1978), is attracting increasing interest in economic research. This is probably due to the fact that economists today use ever more sophisticated models, which often involve non-linearities and multiplicative uncertainty: these are two features that render the use of stochastic control methods computationally expensive and difficult to apply, especially when models of large dimensions are considered.

As we shall see in this section, the robustness approach represents a way out of these difficulties, since it makes it possible to analyse how specific properties of the model under control are affected by exogenous disturbances, by using deterministic control methods. Furthermore, it is possible to reformulate the optimal control problem so as to obtain controls that are *robust*, in the sense that will be defined below.

The concept of robustness is rather close to that of sensitivity; indeed, the two concepts are often mixed up in the economic literature. It is therefore important to highlight the distinction between the two, a distinction which is clearly drawn in the control literature (see, for example, Petkovski, 1989). Although the two concepts have a common feature – they both concern the preservation of various system properties in the face of variations in the model considered – *sensitivity* analysis mainly deals with the relationship between *infinitesimal* variations in the parameters of the system (or other exogenous shocks) and the corresponding system property, whereas *robustness* analysis concerns the relationship between *finite* variations in the parameters of the system (or other exogenous shocks) – which must take place within a finite pre-specified region (not necessarily small) – and the corresponding system property.

Sensitivity analysis has mainly been used in the literature for checking the sensitivity of the *stability* property of a system to infinitesimal variations in the parameters of the system itself. In particular, the sensitivity of the eigenvalues of the dynamic (linear or linearized) system to these variations is usually considered. However, sensitivity analysis has also been used in a wider sense, to test the sensitivity of other features of the model to changes in parameters, for example the sensitivity of the state solution, the eigenvector matrix, etc.[21]

Robustness analysis, on the other hand, is more often applied to investigate the properties of *controlled* systems. The aim of the analysis is to obtain *robust controls*, that is controls under which a specific property of the system is preserved, even in the face of finite variations in the external environment. The importance of robust policies in economics is straightforward, since in general policy-makers are poorly informed about prospective disturbances that might hit the economic system; it is therefore desirable to design policies that perform 'reasonably' well under different types of possible shock.

The robustness concept, however, is not always considered in the economic literature exactly in the sense defined above. Two different ways to deal with robustness have mainly been followed in economic applications:

(a) The first consists in checking the specific system property with the nominal model and a given control rule, and then in testing whether this property is modified or not, and by how much, under different values of the system parameters. The variations of these parameters may not be small and are usually arbitrarily chosen. For example, if stability robustness is to be checked, the problem is to test whether a feedback control rule that stabilizes the economic system considered is still a stabilizing rule when the parameters of the model undergo some specific modifications. If this is so, the control rule used can be considered *robust*.

Alternatively, it is possible to test other characteristics of the controlled model, as, for example, how optimal paths of target variables, or the optimized value of an objective function, are modified as a consequence of variations in the model, where these variations can also be due to exogenous shocks, to different lengths of the planning horizon, to different priorities, and so on. This type of approach to the robustness problem is quite common in applied policy analysis (see, for example, Karakitsos and Rustem, 1984; Levine and Currie, 1985, 1987b; Ghosh *et al.*, 1987). In general, in these 'robustness exercises', the choice of the elements of the model to be modified, the magnitude of these modifications and the criteria to establish robustness are purely arbitrary and subjective, or, at the most, based on previous experimental results.[22] This is of course a shortcoming of this type of approach.

(b) A second way to deal with robustness is to define a specific objective function whose optimization provides control rules that are *robust* in the sense defined above. The problem is usually formulated as the minimization of a performance index which has among its arguments a sensitivity term. For example, if the problem is that of obtaining control rules that preserve the invariance of the value of the policy-maker's objective function with respect to exogenous shocks (i.e. performance robustness), the partial derivative of this function with respect to a vector of uncertain parameters or residual variables is minimized, together with the minimization of the policy-maker's function itself (see Karakitsos, *et al.*, 1980; Rustem, 1989). By including different sensitivity terms in the performance index, it is possible to obtain control rules that preserve other features of the system, such as the invariance of the optimal paths of the target variables with respect to exogenous disturbances (see Deissenberg, 1985; Rustem, 1989).

The optimal control solutions obtained from this type of minimization problem will therefore be more robust, in the sense specified above, than any other solution obtained without taking into account the sensitivity term. This is a case in which the robustness approach is based on sensitivity analysis, since it is the influence of infinitesimal variations in the (uncertain) parameters that are minimized to obtain a *robust* control.

The robustness approach can be extended to deal with the problem of *rival models* (see section 5.14). In this framework, a *robust* control is a control that performs 'reasonably' well for any one of the models considered. The problem for a policy-maker, in this case, is that of taking into account the consequences of basing his policy on one specific model and then of realizing that the 'real' world is instead represented by a different model. The extent of the losses which may occur when the problem of model uncertainty is ignored can be large, as emerges from an empirical test performed by Becker *et. al.*, 1986. The test consisted in simulating optimal policies obtained from a specific econometric model of the U.K., on a different model of the same economy, and vice versa.

An approach for obtaining robust policies in the case of model uncertainty is proposed by the same authors for the case of two rival models. It consists in optimizing a performance index defined as a weighted sum of the two objective functions associated with each model, under the constraints given by the two dynamic models. The weights to be attributed to each objective function can be determined by using the minimax criteria from the theory of choice under uncertainty.[23] This provides an optimal control solution which, although sub-optimal for each single model, is robust in the face of model uncertainty, in the sense that it produces the same value of the (combined) performance index, independently of which of the rival models turns out to be the best representation of the real world.

It is important to note that the problems highlighted in sections 5.14, 5.15 and in this section – referring to the economic implications of the use of optimal control techniques – also extend to the use of dynamic games in the case of decentralized policy-making.

5.17 Other uses of optimal control in macroeconomics

Policy selection is not the only reason for using optimal control in applied macroeconomics. There are other no less important applications which may have only an indirect bearing on the policy-making process (see, for example, HMSO, 1978). These concern in particular (i) the evaluation of the dynamic properties of econometric models, (ii) the testing of the robustness of the economic policies considered, (iii) the evaluation of alternative views on the priorities assigned to different policy targets (or on the ideal values of those targets) and (iv) the reconstruction of the preferences of policy-makers during a given historical period.

As regards point (i), optimal control makes it possible to investigate the dynamic properties of econometric models more completely and efficiently than other methods such as, for example, simulations. Optimal control exercises may show important links between the main components of the model, that is between target and control variables and between targets themselves. These exercises can also be useful for highlighting any shortcoming of economic models which it would have been difficult otherwise to identify. The specification of an econometric model can therefore be improved by the use of this additional information.

It may also be important to examine the robustness of given optimal policies (point (ii)) with respect to the choice of the econometric model, with respect to variations in the parameters of the model considered, and so on. In this case, we have to observe to what extent the feedback policies or the optimal control paths are modified by considering different specifications of the model itself.

As for point (iii), the evaluation of alternative views regarding the priorities assigned to the targets (or regarding the ideal values of those targets) can be carried out by considering different objective functions, that is, by changing the weights assigned to the different targets (or by changing their ideal values) iteratively. These exercises will produce *optimal* tradeoffs between the targets and will provide the economist with a view of the possible optimal results that can be obtained by using alternative optimal policies (see Chow, 1981, chapter 7, and section 7.8 of this volume).

Finally, it is possible to trace back the specific form of the objective function used by policy-makers in selecting optimal policies (point (iv)) by considering the *inverse* optimal control problem. It is possible in fact to obtain an (approximate) specification of the preferences of the decision-makers that have characterized a given time period by making use of the economic results effectively obtained during that period (see sections 6.7 and 6.8).

6   The objective function

6.1 Optimal economic planning

In the previous chapter we have seen the heavy dependence of the optimal control solution on the objective function and on the economic model which constitutes a set of constraints on the optimization problem. Moreover, when dealing with *quantitative* policy problems, optimal control decisions must be based on a *macroeconometric* model which describes the behaviour of the economic system considered. Therefore, the choice of the model which best describes that economic system becomes indeed an important problem, as well as the definition of an objective function which represents the preferences of policy-makers appropriately.

It is well known that one of the main drawbacks of optimal control applications to macroeconomic planning is the lack of information on planners' preferences, which makes it very difficult to give a mathematical and numerical specification to the criterion function. Very often policy-makers' preferences are described simply on the basis of theoretical assumptions about them, whereas they should really be determined on the basis either of observation or of direct interaction with the planners themselves. The problem of an appropriate specification of the objective function is now attracting growing attention and in recent literature new methods for the numerical determination of this function have been proposed.

In the previous chapter we considered quadratic objective functions since this is the form most often used in economic applications. In fact, as we shall see, quadratic functions present many advantages, but there are also some drawbacks which the economist must be aware of.

The aim of this chapter is to deal with the main elements concerning the specification of the planners' objective function, in particular with (a) the mathematical form of the function and (b) the numerical determination of the parameters of the same function, which is a crucial point when a quantitative analysis is to be made.

Since these are long-standing problems, we shall dedicate the next section to an examination of how they have been tackled in the past; there is always much to be learnt from those who first laid the ground-work for this kind of analysis. Indeed, much of the material that will be examined in the following sections is largely based on the pioneering work of economists like Frisch and Theil, who were the first to propose the optimization of a social preference function as a new theoretical approach to policy-decision analysis.[1]

6.2 Ragnar Frisch and the social preference function

The idea of maximizing an objective function which is the expression of social welfare is certainly not new in economics. It constitutes a fundamental feature of welfare economics and is also the basis of economic (linear and non-linear) programming. It is therefore important to examine how this function has been formulated in the past by those economists whose intention was to provide a rigorous treatment of economic policy problems.

It was Frisch, in particular, who conceived a social preference function not as an aggregation of individual welfare functions but as the expression of the preferences of policy-makers as regards public welfare. In fact, Frisch maintained that this kind of function cannot be called the 'welfare function' in the welfare theory sense, since it is not a measure of social (collective) welfare, but of the preferences of the decision-making authority;[2] the function was meant to be an 'indicator of choice' so as to provide all those alternatives to which the policy authorities are indifferent and those which are preferred to others, as in a map of indifferences curves.

Frisch was aware of all the difficulties that the specification of such an objective function implied, and emphasized the importance of cooperation between politicians and economists[3] in carrying out this task. He suggested the method of interviewing policy-makers: 'One way to approach the decision-maker is through *interview questions*. It is well known that people will not always behave in an actual situation exactly in the way they *said* in an interview question that they *would* behave in such and such situation. But still, I think, it remains that valuable information may be obtained through interview questions, provided the questions are wisely formulated'. He also adds: 'The interview approach to the preference function is only a *first stage* in an iterative process which in each step proceeds by an optimal solution of the model' (Frisch, 1969, p. 7). That is, once an objective function has been outlined as a result of the interviews, this function must be optimized, under the constraint of the econometric model considered, so that policy-makers can realize what the results are that would be effectively achieved. This point will be made clearer in section 6.2.2.

A description of the interview method will be provided in that section, after a brief review, in section 6.2.1, of the mathematical forms that can be given to the objective function, as suggested by Frisch himself. The choice of the mathematical form is, as we have seen, another important problem as regards the specification of that function.

6.2.1 The mathematical form

In principle the economist should define the mathematical form of the objective function before interviewing the policy-makers, since the information derived from the interviews should be used to obtain the numerical values of the coefficients of that function. However, Frisch suggested that the interviews could also provide useful information for checking the correctness of the mathematical specification. For example, when using linear objective functions, information could be obtained on significant deviations from linearity indicating the advisability of substituting the function by one of a higher order. Similarly, when using quadratic functions, the information obtained could provide indications of the advisability of using different specifications.

The functional forms considered by Frisch are essentially the following:

(a) *Linear functions*

$$J(x_1, x_2, \ldots, x_n) = q_0 + \sum_{i=1}^{n} q_i x_i \tag{6.1}$$

where the variables x_i, $i = 1, \ldots, n$, are endogenous (target) variables;[4] q_0 is the (constant) intercept of the function and q_i $(i = 1, \ldots, n)$ are constant coefficients which, as we shall see, represent marginal preferences in this case. Some of the q_i can be set to zero when the corresponding endogenous variable x_i is not to be considered as a policy target.

(b) *Quadratic functions*, either of a simple type

$$J(x_1, x_2, \ldots, x_n) = q_0 + \sum_{i=1}^{n} (q_i x_i + \tfrac{1}{2} q_{ii} x_i^2) \tag{6.2}$$

or of a more general type, with cross-products

$$J(x_1, x_2, \ldots, x_n) = q_0 + \sum_{i=1}^{n} q_i x_i + \frac{1}{2} \sum_{i=1}^{n} \sum_{j=1}^{n} q_{ij} x_i x_j \tag{6.3}$$

(c) *Cubic functions* of the type

$$J(x_1, x_2, \ldots, x_n) = q_0 + \sum_{i=1}^{n} (q_i x_i + \tfrac{1}{2} q_i x_i^2 + \tfrac{1}{3} r_i x_i^3) \tag{6.4}$$

where, as above, q_0 is the intercept and all the other coefficients are assumed to be constant. As before, some of them can be zero.

The choice of a *linear function* implies the assumption of constant marginal preferences and marginal rates of substitution between the targets. From (6.1) we have

$$\frac{\partial J(x_1, x_2, \ldots, x_n)}{\partial x_h} = q_h, \quad h = 1, 2, \ldots, n \tag{6.5}$$

that is, the marginal preference with respect to any target variable is a (non-negative) constant and therefore independent of the level of the variable considered. This is an obvious drawback in policy applications since it means that, for example, a 2 per cent increase in the rate of employment gives rise to an equal increase of the preference function both in the case of an initial rate of employment of 50 per cent and in the case of 98 per cent, which is clearly absurd.

The same problem arises for the marginal rate of substitution between two different targets

$$\frac{dx_k}{dx_h} = -\frac{\partial J/\partial x_h}{\partial J/\partial x_k} = -\frac{q_h}{q_k}, \quad h, k = 1, 2, \ldots, n; \quad h \neq k \tag{6.6}$$

which is also independent of the levels of the two variables considered.

These limitations may be overcome by considering non-linear functions. Among this class of functions the simplest one is the *quadratic function* (6.2), which is characterized by marginal preferences that depend only on the level of the target variable with respect to which the derivative is taken, i.e.

$$\frac{\partial J(x_1, x_2, \ldots, x_n)}{\partial x_h} = q_h + q_{hh} x_h, \quad h = 1, 2, \ldots, n \tag{6.7}$$

where q_{hh} is assumed to be negative (principle of decreasing marginal utility; $\partial^2 J/\partial x_h^2 = q_{hh} < 0$).

Also the marginal rate of substitution is a function only of the level of the two target variables concerned.[5] In particular, if we consider the marginal rate of substitution between x_k and x_h, this will be given by

$$\frac{dx_k}{dx_h} = -\frac{\partial J/\partial x_h}{\partial J/\partial x_k} = -\frac{q_h + q_{hh} x_h}{q_k + q_{kk} x_k}, \quad h, k = 1, 2, \ldots, n; \quad h \neq k \tag{6.8}$$

The quadratic function of the more general type (6.3) also exhibits similar characteristics, but in this case marginal preferences are given by

$$\frac{\partial J(x_1, x_2, \ldots, x_n)}{\partial x_h} = q_h + q_{hh} x_h + \sum_{i \neq h} q_{ih} x_i, \quad h = 1, 2, \ldots, n \tag{6.9}$$

which, as can easily be seen, depend not only on the level of the variable x_h (as in (6.7)), but also on the level of the other target variables x_i ($i \neq h$). It follows that the marginal rate of substitution between x_k and x_h is also a function of all the target variables, i.e.

$$\frac{dx_k}{dx_h} = -\frac{\partial J/\partial x_h}{\partial J/\partial x_k} = -\frac{q_h + q_{hh}x_h + \sum_{i \neq h} q_{ih}x_i}{q_k + q_{kk}x_k + \sum_{i \neq k} q_{ik}x_i}, \quad h, k = 1, 2, \ldots, n; \quad h \neq k \qquad (6.10)$$

Finally, cubic functions such as (6.4) also exhibit marginal preferences and marginal rates of substitution which are functions only of the levels of the variables considered, i.e.

$$\frac{\partial J(x_1, x_2, \ldots, x_n)}{\partial x_h} = q_h + p_h x_h + r_h x_h^2, \quad h = 1, 2, \ldots, n \qquad (6.11)$$

and

$$\frac{dx_k}{dx_h} = -\frac{\partial J/\partial x_h}{\partial J/\partial x_k} = -\frac{q_h + p_h x_h + r_h x_h^2}{q_k + p_k x_k + r_k x_k^2}, \quad h, k = 1, 2, \ldots, n; \quad h \neq k \qquad (6.12)$$

Obviously, more complex cubic functions could be considered but they would be difficult to deal with analytically.

The features of the functions just examined induced Frisch – as well as Theil and most of the economists who have followed their theoretical approach – to adopt mainly the quadratic functional form. This form not only does not present the limitations of the linear functions, but is also more tractable, from a mathematical point of view, than the functions of a higher order. Furthermore quadratic functions exhibit other important properties which we shall examine in section 6.4. In section 6.11, other functional forms like piecewise quadratic and exponential functions will also be examined.

6.2.2 The numerical form: the interview method

To give a mathematical form to the objective function is not enough when dealing with quantitative policy analysis: the numerical determination of this function is also required. This was one of the main issues in Frisch's work; he writes:

one must have available a method of actually determining in concrete numerical form the preference function that will express the desires of the responsible political authority... An effective method of organizing the co-operation that is needed between the political authorities and the analytical technicians for an effective determination of the preference function is one of the most important aspects – if not the most important aspect – of macroeconomic programming (Frisch, 1957 [1961], p. 43).

The method that Frisch proposed in order to give a numerical form to the objective function lies in the convinction that policy-makers are not able to express their priorities with precision, making it necessary to use an indirect approach in order to help them to investigate their own preferences and to obtain the information required. Frisch believes that it is during the process of formulation and solution of different alternative policy problems that policy-makers come to realize, in a more definite way, what are their 'true' priorities. In other words, it is the knowledge of the numerical solutions of different policy optimization problems that leads the planners to realize which are effectively their preferences and priorities: policy-makers learn through an iterative process.

The interview method[6] – which was based upon those premises – has greatly influenced economic planning since the fifties, and new methods for the numerical determination of objective functions in dynamic policy analysis are still based upon it today (see sections 6.8 and 6.9). It therefore seems important to outline it here (for a wider discussion on the complex problem of the numerical specification of preferences, the reader is referred to section 6.7).

The method is based on an iterative process of the 'trial and error' type. The process requires a close cooperation between the economist and the planners and can be summarized in four phases. In the *first, preparatory phase*, the economist must try to form for himself a general idea about the preferences of decision-makers on the basis of his knowledge about the economic situation and about current policy programmes. He will then try to formalize these preferences approximately and build a system of interviews appropriate to obtain, in the *second phase*, a specification of the function closer to the preferences in question.

The interview questions suggested by Frisch were basically: (a) questions concerning the ranking of alternatives according to the policy-makers' preferences; (b) 'dichotomic' questions concerning the choice between pairs of alternatives; and (c) distribution questions, where the decision-maker has to distribute a given numerical (total) value among different items, for different values of the total.

According to the answers given to these different questions it becomes possible to build an objective function by processing the interview data. Note that the first type of question was generally used for the construction of linear preference functions while the second and third types were used for the specification of quadratic functions.

In a *third phase* the function thus obtained must be maximized under the constraint of the macroeconometric model considered. The maximization procedure gives rise to an optimal solution for the planning problem, a solution that will be presented to policy-makers so that they express their positive, or negative, opinion about it. If their opinion is positive, the iterative process ends at this point. Otherwise, policy-makers will express their dissatisfaction, indicating those values that they would like to see modified. Through these indications, in a *fourth phase*, the economist can introduce into the preference function the necessary modifications that will allow him to obtain an optimal solution closer to the policy-makers' desires.

The third and fourth phases can be repeated as many times as required until an objective function is defined the maximization of which yields an optimal solution which the planners consider wholly acceptable.

However, it is important to emphasize at this point that it could well happen, for example, that (a) policy-makers cannot (or do not wish to) give truthful answers to the hypothetical questions made; or that (b) the questions do not exhaust *all* the admissible policy alternatives. Therefore, an objective function obtained through interview methods should always be considered simply as an approximation to the 'true' one (in the assumption that such a 'true' one exists, which is itself debatable; see, for example, Bruno, 1986).

6.3 Quadratic functions and quadratic forms

Since quadratic objective functions are those most frequently used in economic applications, it is important to examine their main characteristics and to point out their advantages and limitations. This will be done in this and the following sections.

As we have already seen in section 6.2.1, the general form of a quadratic function is given by (6.3) that we rewrite here for convenience

$$J(x_1, x_2, \ldots, x_n) = q_0 + \sum_{i=1}^{n} q_i x_i + \frac{1}{2} \sum_{i=1}^{n} \sum_{j=1}^{n} q_{ij} x_i x_j \tag{6.13}$$

or, in matrix form

$$J(x) = q_0 + q'x + \tfrac{1}{2}(x'Qx) \tag{6.14}$$

where $x \in R^n$ is a vector of endogenous (target) variables, q is a constant vector and Q is an $n \times n$ constant matrix that is assumed to be *symmetric*. As can easily be seen from (6.13), the product of the variables $x_i x_j$ $(i \neq j)$ is multiplied by the sum $q_{ij} + q_{ji}$; therefore, by substituting both q_{ij} and q_{ji} by the value $\tfrac{1}{2}(q_{ij} + q_{ji})$, the value of the function J does not change and matrix Q becomes symmetric. It can therefore be defined as a symmetric matrix from the beginning.

Very often quadratic functions used in macroeconomic analysis exclude constant and linear terms and retain only quadratic ones. This kind of function is homogeneous of the second degree and is usually called *quadratic form*, that is

$$J(x_1, x_2, \ldots, x_n) = \frac{1}{2} \sum_{i=1}^{n} \sum_{j=1}^{n} q_{ij} x_i x_j \tag{6.15}$$

or, in matrix form

$$J(x) = \tfrac{1}{2}(x'Qx) \tag{6.16}$$

The quadratic form (6.16) is said to be *positive definite* if and only if

$$x'Qx > 0$$

for all

$$x \neq 0$$

negative definite if and only if

$$x'Qx < 0$$

for all

$$x \neq 0$$

positive semidefinite if and only if for all $x \neq 0$

$$x'Qx \geqslant 0$$

with the equality holding for at least one $x \neq 0$,

and *negative semidefinite* if and only if for all $x \neq 0$

$$x'Qx \leqslant 0$$

with the equality holding for at least one $x \neq 0$.

A *necessary* condition for positive (negative) definiteness is that matrix Q be *non-singular*.

Up to now we have considered 'static' objective functions, that is, functions whose arguments are not functions of time. However, as we have seen in chapter 5, when optimal control problems are considered the corresponding objective functions refer to a given time interval over which they have to be maximized (minimized). In this case the variables that enter the objective function are functions of time and we therefore need to specify whether, as such, they are discrete or continuous. If we consider the interval $[t_0, t_f]$ and refer to quadratic functions as above, we have, in the first case, an objective function specified in discrete time, i.e.:

$$J(x_t) = \sum_{t=t_0}^{t_f} q_0 + q'x_t + \tfrac{1}{2}(x_t'Qx_t) \tag{6.17}$$

and, in the second case, an objective function specified in continuous time, i.e.:

$$J[x(t)] = \int_{t_0}^{t_f} \{q_0 + q'x(t) + \tfrac{1}{2}[x'(t)Qx(t)]\} \, dt \qquad (6.18)$$

It should also be noted that, as we have seen in chapter 5, the optimization problem is generally constrained by a set of dynamic relations (an economic model) that describe the evolution over time of the endogenous variables considered. This means that the arguments of the objective function – that usually constitute a subset of the endogenous variables of the model – are linked by these dynamic relations and must therefore be specified in the same (discrete- or continuous-time) form.

Note finally that, when considering intertemporal objective functions, their coefficients can also be assumed to be time-varying so as to allow for a possible evolution over time of the preference structure.

6.4 Properties of quadratic functions

We shall now examine those properties of quadratic functions which render them particularly useful for economic applications. We shall see that most of these properties represent an advantage as regards their use in macroeconomic planning, although some (very few) of them may represent a limitation. This discussion will help us to understand why quadratic functions are so widely used in economic policy analysis.

In order to simplify the exposition we shall refer here to static functions, unless otherwise specified. The properties examined apply equally to intertemporal quadratic functions.

The most important of these properties are the following:

(i) As we have seen in section 6.2.1, marginal preferences and marginal rates of substitution are not constant and depend either on the levels of the relevant variables considered (when Q is diagonal), or on the levels of all the variables that enter the function (when Q is not diagonal).

We must note however that, when considering quadratic forms of the simpler type (with diagonal Q), the marginal rate of substitution between variable k and variable h is given by

$$\frac{dx_k}{dx_h} = -\frac{q_{hh}x_h}{q_{kk}x_k}, \quad h \neq k \qquad (6.19)$$

It follows that for a *given ratio* $r = x_h/x_k$, the marginal rate of substitution is constant and is given by $-(q_{hh}/q_{kk})r$. This means, for example, that the marginal rate of substitution between unemployment and inflation is the same, both in a situation of 4 per cent inflation and 2 per cent unemployment and in a situation of 20 per cent inflation and 10 per cent unemployment, which is rather unrealistic. However this problem can be avoided by putting $q \neq 0$ in (6.14) (see Hughes Hallett and Rees, 1983, chapter 10).

(ii) Assume x^* to be the vector which maximizes (minimizes) the quadratic function $J(x)$. Then, any discrepancy between vector x and vector x^* gives rise to a *quadratic* reduction (increase) in the value of that function. Therefore $J(x)$ decreases (increases) more than proportionally with respect to an increase in the discrepancy between x and x^*. This can be easily seen by considering $J(x)$ as a function of only one variable (a parable).

This well-known mathematical property of quadratic functions has important consequences in economic applications since it implies that, for example, the policy-maker's objective function is more sensitive to a change in the rate of inflation when the latter increases from, say, 10 to 12 per cent than when it increases from 2 to 4 per cent (assuming that the minimum corresponds, say, to a zero rate of inflation).

(iii) The form of the quadratic function $J(x)$ depends on the *absolute value* of the discrepancy between x and the extremal x^*. Again this can easily be seen by considering $J(x)$ as a function of only one variable; in fact $J(x)$ takes the same value both for $x = x^* + k$ and for $x = x^* - k$, for any k. This property – whose validity holds whatever the space of definition of $J(x)$ is – means simply that quadratic functions are *symmetric*.

The symmetry of quadratic functions gives rise to a complex problem when these functions are used in economics. We shall take up this important point again in sections 6.10 and 6.11.

(iv) Negative (positive) definiteness of a quadratic form implies the strict concavity (convexity) of the function and thus the existence of a *unique* maximum (minimum). The importance of this property has already been stressed in section 5.7.

(v) A quadratic function can be considered as a *second-order approximation* around the optimum point of a function of a higher order.
Let

$$J(x) = J(x_1, x_2, \ldots, x_n) \tag{6.20}$$

be a generic objective function and let x^* be the vector which maximizes (minimizes) $J(x)$. Assuming (6.20) to be at least twice differentiable, by expanding it in Taylor series around x^* and ignoring the terms of a higher order than the second, we get

$$J(x)=J(x^*)+\left(\frac{\partial J}{\partial x}\right)'_{x^*}(x-x^*)+\tfrac{1}{2}(x-x^*)'\left(\frac{\partial^2 J}{\partial x\partial x'}\right)_{x^*}(x-x^*) \quad (6.21)$$

By performing the multiplications indicated, (6.21) can also be written

$$J(x)=q_0 +q'x+\tfrac{1}{2}x'Qx \qquad (6.22)$$

which is a quadratic function where

$$Q=\left(\frac{\partial^2 J}{\partial x\partial x'}\right)_{x^*}$$

$$q=\left(\frac{\partial J}{\partial x}\right)_{x^*}-\left(\frac{\partial^2 J}{\partial x\partial x'}\right)_{x^*}x^* \qquad (6.23)$$

and

$$q_0 = J(x^*)-\left(\frac{\partial J}{\partial x^*}\right)_{x^*}x^* +\tfrac{1}{2}x^{*'}\left(\frac{\partial^2 J}{\partial x\partial x'}\right)_{x^*}x^*$$

A function such as (6.22) can therefore be interpreted as a local approximation to the 'true' and more general objective function of the planners.

(vi) When the objective function is quadratic and the model which describes the economic system considered is linear the optimal solution for the policy instruments can be expressed as a linear function of the target variables, that is

$$u = Gx \qquad (6.24)$$

where G is a constant matrix.

This feature of quadratic functions assumes particular importance when *dynamic* optimization problems are considered. In this case, if the intertemporal objective function is quadratic and the dynamic model is linear, the optimal control solution can be described as a *feedback rule* of the type (see section 5.10)

$$u(t)= G(t)x(t) \qquad (6.25)$$

if the optimal control problem is defined in continuous time, or

$$u_t = G_t x_t \qquad (6.26)$$

if the optimal control problem is specified in discrete time. In both cases, matrix G is time-varying. Only when the time horizon of the optimization problem goes to infinity does the optimal feedback rule become a constant one (see Athans and Falb, 1966, chapter 9; see also section 5.10).

(vii) As mentioned in section 5.14, when the objective function is quadratic and the dynamic model considered is linear, the principle of *certainty equivalence* holds. This principle – introduced by Theil (1954, 1957) and Simon (1956) – states that, if the above-mentioned conditions are satisfied and the type of uncertainty considered refers only to the additive structure of the model, the solution of a stochastic optimization problem is the same as the solution of the corresponding deterministic one. The solution of the stochastic problem is obtained by maximizing (minimizing) the mathematical expectation of the objective function under the constraint of the stochastic model considered.

This result, obtained for the case in which the optimization problem refers to only one period, can be extended to the case of dynamic optimization (see Chow, 1975, chapter 8), provided that the objective function is still quadratic and the dynamic model is linear with additive disturbances. In this case the following *multiperiod certainty equivalence* principle holds: the optimal (feedback) control rule obtained from the optimization of a quadratic function under the constraint of a linear stochastic model is also the solution – in the sense that the coefficients of the rule are the same – of the corresponding deterministic problem. As in the static case, the solution of the stochastic optimal control problem is obtained by maximizing (minimizing) the mathematical expectation of the objective function under the constraint of the stochastic model, given the information available.

It should however be observed that the importance of this principle is limited for the following reasons:

(a) even if the certainty equivalence principle makes it possible to consider uncertainty, this can only be of the additive type.

(b) the optimal control rule obtained as a result of the optimization problem is independent of the moments of a higher order than the first concerning the distribution of the stochastic variables. This rule is called *risk neutral*. If we want to introduce risk into stochastic control problems, we have either to abstract from quadratic functions and adopt different functional forms (see, for example, Waud, 1976; Johansen, 1980; Whittle, 1983; Caravani, 1987) or to consider higher moments of the probability distribution, while retaining the quadratic specification (see Hughes Hallett, 1984b and c; see also section 5.15 of this volume).

It can be observed that with the exception of point (iii), concerning the problem of the symmetry of quadratic functions – to which we can add the problem of risk neutrality just mentioned – the properties now analysed show many positive aspects of quadratic functions and therefore serve to justify their extensive use in economic applications. Furthermore, it is possible, by suitable modifications, to consider 'piecewise' quadratic functions which are *asymmetric* (see Friedman, 1975 and section 6.11.1 below) and to obtain *risk sensitive* solutions by solving stochastic control problems through the minimization, not only of the mathematical expectation of quadratic functions, but also of their variances, as just mentioned.

A further, and not irrelevant, advantage of quadratic functions is that they are tractable from a mathematical point of view. Evidently, in many cases, more complicated functions could represent the preferences of policy-makers more appropriately, but, as Chow argues:

An alternative is to make the objective function mathematically more complicated. This may make the computation of an optimal solution for the policy variables more difficult or even impossible. There will then be a choice between an exact solution to an approximate formulation of the problem and an approximate solution to an exact formulation of the problem. (Chow, 1975, p. 151)

As is well known, the first alternative is the one usually chosen.

6.5 Policy instruments and loss functions

Quadratic objective functions have been definitively adopted in economic policy analysis following Theil's important contributions, where a rigorous treatment of the problem of policy optimization was carried out (see Theil, 1958, 1964). Theil generalized the Tinbergen fixed-target approach (see section 3.2) by using the mathematical tools of utility theory on which Theil's previous research had mainly focussed (on this point, see Hughes Hallett, 1989). By introducing an explicit objective function he transforms Tinbergen's approach to policy decision into a *flexible-target* approach, where the values obtained for the target variables are not determined a priori, but are the result of the optimization of the policy-maker's objective function.

Also due to Theil is the idea of introducing policy instruments as specific arguments of the objective function by arguing that the use of these instruments may, by itself, produce positive or negative changes in social welfare. Thus, for example, an increase in public expenditure that aims to increase employment may also have direct welfare consequences due, for example, to the construction of schools, hospitals, roads or any other activity (Theil, 1958, 1964). On the other hand, the negative effects of the use of some policy instruments are generally due to the costs that the society must bear in order to change these instruments substantially. It should suffice to think, for example, of the cost of a tax reform or, more simply, of a modification in the existing tax legislation.

However, Theil's argument for the direct introduction of the policy instruments into the objective function implies accepting a non-totally correct specification of this function. Indeed, if the objective function was correctly specified it should be possible to account for the (positive or negative) effects produced by the use of the instruments without the need to introduce them explicitly. But since it is very difficult, if not impossible, to take into consideration all these possible side effects, the presence of the control variables in the objective function can be interpreted as a device to account for them.

Another argument put forward by Theil (1956, 1964) for the introduction of policy instruments into the objective function is that these instruments, as well as the policy targets, normally have preferred values. Therefore, if the optimization problem is conceived as that of minimizing the deviations of the variables that enter the objective function from ideal values (see below), the presence of the instruments in that function makes it possible to avoid large deviations of these latter variables from their corresponding ideal values. The introduction of the policy instruments into the objective function can therefore be considered, in this case, as a device to impose some kind of constraint on the control variables, while avoiding the introduction of specific bounds on the controls which may complicate the mathematical computation of the optimal control solution and may give rise to bang-bang controls.

Finally, the influence of the engineering literature and, in particular, of optimal control theory on economic policy analysis has undoubtedly been decisive in this sense. As we have seen in chapter 5, the presence of control variables in the objective function is often an essential feature of optimal control problems (like the classical minimum-fuel and minimum-energy problems).

Let us now briefly examine the form of the quadratic function (6.14) when policy instruments are introduced. Omitting the term $1/2$ for simplicity we get

$$J(x, u) = q_0 + q'x + r'u + x'Qx + u'Ru + x'Nu + u'N'x \qquad (6.27)$$

where $u \in R^r$ is a vector of policy instruments, r is a constant vector and R, N are constant matrices of appropriate dimensions.

If we now consider only quadratic terms in (6.27), we obtain a simpler quadratic function

$$J(x, u) = x'Qx + u'Ru + x'Nu + u'N'x \qquad (6.28)$$

which is described by the sum of two quadratic forms $x'Qx$ and $u'Ru$ plus he sum of two so-called *bilinear forms* $x'Nu$ and $u'N'x$, which are equal ،each being the other's transpose and both being scalars). Equation (6.28) can also be written in matrix form by making use of a partitioned matrix, i.e.

$$J(x, u) = [x'\,u'] \begin{bmatrix} Q & N \\ N' & R \end{bmatrix} \begin{bmatrix} x \\ u \end{bmatrix} \tag{6.29}$$

or, more compactly, as a quadratic form

$$J(x, u) = z'Mz \tag{6.30}$$

where $z' = [x'\,u']$ is an $(n+r)$-dimensional vector and $M = \begin{bmatrix} Q & N \\ N' & R \end{bmatrix}$ is a symmetric $(n+r) \times (n+r)$ matrix.

As we have seen in section 5.5, an objective function very often used in macroeconomic applications is a quadratic form defined as the sum of deviations of the target variables from 'ideal' or 'desired' values, that is

$$J(x) = (x - x^D)'Q(x - x^D) \tag{6.31}$$

where x^D represents ideal values. The aim of policy authorities is obviously to obtain x^D or, what amounts to the same thing, to obtain a value of $J(x)$ equal to zero which is the unconstrained minimum of (6.31). Positive values of $J(x)$ are therefore a measure of the *loss* or *cost* incurred whenever it is not possible to obtain exactly the desired values of the targets; indeed, (6.31) is often called the *cost function* or *loss function*.

This particular specification of the objective function is clearly a result of the influence of the optimal control literature, where the optimal control problem based on this type of function (in its dynamic version) is known as the 'tracking' problem (see section 5.13). However, it is possible to find traces of this type of function also in the economic literature: Ramsey, in his well-known paper of 1928, suggested the minimization of the deviations of the target variable (the rate of enjoyment) from an 'ideal' value represented by the greatest rate of enjoyment economically obtainable and which he calls the *bliss* point.

It should also be noted that, if we perform the operations indicated in (6.31), we obtain a quadratic function of the general form (6.13) containing quadratic, linear and constant terms.[7] The use of quadratic loss functions therefore involves no loss of generality from the mathematical point of view.

As in (6.28), the quadratic loss function (6.31) can also include policy instruments; as we have just seen it may be important for planners to ensure that these instruments do not deviate excessively from given desired values. In this case, we obtain the loss function

$$J(x, u) = (x - x^D)'Q(x - x^D) + (x - x^D)'N(u - u^D)$$
$$+ (u - u^D)'N'(x - x^D) + (u - u^D)'R(u - u^D) \tag{6.32}$$

or, equivalently,

$$J(z) = \bar{z}' M \bar{z} \qquad (6.33)$$

where $\bar{z}' = [z - z^D]' = [(x - x^D)'(u - u^D)']$ and M is defined as above.

The properties of quadratic functions examined in the previous section apply also for quadratic loss functions like (6.32). It follows that, because of property (ii) of section 6.4, large deviations from desired values are more strongly penalized than small ones, this being a positive feature of these functions. Limitations are however represented by risk neutrality and by the symmetry of quadratic forms which implies that positive and negative deviations are equally penalized.

On the other hand, the use of linear functions as loss functions is not recommended, since cancellation of positive deviations with negative ones may result in very low values of the function even when large deviations from desired values are present. Absolute values of the deviations could also be considered, but, in this case, large or small deviations would be penalized equally without the problem of symmetry being avoided.

Quadratic loss functions are largely employed in optimal policy design. However, when quantitative policy analysis is involved, its numerical specification remains a rather difficult problem to which we shall dedicate the following sections.

6.6 The parameters in the loss function

Before tackling the problem of the numerical determination of the parameters in the quadratic loss function, it seems important to examine briefly the meaning of these parameters,[8] that is, of the elements of the matrices Q, R and N, which represent the structure of policy-makers' preferences. In particular, and in relation to some normalization:

(a) the elements on the main diagonal of matrix Q represent the weights or penalties assigned to squared deviations of target variables from their corresponding desired values. Thus, for example, a certain degree of importance (weight) may be attached to a deviation of employment from its ideal value, and this weight may be larger or smaller than that on a deviation of inflation from its ideal. It should be remembered that, given property (ii) of section 6.4, the presence of quadratic terms implies that deviations from desired values are more severely penalized when they are large than when they are small.

(b) the off-diagonal elements of Q show the weights assigned to simultaneous deviations of two target variables from their corresponding desired values; these elements are multiplying cross-products of target deviations. For example, it may be important to stress the seriousness of a situation in which a high rate of unemployment is accompanied by a high rate of inflation, and this can be done by penalizing the joint deviations of the two variables in addition to their individual penalties under (a). This penalty means that the weight assigned to inflation also depends on the rate of unemployment, and vice versa.

Note that this additional weight on one variable may have a negative or a positive sign depending on the sign of the deviation of the other variable from its ideal. The sign of these off-diagonal elements of matrix Q should therefore be carefully chosen on the basis of the economic meaning to be attached to each extra-penalty (see point (d) below for an example).

(c) The diagonal elements of matrix R represent the weights attached to deviations of policy instruments from their corresponding desired values. A high penalty reflects the high cost that the use of the corresponding instrument represents when it moves away from the ideal value, whereas a low penalty indicates a greater freedom in the use of the instrument.

(d) The off-diagonal elements of R show the weights assigned to joint deviations from their corresponding desired values of two policy instruments. For example, in certain situations, a simultaneous penalization both for deviations of public expenditure and of taxation may be required, in order to emphasize the importance of not creating a high budget deficit. In this case the weight on public expenditure should increase as revenues from taxation decrease. This means that the weight on the product term should be set in such a way that overshooting the ideal value of public expenditure has an extra penalty if, at the same time, tax revenues fall below the corresponding desired level; i.e. the corresponding element of matrix R should be negative.

(e) Finally, the elements of N represent the weights attached to joint deviations of one target and one control variable from their corresponding desired values. Very often, in economic applications, these matrices are set to zero.

We wish to note here that whenever the quadratic function represents *intertemporal* preferences, as is the case in optimal control problems, the elements of each of the matrices just mentioned can be functions of time, and therefore different at each moment of the planning horizon. As mentioned in section 6.3, when formulated in discrete time, the quadratic loss function (6.33) becomes

$$J(z) = \sum_{t=t_0}^{t_f} \bar{z}_t' M_t \bar{z}_t \tag{6.34}$$

where $\bar{z}_t' = [z_t - z_t^D]'$ and $M_t = \begin{bmatrix} Q_t & N_t \\ N_t' & R_t \end{bmatrix}$; and, when formulated in continuous time

$$J(z) = \int_{t_0}^{t_f} [\bar{z}'(t) M(t) \bar{z}(t)] \, \mathrm{d}t \tag{6.35}$$

where $\bar{z}'(t) = [z(t) - z^D(t)]'$ and $M(t) = \begin{bmatrix} Q(t) & N(t) \\ N'(t) & R(t) \end{bmatrix}$, which is the form introduced in section 5.5 (equation 5.24). The variability of the elements of M makes it possible to attach different penalties to deviations of the same variables at different moments of time. So, for example, the penalties on failing to get good results on targets such as inflation and consumption may rise near election dates.

An alternative way of specifying an intertemporal objective function in discrete time is to consider each of the variables evaluated at different moments of time as different variables; the resulting objective function therefore looks like the 'static' function (6.32), with the difference that the vectors x and u are now stacked vectors whose dimension is $n(t_f - t_0 + 1)$ and $r(t_f - t_0 + 1)$ respectively. This way of formulating an intertemporal objective function was first suggested by Theil (1958, 1964), who made extensive use of it, and is still widely used in recent literature (see, for example, Hughes Hallett and Rees, 1983; Rustem and Velupillai, 1984 and sections 6.8, 6.11.1 and 6.12 of this chapter). Notice that in this case the matrix of the quadratic form may contain elements which penalize joint deviations of targets and/or control variables evaluated at different moments of time. The presence of these intertemporal weights renders the preferences intertemporally dependent (Samuelson, 1971) – i.e. the objective function is no longer separable with respect to time.[9]

6.7 The numerical determination

When optimal control methods are to be used in quantitative policy analysis, the economist has to define an objective function: he has to select the relevant variables to include in this function and to choose an appropriate mathematical form whose parameters must be determined numerically. Therefore, assuming that the mathematical form chosen is a quadratic loss function – which, as we have seen, can be interpreted as a second-order approximation to a more general function – and once the target and control variables have been selected, the economist still has before him the difficult task of giving a numerical content to this function; in particular, to the desired values of the variables (vectors x^D and u^D) and to the weights to be attached to these variables (matrices Q, R and N, whose meaning has been discussed in the previous section).

As we have seen in section 6.2, the specification of an objective function which adequately reflects the preferences of the Government as to collective welfare is not a new problem; it was already an important issue in the fifties, as can be seen from Frisch's work, and the interview method that this author proposed (section 6.2.1) is today the starting point of the more recent, so-called 'interactive' methods. The problem of the numerical specification of the objective function has also been considered outside the sphere of economic policy analysis, in the wider framework of decision theory, and, in particular, in the literature on *multicriteria decision-making*.[10]

However, the numerical determination of preferences still remains one of the major difficulties in optimal economic planning. The fundamental point is that this function is not usually known, even by the policy authorities themselves. Indeed, a function that specifies the structure of preferences of policy-makers may not even exist, in the sense that it may exist only *implicitly*, but not be known a priori; policy options are often only clearly distinguished qualitatively rather than quantitatively. Furthermore, it may not be in the interest of policy-makers to reveal their preferences even in the happy event of their knowing them.

The task of the economist thus becomes that of obtaining the required information from decision-makers, in order to determine explicitly the objective function that best represents their preferences. Two different approaches can be followed in carrying out this task: (a) that of *observing* the past behaviour of planners, which is at the basis of the *methods of estimation* and (b) that of cooperating with these planners – following the line suggested by Frisch – in such a way that the *interaction* between politicians and economists leads the former to render explicit their own preferences, thus allowing the latter to build the required objective function; *interactive methods* rely on this approach. Both methods will be discussed in detail in section 6.7.1 and 6.7.2 respectively.

Before concluding this section it seems important to give at least a brief description of another approach: the *imaginary interview* suggested by van Eijk and Sandee (1959). These authors extend Frisch's interview method to the case in which direct cooperation with policy-makers is not possible. In this case the economist must try to obtain all available information about policy goals and priorities from official documents and policy statements and then play the double role of interviewer and interviewed: 'This means that interviews must be imaginary. All available knowledge of private and public utterances of members of the government or its advisers must be used... In short, the presumable outcome of a real interview must be forecast' (van Eijk and Sandee, 1959, p. 4). Thus, by imagining the results that policy-makers would like to obtain on the basis of the information available, the economist must iteratively modify the weights and/or desired values of the variables that appear in the objective function until he gets the results that he assumes would be considered 'the best': the weights and ideal values finally selected are those underlying these 'best' results.

This approach was followed by van Eijk and Sandee (1959) in an exercise of policy planning for the Netherlands, using information derived from the transcripts of the meetings of the Social and Economic Council that was advising the Netherlands Government in 1957. The approach suggested by these authors is frequently followed in optimal policy analysis, especially in academic research work, whenever it is not possible to interview policy authorities directly (see section 7.3 for an example).

In fact, in recent applications of optimal control to economic planning, it has been suggested that the optimal trajectories followed by the relevant variables should be examined first, and then the parameters in the objective function should be modified following an iterative procedure (see, for example, Chow, 1975 and 1981). In this way, if the time behaviour of one or more variables, as results from a given optimal policy, is not considered satisfactory by the economist, the penalties and/or the desired values of these variables can be modified in the direction suggested by the results, so as to improve their behaviour compatibly with an acceptable worsening in the behaviour of the remaining variables. Following this approach it is possible, after successive adjustments based on the information available, to obtain the objective function required.

6.7.1 Estimation methods

One way of getting to the numerical determination of the objective function consists in the estimation of the parameters of that function which are implicit in the past behaviour of policy-makers, that is in the behaviour observed over a given time interval.[11] This behaviour is described by the so-called *policy reaction functions* which, as is well known, specify the dependence of control variables on target variables.

The idea of obtaining the numerical values of the parameters of the objective function through the estimation of reaction functions had its major development in the sixties and seventies and was applied to static optimization problems. This approach was suggested initially by Dewald and Johnson (1963) and Reuber (1964) and successively developed by

Pissarides (1972), Friedlander (1973) and Makin (1976), among others. However, the method and its extension to a dynamic framework developed by Chow (1980b, 1981) attracted little subsequent attention. Nevertheless, we consider it of sufficient importance to provide at least a brief description, referring the reader to Makin (1976) and to Chow (1981, chapter 16) for further details concerning the estimation process in a static and in a dynamic context respectively.

Since our attention is mainly addressed to dynamic problems, we shall focus here on the method described by Chow. Furthermore, the logical premises which underlie it are substantially the same as those underlying the static method.

Chow's approach is based on optimal control theory and takes as its starting point the fact that the optimal control solution of a linear-quadratic problem is given by an optimal feedback rule, which can be considered as a policy reaction function. The optimal feedback rule is given by

$$u(t) = G(t)x(t) + g(t) \tag{6.36}$$

if the optimal control problem is formulated in continuous time, and by

$$u_t = G_t x_t + g_t \tag{6.37}$$

if formulated in discrete time.

As we have seen in section 5.13 (equation (5.158) and (5.159)), the coefficients of (6.36) (and (6.37)) are known functions of the coefficients of the dynamic model considered and of the parameters of the objective function (both weights and ideal values); it is therefore possible to derive these parameters from the optimal feedback rule through the following procedure. Estimate *simultaneously* a dynamic linear[12] econometric model and a set of reaction functions of the form of (6.36) (or (6.37)) which describe the relation between the policy instruments (control variables) and the state variables over a given time interval. The two systems are estimated by making use of data on the state and control variables (which are now endogenous) and on any exogenous variables entering the econometric model.

The estimation procedure – developed by Chow in discrete time – provides the values of the parameters of the objective function, since the likelihood function is not maximized with respect of G_t and g_t but with respect to M_t and z_t^D (see (6.33)) of which G_t and g_t are functions. This approach is technically related to the so-called *inverse optimal problem* (see Kurz, 1969). The problem considered here can in fact be seen as the converse of a standard optimal control problem. As we have seen, an optimal control problem can be defined in the following terms: *given* a dynamic econometric model and *given* a dynamic objective function, *find* the coefficients of the optimal feedback rule. Conversely, the problem of the estimation of the objective function is the following: *given* a dynamic econometric model and *given* the policy reaction functions (feedback rule), *find* the parameters of the objective function.

Though the method proposed by Chow has been specified in discrete time, it could also be extended to the continuous-time case by using methods of simultaneous estimation in continuous time (see, for example, Gandolfo, 1981, and the references therein).

The simplicity of the estimation method is however only apparent, since many technical difficulties are involved the solution of which requires drastic simplifications. For example, specific conditions need to be imposed so that the weighting matrices obtained are positive semidefinite; furthermore, the scarcity of data in relationship to the large number of parameters to be estimated makes it necessary to impose some arbitrary constraints on the objective function that may have no theoretical justification, like setting $N_t = 0$ and defining the weighting matrices Q_t and R_t and ideal values z_t^D as constants.[13] In this way the number of parameters to be estimated decreases, but their economic interpretation becomes difficult, specially if we consider that the time horizon must necessarily be very long.

Indeed, besides the problem of the scarcity of data with respect to the number of parameters, another technical problem arises from the variability of the coefficients of the optimal feedback rule. For estimation purposes these coefficients are assumed to be constant, but this assumption can be made only when the parameters of the objective function are time-invariant and the time horizon considered is very long (long enough for the system to approach a steady state; see Chow 1975, chapter 7). The parameters obtained from the estimation procedure therefore represent penalties and ideal values which are constant over the whole time interval considered in the estimation. This seems quite unrealistic since usually Governments change their priorities and ideal values of policy variables over time, especially when a long period is considered, as is the case here. A way out of this difficulty is to interpret these constant parameters in the objective function as average values over the planning period.

In any case it is difficult to tell how much the results obtained are distorted by the arbitrariness of the assumptions involved.

Other more general drawbacks of the estimation method should be mentioned:

(a) to obtain the objective function from past behaviour of decision-makers and through the optimal feedback rule implies the assumption that the policy rules followed in the past were the result of an *optimal* behaviour of the Government. But, in general, there is no evidence to support this assumption. Nevertheless, the 'as if' assumption is usually accepted.

(b) Estimation methods also imply that policy-makers know the 'true' model of the economy, since the outcomes observed are assumed to be the result of the actions taken on the basis of a model that describes the behaviour of that economy. If the model is not the 'true' one, observed behaviour may not reflect the 'true' preferences of policy-makers. 'From actually observed policy-actions and results of policy we may therefore draw wrong inferences about the preference function if we proceed as if the politicians know the real mode of operation of the economy' (Johansen, 1974, p. 49).

(c) Even if we accepted past policy decisions as optimal, there is no reason to assume that the objective function obtained from the observation of past behaviour (and the *distant* past) will still be the same today. Usually, as time goes by, not only can Governments change, but the desired values and priorities of the same Government may be also modified. Therefore, there may be no justification, in certain situations, for projecting the structure of preferences concerning the past into the future. Obviously this last criticism no longer holds whenever past policy behaviour alone is to be analysed.

A similar approach to the one just outlined – also based on the *inverse optimal problem* – has been used to estimate the private-sector preferences and technology, in order to obtain, from the optimization of these functions, optimal decisions on consumption, investment, and so on (see, for example, Hansen and Sargent, 1980, 1982; Hansen and Singleton, 1982; Singleton, 1988). This way of obtaining private decisions – as opposed to the usual direct estimation of behavioural relations – allows us to take into account possible modifications in the structure of these relations as a consequence of variations in economic policy rules, and therefore to overcome the so-called 'Lucas critique'. How and why this can be done we shall see in chapter 10.

6.7.2 Interactive methods

Like the estimation method examined in the previous section, interactive methods make possible the determination of policy-makers' implicit preference structure. The difference from estimation methods is that the latter are not based on *observed* (past) behaviour but on the *present*, though implicit, preferences of policy-makers. These methods are based on a sequential search for the parameters in the objective function; starting from arbitrary values, an iterative process takes place until a set of parameters – weights and ideal values of the relevant variables – is obtained that gives rise to those results 'implicitly' preferred by policy-makers. Interactive methods are based on the same premises that characterize Frisch's approach, i.e., that it is not possible to establish which set of parameters is 'better' than another independently of the optimal results obtained through them; and also that it is easier for policy-makers to express an opinion on policy results rather than on policy priorities. These methods can be considered as more or less sophisticated extensions of the interview method proposed by Frisch (section 6.2.2). Interactive methods are based on interviewing techniques, since also in this case the economist needs to obtain as much information as possible directly from policy-makers.

The sequential search for the parameters in the objective function is carried out jointly by the economist (who has to construct it) and the planners; and it is from this *interaction* that both parties increase their information along the iterative process. The results obtained by the economist at each iteration (through the optimization of an objective function) allow the policy-makers to understand better what can effectively be performed and to increase the knowledge of their own preferences. At the same time, this information makes it possible for the economist to reformulate new objective functions which give rise to more satisfying results, closer and closer to those desired, consciously or unconsciously, by the planners. Finally, the objective function sought is the one that gives rise to the best optimal results.

A brief comment is in order at this point on this, in some way special, concept of optimality. If the planners' objective function were a given *known* function, the solution obtained from its optimization would be *the* optimal solution. In this case, however, it is the policy-makers themselves who decide which of the optimal solutions obtained is the best, and it is then that the solution chosen becomes *the* optimal solution. The concept of optimality is therefore to some extent subjective. In fact, all the solutions obtained from the optimization of an objective function are optimal by definition; but here it is the policy-makers who decide which, among the optimal solutions obtained along the iterative procedure, is superior to the others (on this point, see Gruber, 1983).

We also note that, even if the preference structure of policy-makers is not known a priori, it is assumed that a preference ordering exists, at least at a local level, and that this ordering satisfies a minimal set of elementary axioms consistent with rational choices like completeness, reflexivity, transitivity and convexity (see Hughes Hallett and Rees, 1983, chapter 10). This assumption is also crucial to guarantee the convergence of the iterative process.

Since interactive methods have been largely applied in multicriteria decision problems they are also known as *interactive multicriteria decision methods*. These methods were developed mainly in the seventies, but are still often used today in many decision problems, even outside the economic field. They are based on a process which unfolds as follows: a set of possible combinations of values of instruments (decision variables) and targets – compatible with the constraints imposed by the economic model considered and obtained through the optimization of a variety of different objective functions – is presented to the decision-makers. The set of all these possible alternative combinations of values of the variables considered is called a 'scenario' or 'menu'.

After examining and evaluating this scenario, one combination is chosen. This combination is obviously preferred to the others, but is still not sufficiently satisfying. The economist must therefore modify the relevant objective function (i.e. the one which has produced the combination chosen) so as to generate a different set of objective functions whose optimization gives rise, in the following iteration, to a new scenario of possible alternatives which lie in the neighbourhood of the combination chosen in the previous iteration. The process is repeated, until it is no longer possible to find, in the neighbourhood of the last combination, other combinations preferred to it; the objective function which gives rise to this last combination is the objective function sought. A major problem that these methods involve is that of the convergence of the iterative process.

The development of multicriteria decision methods has been favoured in recent years by the growing use of computers and of increasingly sophisticated algorithms. However, the applications to economic policy problems are not numerous and are mostly restricted to the static framework. The extension of these methods to dynamic problems involves further difficulties, and in particular those which arise from the large amount of data which decision-makers are necessarily confronted with (see Deissenberg, 1983, and references therein). In the dynamic case each of the combinations that is part of a scenario is given by the product of the number of variables considered at each period by the number of periods. The increase in the amount of data makes it harder to choose among all the possible combinations.[14] However, new interactive methods concerning dynamic decision problems and applications to economic analysis have recently been proposed, and it is to these that we shall dedicate the following section.

6.8 The specification of implicit preferences[15]

A method for the determination of an intertemporal objective function in macroeconomic *dynamic* problems which relies very much both on Frisch's approach and on multicriteria decision methods has been proposed by Rustem, Velupillai and Wescott (1978) (successively developed by Rustem and Velupillai, 1983 and 1984, and by Hughes Hallett, 1979, Ancot, Hughes Hallett and Paelinck, 1982, Hughes Hallett and Ancot, 1982 and 1983). With this method – which belongs to the class of interactive methods – the authors solve the problem of the great amount of data which characterize dynamic multicriteria decision-making simply by calculating only *one* optimal solution at each iteration. In this way, the need for policy-makers to rank a set of alternatives, each containing a large amount of data, is avoided; policy-makers are simply asked to provide indications as to preferred directions from the last optimal results obtained, and these indications are then translated into corrections of the weighting matrix through a rank-one algorithm of the variable-metric type.

In order to provide a description of this method we shall consider a discrete-time framework, since dynamic interactive methods have been developed in discrete time. Their extension to continuous time is not so straightforward since, as we shall see, the property of discrete-time systems to be specified in stacked-up form is fundamental to the application of the variable-metric algorithm used in the iterative process. The possibility of defining both the econometric model and the objective function in stacked-up form permits us to work with a weighting matrix of constant elements, each representing the penalty assigned to each different variable at each different moment of time. On the contrary, the weighting matrix of an objective funtion specified in continuous time is itself a continous function of time, unless the penalties are assumed to remain constant over the whole planning horizon.[16]

Therefore, we assume that the objective function whose parameters must be determined through interaction with policy-makers is a discrete-time quadratic loss function

$$J(z) = \frac{1}{2} \sum_{t=t_0}^{t_f} \bar{z}_t' M_t \bar{z}_t \tag{6.38}$$

where, as above, $\bar{z}_t' = [z_t - z_t^D]' = [(x_t - x_t^D)' (u_t - u_t^D)']$, $x_t \in R^n$ is a vector of target variables, $u_t \in R^r$ is a vector of control (policy instrument) variables, and $M_t = \begin{bmatrix} Q_t & N_t \\ N_t' & R_t \end{bmatrix}$ is a positive semi-definite matrix to be determined, for $t = t_0, \ldots, t_f$. As we have seen in section 6.4, (6.38) can be taken as a second-order approximation to some general convex criterion function.

The dynamic model which describes the behaviour of the economy is given by

$$x_t = Ax_{t-1} + Bu_t + Cs_t \tag{6.39}$$

where A, B and C are constant matrices, and s_t represents other exogenous non-control variables.

The planning problem is therefore the usual one of dynamic optimization, that is, to minimize (6.38) given (6.39). However, this problem cannot be solved until M_t is known.

System (6.39) can also be written, by stacking it up for $t = t_0, \ldots, t_f$, as

$$x = Fu + s \tag{6.40}$$

where $x \in R^{n(t_f - t_0 + 1)}$, $u \in R^{r(t_f - t_0 + 1)}$, $s \in R^{n(t_f - t_0 + 1)}$ and[17]

$$F = \begin{bmatrix} F_{t_0} & 0 \ldots \ldots .0 \\ F_{t_1} & F_{t_0} & 0 \ldots 0 \\ \ldots \ldots \ldots \ldots \ldots \\ F_{t_f} & F_{t_f-1} \ldots F_{t_0} \end{bmatrix} \tag{6.41}$$

is a constant matrix of instant and delay multipliers of instruments on targets.

System (6.40) can also be rewritten in terms of $\bar{z}$, that is

$$H\bar{z} = b \tag{6.42}$$

where $\bar{z} = z - z^D$ (z^D being the vector whose elements represent ideal values of targets and instruments at each time interval), $H = [I \vdots -F]$ and $b = s - Hz^D$.

In the same way, the objective function (6.38) can be redefined in terms of deviations of policy variables referring to different moments of time, that is

$$J(z) = \tfrac{1}{2}\bar{z}' M\bar{z} \tag{6.43}$$

Since M is not assumed to be diagonal, its off-diagonal elements represent either penalties on simultaneous joint deviations of policy variables or penalties on joint deviations of these variables corresponding to different moments of time, as mentioned in section 6.6.

Let Φ be the set of *feasible* values of z, that is the set of z which satisfies the constraint imposed by the model

$$\Phi = \{z | H\bar{z} = b\} \tag{6.44}$$

The optimal policy problem is therefore

$$\min_z \{\tfrac{1}{2}\bar{z}' M\bar{z} | z \in \Phi\} \tag{6.45}$$

It can be observed that a dynamic optimization problem has been reduced to a static one, where the weighting matrix to be derived is a matrix M of constant elements.

Let us assume now that the ideal values of z are not feasible, that is $z^D \notin \Phi$ (otherwise z^D would be the obvious solution of the optimization problem (6.45)), and define a convex set Ω of *admissible* values of z, that is of values that are acceptable to policy-makers (though inferior to the desired ones). Therefore, the solution of (6.45) must belong to Ω (and, obviously, $z^D \in \Omega$). We also assume that the intersection between Φ and Ω is not empty, i.e.

$$\Phi \cap \Omega \neq \emptyset \qquad (6.46)$$

which ensures that an acceptable solution exists which is also feasible. In fact, the optimal solution must be such that

$$z^* \in \Phi \cap \Omega \qquad (6.47)$$

A difficult problem in economic planning is to define the set Ω, since this set is usually not known to the economist and not even to the decision-makers themselves. The interaction between the latter and the economist will lead to the definition of this set and, at the same time, to the determination of the M matrix.

The basic point in the process of determination of the weighting matrix M is the following: the optimal value of vector z obtained from the solution of (6.45) is given by

$$\bar{z}^* = M^{-1}H'(HM^{-1}H')^{-1}b \qquad (6.48)$$

which is derived from the first-order conditions of a static optimization problem. Since, as we have just seen, $b = s - Hz^D$ and $\bar{z} = z - z^D$, we obtain, from (6.48) the optimal (target and control) vector

$$z^* = [I - M^{-1}H'(HM^{-1}H')^{-1}H]z^D + M^{-1}H'(HM^{-1}H')^{-1}s \quad (6.49)$$

It should be noted from (6.48) that $\bar{z}^*$ cannot be obtained if M is not known. On the other hand, M could only be obtained if $\bar{z}^*$ were known since, as we have seen in section 6.4, $M = (\partial^2 J / \partial z \partial z')_{\bar{z}^*}$; that is, M is derived from the second-order approximation of a general objective function $J(\bar{z})$ about some feasible $\bar{z}^*$. Therefore, M is needed to obtain $\bar{z}^*$ and $\bar{z}^*$ is needed to obtain M. In order to solve this problem – that is to solve simultaneously both for the value of $\bar{z}^*$ and for that of M – use is made of search procedures based on variable-metric algorithms.

We shall assume for simplicity that there is only one decision-maker and that he is able to define a policy vector $z_p \in \Omega$ which is a preferred, but generally unfeasible, 'second best', while z^D remains the ideal. As we have seen, z_p contains preferred values of each policy variable (targets and instruments) at each time interval of the planning horizon. When setting z_P

the policy-maker is supposed to use his implicit, but unspecified, preferences; he is also supposed to consider elements like risk, timing of policy
decisions, coordination, continuity in policies and objectives, and so on.

We also assume that the policy-maker takes into consideration some
sequence of candidate vectors $z^{(s)} \in \Phi$, $s = 0, 1, \ldots$ obtained through the
constrained minimization of (6.43) after setting $M = M^{(s)}$. The iterative
process used to obtain the structure of preferences M and the corresponding optimal values of z consists in updating $M^{(s)}$ by using the following
rank-one algorithm

$$M^{(s+1)} = M^{(s)} + (\mu_s - 1) \frac{M^{(s)} \delta^{(s)} \delta^{(s)'} M^{(s)}}{\delta^{(s)'} M^{(s)} \delta^{(s)}} \tag{6.50}$$

and

$$z^{(s+1)} = z^{(s)} + \alpha_s P^s \delta^s \tag{6.51}$$

where $\delta^{(s)}$ is the displacement vector defined as

$$\delta^{(s)} = z_P - z^{(s)}; \quad \text{and where} \quad \alpha_s = \frac{(\mu_s - 1)a^{(s)}}{(\mu_s - 1)b^{(s)} - \mu_s \delta^{(s)'} M^{(s)} \delta^{(s)}};$$

$$a^{(s)} = \delta^{(s)'} M^{(s)} \bar{z}^{(s)}; \quad b^{(s)} = \delta^{(s)'} M^{(s)}(I - P^{(s)})\delta^{(s)}$$

and

$$P^{(s)} = I - M^{(s)-1} H'(HM^{(s)-1} H')^{-1} H$$

The fixed points $z^{(p)} = \lim_{s \to \infty} z^{(s)}$ and $M^{(p)} = \lim_{s \to \infty} M^{(s)}$ are the solutions of the
iterative process and are obtained from the iterations (6.50) and (6.51), given
an arbitrary initial symmetric positive definite $M^{(0)}$ and arbitrary given
values z_P and z^D (see Hughes Hallett and Ancot, 1982, for a demonstration
of the convergence of the iterative process and the (local) uniqueness of the
solution).

The local validity of the results obtained with this type of method should
however be stressed since, as we have seen, it is based on *one* specific
preferred trajectory for the policy variables.

6.9 An extension to the determination of revealed preferences

The method now described can also be used to 'estimate' past preferences
where the word 'estimate' 'is used . . . as a synonym for "providing a suitable
approximation" rather than for optimizing some statistical criterion of fit
and basing inferences on the distributional characteristics of the results'
(Hughes Hallett and Ancot 1982, p. 150). The assumptions which underlie
this estimation method are very similar to those at the basis of the method

proposed by Chow (1981) (see section 6.7.1); it is assumed that the outcomes *observed* are either the result of optimal past decisions or can be treated as such and, therefore, that it is possible to infer the structure of preferences from the observed outcomes. Consequently, part of the criticisms raised to Chow's method still apply in this case, in particular those reported in points (a) and (b) of section 6.7.1. It should be stressed, however, that this method overcomes some of the restrictions imposed by methods based on reaction functions, like, for example, those referring to the assumption of time invariance of the parameters of the objective function and to the absence of penalties on joint deviations of targets and instruments. Furthermore, in this case, a long data series is not required for estimation purposes. The method can also be applied to the estimation of those policy preferences that have characterized short historical periods.

The approach is based on the assumption that *observed* policies (decisions implemented and outcomes obtained from these decisions) define the vector $z^{(p)}$, that is, the solution of the iterative process (see section 6.8). Then, by making $z^{(p)}$ play the role of z_p (preferred policies), it is possible to apply the same algorithm described by (6.50) and (6.51) starting from arbitrary $M^{(0)}$, $x^{(0)}$, until convergence; the solution of the iterative process provides that matrix which yields the given (observed) optimal policy choice z_p (or at least the closest policy choice to z_p). The final matrix obtained ($M^{(p)}$) reflects the implicit preferences of policy-makers over the (past) period considered. It is assumed that policy-makers have used these (implicit) preferences in accepting z_p as the best of the feasible choices.

Another important requirement for inferring implicit preferences from observed outcomes is that both the econometric model used by policy-makers for planning over the period considered and the ideal vector z^D over the same period should be known. Otherwise it may be possible to obtain them from reports and documents concerning the period under analysis.

Applications of this method have been carried out concerning the American economy during the periods 1933–6 and 1957–62, the Dutch economy over the period 1976–80, and the Soviet economy over the period 1966–75 (see Hughes Hallett and Ancot 1982; Ancot and Hughes Hallett, 1982, respectively). The estimation of the corresponding preferences yields intertemporal as well as contemporaneous weights on targets and instruments and on joint failures of both. Interesting information concerning electoral cycles can also be inferred from the results.

6.10 The problem of symmetry of quadratic functions

As we have seen in section 6.4, a quadratic function assumes the same value for deviations, in opposite directions (and of like magnitude), of its arguments from the optimal point. Moreover, the unconstrained minimum of a quadratic loss function

$$J(z) = \bar{z}' M \bar{z} \tag{6.52}$$

is $J^* = 0$, which corresponds to $\bar{z}^* = 0$; therefore, (6.52) will take on the same values both for positive and for negative values of $\bar{z}$, provided that the absolute values are the same. This means that deviations of targets and instruments from their ideals have the same effects on the objective function independently of the direction of the deviation: deviations in the 'right' or in the 'wrong' direction are equally penalized. This obviously has important consequences in economic applications since if, for example, the ideal rate of inflation is 3 per cent, a rate of inflation of 1 per cent is penalized in the same way as a rate of inflation of 5 per cent. This is a well-known problem, but the suggestions for solving it have up to now been quite rare.

The simplest way to resolve the problem of symmetric penalties is to set very high (low) ideal values for the policy variables, that is, values that will be very difficult for the variables to achieve (see, for example, Chow, 1975, chapter 7; Rustem and Velupillai, 1984). In this way it becomes very unlikely that these variables overshoot (or undershoot) these values. If, for example, the ideal rate of inflation is set equal to zero, it is very unlikely that the actual solution will fall below the ideal. Very often overshooting (or undershooting) of ideal values is the result of a misspecification of these values.

Clearly, the best way to solve the problem of the symmetry of quadratic forms is to replace them with asymmetric ones. Along this line, a suggestion is to replace the quadratic form, which is perfectly symmetric around $\bar{z} = 0$ (and therefore around $z = z^D$), with a quadratic function of the form (Hughes Hallett and Rees, 1983, chapter 10)

$$J(z) = q' \bar{z} + \bar{z}' M \bar{z} \tag{6.53}$$

which is no longer symmetric about zero. Since $\partial J / \partial \bar{z} = q$, the sign and size of q determine the form of asymmetry. However, to define the vector q a priori, so as to give the quadratic function the desired asymmetry about zero, is not an easy task, especially if the number of policy variables is large.

Asymmetric objective functions have been proposed in the literature, which make it possible to assign different weights to errors of overshooting, or of shortfall below, ideal values. These functional forms will be dealt with in the next section.

6.11 Asymmetric forms

The search for asymmetric objective functions has been undertaken in two different directions. One still characterized by quadratic functions, but such that positive and negative deviations from ideal values may be differently penalized. Function (6.53) examined in the previous section and a *piecewise quadratic* function introduced by Friedman (1972, 1975) belong to this type of functional form. Conversely, other authors have definitely abandoned the quadratic specification and have introduced asymmetric forms formulated as *exponential* loss functions (Johansen, 1980; Kunstman, 1984). These two types of function will be examined in detail in what follows.

6.11.1 A piecewise quadratic function

Consider again the quadratic function introduced in section 6.8

$$J(z) = \tfrac{1}{2} \bar{z}' M \bar{z} \tag{6.54}$$

where $M = \begin{bmatrix} Q & N \\ N' & R \end{bmatrix}$ but with $N = 0$ and diagonal Q and R. Since these assumptions exclude cross-products of the variables, (6.54) can be written as

$$J(x, u) = \tfrac{1}{2} [\bar{x}' Q \bar{x} + \bar{u}' R \bar{u}] \tag{6.55}$$

where x and u are related by the linear system

$$x = Fu + s \tag{6.56}$$

As above, system (6.56) represents a dynamic discrete-time system specified in stacked-up form. Therefore, vectors x and u – in both (6.55) and (6.56) – are stacked vectors, as defined in section 6.8. Q and R are matrices of conformable dimensions representing the weights attached to deviations from ideal values at each moment of time.

Since Q and R are diagonal matrices, we can also write (6.55), for expositional purposes, as

$$J(x, u) = \frac{1}{2} \left(\sum_{i=1}^{n(t_f - t_0 + 1)} q_{ii} \bar{x}_i^2 + \sum_{j=1}^{r(t_f - t_0 + 1)} r_{jj} \bar{u}_j^2 \right) \tag{6.57}$$

Now assume that, for each target variable x_i (which does not necessarily coincide with each state variable, since some of the q_{ii} can be set equal to zero), three different convex sets are defined:

(i) An intermediate closed and limited set $I(x_i)$ which represents desired values of target variables. A zero weight is attached to all values of x_i corresponding to this set.

(ii) A set $U(x_i)$, which represents values of target variables that are higher than those belonging to $I(x_i)$; this set has only a lower bound x_i^U and is not closed. Non-negative weights are assigned to values of x_i belonging to this set.

(iii) A set $L(x_i)$ of values of target variables that are lower than those belonging to $I(x_i)$; this set has only an upper bound x_i^L and is not closed. Non-negative weights are also attached to elements of this set, though different from those defined for $U(x_i)$.

It follows that each element q_{ii} of the weighting matrix Q will be defined as

$$q_{ii} = \begin{cases} q_{ii}^U & \text{if } x_i \in U(x_i) = \{x_i | x_i > x_i^U\} \\ 0 & \text{if } x_i \in I(x_i) = \{x_i | x_i^L \leqslant x_i \leqslant x_i^U\} \\ q_{ii}^L & \text{if } x_i \in L(x_i) = \{x_i | x_i < x_i^L\} \end{cases} \quad (6.58)$$

$i = 1, \ldots, n(t_f - t_0 + 1)$

where

q_{ii}^U is the weight attached to values of x_i belonging to $U(x_i)$,

q_{ii}^L is the weight attached to values of x_i belonging to $L(x_i)$ $(q_{ii}^U \neq q_{ii}^L)$,

x_i^U is the upper bound of the intermediate set $I(x_i)$ and

x_i^L is the lower bound of the same set $I(x_i)$.

Furthermore, for each x_i in (6.57), the usual deviations $\bar{x}_i = x_i - x_i^D$ are substituted by

$$\bar{x}_i = \begin{cases} (x_i - x_i^U) & \text{if } x_i \in U(x_i) \\ (x_i - x_i^U) \text{ or } (x_i^L - x_i) & \text{if } x_i \in I(x_i) \\ (x_i^L - x_i) & \text{if } x_i \in L(x_i) \end{cases} \quad (6.59)$$

$i = 1, \ldots, n(t_f - t_0 + 1)$

The choice between $(x_i - x_i^U)$ and $(x_i^L - x_i)$ in the second equality is arbitrary, since q_{ii} is equal to zero in this case, as can be seen from (6.58). The definitions (6.58) and (6.59) provide the elements $q_{ii}\bar{x}_i^2$ in (6.57).

Similarly, three different sets $I(u_j)$, $U(u_j)$ and $L(u_j)$ are defined for the control variables – as well as the corresponding values u_j^U, u_j^L, r_{ii}^U and r_{ii}^L – in order to obtain the elements $r_{ii}\bar{u}_i^2$ in the objective function (6.57).

Considering for simplicity a piecewise quadratic function in only one variable, the values of this function will be given by

$$J(x) = \begin{cases} q^U(x - x^U)^2 & \text{if } x \in U(x) = \{x | x > x^U\} \\ 0 & \text{if } x \in I(x) = \{x | x^L \leqslant x \leqslant x^U\} \\ q^L(x^L - x)^2 & \text{if } x \in L(x) = \{x | x < x^L\} \end{cases} \quad (6.60)$$

which can be represented graphically as in figure 6.1. The three pieces into which the quadratic function is divided can easily be seen from the figure, where the asymmetric form of the function is guaranteed by the fact that $q^U \neq q^L$.

It should also be observed that the piecewise quadratic function now defined is convex, but not strictly convex. In fact it takes on the minimum value (zero) for all values of $x \in I(x)$, that is for $x^L \leqslant x \leqslant x^U$. This property, in

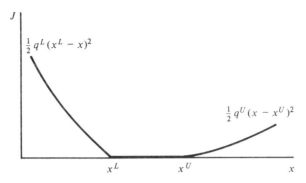

Figure 6.1   A piecewise quadratic function

contrast to strict convexity, makes it possible to consider a set of ideal values of the variables, and not only one ideal value for each variable. Policy-makers may have in mind more than one value for targets and/or control variables that they consider acceptable and may therefore wish to assign a zero weight to deviations from any of those values.

Let us assume, for example, that the target variable considered is the rate of exchange between the dollar and the Deutschmark and that an exchange rate in the range between 1.5 and 2 Deutschmarks to the dollar is considered acceptable by U.S. policy-makers. This means that $x^L = 1.5$ and $x^U = 2$. Therefore, when the exchange rate takes on values between 1.5 and 2, a zero weight will be attached to deviations from any one of these two values: these deviations do not alter the planners objective function. However, assuming that the American monetary authorities are more concerned about devaluation than about revaluation, deviations from 1.5 will be heavily penalized when the exchange rate falls below this value, whereas, when the exchange rate rises above 2, a lower weight will be assigned to deviations from this latter value.

As Q and R are diagonal matrices by assumption, piecewise quadratic functions can also be defined as a sum of piecewise quadratic functions in one single variable, i.e.

$$J(x, u) = \sum_{i=1}^{n(t_f - t_0 + 1)} J_i(x_i) + \sum_{j=1}^{r(t_f - t_0 + 1)} J_j(u_j) \tag{6.61}$$

where J_i and J_j are convex and asymmetric functions as represented in figure 6.1. Since addition preserves both convexity and asymmetry, the resulting function (6.61) will also be convex and asymmetric. (This does not prevent some of the J_i or J_j from being symmetric and/or strictly convex).

Quadratic functions can be considered as a particular case of piecewise

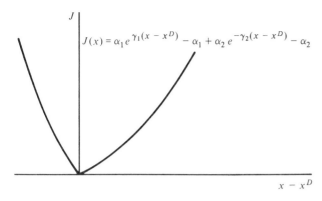

$$J(x) = \alpha_1 e^{\gamma_1(x - x^D)} - \alpha_1 + \alpha_2 e^{-\gamma_2(x - x^D)} - \alpha_2$$

Figure 6.2   An exponential function

quadratic ones whenever $q_{ii}^U = q_{ii}^L$ (which provides symmetry) and $x_i^U = x_i^L$ (which provides strict convexity).

Piecewise quadratic functions can easily be specified in continuous time; a function like (6.61) can be defined as

$$J(x, u) = \int_{t_0}^{t_f} \left\{ \sum_{i=1}^{n} J_i[x_i(t)] + \sum_{j=1}^{r} J_j[u_j(t)] \right\} dt \qquad (6.62)$$

where J_i and J_j are defined as in (6.60) for each i, j. However, the optimization of a function like (6.62) will pose significant computational difficulties. Conversely, standard static optimization techniques can be used to minimize (6.61) since, as we have seen, a discrete-time optimization problem is reduced to a static one when the relevant vectors are stacked.[18]

6.11.2 Exponential functions

Utility functions defined as a sum of exponentials were already adopted by Chipman (1965) and then used by Pollak (1971) in the framework of consumer demand theory. As an alternative to standard quadratic forms, exponential objective functions were also considered by Pratt (1964) and Johansen (1980) for investigating the problem of decision-making under uncertainty, and subsequently used by Kunstman (1984) in the context of an optimal control problem. This type of function makes it possible to define asymmetric forms about the optimum and therefore to consider differences in the penalties attached to deviations, depending on whether they are deviations of overshooting or of shortfall below ideal values.

This objective function consists of a weighted sum of two exponentials for each policy variable considered. Its convexity and asymmetry may be ensured by an appropriate choice of parameters.

Considering initially a static function in only one variable, the exponential objective function can be defined as

$$J(x) = \alpha_1 e^{\gamma_1(x - x^D)} - \alpha_1 + \alpha_2 e^{-\gamma_2(x - x^D)} - \alpha_2 \tag{6.63}$$

where α_1, α_2, γ_1 and γ_2 are positive constants and the exponents represent deviations from the ideal value weighted by parameters of the opposite sign. The subtraction of α_1 and α_2 in (6.63) makes it possible to have the minimum value of J $(J = 0)$ for $x = x^D$.

The first-order condition for a minimum is given by

$$\frac{\partial J}{\partial x} = \alpha_1 \gamma_1 e^{\gamma_1(x - x^D)} - \alpha_2 \gamma_2 e^{-\gamma_2(x - x^D)} = 0 \tag{6.64}$$

From the second-order condition we have

$$\frac{\partial^2 J}{\partial x^2} = \alpha_1 \gamma_1^2 e^{\gamma_1(x - x^D)} + \alpha_2 \gamma_2^2 e^{-\gamma_2(x - x^D)} > 0 \tag{6.65}$$

which is satisfied if

$$\alpha_1 > 0, \qquad \alpha_2 > 0 \tag{6.66}$$

This condition guarantees the convexity of J. Furthermore, since $x = x^D$ at a minimum, (6.64) becomes

$$\alpha_1 \gamma_1 - \alpha_2 \gamma_2 = 0 \tag{6.67}$$

that is

$$\frac{\alpha_1}{\alpha_2} = \frac{\gamma_2}{\gamma_1} \tag{6.68}$$

When $\gamma_1 = \gamma_2$, $(\alpha_1 = \alpha_2)$ function $J(x)$ becomes symmetric and provides results which are close to those of a quadratic form. The shape of (6.63) depends on the values of γ_1 and γ_2: if $\gamma_1 > \gamma_2$, penalties are higher for positive deviations, and vice versa. Figure 6.2 represents a function of the type (6.63), showing how positive and negative deviations from the desired value are differently penalized.

The exponential function (6.63) can be extended to the multivariable dynamic case simply by considering n variables and a given time interval $[t_0, t_f]$ along which the objective function must be minimized, i.e.

$$J(x_t) = \sum_{t=t_0}^{t_f} \sum_{i=1}^{n} [\alpha_{i1} e^{\gamma_{i1}(x_{it} - x_{it}^D)} - \alpha_{i1} + \alpha_{i2} e^{-\gamma_{i2}(x_{it} - x_{it}^D)} - \alpha_{i2}] \tag{6.69}$$

in the discrete-time case, or

$$J[x(t)] = \int_{t_0}^{t_f} \left\{ \sum_{i=1}^{n} \left[\alpha_{i1} e^{\gamma_{i1}[x_i(t) - x_i^P(t)]} - \alpha_{i1} \right. \right.$$

$$\left. \left. + \alpha_{i2} e^{-\gamma_{i2}[x_i(t) - x_i^P(t)]} - \alpha_{i2} \right] \right\} dt \qquad (6.70)$$

in the continuous-time case. Methods of solution and numerical examples are described in Kunstman (1984).

We wish only to note, before concluding, that certainty equivalence no longer holds in general either for this type of function or for the piecewise quadratic one described in section 6.11.1. Asymmetric functions are often used when the effects of uncertainty on optimal decisions are to be considered (see, for example, Waud, 1976; Johansen, 1980). In fact, the solution of the minimization of the expectation of (6.63) under the constraint of a linear model with an additive disturbance is a function of the variance of this disturbance which makes it possible to take into account risk aversion and its effects on optimal decisions.

In general, however, focussing on asymmetric functions entails loosing the advantages that derive from the mathematical tractability of standard quadratic functions. This is probably the reason why their use in macroeconomic planning has not been as extensive as might have been expected.

6.12 Planning without an explicit specification of priorities

Throughout this chapter we have analysed the problems which arise when it is necessary to provide an explicit formulation of an objective function. Old and new methods introduced in order to evaluate the (implicit) preferences of policy-makers have been examined. The conclusion is that the specification of an objective function which correctly reflects the planners' priorities is a very difficult task: any objective function adopted for optimal planning will always have the nature of an approximation to the 'true' one. If, in addition, we consider that usually policy decisions are not taken by one single decision-maker, but are the result of a compromise between different political groups, then we also need to take into account the fact that as many objective functions may exist as there are pressure groups. For all these reasons the economist often feels uneasy when using optimization methods for economic planning, since this necessarily involves defining a specific objective function.

Obviously, other planning techniques exist which do not require the explicit formulation of an objective function. For example, methods based on the controllability approach see chapter 3) or, more simply, the usual and widespread technique of simulating the results of different exogenous policies within a given econometric model. However, the selection of policies through these techniques implies a high degree of arbitrariness and, of course, does not provide optimal results.

An immediate question therefore arises: is it possible to obtain *optimal* policies without the need to specify an explicit objective function? Recent research is moving along these lines and interactive methods known as *vector optimization models* have been proposed to give a positive answer to this question (see Streuff and Gruber, 1983, for details).

We shall examine here a method which also moves along this line (Hughes Hallett and Rees, 1983, chapter 10) and is based on the idea of selecting policies (targets and instruments) which are the closest to a given *preferred* vector z_p. The interaction between the economist and the policy-makers leads, after an iterative process in which z_p is modified, to the selection of the 'best' policies.

It should however be emphasized that this type of method makes it possible to avoid the numerical specification of the weights in the objective function (as we shall see all the weights are set equal to one), but not the numerical specification of the desired values of the policy (target and control) variables, which are parameters of the objective function as well.

Using the terminology introduced in section 6.8, assume that $z'_p = [x'_p, u'_p]$ is an unfeasible preferred policy vector and that z^D is the ideal one. Assuming also that there is a single planner who makes rational choices – that is choices which satisfy a minimal set of elementary axioms consistent with rational behaviour (see section 6.7.2) – this planner chooses from among all the feasible alternatives $z^{(s)} \in \Phi, s = 0, 1, \ldots$, ranking them according to

$$\| z^{(s+1)} - z_p \|_2 < \| z^s - z_p \|_2 \tag{6.71}$$

where $\| \ldots \|_2$ represents the Euclidean distance between the two vectors considered.

The policy selection takes place by choosing the closest vector to z_p among the feasible vectors considered; that is a vector $z^{(p)}$ such that

$$z^{(p)} = \arg \min_z \{ \| z - z_p \|_2 \mid H\bar{z} = b \} \tag{6.72}$$

i.e.

$$z^{(p)} = (I - H'(HH')^{-1}H)z_p + H'(HH')^{-1}s \tag{6.73}$$

which is a special case of (6.49) with $M = I$ and $z^D = z_p$. If the policy-maker realizes that the selected vector $z^{(p)}$ does not represent what he really expected to achieve, he will modify his preferred vector z_p in the desired direction, so that the economist can obtain a new $z^{(p)}$ from (6.72). This process can be repeated until the policy-maker declares himself satisfied with the results obtained.

By changing the preferred vector z_p it is possible to obtain different vectors $z^{(p)}$ which form a Pareto optimal frontier. Assuming the feasible set to be convex, this frontier can be represented, in the bi-dimensional case, as in figure 6.3, where $z_1^{(p)}$, $z_2^{(p)}$ and $z_3^{(p)}$ are three representative points of the frontier, which indicate the closest ones to the corresponding preferred points z_p^1, z_p^2 and z_p^3. In this way each planner can sample and evaluate all points in the Pareto optimal frontier.

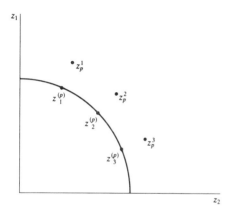

Figure 6.3 The policy possibility frontier

When decisions are taken by several decision-makers each of them might wish to choose a different point on the Pareto frontier corresponding to a different preferred point z_p, provided that they all agree on z^D (which establishes the direction of the z_p) and on the econometric model considered.[19] All feasible best policy alternatives can therefore be compared without the need to specify a particular objective function, that is, without the need to specify particular priorities, for the mathematical form of the function (a quadratic; see equation (6.72)) and the ideal values of the variables (vector z_p) have to be specified.

The method is based on the consideration that the set of optimal policies that form the Pareto optimal frontier can be obtained either by varying the weighting matrix M in the objective function while keeping z_P fixed, or by varying z_P while keeping M fixed. In the case considered here, M is fixed and equal to the identity matrix I, while z_P changes. The optimal policies obtained are the same, but in the latter case they are derived without the need to give specific numerical values to the weights in the objective function. Policy-makers are only asked to indicate preferred policy vectors but not priorities over the policy variables. And this is supposed to be a much easier task, since planners usually think in terms of numerical values of policy variables rather than in terms of numerical priorities.

The simplicity of this approach makes it possible to extend it easily to the continuous-time case. An optimal policy path will then be given by

$$z^*(t) = \arg \min_z \left\{ \int_{t_0}^{t_f} \| z(t) - z_P(t) \|_2 \, dt \mid \dot{x}(t) = Ax(t) + Bu(t) \right\} \quad (6.74)$$

where $z'(t) = [x'(t), u'(t)]$. By changing $z_P(t)$ in (6.74), different optimal paths can be obtained and evaluated.

The fact that the same optimal solutions for policy variables can be derived either by changing the weighting matrix or by changing the ideal values is a very important point for economic planning and can easily be seen from equation (6.49) in section 6.8. Indeed, given the other vectors and matrices, the same z^* can be obtained either by iterating M while keeping z^D fixed, or by iterating z^D while keeping M fixed. The first alternative is the basis of the method for the determination of implicit preferences examined in section 6.8. The second alternative is the basis of the method examined in this section, which makes it possible to obtain optimal policies while avoiding the a priori specification of priorities.

7   Applications of optimal control*

7.1 Optimal control in continuous-time modelling

So far the discussion has been mainly kept in general terms, also considering the fact that most of the mathematical methods presented in previous chapters can be applied equally both to theoretical and empirical economic models. We wish now to consider a specific econometric model estimated in continuous time in order to illustrate how some of the methods examined above can be effectively used for applied policy analysis.

The model we shall consider is described by a system of 23 equations. The size of a continuous-time econometric model is usually limited to no more than 20 or 30 equations; this is important in our case because it would be very complicated – from a computational point of view – to handle a bigger model. Since the method we shall follow to solve the optimal control problems (and also to solve the differential games of chapter 9) is Pontryagin's minimum principle, a two-point boundary system of canonical equations has to be solved in order to obtain the optimal trajectories of state, costate and control variables within a linear-quadratic framework, as is the case considered here. This means that if we deal with a model of 20 equations we have to solve double that number (20 state and 20 costate equations) in optimal control problems and three and four times that number in Nash and Stackleberg solutions of differential games respectively. Now, although the program we use ('Continest' by C.R. Wymer) can be extended to solve any number of differential equations, it clearly becomes rather cumbersome to handle a very big model and, besides, the required capacity of the computer becomes extremely high. The procedure is even more complicated if we try to obtain the optimal control trajectories by solving the matrix Riccati equation since, as we have seen in section 5.9, the system in that case is given by $n(n+1)/2$ non-linear differential

*The results presented in this chapter have been taken from Gandolfo and Petit, 1987, 1988 and from Hughes Hallett and Petit (1988a and c).

equations, where n is the number of dynamic (state) equations in the model.

As a matter of fact, many of the simplifying assumptions made in this chapter and in chapter 9 (where differential games are applied to the same econometric model) are due to the computational problems that the continuous-time techniques used involve, given the size of the econometric model.

As already stressed in section 1.4, an important feature, from the point of view of control theory, of continuous-time econometric models[1] is the possibility of obtaining information on the optimal paths of target and control variables at each point in time and not only at discrete intervals, as is the case with discrete-time models. Of course, continuous paths of the exogenous variables are needed, which have been obtained here by interpolation; also continuity of optimal control trajectories is required, but this is ensured in the linear-quadratic case considered here.

Let us now see how optimal control methods can be applied to continuous-time econometric models, and refer the reader to chapter 9 for an illustration of the use of differential games within the same context.

7.2 An overview of the model

The model chosen in order to illustrate the use of optimal control techniques in a continuous-time framework is a dynamic econometric model of the Italian economy estimated in continuous time over the period 1961–81 inclusive (see the appendix of this chapter, tables A.7.1, A.7.2 and A.7.3 and, for a detailed description, Gandolfo and Padoan, 1984). It is specified as a system of 23 equations, of which 20 are stochastic differential equations and three definitional ones. Most of the dynamic equations are defined as partial adjustment equations, where each endogenous variable considered adjusts towards its 'desired' or partial equilibrium level with a speed of adjustment α.[2]

The model describes the stock-flow behaviour of an open economy in which both price and quantity adjustments take place. Stocks are introduced with reference to the real sector (where adjustments of fixed capital and inventories to their respective desired levels are present) and to the financial sector which includes the stock of money, the stock of commercial credit, the stock of net foreign assets and the stock of international reserves. Real and financial feedbacks are therefore considered in the model. Government expenditure and revenues (taxation) are also present so that the effects of endogenous public deficits are included.

Quantity behaviour equations are considered for the traditional macroeconomic variables in real terms: private consumption, net fixed investment, imports and exports of goods and services, inventories and net domestic product. Employment is not explicitly considered in the model; however its level can be (approximately) derived from domestic product, given the value of productivity (which appears in the price equation). Expectations are present through an adaptive mechanism concerning expected output. Therefore the problems caused by dynamically inconsistent decision-making will not arise (see section 10.2).

A price block is included, which determines the domestic price level, the nominal wage rate, and the export price level. Endogenous determination of the latter was considered crucial for an export-led economy such as Italy's, while wage-price spiral effects are explicitly taken into account. The specification of a financial sector was completed by the inclusion of an interest rate determination equation.

Although the model is a closely interlocked system of simultaneous differential equations, it is important to pick out the following causal links. The growth process is both export-led and expectations-led. Given foreign demand and prices, real exports grow according to domestic competitiveness and to supply constraints. Export growth enhances output growth which in turn modifies expectations and, consequently, real capital formation. Output growth also influences real imports, aggregate public consumption, direct taxes and the level of private consumption through the determination of disposable income. Changes in inventories, whose desired level is linked to expected output, act as a buffer in output determination.

The performance of real aggregates is also influenced by price behaviour based essentially on cost-push mechanisms. Prices also enter in the determination of financial variables whose behaviour is closely connected with that of real variables.

A central place in the model is occupied by credit whose expansion, as determined by the behaviour of banks, influences real capital accumulation as well as exports of goods and services and capital movements. An important role is also played by the rate of interest, because it influences the demand for money (and hence real consumption), credit expansion, and the accumulation of net foreign assets. The rate of interest is determined, given the foreign rate of interest and the demand for money, by the supply of money whose expansion is determined by the monetary authorities, given their own policy targets and the other channels of money creation represented by the Government and the balance of payments.

The size of the model is sufficient to illustrate the application of the mathematical techniques described in this book, and yet not so large as to be too cumbersome for computational purposes. Evidently, its moderate dimension also implies some limitation in terms of detail, particularly from the point of view of policy instruments where a higher level of disaggregation would have rendered the policy exercises more realistic. However, most of the familiar targets and instruments of macroeconomic policy are present, as can be seen in the appendix, table A.7.2.

Apart from a few exceptions, the equations of the model are expressed in logarithmic form and some of them are non-linear in the logarithms. These equations have been linearized for estimation purposes and have been used in their linearized form in all the exercises performed in this chapter. Furthermore, since some equations of the model contain second-order derivatives (equations A.7.2, A.7.5, A.7.7, A.7.12 and A.7.13), the dynamic system has been transformed into state-space form by defining the corresponding state variables (see chapter 2).

Finally the model has good structural properties. It has a steady-growth path which is locally stable. Structural stability has also been demonstrated analytically (Gandolfo and Padoan, 1984). These properties, plus satisfactory parameter estimates, suggest that the model is a suitable vehicle for policy analysis through dynamic optimization methods and also for effectively studying policy options for the Italian economy.

7.3 Definition of the objective function

The policy problem that we intend to solve by using optimal control methods consists in the optimization, over a given period of time, of an intertemporal objective function which defines the structure of preferences of policy-makers. Moreover, since the time behaviour of the variables that appear in this function is described by the dynamic equations of the macroeconomic model considered, the optimization problem will be constrained by this dynamic system.

Therefore, once the econometric model has been chosen, the next step is to define the objective function of the policy authorities, taking into account the fact that the target variables that can be considered in this function must be the same as (or a subset of) the endogenous variables that appear in the model itself. The objective function we shall here consider is a quadratic loss function in which deviations of the variables from their assumed ideal paths are penalized (see section 5.5). Advantages and limitations of quadratic functions have been widely discussed in chapter 6; all we wish to observe here is that we have tried to overcome the problem of the symmetry of this type of function simply by assigning 'ambitious' values to the ideal paths, so as to render unlikely an overshooting (or undershooting) of the path in the 'wrong' direction (see section 6.10).

In order to build an objective function for purposes of policy selection, four points in particular should be considered:

   (i) the planning horizon,
   (ii) the policy targets,

(iii) the policy instruments,
(iv) the numerical weights.

(i) The planning horizon considered extends from the beginning of 1977 to the end of 1981. The control exercises are therefore 'in sample' exercises, as 1981 is the last year of the sample period considered in estimation.[3] The results might therefore be interpreted as 'what the government could have done'. This is not however the main purpose since we are aware of the limits of deriving such conclusions from econometric models.[4] However, the results obtained can give an idea of whether actual policy decisions could have been improved upon and better outcomes attained.

In any case, control exercises are important for an evaluation of the dynamic properties of the model and an analysis of the optimal policy responses to different choices of targets and instruments.

The optimal trajectories of both the targets and the instruments are expressed in quarterly data. The results go therefore from the first quarter of 1977 to the last quarter of 1981. The choice of the quarter as the unit of time has been made for uniformity with the time series (quarterly data) used in estimation but, as mentioned in section 7.1, as the model is a continuous-time model, the same results could be obtained on any basis (monthly, weekly, etc.).

(ii) The targets considered are the domestic price level (P), the real domestic product (Y) and the international reserves (R). The conditions we impose are that the Italian rate of inflation tracks the European rate of inflation (EEC average rate of inflation), that the rate of growth of output follows as closely as possible the average rate of growth of EEC countries, and that international reserves grow at a rate close to the average rate of growth of reserves in EEC countries. We therefore assume reference-time paths that grow at those given rates, which are taken as the 'ideal' rates; taking into account the poor performance of the Italian economy during the period considered, the EEC average rates can be considered as 'ambitious' ones. The initial values of the ideal paths are the corresponding observed values of the target variables at the initial time.

(iii) As regards the instruments our choice fell on three policy variables: public expenditure (G), taxes (T) and money supply, in particular the rate of growth of money supply, (m). It is assumed that the three policy variables can be used independently of one another. Actually, G, T and m are related by the financing of the public deficit; nonetheless – for the reasons explained in Gandolfo and Padoan (1984, chapter 2) – they can be managed independently, within certain limits. Other possible policy variables, the exchange rate and the wage rate, will be considered later (sections 7.6 and 7.7 respectively).

As we have seen in section 6.5, the inclusion of the policy instruments in the objective function serves to avoid large deviations of those variables from their ideal paths, or at least to prevent the policy variables from assuming values which would be absurd from an economic point of view. Furthermore, since the problem we have to solve is a continuous-time linear-quadratic minimization problem, the weighting matrix of the control variables must be positive definite, as we have seen in section 5.8. Consequently, the policy instruments have to be included in the objective function.

As ideal rate of growth of the money supply, we chose the average rate of growth observed, during the same time-interval, in the other EEC countries (which was lower than the Italian rate), and we tried to stabilize public expenditure and taxes by penalizing deviations from a very low rate of growth. We observe that, as taxes are the amount of money collected by the Government, a high rate of growth of taxes does not necessarily mean a restrictive policy, but can be the result of growing nominal income.

(iv) As we have seen in chapter 6, a complex problem inherent in the quantitative definition of the objective function is the determination of weights. In fact estimation methods present great limitations besides considerable computational difficulties (see section 6.7.1); and, more important, the relevant software for the continuous-time case is not, as yet, available. On the other hand, variable metric algorithms which are used in revealed preference methods (section 6.9) can only be applied to models specified in stacked-up form and, therefore, to discrete-time models.[5] Since interview methods are also ruled out in a historical (in sample) exercise, the choice of a method to define the numerical weights to be attributed to the targets was not particularly wide; consequently the line suggested by van Eijk and Sandee (1959) has been followed, based on imaginary interviews of the policy-maker. As we have seen in section 6.7, the method substantially consists in determining the priorities on the basis of an evaluation of the results obtained from the optimization process.

From the information available, we tried to imagine what a policy-maker, at the beginning of 1977, would have chosen from the 'menu' of results submitted for his choice. These results are obtained by iteratively modifying the weights in the loss function until we get the results that we assume would be considered 'the best'. The method can therefore be considered as an iterative process which works as follows:

(1) Optimize the objective function with arbitrary (though sensible) weights.

2) Examine the results obtained (the optimal time paths of instruments and targets). If the results are not satisfactory (for example, if the rate of inflation is too high though output grows at a satisfactory rate), then

(3) modify the weights in the direction indicated by the results (i.e. a higher weight should be assigned to inflation relative to the weight assigned to output growth), and

(4) optimize again the new objective function. If the results are still unsatisfactory, go back to point (3).

Successive adjustments make it possible to find out whether the behaviour of some of the targets can be improved upon, provided that (any) consequent deterioration in the behaviour of the other targets is acceptable (on this point, see Chow, 1975, chapter 9). The weights finally chosen are those that underlie the 'best' results. In this way we have assigned to inflation a weight four times the weight assigned to output growth, and to reserves a weight 0.4 times the latter, that is $w_P = 4$, $w_Y = 1$ and $w_R = 0.4$.

Since, in our case, the variables are expressed in logarithms, the problem of proportioning the weights to the numerical magnitudes of the variables doesn't arise. In fact, when the variables are expressed in logarithmic form, the deviations from the ideal values are percentage deviations from those values. For example, a logarithmic deviation $d = 0.01$ of a variable from its ideal path represents a deviation of approximately 1 per cent.

Therefore the weights $w_Y = 1.0$, $w_P = 4.0$ and $w_R = 0.4$ mean that a 1 per cent deviation in the price level (for example, a price level which is 1 per cent higher than its ideal value) is penalized four times as much as a 1 per cent deviation in output (for example, an output level which is 1 per cent lower than its ideal value), and that a 1 per cent deviation in reserves (for example, a reserve level which is 1 per cent lower than its ideal value) is penalized 0.4 times as much as a 1 per cent deviation in output.

As for the instruments, we first considered the advisability of assigning an equal and low weight (under unity) to the three policy variables, in order to allow them to behave as freely as possible. However, in the optimization problem considered, monetary policy and public expenditure turned out to be more effective policies than taxes (see the following section), and the optimal control trajectories of these two variables presented deviations from the corresponding desired paths which were large in comparison with taxes, which were characterized by a very stable behaviour. This obliged us to assign to the rate of growth of money supply and to public expenditure a weight 3.3 times the weight assigned to taxes, that is $w_m = 1.0$, $w_G = 1.0$, $w_T = 0.3$.

The objective function to be optimized is therefore the following (for the symbols, see the appendix, table A.7.2)

$$J = \int_{77}^{81} \{ w_Y [\log Y(t) - \log Y^D(t)]^2 + w_P [\log P(t) - \log P^D(t)]^2$$

$$+ w_R [\log R(t) - \log R^D(t)]^2 + w_m [m(t) - m^D(t)]^2 \qquad (7.1)$$

$$+ w_G [\log G(t) - \log G^D(t)]^2 + w_T [\log T(t) - \log T^D(t)]^2 \} \, dt$$

where

$$\log Y^D(t) = \log Y(t_0) + 0.01t; \quad \log P^D(t) = \log P(t_0) + 0.02t$$

$$\log R^D(t) = \log R(t_0) + 0.01t; \quad m^D(t) = 0.03$$

$$\log G^D(t) = \log G(t_0) + 0.01t; \quad \log T^D(t) = \log T(t_0) + 0.01t$$

$$t_0 = 1976 - IV, \text{ and the weights are}$$

$$w_Y = 1.0, w_P = 4.0, w_R = 0.4, w_G = 1.0, w_m = 1.0, w_T = 0.3$$

7.4 The policy problem

Most exercises in the field of dynamic optimization of econometric models have been carried out by means of discrete-time techniques, mostly following the line of Bellman's dynamic programming. Since we are here considering both a model and an objective function specified in continuous time, continuous-time optimization techniques have to be used and Pontryagin's minimum principle is certainly the most appropriate in this case.

Pontryagin's method has been widely discussed in chapter 5 and therefore we simply need now to apply it to our policy problem. Before doing so, however, we wish first to recall briefly the mathematical form that a continuous-time model may assume. In general, a continuous-time model will be of the type

$$\Psi[y(t), \dot{y}(t), \overset{(2)}{y}(t), \ldots, u(t), z(t)] = \varepsilon(t) \qquad (7.2)$$

where Ψ is a vector of continuously differentiable functions, $y(t)$ is a vector of endogenous (output) variables, $u(t)$ a vector of control variables, and $z(t)$ a vector of all the non-controlled exogenous variables; $\varepsilon(t)$ is a vector of disturbances with classic properties (white noise). Henceforth we shall consider the deterministic part of the model, i.e. $\Psi(\ldots) = 0$. Provided that the appropriate conditions are satisfied, it is possible to linearize system (7.2) and to transform it into state-space form

$$\dot{x}(t) = Ax(t) + Bu(t) + Cz(t) \qquad (7.3)$$

$$y(t) = Fx(t), \qquad (7.4)$$

where $x(t)$ is the vector of state variables and A, B, C and F are constant matrices of the required dimensions; system (7.4) represents the output equations of the system. Since the dynamic system considered is observable (i.e. it is possible to obtain unique values of $x(t)$ from the output variables $y(t)$; see section 3.9), in what follows we shall consider only system (7.3), which describes the dynamics of the model. We can therefore define the objective function in terms of the state variables so that optimal trajectories of these variables will be obtained. Optimal trajectories of the output variables can be straight-forwardly derived from (7.4).[6]

Using the matrix form introduced in section 5.5 to specify the objective function (7.1), the policy problem can be described as that of minimizing

$$J(u) = \int_{77}^{81} [\bar{x}'(t)Q\bar{x}(t) + \bar{u}'(t)R\bar{u}(t)]\,dt \tag{7.5}$$

subject to

$$\dot{x}(t) = Ax(t) + Bu(t) + Cz(t) \tag{7.6}$$

where the matrix Q is a diagonal (constant) matrix whose elements along the main diagonal are the three weights assigned to output, inflation and reserves, with zeros elsewhere, and the matrix R is also a (constant) diagonal matrix whose elements along the main diagonal are the weights assigned to public expenditure, taxes and the rate of growth of money supply; the bars over the variables, as usual, indicate deviations from ideal paths.

In order to solve this optimization problem by applying Pontryagin's principle we first need to define the Hamiltonian

$$H = \bar{x}'(t)Q\bar{x}(t) + \bar{u}'(t)R\bar{u}(t) + \lambda'(t)[Ax(t) + Bu(t) + Cz(t)] \tag{7.7}$$

Since the control variables are unconstrained and no terminal cost is considered in the objective function, the optimal trajectories of the state, costate and control variables can be obtained by solving the following system of equations (see section 5.8)

$$\dot{x}(t) = \frac{\partial H}{\partial \lambda} = Ax(t) + Bu(t) + Cz(t) \tag{7.8}$$

$$\dot{\lambda}(t) = -\frac{\partial H}{\partial x} = -2Q\bar{x}(t) - A'\lambda(t) \tag{7.9}$$

$$\frac{\partial H}{\partial u} = 2R\bar{u}(t) + B'\lambda(t) = 0 \tag{7.10}$$

$$x(t_0) = x, \qquad \lambda(t_f) = 0 \tag{7.11}$$

where (7.8) is the set of 20 differential equations which characterize the macroeconomic model, (7.9) is the set of 20 differential equations which describe the dynamics of the costate variables, (7.10) are the three static equations corresponding to the three control variables considered and (7.11) are the boundary conditions.

The optimal control policies obtained from the solution of this system is of the open-loop type. However, since we consider only the deterministic part of the model, feedback and open-loop control coincide in our case (see section 5.10). The choice of the open-loop form is due to its greater simplicity from both a computational and a descriptive point of view. From a computational point of view the calculation of the feedback rule would have implied the solution of the non-linear dynamic Riccati equations that, as stressed in section 7.1, is computationally more cumbersome than the solution of the canonical system (7.8)–(7.11). From a descriptive point of view, optimal feedback rules have a complicated form since, in the case of a finite time horizon, they are time-varying functions of all the state variables in the model. Control rules are therefore, in general, more easily understood if specified as (open-loop) time paths of the policy instruments rather than as complicated time-varying (feedback) rules (see also section 5.14.1).

The canonical system described by (7.8)–(7.11) has been solved with 'Continest', giving rise to the results that we shall comment upon in the next section.

7.5 Optimal management of fiscal and monetary policy

In order to point out the effectiveness of each of the instruments considered, six more control problems have been solved (besides the one defined by (7.1)), taking into account all possible alternatives: one instrument at a time and combinations of two instruments. In table 7.1 a very general idea of the performance of the targets under various combinations of the control variables is provided. The figures are average annual growth rates over the control period. In all exercises the weights are the same.

It is interesting to note that the 'best' set of instruments is (G, m), namely a combined use of public expenditure and monetary policy. If we take (G, m) as the benchmark, we can observe that:
(a) when only one control variable is used the results are clearly inferior. Notice also that acceptable results are obtained only with public expenditure;
(b) the combination (T, m) gives practically the same results as regards the rate of growth of income and of reserves, but worse results as regards the rate of inflation;
(c) the combination (G, T) gives practically the same results as regards the

Table 7.1   *Average annual growth rates of the targets under various combinations of the instruments, 1977–1981*

	Instruments used							
Target	G, T, m	G, m	T, m	G, T	G	T	m	Base run
Y	8.09	8.03	8.34	8.15	8.17	0.87	14.26	3.22
P	8.49	8.41	10.17	8.37	8.30	8.60	5.37	12.42
R	22.36	22.79	24.03	13.49	13.31	104.00	−8.13	11.90

rate of growth of income and of prices but much worse results as regards reserve growth;

(d) finally, the combination (G, T, m) gives practically the same results as regards all targets and so, on the basis of the principle of parsimony, is to be considered inferior.

These results deserve a few comments. First of all, result (a) underlines the fact that, when the policy-maker can use only one instrument as control variable, the choice should fall on public expenditure. Taxes alone and monetary policy alone are not capable, even when used optimally, of driving the system close to the given ideal paths. Results (a) and (b) taken together mean that, considering the two instruments which make up fiscal policy (i.e. Government expenditure and taxation), the choice should fall on G rather than on T. This has both theoretical and institutional implications.

From the theoretical point of view it means that fiscal policy is better manoeuvered through Government expenditure than through taxation: thus, for example, a fiscal expansion is better engineered through an increase in G rather than through a decrease in T. It should be stressed that this is not the old textbook result that the multiplier of an increase in G is larger than the multiplier of an equal decrease in T, as we are in the context of the control of an economy-wide model, of which the results given in the table are a summary; as a matter of fact, the better results of the use of G instead of T consist of a lower rate of inflation (which, in any case, cannot be ascribed to G as such, but derives from the working of the model).

The institutional implications are also important. In the exercises it is not possible to account for the problems related with the practical implementation of the optimal paths of the control variables, but these should be kept in mind when looking at the results of the exercises. Now, in general, the implementation of changes in taxation is much more difficult to achieve than the implementation of changes in Government expenditure. Therefore it is important to know that the results of the optimal control exercises go in the direction of suggesting the use of G rather than of T.

Let us now consider result (c). It stresses the importance of monetary policy or, more generally, of the fact that fiscal policy alone – although split into its two instruments, G and T – is unable to achieve the same results that can be obtained by combining it with monetary policy.

Finally, result (d), if compared also with (b) and (c), is a welcome result for the same institutional reasons discussed above.

In what follows, therefore, we shall concentrate on the description of the results of the (G, m) combination, which are presented graphically in figure (7.1). Only the results concerning target variables and control variables are reported . This does not mean that no account has been taken of the overall behaviour of the model, but only that lack of space prevents us from presenting the trajectories of all the endogenous variables. The diagrams are expressed in logarithms, except for m, which is the rate of growth of the money supply M $(m = D \log M)$.

The three targets aimed at (higher output growth, lower inflation and increasing reserves) are met entirely through optimal control policies. It seems therefore that the poor behaviour of the Italian economy, as described by the solution of the model (base run) in that period,[7] could have been improved upon through adequate policies.

If we look at the base run during the years 1977–81 we see that the average yearly rate of inflation was 12.4 per cent and that the corresponding rate of growth in output was 3.2 per cent, while reserves grew at 11.9 per cent. If we then note the monetary and fiscal policies followed in that period, we can also observe that these policies presented a clearly expansionary tendency. The money supply grew at 10.3 per cent (yearly average), and public expenditure also grew at 3.4 per cent, while taxes (in real terms) grew at 1.4 per cent; since output increased by 3.2 per cent, this also reflects an expansionary tax policy.

The expansionary policy followed in those years by Italian policy-makers reflects a priority of growth over inflation. Although the rate of inflation was dramatically high, the problem of unemployment was probably felt more strongly by both trade unions and public authorities.

Our control exercises reflect instead the fact that, if the policy-makers had inverted their priorities, better results could have been obtained, as regards not only inflation but also growth (and international reserves). This means that if a less expansionary monetary policy had been followed – together with a higher (though decreasing) public expenditure – the rate of inflation would have been much lower, and output growth much higher (see, on this point, section 7.9 and Hughes Hallett and Petit, 1988a and c). The exercises show that with an adequate (optimal) policy mix the rate of inflation could have been lowered to a yearly (average) rate of 8.4 per cent, while the rate of growth of output could have been pushed up to 8 per cent;

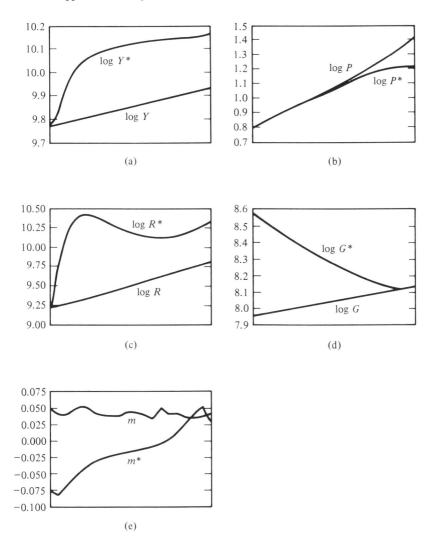

Figure 7.1 Performance of the economy under the (G, m) combination (1977.1–
1981.4)
(a) Output
(b) Price level
(c) Reserves
(d) Public expenditure
(e) Rate of growth of the money supply
Note: The starred symbols indicate the optimal trajectories. The
non-starred symbols indicate the base run.

at the same time reserves would have been growing at more than 22 per cent per annum.

It is interesting to observe that this conclusion is qualitatively the same as that obtained by other researchers in a traditional non-optimising framework: for example, Perkins (1985) has shown that a shift to a less inflationary policy mix can bring about macroeconomic benefits (higher output and lower inflation).

Although it is not possible to keep track of all the effects of the optimal policy, an approximate idea of its working can be given. A restrictive monetary policy has favourable effects on inflation (equation A.7.7 of the model). The lower rate of inflation stimulates internal demand, as does the increased public expenditure, hence the increase in output, which feeds back on internal demand (of both consumption (equation A.7.1) and investment goods (equation A.7.2)). International reserves grow because the improvement in the capital account more than offsets the deterioration in the current account.

It is clear from this description that the optimal control results obtained here and in the following sections depend heavily on the model used, as well as on the objective function assumed to represent the preferences of policy-makers. This dependence should always be kept in mind when using control methods for policy selection and advice, since, as stressed in section 5.14, a model is always an approximate description of reality and an objective function is only an approximation to the true policy-maker's preferences.

7.6 The optimal path of the exchange rate

In this section we shall consider the exchange rate as a control variable in order to determine its optimal trajectory over the planning period. However, a few words are in order on the use of the exchange rate as a control variable. In principle, the exchange rate cannot be taken as a 'full' control variable. Although under a dirty-float regime (which prevailed in the period considered) the exchange rate is managed by the monetary authorities, the latter do not have the power to make it take on any value they wish (a power which they may (relatively) have over other conrol variables like, say, public expenditure).

Therefore the optimal control exercise in which the exchange rate is used as a control variable has a different meaning from the other exercises: it determines an optimal path of the exchange rate which has the nature of a *guideline* for the monetary authorities in their management of the actual rate. What we are looking for with this exercise is an answer to a moot question: that of the criteria which policy-makers should follow in managing the exchange rate.

For this purpose we have introduced the spot exchange rate E (which enters the model as an exogenous variable) in the objective function (7.1) so that the optimization problem becomes that of minimizing

$$J = \int_{77}^{81} \{ w_y [\log Y(t) - \log Y^D(t)]^2 + w_p [\log P(t) - \log P^D(t)]^2$$

$$+ w_R [\log R(t) - \log R^D(t)]^2 + w_m [m(t) - m^D(t)]^2$$

$$+ w_G [\log G(t) - \log G^D(t)]^2 + w_T [\log T(t) - \log T^D(t)]^2$$

$$+ w_E [\log E(t) - \log E^D(t)]^2 \} \, dt \qquad (7.12)$$

subject to

$$\dot{x}(t) = Ax(t) + Bu(t) + Cz(t)$$

where the target and control variables and corresponding ideal paths are the same as those described in section 7.3, and where $\log E^D(t) = \log E(t_0) + 0.006t$; $t_0 = 1976(\text{IV})$ and $w_E = 3.0$.

The ideal rate of variation of the exchange rate was chosen so as to guarantee the international competitiveness of domestic products; it was therefore defined as the difference between the proportional rate of change of export prices and the proportional rate of change of foreign competitors' prices on international markets. This gave the ideal rate of growth of the exchange rate of 0.6 per cent per quarter. The penalty (w_E) assigned to the deviations of the exchange rate from its ideal path was set equal to 3 in order to avoid too large oscillations of the optimal control trajectory.

Since the exercises performed in this section can also be regarded as tests of the effectiveness of a managed exchange rate on the overall behaviour of the economy, we have run the same exercises described in section 7.5, introducing the exchange rate as a control variable in each of them. For purposes of comparison, in all cases the weights were kept at the same values as those defined in section 7.3.

A general idea of the performance of the targets when the exchange rate is introduced as a control variable is given in table 7.2, where average annual growth rates of the targets over the planning period are reported.

From an examination of table 7.2 and a comparison with the results given in table 7.1 we can observe the following:

(a) when the exchange rate is introduced as a policy variable in a situation in which two (or three) instruments are already following optimal control trajectories – as is the case in combinations (G, m, E), (T, m, E), (G, T, E) and (G, T, m, E) – the additional effect of an optimally managed exchange rate is very small. The improvement in the behaviour of the targets is negligible

Table 7.2   *Average annual growth rates of the targets under various combinations of the instruments including the exchange rate, 1977–1981*

| | Instruments used | | | | | | | |
Target	G, T, m, E	G, m, E	T, m, E	G, T, E	G, E	T, E	m, E	Base run
Y	7.98	7.94	12.60	8.69	8.84	10.90	12.50	3.22
P	8.00	7.93	8.91	7.18	7.13	8.19	8.89	12.42
R	23.90	24.27	−5.51	20.42	21.30	37.90	−51.00	11.90

and in one case (combination T, m, E) the improvement in growth and inflation is paid with a decrease in reserves.

This result however is not unexpected. The introduction of a new control variable in a context in which there are already two or three policy instruments optimally managed (and with positive effects on the targets) can hardly improve the situation. A very similar conclusion can be drawn for other control variables by observing table 7.1. The improvement obtained by using three instruments – combination (G, T, m) – is almost negligible when compared with the results obtained by using only two of them.

It would therefore be incorrect to conclude from these exercises that the management of the exchange rate is useless. The correct conclusion is that moving two adequately chosen instruments in an optimal way is sufficient to obtain very satisfactory results for the three targets aimed at, and that the results obtained in this way can hardly be improved upon.

(b) These conclusions no longer hold as regards the introduction of the exchange rate as a control variable when the policy-maker has only one other control variable available. In this case, the results obtained depend on which the other control variable is.

In the case in which the other control variable is a fiscal instrument (G, or T), the introduction of the exchange rate improves the behaviour of the targets. Since, as we have pointed out in section 7.5, public expenditure is a more effective instrument than taxes, the behaviour of the economy is fairly good when using only public expenditure as a control variable, while it is very unsatisfactory when using taxes alone. In both cases the management of the exchange rate clearly improves the results.

Things are different when management of the exchange rate is combined with monetary policy. The results obtained are worse when the exchange rate is introduced as a further instrument, showing in particular a strong decrease in international reserves.[8]

Nothing has been said yet about the *optimal path* of the exhange rate obtained as the solution of the previous exercises. Since, as before (see section 7.5), the best results are obtained with the combination of public expenditure and monetary policy, with the addition, in this case, of the exchange rate, we again take (G, m, E) as the benchmark and give the results in figure 7.2. Figure 7.2(f) shows the optimal path of the exchange rate; as

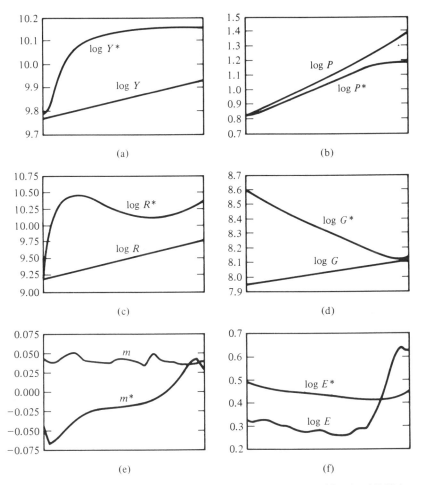

Figure 7.2   Performance of the economy under the (G, m, E) combination (1977.1–1981.4)

    (a) Output
    (b) Price level
    (c) Reserves
    (d) Public expenditure
    (e) Rate of growth of the money supply
    (f) Exchange rate

can be observed, the optimal path of this variable shows, when compared with the historical path, that the lira/dollar exchange rate was overvalued during most of the period under consideration; to be precise, from 1977 up to end of 1980, when a heavy devaluation occurred. The optimal exchange rate path shows that, if the exchange rate had been kept higher in that period, it would not have been necessary for the lira to undergo such a relatively high devaluation *vis-à-vis* the dollar in 1980–1.

7.7 The optimal degree of wage indexation

In the late seventies and early eighties the high rate of inflation prevailing in many industrialized countries led economists and politicians to analyse more deeply the effects of wage indexation on prices. In Italy, a heated debate took place regarding the modifications in the wage indexation mechanism which were needed in order to fight inflation. It would therefore be an interesting point to examine what the optimal path of the money wage rate would have been over the period considered, and to derive from this path the optimal degree of wage indexation over the period.

For this purpose we have to consider the wage rate as if it were a control variable, as was done in the previous section with the exchange rate. In fact, not even the wage rate can be considered as a 'full' control variable since many different factors enter into its determination and, therefore, policymakers do not have the power of making it assume any value they want. Consequently, as for the exchange rate, the results that we obtain can be considered as a guideline for wage indexation policies.

In order to obtain the optimal path of the money wage rate (W) we introduce this variable into the objective function (7.1). The problem thus consists in minimizing.

$$
\begin{aligned}
J = \int_{77}^{81} & \{ w_Y [\log Y(t) - \log Y^D(t)]^2 + w_P [\log P(t) - \log P^D(t)]^2 \\
& + w_R [\log R(t) - \log R^D(t)]^2 + w_m [m(t) - m^D(t)]^2 \\
& + w_G [\log G(t) - \log G^D(t)]^2 + w_T [\log T(t) - \log T^D(t)]^2 \\
& + w_w [\log W(t) - \log W^D(t)]^2 \} \, dt
\end{aligned}
\tag{7.13}
$$

subject to

$$\dot{x}(t) = Ax(t) + Bu(t) + Cz(t)$$

where the target and control variables, ideal paths and weights are the same as those described in section 7.3 and where $\log W^D(t) = \log W(t_0) + 0.02t$; $t_0 = 1976\text{–IV}$, and $w_w = 0.5$. The ideal rate of growth of the wage rate was

Table 7.3 *Average annual growth rates under various combinations of the instruments, 1977–1981*

Variable	Instruments used				Base run
	W	*G, W*	*G, T, W*	*G, T, m, W*	
Y	11.00	8.52	8.54	8.60	3.22
P	10.24	9.68	9.66	6.95	12.42
R	9.41	19.81	20.65	23.68	11.90
W	5.64	5.71	6.15	7.08	12.93

chosen so as to keep real wages constant over the period and a low weight on the variable was chosen in order to allow it the greatest possible freedom of behaviour.

The same exercises as described in section 7.5 have been carried out (using the wage rate as a control variable in each of them) in order to have an idea of the performance of the targets and of the wage rate under various combinations of the instruments. Only the most significant results have been given in table 7.3 (however, they do not change substantially when other possible combinations of the instruments are considered). The figures are, as usual, average annual growth rates over the planning period.

Several interesting observations can be made regarding these results. First of all, the wage rate turns out to be an effective policy instrument: when used alone, it gives rise to a great increase in the rate of growth of income and to a decrease in the rate of inflation. But the cost of these results is a huge nominal wage squeeze and – what matters most – of a huge reduction in real wages.

The use of one or two additional instruments improves the situation as regards inflation (and international reserves), but the rate of growth of income is lower; the rate of growth of real wages, however, is still negative, although to a lesser extent.

It is only when *all four* instruments are used together optimally that it is possible to obtain a drastic reduction in inflation together with an improvement in income growth *with no real wage loss*, as this is the only case in which nominal wages and prices grow at approximately the same rate.

The optimal paths of *W* and *P* in the case of the four-instrument combination are given in figure 7.3.

The optimal degree of wage indexation concerning the period considered could be inferred, if desired, from these paths. However, it should be noted that table 7.3 shows the total percentage change in *W* with respect to the

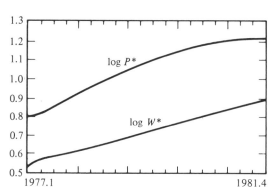

Figure 7.3   Optimal paths of W and P

total percentage change in P over the period, a relation that could have been implemented in several ways (for example, through annual, quarterly or monthly adjustments) according to the agreements between the parties concerned. It appears therefore more illuminating to refer to the optimal path of W as the required guideline.

We can however conclude from the results that a 100 per cent indexation, like that which existed in Italy in the second half of the seventies, could have been maintained – in the sense of being able to keep at the same time a high rate of growth of output and acceptable rates of inflation and of reserve growth – only if the other three instruments (G, T and m) were used optimally together. Otherwise, as can be seen from table 7.3, the achievement of these policy targets is totally incompatible with a complete wage indexation and, on the contrary, requires a considerable reduction of real wages over the period.

The optimal control exercises performed in this section confirm the point stressed in section 5.17 (i). They provide useful information about the econometric model considered, showing important links between variables that would have been difficult to highlight with other methods. In our case, for example, an important link between output and prices is highlighted, showing that the relation between these two variables can be a negative one. An implication of this result is that the conventional output-inflation tradeoff may be reversed, as we shall see in the following sections.

7.8 The policy possibility frontier

It is well known that an important problem for policy-makers is to maintain low inflation rates without depressing the rate of growth of output. The output-inflation tradeoff is still a dominant paradigm in most economists' thinking and in their models. However, the inflation-output combinations that are compatible with a given econometric model can be determined in many ways. For example, it is possible to derive the rates of inflation corresponding to different rates of growth by simulating the model under the assumption of no change in policies or that the policy variables follow various pre-assigned patterns of behaviour. Arbitrary changes in the policy variables can therefore produce an infinite number of inflation-output combinations, some better than others.

By using optimal control methods, it is possible to identify the *best* inflation-output combinations available, as suggested in Chow and Megdal's (1978) pioneering paper. Once the targets and the policy instruments are chosen, different optimal values can be obtained from the minimization of an objective function, either by changing the relative weights assigned to prices and output or by changing the desired (target) trajectories. In both cases, the inflation-output combinations obtained will yield a set of points, or an *efficient policy frontier*, which cannot be dominated.

In this section we shall briefly examine how these efficient tradeoffs are calculated in order to identify, in the following section, the best inflation-output combinations available for the Italian economy.

Suppose, for simplicity, that we are only concerned with the traditional tradeoff between two targets x_1 (inflation) and x_2 (output) and that two policy instruments, for example, u_1 (public expenditure) and u_2 (the money supply) are available. Then, if Q and R are diagonal, the objective function is given by

$$J = \int_{t_0}^{t_f} \{[x_1(t) - x_1^D(t)]^2 + \alpha[x_2(t) - x_2^D(t)]^2$$

$$+ \beta[u_1(t) - u_1^D(t)]^2 + \gamma[u_2(t) - u_2^D(t)]^2\} \, dt \qquad (7.14)$$

By minimizing (7.14), subject to a model describing the behaviour of the economy (see equation 7.3), optimal paths for $x_1(t)$, $x_2(t)$, $u_1(t)$ and $u_2(t)$ are obtained.

Optimal (non-dominated) combinations of target values can be generated by varying the relative priority on output (α) over the interval $(0, \infty)$ and keeping the rest of (7.14) constant. This may be done for a single time period, or as average target values over T periods (Chow, 1981; see also Henry *et al.*, 1982), or in terms of average rates of growth over T periods (Hughes Hallett and Petit, 1988a and c).

In a conventional set up, by varying α in (7.14) will yield the Pareto-efficient frontier FF' in figure 7.4. Above FF' are the inefficient but feasible

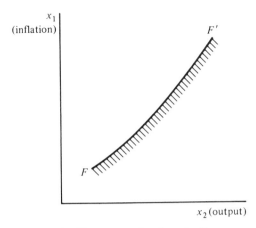

Figure 7.4   The conventional tradeoff

target combinations; below FF' are superior but not feasible target values. The ideal point lies towards the bottom right of the diagram – the point $(\infty, 0)$ – and the policy-maker's problem is one of choosing the most desirable position on this tradeoff between attainable target values.

However, in the absence of further restrictions, there is actually no guarantee that the optimal tradeoff will have the traditional upward sloping form of figure 7.4. For certain values of the relative priorities (α), for certain specifications of the ideal trajectories ($x^D(t)$), or for certain expectations or realization of the non-controllable (exogenous) variables, the tradeoff curve FF' can switch to the downward sloping form in figure 7.5. This policy switch implies that there is no policy conflict since the ideal point lies towards $(\infty, 0)$; the policy-maker can obtain lower rates of inflation while increasing the rate of growth of output. The policy-maker's aim is to bring the system to point F' which is the best available point of the reversed policy possibility frontier. The policy problem then boils down to deciding how close to F' the most desirable position would be, since stronger interventions are required in order to get better target outcomes in a situation where the tradeoff between targets has become a groupwise tradeoff between targets and instruments. Therefore the sophisticated policy-maker will here be trading intervention 'effort' against target 'success'. In this case the decision problem is considerably simplified.

There are two possible explanations for this situation. It could be good fortune, in that a particular configuration of external 'shocks' are expected to push both targets together in a favourable (or unfavourable) direction. But it could also be that there is some underlying structural link between the targets, which moves one target in a favourable direction if there is

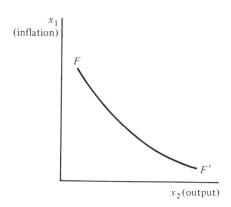

Figure 7.5   The reversed tradeoff

a favourable movement in the other.[9] It is obviously vital to be able to distinguish the two cases since the former only holds by chance, whereas the latter means that hard choices can be avoided, since only one constraint is actually binding.

7.9 The inflation-output tradeoff: numerical results

The efficient tradeoff between output growth and inflation for the Italian economy has been calculated by using the quadratic loss function defined by (7.1). This function has been minimized under the constraint of the continuous-time econometric model of the Italian economy described in section 7.2 (see also the appendices to this chapter). As we have seen in section 7.4, this model can be summarized by system (7.3).

As above, the planning horizon considered goes from the beginning of 1977 to the end of 1981 and the optimization technique used is Pontryagin's minimum principle. As we have seen in the previous section, once the targets and control variables are chosen, different optimal results can be obtained from the minimization of the loss function (7.1), either by changing the relative weights assigned to prices and output or by changing the desired trajectories of these two targets. In both cases, the inflation growth combinations obtained will form an *efficient policy frontier*. In this exercise, the efficient policy frontier for the Italian economy has been computed by changing the relative weights assigned to prices and output in (7.1).

Table 7.4 and the curve AA in figure 7.6 present the output-price tradeoff available to the Italian economy during the period 1977–81. The figures quoted are the mean output and price levels (expressed in logarithms) obtained over that period, and correspond to a 100-fold change in priority

Table 7.4   *Average price-output tradeoff (in levels) for the Italian economy, 1977–1981*

Inflation weight (w_2)	Output (log $\bar{Y}$)	Prices (log $\bar{P}$)
0.1	9.890	2.228
0.3	9.984	1.594
0.5	10.018	1.396
0.7	10.037	1.299
1.0	10.048	1.221
1.4	10.065	1.165
2.0	10.083	1.091
3.0	10.085	1.072
5.0	10.093	1.049
10.0	10.096	1.026

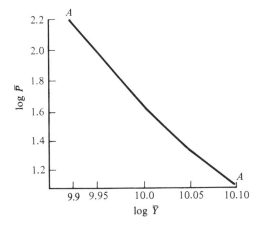

Figure 7.6   The output-inflation tradeoff (average values)

given to restraining inflation compared to raising output. Recall that weights in (7.1) penalize percentage deviations from the ideal path equally, so that table 7.4 represents policies where proportional failures in the inflation target are treated as 10 times less important, through to 10 times more important, than the same failures in output.

These results clearly show a tradeoff 'reversal', with no conflict arising between the output and price targets. Indeed there is no question of which policy package should be selected on this tradeoff; increasing the weight on the inflation target ($w_2 \rightarrow 10$) generates *higher* output levels together with a *smaller* increase in prices than do policies which give a lower priority to inflation.

Table 7.5 *Average growth-inflation tradeoff for the Italian economy, 1977–1981*

Inflation weight (w_2)	Output ($\dot{Y}/Y$)	Prices ($\dot{P}/P$)
0.1	−4.50	38.22
0.3	1.93	21.93
0.5	4.16	16.62
0.7	5.29	14.08
1.0	6.22	12.10
1.4	6.91	10.77
2.0	7.57	9.35
3.0	7.88	8.79
5.0	8.23	8.50
10.0	8.46	8.02

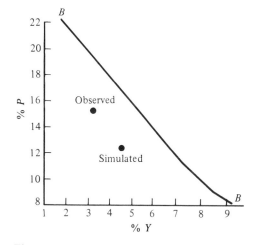

Figure 7.7   The output-inflation tradeoff (rates of growth)

The same kind of results are obtained by considering a more familiar form of the output-inflation conflict directly in terms of rates of growth. That is done in table 7.5 and line *BB* of figure 7.7. The observed output-inflation outcome has also been plotted in figure 7.7, along with the outcome obtained by simply simulating the base-run solution. The latter is clearly superior to the former, but neither of them lies anywhere near the optimal policy possibility frontier *BB*. This confirms that large gains could have been made by introducing policy optimization methods to construct the *best* output-inflation tradeoff available and asking policy-makers to pick their preferred position on this frontier (i.e. towards the lower end of *BB*).

These results appear to confirm exactly the strategy based on the argument that the first priority should be to reduce inflation because recovery, output growth, investment and employment would then automatically follow. The thesis that, if the industrialized countries had followed a less inflationary policy mix in the seventies, then they could have obtained much better results not only as regards a lower rate of inflation, but also as regards a higher growth-rate of output, can be found, for example, in Perkins (1985). In terms of *efficient* policy selection this argument amounts to saying that the weight given to inflation (in that period) should have been much greater than the weight given to the rate of growth of output, so as to induce the authorities to follow a less inflationary policy. This thesis is also confirmed by the results of section 7.5.

The actual outcomes in Italy in recent years have been consistent with the tradeoff shown in figure 7.7. Output growth in Italy rose from -0.5 per cent per annum in 1982 to $+3$ per cent per annum in 1986 while the inflation rate fell from 17.8 per cent per annum to 5 per cent per annum over the same period. Undoubtedly the fall in oil prices and the US dollar contributed to those achievements – but those two factors would only influence events in 1986; not in the 1982–5 period and still less the 1977–81 policy possibilities revealed by tables 7.4 and 7.5 and figures 7.6 and 7.7.

The interesting result here is that this opportunity to boost output while at the same time reducing inflation also existed, at least in Italy, for the earlier period when oil prices more than doubled and when the recovery of 1977–8 turned into the world recession of 1979–81. But the policy-makers appear not to have made use of their opportunity to start a recovery by reducing inflation in that period.

Appendix – The econometric model

Table A.7.1   *Equations of the model**

Private consumption

$$D \log C = \alpha_1 \log(\hat{C}/C) + \alpha_2 \log(M/M_d) \tag{A.7.1}$$

where

$$\hat{C} = \gamma_1 e^{\beta_1 D \log Y} \left(\frac{P}{PMGS}\right)^{\beta_2} (Y - T/P), \beta_1 \lessgtr 0, \beta_2 \lessgtr 0.$$

$$M_d = \gamma_2 i_{TIT}^{-\beta_3} P^{\beta_4} Y^{\beta_5}, \beta_3 \lessgtr 0 \tag{A.7.1.1}$$

Rate of growth in fixed capital stock

$$Dk = \alpha_3 [\alpha' \log(\hat{K}/K) - k] + \alpha_4 Da \tag{A.7.2}$$

where

$$\hat{K} = \gamma_3 \tilde{Y}, \quad \gamma_3 = \kappa u \tag{A.7.2.1}$$

Expected output

$$D \log \tilde{Y} = \eta \log(Y/\tilde{Y}) \tag{A.7.3}$$

Imports

$$D \log MGS = \alpha_5 \log(M\hat{G}S/MGS) + \alpha_6 \log(\hat{V}/V) \tag{A.7.4}$$

where

$$M\hat{G}S = \gamma_4 P^6 PMGS^{-\beta_7} Y^{\beta_8}, \quad \hat{V} = \gamma_5 \tilde{Y} \tag{A.7.4.1}$$

Exports

$$D \log XGS = \alpha_7 \log(X\hat{G}S/XGS) - \alpha_8 Da \tag{A.7.5}$$

where

$$X\hat{G}S = \gamma_6 (PXGS/PF)^{-\beta_9} YF^{\beta_{10}} (\gamma_3 Y/K)^{-\beta_{11}} \tag{A.7.5.1}$$

Output

$$D \log Y = \alpha_9 \log(\tilde{Y}/Y) + \alpha_{10} \log(\hat{V}/V) \tag{A.7.6}$$

201

Table A.7.1—*contd.*

Price of output

$$D \log P = \alpha_{11} \log(\hat{P}/P) + \alpha_{12} Dm \qquad \text{(A.7.7)}$$

where

$$\hat{P} = \gamma_7 PMGS^{\beta_{12}} W^{\beta_{13}} PROD^{-\beta_{14}} \qquad \text{(A.7.7.1)}$$

Price of exports

$$D \log PXGS = \alpha_{13} \log(P\hat{X}GS/PXGS) \qquad \text{(A.7.8)}$$

where

$$P\hat{X}GS = \gamma_8 P^{\beta_{15}} PF^{\beta_{16}} \qquad \text{(A.7.8.1)}$$

Money wage rate

$$D \log W = \alpha_{14} \log(\hat{W}/W) \qquad \text{(A.7.9)}$$

where

$$\hat{W} = \gamma_9 P^{\beta_{17}} e^{\lambda_5 t} \qquad \text{(A.7.9.1)}$$

Interest rate

$$D \log i_{TIT} = \alpha_{15} \log(M_d/M) + \alpha_{16} \log(\gamma_{10} i_f/i_{TIT}) \qquad \text{(A.7.10)}$$

Bank advances

$$D \log A = \alpha_{17} \log(\hat{A}/A) \qquad \text{(A.7.11)}$$

where

$$\hat{A} = \gamma_{11} i_{TIT}{}^{\beta_{18}} M, \quad \beta_{18} \lesseqgtr 0 \qquad \text{(A.7.11.1)}$$

Net foreign assets

$$D \log NFA = \alpha_{18} \log(N\hat{F}A/NFA) + \alpha_{19} Da \qquad \text{(A.7.12)}$$

where

$$N\hat{F}A = \gamma_{12} i_{TIT}{}^{-\beta_{19}} i_f{}^{\beta_{20}} (PY)^{\beta_{21}} (PF \cdot YF)^{-\beta_{22}} Q^{\beta_{23}}, \quad \beta_{23} \lesseqgtr 0 \qquad \text{(A.7.12.1)}$$

Monetary authorities' reaction function

$$Dm = \alpha_{20}(\hat{m} - m) + \delta_3 Dh + \delta_4 Dr \qquad \text{(A.7.13)}$$

where

$$\hat{m} = \delta_1 \log(R/\gamma_{13} PMGS \cdot MGS) - \delta_2(D \log P - D \log PF) \qquad \text{(A.7.13.1)}$$

Taxes

$$D \log T = \alpha_{21} \log(\hat{T}/T) \qquad \text{(A.7.14)}$$

where

$$\hat{T} = \gamma_{14}(PY)^{\beta_{24}} \qquad \text{(A.7.14.1)}$$

Table A.7.1—*contd.*

Public expenditure

$$D \log G = \alpha_{22} \log(\gamma_{15} Y/G) \tag{A.7.15}$$

Inventories

$$DV = Y + MGS - C - DK - XGS - G \tag{A.7.16}$$

International reserves

$$DR = PXGS \cdot XGS - PMGS \cdot MGS$$
$$+ (UT_a - UT_p) - DNFA \tag{A.7.17}$$

Fixed capital stock

$$D \log K = k \tag{A.7.18}$$

Rate of growth in bank advances

$$a = D \log A \tag{A.7.19}$$

Rate of growth in money supply

$$m = D \log M \tag{A.7.20}$$

Public sector's borrowing requirement

$$DH = PG - T \tag{A.7.21}$$

Rate of growth in H

$$h = D \log H \tag{A.7.22}$$

Rate of growth in international reserves

$$r = D \log R \tag{A.7.23}$$

Note: *For economy of notation, the disturbance terms are omitted and the model is written in deterministic terms. A hat ($\hat{\ }$) refers to the partial equilibrium level or desired value of the hatted variable, a tilde ($\tilde{\ }$) to expectations; the symbol D denotes the differential operator d/dt, and log the natural logarithm. All parameters are assumed positive, unless otherwise specified.

Table A.7.2   *Variables of the model*

Endogenous

A	= nominal stock of bank advances
a	= proportional rate of growth of A
C	= private consumption expenditure in real terms
G	= public expenditure in real terms
H	= public sector borrowing requirement
h	= proportional rate of change of H
i_{TIT}	= domestic nominal interest rate
K	= stock of fixed capital in real terms
k	= proportional rate of change of K
M	= nominal stock of money ($M2$)
m	= proportional rate of change of M
MGS	= imports of goods and services in real terms
NFA	= nominal stock of net foreign assets
P	= domestic price level
$PXGS$	= export price level
R	= nominal stock of international reserves
r	= proportional rate of change of R
T	= nominal taxes
V	= stock of inventories in real terms
W	= money wage rate
XGS	= exports of goods and services in real terms
Y	= real net domestic product and income
$\tilde{Y}$	= expected real net domestic product and income

Exogenous

i_f	= foreign nominal interest rate
PF	= foreign competitors' export price level
$PMGS$	= import price level
$PROD$	= labour productivity
Q	= ratio of the forward to the spot exchange rate
t	= time
$(UT_a - UT_p)$	= net unilateral transfers, in nominal terms
YF	= real world income

Table A.7.3   *Estimated adjustment parameters*

Parameter	Entering equation number	Point estimate	Asymptotic standard error	Mean time lag (quarters)	Standard error of mean time lag
α_1	(1)	1.423	0.188	0.702	0.093
α_2	(1)	0.151	0.050		
α_3	(2)	1.334	0.220	0.750	0.123
α_4	(2)	0.122	0.011		
α_5	(4)	1.409	0.196	0.710	0.099
α_6	(4)	0.556	0.142		
α_7	(5)	0.673	0.124	1.486	0.275
α_8	(5)	0.902	0.153		
α_9	(6)	1.932	0.287	0.518	0.077
α_{10}	(6)	0.346	0.070		
α_{11}	(7)	0.145	0.056	6.897	2.694
α_{12}	(7)	0.211	0.071		
α_{13}	(8)	0.208	0.059	4.808	1.370
α_{14}	(9)	1.365	0.281	0.733	0.151
α_{15}	(10)	−0.007	0.045		
α_{16}	(10)	0.076	0.019	13.158	3.289
α_{17}	(11)	0.111	0.019	9.009	1.548
α_{18}	(12)	0.286	0.029	3.497	0.354
α_{19}	(12)	1.356	0.062		
α_{20}	(13)	3.445	0.604	0.290	0.051
α_{21}	(14)	0.181	0.079	5.525	2.402
α_{22}	(15)	0.281	0.070	3.559	0.892
α'	(2)	0.050	0.003	20.000	1.213
η	(3)	0.156	0.064		

Table A.7.4   *Other estimated parameters*

Parameter	Entering equation number	Point estimate	Asymptotic standard error
β_1	(1)	-0.813	0.168
β_2	(2)	0.000*	
β_3	(1), (10)	0.104	0.198
β_4	(1), (10)	0.864	0.145
β_5	(1), (10)	2.497	0.289
β_6	(4)	0.505	0.105
β_7	(4)	0.507	0.078
β_8	(4)	1.257	0.102
β_9	(5)	0.004	0.160
β_{10}	(5)	0.643	0.214
β_{11}	(5)	1.225	0.161
β_{12}	(7)	0.392	0.164
β_{13}	(7)	0.474 ·	0.108
β_{14}	(7)	0.000*	
β_{15}	(8)	0.713	0.159
β_{16}	(8)	0.286	0.128
β_{17}	(9)	0.682	0.040
β_{18}	(11)	-0.305	0.040
β_{19}	(12)	-0.116	0.150
β_{20}	(12)	0.169	0.056
β_{21}	(12)	1.051	0.120
β_{22}	(12)	0.940	0.113
β_{23}	(12)	2.694	0.436
β_{24}	(14)	0.871	0.066
λ_5	(9)	0.019	0.001
δ_1	(13)	0.000*	
δ_2	(13)	0.077	0.026
δ_3	(13)	0.275	0.039
δ_4	(13)	0.169	0.019
$\log \gamma_1'$	(1)	-0.316	0.018
$\log \gamma_2$	(1), (10)	-18.935	2.703
$\log \gamma_3$	(2)	1.437	0.015
$\log \gamma_4$	(4)	2.987	0.807
$\log \gamma_5$	(4), (6)	0.115	0.197
$\log \gamma_6$	(5)	-0.405	1.161
$\log \gamma_7$	(7)	0.351	0.012
$\log \gamma_8$	(8)	-0.091	0.028
$\log \gamma_9$	(9)	-0.324	0.091
$\log \gamma_{10}$	(10)	0.000*	
$\log \gamma_{11}$	(11)	-3.967	0.093
$\log \gamma_{12}$	(12)	8.002	0.913
$\log \gamma_{13}$	(13)	0.000*	
$\log \gamma_{14}$	(14)	-0.319	0.529
$\log \gamma_{15}$	(15)	-1.439	0.033

Note: *Value imposed

8 Decentralized decisions and differential games

8.1 The problem of decentralized decisions

The optimal control approach to economic policy design that we have analysed in previous chapters implies the assumption either that all policy decisions are taken by a single institution or that the political institutions concerned with planning act in complete agreement. The same assumption of centralized decisions is implicit in the controllability and stability approaches described in chapters 3 and 4; in fact, when we look for those policies which make it possible to control the economic system or to stabilize it, we are assuming that a single political institution will be able to manage the policy instruments under consideration.

However, in most countries, more than one decision-making institution co-exists. Think for example of the Treasury, the Central Bank, trade-unions, industrial organizations, and so forth. These decision-makers do not always succeed in reaching binding agreements as to the policy targets to aim for and/or the priorities to be assigned to these targets. Therefore, optimal policy decisions are no longer the result of a single optimization problem but are the result of a dynamic game between different policy-makers.

The problem of decentralized decisions has already been mentioned in chapter 4, when dealing with the *assignment* problem (section 4.4) and with the *decoupling* problem (section 4.6). These two approaches make it possible to consider the case of decentralization, since it can be assumed that each decision-maker is able to influence the behaviour of only one policy target (or a group of targets), by moving only one control variable (or a group of control variables). Though the assignment of instruments to targets is not necessarily one to one, each policy-maker is assumed to have his own targets and his own instruments, which cannot be shared by other policy-makers. However, as we have already mentioned in chapter 4, the dynamic game approach to the problem of decentralized decisions presents some important characteristics that are absent from the other approaches. Among these, the following features can be singled out:

(a) Dynamic games make it possible to make a selection from among all those policy rules that are able to stabilize or to control the system in a decentralized manner. This selection can be performed only by considering some criterion of choice, and, in the case of decentralized decisions, dynamic games constitute a method which provides this criterion.

Conversely, as we have seen in chapter 4, the assignment (stability) approach simply provides the conditions that the economic system must satisfy so that it is possible to pair off instruments with targets and makes it possible to find out which is the assignment of instruments to targets that stabilizes the economic system. The decoupling (controllability) approach allows us to find out only if there exists a control rule by which the economic system can be decoupled, i.e. can be controlled by assigning a specific control to a specific target variable. However, there may be more than one policy rule which is able to stabilize or to decouple the economic system, and neither of these two approaches provides any kind of criteria which makes possible the choice of a particular one of these different policy rules.

(b) Dynamic games make it possible to consider policy-makers that share the same targets. For example, inflation and employment may be common targets for both the Government and the trade-unions, and conflict may arise simply from other, different targets and/or from different priorities. Therefore, even if it is assumed that each decision-maker can only move its own control variables, it is not necessary for these variables to be assigned to different specific targets, as is conversely the case with the other two approaches. This means that the problem of decentralized decisions can be analysed by means of dynamic games even in those cases in which the system is not decouplable.

(c) Dynamic games make it possible to consider the *interaction* between the different decision-makers, since, as we shall see, each of them will formulate their own decisions by taking into account the decisions of all the others. Different assumptions can be made about the type of interaction between the players of a dynamic game, which will lead to different equilibrium solutions. Furthermore, the intertemporal feature of dynamic games makes it possible for each policy-maker to take into account not only *current* decisions of the other policy-makers, but also their *future* decisions: the strategies of the other players may enter the objective function of each player either directly or indirectly through the target variables whose time behaviour is influenced by the decisions of *all* the players. Intertemporal interaction between policy-makers can therefore be taken fully into account.

This of course is not possible with the other approaches where the implicit idea is that each policy-maker, once the assignment has been established, moves its control viariable(s) only by focussing on its own objective(s), while taking all the rest (including the actions of the others) as given.

Another important problem which can be analysed by using dynamic game methods is that concerning the interaction between the Government (or policy-makers in general) and the private sector. As we shall see in chapter 10, dynamic games can describe this interaction in the case in which the private sector forms expectations about future policy actions, and they also make it possible to overcome the Lucas critique (see section 10.9).

Dynamic games undoubtedly are a powerful mathematical tool for analysing macroeconomic policy problems, both in the framework of a single economic system and in that of an international system. However, since very competent and clearly written books on game theory have been published in recent years – to which we shall often refer the reader in this and in the following chapters – we shall not present here a complete review of dynamic games, but only consider some specific features that have not been so often treated in the literature on economic policy analysis. Ours can thus be considered as a brief introduction to dynamic games, which will be useful for the application of this method to a macroeconometric model (that will be undertaken in the following chapter) and for the discussion on some of the topics that will be considered in the last chapter. Therefore, many points will necessarily be left out of consideration.

Following the main line of the book we shall focus here on infinite dynamic games specified in *continuous time* – also known as *differential* games – and defined on a finite time horizon; in this type of game a continuum of levels of play is considered, and not a finite number of them, as is the case for discrete-time games. In the following sections we shall first examine non-cooperative solutions and then axiomatic bargaining theory, which provides a framework for determining cooperative solutions.

8.2 Differential games: a general view

In order to describe a problem of decentralized economic planning by using differential game methods the following elements have to be considered:
  (i) an index set N (the player set), which defines the number of decision-makers considered in the policy game, i.e. $N=(1, 2, \ldots, N)$.
 (ii) a given time interval $[t_0, t_f]$ during which the decision process is

defined and which denotes the duration of the game, i.e. the planning horizon.

(iii) an infinite set[1] U_i defined for each $i \in N$ called the control space of player i. The elements of each U_i are the control functions defined over the whole time interval, i.e., $u_{i|[t_0, t_f]}$. Furthermore, there exists a set S^i so that for each fixed $t \in [t_0, t_f]$, $u_i(t) \in S^i \subseteq R^{m_i} (i \in N)$.

(iv) a macroeconomic model formulated as a set of differential equations which describe the dynamic evolution of the economic system, that is

$$\dot{x}(t) = f[x(t), u_1(t), \ldots, u_N(t), t] \tag{8.1}$$

where $x(t) \in R^n$ is the state[2] vector and $u_i(t) \in S^i (i \in N)$.

(v) a set-valued function $\eta_i(.)$ defined for each $i \in N$ which characterizes the *information structure* (or *information pattern*) of player i and such that $\eta_i(t)$ defines the information of player i at time $t \in [t_0, t_f]$. The *information structure* of the game is defined by the collection of the information structures of all the players, that is $\eta = (\eta_1, \eta_2, \ldots, \eta_N)$.

(vi) a set Γ_i of permissible strategies γ_i of player i, defined for each $i \in N$. Γ_i is known as the strategy space of the decision-maker i and γ_i defines a mapping from the information space into the action space of each player $i \in N$, i.e. $\gamma_i : \eta_i \to u_i$.

(vii) an objective functional or cost functional J_i defined for each decision-maker $i \in N$ over the planning horizon $[t_0, t_f]$. The value of J_i depends not only on the actions of player i but also on the actions of all the other decision-makers. In game theory, J_i is often called the 'pay-off' function of player i and can be written as

$$J_i(u_i, u_2, \ldots, u_N) = \int_{t_0}^{t_f} I_i[x(t), u_1(t), \ldots, u_N(t), t] \, dt, \quad i \in N \tag{8.2}$$

where, for simplicity, a terminal condition is not considered. We also assume in what follows that the target set is the whole state space R^n. As we have seen in chapter 5, section 5.6, the assumption of different target sets will change the boundary points of the optimality conditions.

The solution of a differential game will be different, depending on the assumptions made about the information structure of the players. The most prevalent types of information structures are (see Basar and Olsder, 1982, chapter 5):

(a) *open-loop*, if

$$\eta_i(t) = \{x_0\}, \quad t \in [t_0, t_f],$$

(b) *closed-loop* (perfect state), if

$$\eta_i(t) = \{x(s), t_0 \leqslant s \leqslant t\}, \quad t \in [t_0, t_f],$$

(c) *closed-loop no-memory* (memoryless perfect state), if

$$\eta_i(t) = \{x_0, x(t)\}, \quad t \in [t_0, t_f],$$

(d) *feedback* (perfect state), if

$$\eta_i(t) = \{x(t)\}, \quad t \in [t_0, t_f].$$

The open-loop information pattern describes the case in which player i at time t recalls only the initial state. Conversely, the closed-loop information pattern describes the case in which player i recalls the whole path of the state up to t; this type of information structure, therefore, incorporates *memory*. The closed-loop no-memory information structure considers the case in which player i recalls only the initial state and knows the current one. Finally, the feedback information pattern considers the case without memory, so that player i knows only the current state.

As we have seen above (point vi), the strategies of each player depend upon his information structure. If the information structure of player i is open-loop, his strategy will be of the form $u_i(t) = \gamma_i(t, x_0)$; an open-loop strategy will therefore only be a function of time, given the initial state. It follows that, since open-loop strategies at each t are constant functions, they can be considered as elements of the set S^i, $i \in N$. On the other hand when the information structure is closed-loop, the strategy of player i will be given by $u_i(t) = \gamma_i(t, x(s); t_0 \leqslant s \leqslant t)$, that is, it will depend on the whole history of the state up to t, while, if it is closed-loop no-memory, the strategy of player i will be of the form $u_i(t) = \gamma_i(t, x_0, x(t))$. Finally, if the information structure of player i is feedback, his strategy will be given by $u_i(t) = \gamma_i(t, x(t))$, that is will depend only on the current state. It follows that in the cases of closed-loop and feedback strategies, the actual values of $u_i(t)$ cannot be determined at the beginning of the game (as is the case with open-loop strategies), but have to be determined as the game evolves, once the actual values of the state variables at each time t become available.

It is important from the beginning to make clear the distinction between *strategies* (or *decision rules*) and *actions* (or *controls*). A *strategy* is a function of one or more quantities that are not (totally) controlled by decision-makers and that are not yet known when the strategies themselves are derived. For example, if the Government has to decide today either to expand or to restrict public expenditure in the following quarter, a strategy would be: 'if demand falls below full-employment output, expand public expenditure; otherwise, restrict it'. An *action*, on the other hand, is simply the consequence of a strategy. In the example above, once the value of demand in the following quarter is known, the Government will know the action to take, which will be either 'expand' or 'restrict'. Therefore, a *constant strategy* – such as an irrevocable decision to follow a restrictive policy – coincides with the notion of *action* (see, for example, Basar and Olsder, 1982, chapter 1). This is the reason why, as we have just seen, when open-loop strategies are considered, the control space coincides, at each t, with the strategy space.

Closed-loop (memory) strategies give rise to *informational non-uniqueness of equilibria*, that is to problems of non-uniqueness of the equilibrium solutions due to the greater information of the players. The increased information of one or more players leaves the solutions obtained with previous inferior information unchanged, but also creates new equilibria (see Basar and Olsder, 1982, chapter 6). For this reason we shall consider here only open-loop and feedback equilibrium solutions, focussing in particular on the computation of open-loop solutions[3] since, as we shall see, the numerical computation of feedback equilibrium solutions in continuous time still presents unresolved problems which can be overcome only by the use of discretization techniques (see Basar, 1986), thus losing the main characteristics and advantages of working with continuous-time models.

Besides the information concerning the state, we shall assume that each player knows[4] the structure of the dynamic model which describes the performance of the economic system considered and its own objective function. Furthermore, if information is *symmetric*, the objective functions of the other players are also assumed to be known. Conversely, in the case of *asymmetric* information, some of the players may not know the objective function of the other players.

An important classification of dynamic games is that between *cooperative* and *non-cooperative* games. In the first case, it is assumed that the players can communicate and negotiate with one another in order to arrive at the determination of a common line of action. In the second case, no kind of communication is considered, so that each player will simply try to optimize his own objective function on the basis of the conjectures that he makes about the behaviour of the others. These different conjectures give rise to different equilibrium strategies, as we shall see in the next section.

A further classification of non-cooperative games is that between zero-sum and non-zero-sum games. In the first case it is assumed that the players have diametrically opposed interests, so that the sum of their pay-off functions is zero (or, more generally, a constant). Conversely, no explicit assumption as to the sum of these functions is made in the second case.

In what follows we shall consider only non-zero-sum games, since a conflicting situation giving rise to a zero-sum game is unlikely to arise in economic policy problems. For simplicity, we shall focus only on *two-player* games; more general cases can be considered simply by extending the concepts introduced for the two-player case.

3.3 Non-cooperative solutions: definitions and properties

In this section, two non-cooperative solution concepts will be considered, the Nash and the Stackelberg equilibrium solutions. The possibility of defining different equilibrium solutions arises as a consequence of the different assumptions made as to the behaviour of the players and/or their information structures.

The Nash equilibrium solution is also known as Cournot–Nash, since it was the French economist, Cournot, who, in 1838, first introduced this solution concept with reference to oligopoly theory. This solution – which was later generalized by Nash (1951) – is based on the assumption that information is symmetric between the two players in the sense mentioned above, that is, each player knows the structure of the model which describes the economic environment and the objective function of the other player (Starr and Ho, 1969a). This symmetry of information makes it possible for the players to determine their strategies *simultaneously*: it is generally assumed that the players act at the same instant of time. The Nash equilibrium solution concept thus provides a good description of those economic problems where the roles of the decision-makers are symmetric, that is, where no policy-maker dominates the decision process.

The Stackelberg equilibrium solution was introduced by Von Stackelberg, in 1934, also in the framework of oligopoly theory. Unlike the Nash solution, the Stackelberg solution is a hierarchical solution concept, since one of the players, the 'leader', has a stronger position in the decision process. This equilibrium solution is the result of sequential decisions: the leader announces his strategy first so that the other player, the 'follower', can only react, subsequently, to the leader's strategy. The strategy of the follower is thus determined when the strategy of the leader is already known.

This type of sequential behaviour may arise because of a difference in the information patterns of the two players; it may be the case that the leader knows the cost function of the follower, but the follower does not know the cost function of the leader (see Cruz, 1975). Consequently the follower does not have enough information to compute a Nash strategy,

instead, allowing for the worst possible behaviour on his rival's part, he may choose to play a minimax strategy whose calculation requires only knowledge of his own performance function. Or, instead of risking such a pessimistic strategy, he may select to play the game *passively*, that is, by waiting until the other player's strategy is announced and then solving an ordinary optimization problem for his corresponding strategy. (Simaan and Cruz, 1973a, p. 534; emphasis added)

It is this passive attitude just described which characterizes the behaviour of the follower in a Stackelberg game.

Sequential behaviour may also be due to faster means of information processing for one of the players, which permits him to compute his strategy first, and thus to announce it before the other player does. The Stackelberg equilibrium solution is a reasonable solution concept to describe those cases in which the roles of the players are asymmetric and one of them has the opportunity to declare his strategy in advance, thus imposing a solution which is favourable to himself.

An important feature of dynamic non-cooperative games is that, unlike optimal control problems, the equilibrium solutions are different for each different information structure considered. Thus, an open-loop equilibrium solution is usually different from a feedback equilibrium solution, even in a deterministic framework (Starr and Ho, 1969b; Simaan and Cruz, 1973b). This is due to the fact that some links between the strategies, through the state variables, are not fully considered in the computation of open-loop equilibrium solutions: when computing open-loop strategies, player i assumes that player j will not adjust his strategy in response to changes in the state of the system, and vice versa. A class of games exists, however, called *state separable* games (see Dockner, Feichtinger and Jorgensen, 1985), for which the open-loop and the feedback Nash equilibrium solutions coincide.

Nash equilibrium strategies have an important property (that, as we shall see, not all Stackelberg equilibrium strategies possess): they satisfy Bellman's principle of optimality, or, in other words, they are *time consistent*. This property has considerable implications in economic policy analysis and will therefore be considered in detail in chapter 10. However, since we shall also deal with this property in the following sections, we provide here a brief definition of time-consistent solutions following Basar, 1986.

Let $\mathscr{G}(t_0, t_f)$ denote a dynamic game defined on the interval $[t_0, t_f]$, and $\mathscr{G}(s, t_f)$ denote the same game, but defined over a shorter interval $[s, t_f], t_0 < s \leqslant t_f$. That is, we assume that the game is truncated to the time interval $[s, t_f]$. Let $\mathscr{S}$ be a solution operator which produces a unique pair of equilibrium strategies for each of these games (each strategy belonging to the corresponding admissible set), i.e.

$$\mathscr{S}[\mathscr{G}(s, t_f)] = (\gamma_1, \gamma_2)_{(s)} \triangleq \gamma_{(s)} \tag{8.3}$$

where the subscript (s) indicates that the game considered is defined on $[s, t_f]$.

A solution operator $\mathscr{S}$ for $\mathscr{G}$ generates a time-consistent solution $\gamma_{(t_0)}$ if, for every $s \in (t_0, t_f]$, the solution operator $\mathscr{S}$ for $\mathscr{G}(s, t_f)$ generates $\gamma_{(s)}$ which is a truncated version of $\gamma_{(t_0)}$, that is

$$[\gamma_1(t, \eta_1(t)), \gamma_2(t, \eta_2(t))]_{(t_0)} = [\gamma_1(t, \eta_1(t)), \gamma_2(t, \eta_2(t))]_{(s)} \qquad (8.4)$$

for all $t, s \leq t \leq t_f$.

An equilibrium solution concept is *time consistent* if the solution operator $\mathscr{S}$ which generates it, generates a solution that satisfies (8.4).

It is important to observe that no reference has been made, in defining time consistency, to the initial state of the truncated game $\mathscr{G}(s, t_f)$. In fact, only the concept of time is important in the definition of time consistency, since the state corresponding to each initial time $s \in (t_0, t_f]$ is the state which corresponds to the same time s along the equilibrium state trajectory of the dynamic game starting at t_0. This means that (8.4) must hold only along the *equilibrium* solution.

Time consistency is a common feature of both open-loop and feedback Nash strategies. There is however another important property of equilibrium strategies, known as *subgame perfectness* (Selten, 1975) that only feedback strategies possess. The property of subgame perfectness, initially defined in the framework of finite games, has been recently redefined in the domain of infinite dynamic games and is known as *strong time consistency* (Basar, 1989). This property, as its name indicates, is stronger than time consistency (redefined as *weak time consistency*) and requires that an equilibrium strategy still remains an equilibrium strategy even when the game is perturbed in some way (i.e. requires the equilibrium strategy to be robust; see section 5.16). In other words subgame perfectness implies that an equilibrium strategy remains an equilibrium strategy for any possible subgame of the original game, where a *subgame* is a truncated game starting from *any date* and *any state*. This is a very strong requirement since it means that a player can be sure to be playing an equilibrium strategy even if the other players deviate from their equilibrium strategies, that is, no matter what strategy the other players select. It follows that *subgame perfectness implies time consistency while the opposite is not true.*

Feedback strategies have the property of subgame perfectness[5] since they are computed by backward recursive methods (dynamic programming) and are thus independent of the initial date and the initial state.

Let us now examine in more detail the Nash and the Stackelberg equilibrium solutions.

8.3.1 The Nash equilibrium solution

By using the normal form description of the game the following definition can be given:

A strategy pair (γ_1^*, γ_2^*) constitutes a Nash equilibrium solution if and only if

$$\gamma_1^* = \arg \min_{\gamma_1 \in \Gamma_1} J_1(\gamma_1, \gamma_2^*) \tag{8.5}$$

$$\gamma_2^* = \arg \min_{\gamma_2 \in \Gamma_2} J_2(\gamma_1^*, \gamma_2) \tag{8.6}$$

We can see from (8.5) and (8.6) that the strategy chosen by each player is the *optimal response* to the strategy chosen by the other player, and vice versa. Therefore, γ_1^* is optimal for player 1 given that player 2 follows γ_2^*, while γ_2^* is optimal for player 2 given that player 1 follows γ_1^*. The Nash solution concept will be more easily understood by introducing the *reaction set* of each player. This set is defined for each $\gamma_j \in \Gamma_j$ by

$$R^i(\gamma_j) = \{\gamma_i^0 \in \Gamma_i : J_i(\gamma_i^0, \gamma_j) \leqslant J_i(\gamma_i, \gamma_j), \forall \gamma_i \in \Gamma_i\}, \quad i = 1, 2; \quad i \neq j \tag{8.7}$$

Set (8.7) defines all the strategies of player i which are optimal responses to each strategy of player j. The intersection of the reaction sets of the two players, if it exists, provides the Nash equilibrium strategies. If the reaction set of each player is a singleton, (8.7) defines a unique mapping $T_i : \Gamma_j \rightarrow \Gamma_i, i = 1, 2; i \neq j$. A Nash equilibrium solution will then be computed as a fixed point of the mapping (Basar, 1986)

$$\begin{aligned} \gamma_1 &= T_1(\gamma_2) \\ \gamma_2 &= T_2(\gamma_1) \end{aligned} \tag{8.8}$$

It follows that a Nash solution is an *equilibrium* concept since none of the players would benefit from unilaterally deviating from it: if one player follows a Nash strategy the best strategy for the other player is also a Nash strategy.

An important feature of the Nash equilibrium strategies is that they are computed without taking explicitly into account the reciprocal influence between the players' strategies. This means that player 1 optimizes his own objective function by considering the strategy of player 2 as independent of his own decisions, and vice versa. This conjecture is clearly inconsistent with the true behaviour of the players, since, as a matter of fact, player 2 *does* take into account the strategy of player 1 when computing his own strategy, and vice versa (on this point, see Johansen, 1982). The inconsistency of conjectures, which characterizes the Nash solution concept, is a very old problem, already pointed out by Fisher (1898), Bowley (1924), Frisch (1933) and von Stackelberg (1934) in connection with the Cournot solution. This feature of Nash strategies, which is often considered as a limit to this solution concept,[6] is also a reason why Nash equilibrium solutions in dynamic games can be derived by simply solving jointly two (or N) optimal control problems and why they, therefore, satisfy Bellman's principle of optimality; i.e. are *time consistent*.

Time consistency is an important feature of Nash equilibria (both open-loop and feedback) and it implies that Nash strategies maintain their Nash equilibrium property over the whole time horizon in which the game is played. It follows that no player will ever be tempted to revise his strategy during the game, since by reoptimizing his objective function at a new date he will simply obtain a truncated version of the optimal strategy calculated at the original date (see 8.4).

Let us now see how an *open-loop Nash* equilibrium strategy can be computed. The method we shall use is Pontryagin's minimum principle, as we did in chapter 5 for the computation of optimal control (single agent) strategies.

Consider again the state equation (8.1) which describes the law of motion of the system and the cost functionals defined by (8.2), that is

$$\dot{x}(t) = f[x(t), u_1(t), u_2(t), t] \tag{8.9}$$

and

$$J_i(u_1, u_2) = \int_{t_0}^{t_f} I_i[x(t), u_1(t), u_2(t), t] \, dt, \quad i = 1, 2 \tag{8.10}$$

Since the information structure is open-loop, the equilibrium strategy of player i will be of the form $\gamma_i^*(t, x_0) = u_i^*(t), t \in [t_0, t_f], i = 1, 2$. In order to obtain these strategies two Hamiltonians, one for each player, must be defined; therefore, omitting t for simplicity, we have

$$H^i(\lambda_i, x, u_1, u_2, t) = I_i(x, u_1, u_2, t) + \lambda_i' f(x, u_1, u_2, t) \tag{8.11}$$

$$t \in [t_0, t_f], \quad i = 1, 2$$

where $\lambda_i(t)$ is the costate vector for player i.

Assuming that the functions $f(\dots)$ and $I_i(\dots)$, $i = 1, 2$, satisfy appropriate conditions of continuity and differentiability, the following relations constitute a set of *necessary* conditions for an *open-loop* Nash solution

$$\dot{x}^*(t) = \frac{\partial H^i(\lambda_i, x^*, u_1^*, u_2^*, t)}{\partial \lambda_i} = f(x^*, u_1^*, u_2^*, t) \tag{8.12}$$

$$\dot{\lambda}_i(t) = -\frac{\partial H^i(\lambda_i, x^*, u_1^*, u_2^*, t)}{\partial x}, \quad (i = 1, 2) \tag{8.13}$$

$$u_1^*(t) = \arg \min_{u_1 \in S^1} H^1(\lambda_1, x^*, u_1, u_2^*, t) \tag{8.14}$$

$$u_2^*(t) = \arg \min_{u_2 \in S^2} H^2(\lambda_2, x^*, u_1^*, u_2, t) \tag{8.15}$$

given the boundary conditions (see section 5.6.3)

$$x^*(t_0) = x_0, \qquad \lambda_i(t_0) = 0, \quad (i = 1, 2) \tag{8.16}$$

where $u_i^*(t)$, $i = 1, 2$, is an open-loop Nash equilibrium strategy, and $x^*(t)$ is the corresponding equilibrium state trajectory.

If we also assume that $H^i(\lambda_i, x, u_1, u_2, t)$ is continuously differentiable and strictly convex on S^i ($i = 1, 2$) which is taken as an open set, relations (8.14) and (8.15) are respectively replaced by

$$\frac{\partial H^1(\lambda_1, x^*, u_1^*, u_2^*, t)}{\partial u_1(t)} = 0 \tag{8.17}$$

$$\frac{\partial H^2(\lambda_2, x^*, u_1^*, u_2^*, t)}{\partial u_2(t)} = 0 \tag{8.18}$$

Under the memoryless perfect state information pattern, account has to be taken – when computing the necessary conditions of the minimum principle (in particular, condition (8.13)) – of the fact that the strategies of the players depend also on the current state of the system. This implies introducing a partial derivative $(\partial u_j^*/\partial x)$ in the costate equation of player i ($i \neq j$), which makes the closed-loop Nash equilibrium solution very difficult (if not impossible) to obtain (see Fershtman and Kamien, 1985) and gives rise to (informationally) non-unique Nash equilibria (Basar and Olsder, 1982, chapter 6). In order to avoid informational non-uniqueness under the memoryless information pattern, the feedback Nash equilibrium solution should be computed, which, as we have seen, depends only on the current time and the current state; this solution, as mentioned above, has to be obtained by making use of dynamic programming methods. However, unlike the discrete-time case – where the computation of the feedback Nash equilibrium solution through dynamic programming can be, in general, easily obtained – in the continuous-time case the numerical computation of the feedback Nash solution requires the solving of a set of partial differential equations, whose solution is usually impossible unless discretization techniques are used (see Basar, 1986).

8.3.2 The Stackelberg equilibrium solution

As we have seen above, the Stackelberg equilibrium solution is a hierarchical solution concept where one of the players (the leader) has the ability to impose his strategy on the other player (the follower).

A pair of strategies (γ_1^*, γ_2^*) constitutes a Stackelberg equilibrium with player 1 as leader and player 2 as follower, if and only if (Basar, 1986)

$$\gamma_1^* = \arg \min_{\gamma_1 \in \Gamma_1} J_1[\gamma_1, T_2(\gamma_1)] \tag{8.19}$$

$$\gamma_2^* = T_2(\gamma_1^*) \tag{8.20}$$

$$T_2(\gamma_1) = \arg \min_{\gamma_2 \in \Gamma_2} J_2(\gamma_1, \gamma_2) \quad \forall \gamma_1 \in \Gamma_1 \tag{8.21}$$

This definition of a Stackelberg equilibrium implies the assumption that the reaction set of the follower defined for each $\gamma_1 \in \Gamma_1$ by (see (8.7))

$$R^2(\gamma_1) = \{\gamma_2^0 \in \Gamma_2 : J_2(\gamma_2^0, \gamma_1) \leqslant J_2(\gamma_2, \gamma_1), \forall \gamma_2 \in \Gamma_2\} \tag{8.22}$$

is a singleton, so that there is a unique mapping $T_2 : \gamma_1 \to \gamma_2$. If this is not the case, the leader may compute his equilibrium strategy by following a minimax approach in order to secure himself against the 'worst' choices of the follower. This *pessimistic* solution is defined as

$$\gamma_1^* = \arg \min_{\gamma_1 \in \Gamma_1} \sup_{\gamma_2 \in R^2(\gamma_1)} J_1(\gamma_1, \gamma_2) \tag{8.23}$$

$$\gamma_2^* \in R^2(\gamma_1^*) \tag{8.24}$$

On the contrary, the leader may expect the follower to make the 'best' choices. In this case, the *optimistic* Stackelberg solution is given by (Basar, 1989).

$$\gamma_1^* = \arg \min_{\gamma_1 \in \Gamma_1} \inf_{\gamma_2 \in R^2(\gamma_1)} J_1(\gamma_1, \gamma_2) \tag{8.25}$$

$$\gamma_2^* \in R^2(\gamma_1^*) \tag{8.26}$$

When the reaction set of the follower $R^2(\gamma_1)$ is a singleton, then the Stackelberg equilibrium solution leads to a situation for the leader which is *no worse* than that corresponding to any of the Nash solutions. This property may no longer hold when $R^2(\gamma_1)$ is not a singleton. As for the follower, his situation can be either better or worse than in any of the Nash equilibria.

The asymmetry which characterizes the Stackelberg solution concept leads to a sequential mode of play. This sequentiality may manifest itself in two different ways, which produce two different types of strategies:

(a) *Global strategies*, which refer to the case in which the leader announces his *whole* course of action (from t_0 to t_f) at the beginning of the game. This case may cover both open-loop and closed-loop strategies. However, it is not possible to compute global closed-loop Stackelberg solutions in dynamic infinite games, such as the ones here considered, by using standard techniques and, in any case, they can only be obtained under very special assumptions.

(b) *Stagewise strategies*, which refer instead to the case in which the leader announces his strategy at each stage of the game. These strategies are assumed to be of the *feedback* type, so that the players know, at each t, the current state and time. Feedback stagewise Stackelberg equilibrium solutions were first introduced by Simaan and Cruz (1973a, b) in the discrete-time framework and then extended to the continuous-time framework by Basar and Haurie (1984). Feedback stagewise strategies can be obtained by using dynamic programming methods, although a rigorous definition in the continuous-time framework can be provided only if the continuous-time feedback strategies are considered as the limit of the corresponding discretized version (see Friedman, 1971; Basar and Haurie, 1984).

It can easily be observed from the definition of the Stackelberg solution concept that, unlike the Nash solution, one player (the leader) takes into account the influence of his strategy on that of the other player (the follower), but not vice versa: that is, the follower, as in the Nash solution concept, considers the leader's strategy as independent of his own decisions. As a consequence of this assumption, the optimization problem of the follower is simply an optimal control problem and his Stackelberg equilibrium strategy is therefore *time consistent*.

On the contrary, the property of time consistency does not generally apply to the leader's strategy. In fact, when the *global* solution is computed, the optimization problem of the leader is not, as we shall see, a standard optimal control problem, and his global strategy is *time inconsistent*: the leader will be tempted to recompute his strategy at each time $s, t_0 < s \leqslant t_f$. It follows that this type of solution characterizes an equilibrium between the players only when the leader pre-commits himself to the announced strategy.

An intuitive explanation of the time inconsistency of the leader's *global* equilibrium strategy is the following: when the leader computes his equilibrium strategy at time t_0, he takes into account the effect that his strategy at *each* $t \in [t_0, t_f]$ will have on the follower's strategy. But if the leader's strategy is computed again at a subsequent moment of time $s \in (t_0, t_f]$ he will take into account only the effect of his strategy on the follower's decisions after s – that is, on the decisions corresponding to each time $t \geqslant s$ – since the decisions of the follower corresponding to $t < s$ are already a given at $t = s$ (on this point see also the single-agent optimization problem described in sections 10.2 and 10.3). The optimal strategy computed at t_0 will therefore be different from that obtained from the truncated game starting at s: relation (8.4) does not hold for the leader's strategy (we shall take up this point again at the end of this section).

On the other hand, the feedback *stagewise* strategy of the leader is time consistent by construction, since it is calculated by using dynamic programming. This method does not make it possible to take thoroughly into account the effects that the strategy of the leader has on that of the follower, effects that we have just described in the previous paragraph (this point will be more closely examined in chapter 10, section 10.2.1). Furthermore, since, as we have already mentioned, dynamic programming is a backward recursive method, it is independent of the initial time and the initial state. It follows that the *Stackelberg feedback stagewise equilibrium strategies*, both of the follower and of the leader, are *time consistent* and *subgame perfect*. As mentioned above, the computation of the Stackelberg feedback equilibrium solution in continuous time still presents, in general, a number of unresolved problems.[7]

Another type of time-consistent Stackelberg solution can be obtained by assuming a closed-loop information pattern with memory. In this case, the leader can formulate threats or incentives in order to force the follower to the team-optimal solution to his own benefit[8] (see Basar and Selbuz, 1979; Papavassilopoulos and Cruz, 1980; Tolwinski, 1981; Zheng *et al.*, 1984; Ehtamo and Hämäläinen, 1986 among others).

Let us now examine the way to obtain the *Stackelberg open-loop* (global) equilibrium solution. As for the Nash solution, we shall follow Pontryagin's minimum principle. Consider again the state equation

$$\dot{x}(t) = f[x(t), u_1(t), u_2(t), t] \tag{8.27}$$

and the cost functionals

$$J_i(u_1, u_2) = \int_{t_0}^{t_f} I_i[x(t), u_1(t), u_2(t), t]\, dt, \quad i = 1, 2 \tag{8.28}$$

and assume that the functions $f(\ldots)$ and $I_i(\ldots)$ satisfy the required conditions of continuity and differentiability.

Since the follower (player 2) derives his optimal strategy by considering the strategy of the leader as independent of his own decisions, his problem is similar to that of a player in a Nash game, and his Hamiltonian is therefore defined by (see 8.11)

$$H^2(\lambda_2, x, u_1, u_2, t) = I_2(x, u_1, u_2, t)$$
$$+ \lambda_2' f(x, u_1, u_2, t), \quad t \in [t_0, t_f] \tag{8.29}$$

where $\lambda_2(t)$ is the costate vector for the follower.

Assuming as above that $H^2(\lambda_2, x, u_1, u_2, t)$ is continuously differentiable and strictly convex on S^2 (which is taken as an open set), there exists a function $\lambda_2(t)$ such that the following relations are satisfied (see Basar, 1980)

$$\dot{x}(t) = \frac{\partial H^2(\lambda_2, x, u_1, u_2^0, t)}{\partial \lambda_2} = f(x, u_1, u_2^0, t) \tag{8.30}$$

$$\dot{\lambda}_2(t) = -\frac{\partial H^2(\lambda_2, x, u_1, u_2^0, t)}{\partial x} \tag{8.31}$$

$$\frac{\partial H^2(\lambda_2, x, u_1, u_2^0, t)}{\partial u_2(t)} = 0, \quad t \in [t_0, t_f] \tag{8.32}$$

$$x(t_0) = x_0, \qquad \lambda_2(t_f) = 0 \tag{8.33}$$

where $u_2^0 \in U^2$ denotes an optimal response of the follower to any given strategy $(u_1 \in U^1)$ of the leader.

The leader also minimizes his objective function, but under the constraints given, not only by the dynamics of the state, but also by the necessary conditions of the optimization problem of the follower, which, as we have seen above, are known to him and are explicitly taken into account. We further assume that there exists a unique $u_2^0 \in U^2$ under which the set of equations (8.30–8.33) is satisfied for each given $u^1 \in U^1$. The Hamiltonian function of the leader is therefore given by

$$\begin{aligned}
H^1 = I_1(x, u_1, u_2, t) &+ \lambda_1' f(x_1, u_1, u_2, t) \\
&+ u'[-\nabla_x H^2(\lambda_2, x, u_1, u_2, t)] \\
&+ v'[\nabla_{u_2} H^2(\lambda_2, x, u_1, u_2, t)], \quad t \in [t_0, t_f]
\end{aligned} \tag{8.34}$$

where $\lambda_1(t)$, $\mu(t)$ are costate vectors corresponding to the constraints (8.27) and (8.31), and $v(t)$ is the vector of Lagrange multipliers associated with the equality constraint (8.32).

Then, under suitable differentiability conditions, if $u_i^*(t)$ $(i = 1, 2)$ is an open-loop Stackelberg solution with player 1 as leader and $x^*(t)$ is the corresponding state trajectory, there exist continuously differentiable functions $\lambda_1(t)$, $\lambda_2(t)$, $\mu(t)$ and a continuous function $v(t)$ such that the following relations are satisfied:

$$\dot{x}^*(t) = \frac{H^1(\lambda_1, \lambda_2, \mu, v, x^*, u_1^*, u_2^*, t)}{\partial \lambda_1} = f(x^*, u_1^*, u_2^*, t) \tag{8.35}$$

$$\dot{\lambda}_2(t) = \frac{\partial H^1(\lambda_1, \lambda_2, \mu, v, x^*, u_1^*, u_2^*, t)}{\partial \mu} \tag{8.36}$$

$$\dot{\lambda}_1(t) = -\frac{\partial H^1(\lambda_1, \lambda_2, \mu, \nu, x^*, u_1^*, u_2^*, t)}{\partial x} \tag{8.37}$$

$$\dot{\mu}(t) = -\frac{\partial H^1(\lambda_1, \lambda_2, \mu, \nu, x^*, u_1^*, u_2^*, t)}{\partial \lambda_2} \tag{8.38}$$

$$\frac{\partial H^2}{\partial u_2(t)}\bigg|_{u_2 = u_2^*(t)} = 0 \tag{8.39}$$

$$\frac{\partial H^1}{\partial u_1(t)}\bigg|_{u_1 = u_1^*(t)} = 0 \tag{8.40}$$

with boundary conditions

$$x^*(t_0) = x_0, \qquad \mu(t_0) = 0, \qquad \lambda_1(t_f) = 0, \qquad \lambda_2(t_f) = 0 \tag{8.41}$$

However, as we have just seen, the equilibrium strategy of the leader $u_1^*(t)$ will be different if recomputed at a subsequent moment of time $s\,(t_0 < s \leqslant t_f)$. The mathematical reason for the time-inconsistency problem can easily be understood if we observe that the leader's optimization is not a standard optimal control problem. The leader's optimality conditions contain two state vectors: $x(t)$ and the follower's costate vector $\lambda_2(t)$ and, therefore, the initial value of the 'state' vector $\lambda_2(t)$ is not predetermined as in the standard case. On the contrary, since it is optimal to select the initial value of the corresponding costate $\mu(t)$ equal to zero, the initial value of $\lambda_2(t)$ will be (optimally) determined in each single case in such a way that its corresponding costate vector satisfies $\mu(t_0) = 0$ (see Miller and Salmon, 1985a; Pohjola, 1986).

But since $\mu(t)$ evolves according to (8.38), it is clearly unlikely that $\mu(s) = 0$ for any $s > t_0$. However, if the leader reoptimizes at a subsequent time s, the initial value of the 'state' vector $\lambda_2(s)$ will again be such that the corresponding costate $\mu(t)$ satisfies $\mu(s) = 0$. Consequently, the optimal trajectory of the costate vector $\mu(t)$ obtained at the initial time t_0 will be different from the one obtained at a subsequent time $s\ (s > t_0)$, thus giving rise to the time inconsistency of the leader's optimal strategy.

Conversely, the follower's equilibrium strategy is time consistent: once the leader has computed and announced his strategy, the follower simply substitutes it into (8.30)–(8.33) in order to obtain his optimal response. He therefore solves a standard optimal control problem and consequently his strategy is time consistent, *given* the optimal strategy of the leader.

8.4 The linear-quadratic case

As we have already seen when dealing with single agent (optimal control) problems, objective functions of policy-makers are often assumed to be quadratic. This type of function can be considered as a second-order approximation of a more general objective function and presents many properties that are useful in applied work, as we have seen in chapter 6.

When dynamic game theory is used for policy analysis, it is often assumed – as in the case of centralized planning – that each policy-maker wants to keep the trajectory of his target variables as close as possible to a given desired path during a given time interval. Also, as in the optimal control case, planners usually wish to avoid large deviations of their policy instruments (control variables) from given pre-assigned values, in order to prevent these instruments from taking on values that might be unrealistic or unsustainable from an economic point of view. All these assumptions can be taken into consideration by using quadratic loss (or cost) functions whose main features have been thoroughly examined in sections 6.4 to 6.6, and to which we refer the reader.

Assuming, as above, two different decision-makers (player 1 and player 2) let us now consider the following linear state equation and quadratic cost functional[9]

$$\dot{x}(t) = Ax(t) + B_1 u_1(t) + B_2 u_2(t) \tag{8.42}$$

$$J_i(u_1, u_2) = \frac{1}{2} \int_{t_0}^{t_f} (\bar{x}_i' Q_i \bar{x}_i + \bar{u}_i' R_{ii} \bar{u}_i + \bar{u}_j' R_{ij} \bar{u}_j) \, \mathrm{d}t \quad (i = 1, 2) \tag{8.43}$$

System (8.42) describes the dynamic economic model considered, which, for simplicity, is assumed time invariant; $x(t) \in R^n$ and $u_i(t) \in R^{r_i}$ $(i = 1, 2)$. Bars over the variables indicate, as usual, deviations from ideal values, that is $\bar{x}_i(t) = x(t) - x_i^p(t)$ and $\bar{u}_i(t) = u_i(t) - u_i^p(t)$, $(i = 1, 2)$. $Q_i(t)$, $R_{ii}(t)$ and $R_{ij}(t)$ are symmetric matrices of appropriate dimensions; in particular, matrices $Q_i(t)$ represent the weights assigned by player i to deviations of the state variables from the corresponding ideal paths $(Q_i(t) \geqslant 0)$, matrices $R_{ii}(t)$ represent the weights assigned by player i to deviations of its *own* control variables from the corresponding ideal paths $(R_{ii}(t) > 0)$ and matrices $R_{ij}(t)$ represent the weights assigned by player i to deviations of the control variables of player j from given pre-specified trajectories $(R_{ij}(t) \geqslant 0)$, $i \neq j$. Matrices R_{ij} are irrelevant in the computation of open-loop Nash strategies, since, as we have seen, player i does not consider the possibility of influencing player j with his own strategy. These matrices are important, on the contrary, in the computation of the Stackelberg (leader) strategy.

We assume the weighting matrices to be time varying, so that deviations corresponding to different moments of time can be differently penalized (see section 6.6).

Let us now see how to compute the Nash and the Stackelberg equilibrium solutions by again following Pontryagin's minimum principle.

(i) *The Nash equilibrium solution*
In this case, the Hamiltonian of the two players will be defined by

$$H^i = \tfrac{1}{2}(\bar{x}'_i Q_i \bar{x}_i + \bar{u}'_i R_{ii} \bar{u}_i + \bar{u}'_j R_{ij} \bar{u}_j) + \lambda'_i(Ax + B_1 u_1 + B_2 u_2),$$
$$i = 1, 2 \quad t \in [t_0, t_f] \tag{8.44}$$

Since the optimization problem is linear quadratic, the necessary conditions defined by (8.12)–(8.15) are also sufficient. Therefore the Nash equilibrium strategies of the two players can be obtained by solving simultaneously

$$\dot{x}^*(t) = \frac{\partial H^i}{\partial \lambda_i} = Ax^* + B_1 u_1^* + B_2 u_2^* \tag{8.45}$$

$$\dot{\lambda}_1(t) = -\frac{\partial H^1}{\partial x} = -Q_1 \bar{x}^* - A' \lambda_1 \tag{8.46}$$

$$\dot{\lambda}_2(t) = -\frac{\partial H^2}{\partial x} = -Q_2 \bar{x}^* - A' \lambda_2 \tag{8.47}$$

$$\frac{\partial H^1}{\partial u_1} = R_{11} \bar{u}_1^* + B'_1 \lambda_1 = 0 \tag{8.48}$$

$$\frac{\partial H^2}{\partial u_2} = R_{22} \bar{u}_2^* + B'_2 \lambda_2 = 0 \tag{8.49}$$

given the boundary conditions

$$x(t_0) = x_0, \qquad \lambda_i(t_f) = 0, \quad i = 1, 2 \tag{8.50}$$

Since we have assumed $R_{11} > 0$ and $R_{22} > 0$, conditions (8.48)–(8.49) define a minimum of (8.44) (see section 5.8).

It can be observed that, if we substitute $u_1^*(t)$ and $u_2^*(t)$ obtained from (8.48) and (8.49) into (8.45), the problem is reduced to solving a system of linear differential equations with two-point boundary conditions, whose solution provides the equilibrium trajectories of the state and costate variables. Furthermore, as we have seen in chapter 5 for the optimal control case (see section 5.9), the costate vector $\lambda_i(t)$ can be written as a function of $x(t)$ of the form

$$\lambda_i(t) = M^i(t)x^*(t), \quad i = 1, 2; \quad t \in [t_0, t_f] \tag{8.51}$$

where $M^i(t)$ are $(n \times n)$-dimensional matrices which satisfy the so-called *coupled matrix Riccati equations*. As with the optimal control problem, the

Nash equilibrium strategies can also be computed, in the linear-quadratic case, by solving a set of $n(n+1)/2$ non-linear differential equations of the Riccati type for each player (we refer the reader to Basar and Olsder, 1982, appendix to chapter 6, for a description of these equations).

(ii) The Stackelberg equilibrium solution

Since, as we have seen in the previous section, the follower considers the strategy of the leader as independent of his own decisions, his Hamiltonian (assuming, as above, that player 1 acts as leader and player 2 as follower) will be given by

$$H^2 = \tfrac{1}{2}(\bar{x}_2' Q_2 \bar{x}_2 + \bar{u}_2' R_{22} \bar{u}_2 + \bar{u}_1' R_{21} \bar{u}_1)$$
$$+ \lambda_2'(Ax + B_1 u_1 + B_2 u_2), \quad t \in [t_0, t_f] \tag{8.52}$$

and the set of equations (8.30)–(8.32) reduce to

$$\dot{x}(t) = \frac{\partial H^2}{\partial \lambda_2} = Ax + B_1 u_1 + B_2 u_2^0 \tag{8.53}$$

$$\dot{\lambda}_2(t) = -\frac{\partial H^2}{\partial x} = -Q_2 \bar{x}_2 - A' \lambda_2 \tag{8.54}$$

$$\frac{\partial H^2}{\partial u_2} = R_{22} \bar{u}_2^0 + B_2' \lambda_2 = 0 \tag{8.55}$$

From (8.55) we get

$$\bar{u}_2^0(t) = -R_{22}^{-1}(t) B_2' \lambda_2(t) \tag{8.56}$$

Since the leader takes into account the optimal reaction of the follower, his Hamiltonian will be defined by

$$H^1 = \tfrac{1}{2}[\bar{x}_1' Q_1 \bar{x}_1 + \bar{u}_1' R_{11} \bar{u}_1 + (\lambda_2' B_2 R_{22}^{-1}) R_{12} (R_{22}^{-1} B_2' \lambda_2)]$$
$$+ \lambda_1'(Ax + B_1 u_1 - B_2 R_{22}^{-1} B_2' \lambda_2 + B_2 u_2^D)$$
$$+ \mu'(-Q_2 \bar{x}_2 - A' \lambda_2), \quad t \in [t_0, t_f] \tag{8.57}$$

where (8.56) has been directly substituted into the leader's Hamiltonian. Thus relations (8.35)–(8.41) are now given by

$$\dot{x}^*(t) = \frac{\partial H^1}{\partial \lambda_1} = Ax^* + B_1 u_1^* - B_2 R_{22}^{-1} B_2' \lambda_2 + B_2 u_2^D \tag{8.58}$$

$$\dot{\lambda}_2(t) = \frac{\partial H^1}{\partial \mu} = -Q_2 \bar{x}_2^* - A' \lambda_2 \tag{8.59}$$

$$\dot{\lambda}_1(t) = -\frac{\partial H^1}{\partial x} = -Q_1 \bar{x}_1^* - A' \lambda_1 + Q_2 \mu \tag{8.60}$$

$$\dot{\mu}(t) = -\frac{\partial H^1}{\partial \lambda_2} = -B_2 R_{22}^{-1} R_{12} R_{22}^{-1} B_2' \lambda_2 + B_2 R_{22}^{-1} B_2' \lambda_1 + A\mu \tag{8.61}$$

$$\frac{\partial H^1}{\partial u_1} = R_{11} \bar{u}_1^* + B_1' \lambda_1 = 0 \tag{8.62}$$

with boundary conditions

$$x^*(t_0) = x_0, \qquad \mu(t_0) = 0, \qquad \lambda_1(t_f) = 0, \qquad \lambda_2(t_f) = 0 \tag{8.63}$$

Since $R_{11} > 0$, $R_{22} > 0$, (8.55), (8.62) define a minimum of H^2 and H^1 respectively.

From the solution of this system it is possible to obtain the state and costate trajectories and the leader's equilibrium strategy $u_1^*(t)$, $t \in [t_0, t_f]$. In order to obtain the follower's equilibrium strategy $u_2^*(t)$, we simply substitute the solution obtained for $\lambda_2(t)$ into (8.56). (See the next chapter for an application of the Nash and Stackelberg solution concepts just described.)

As for the Nash equilibrium solution, the open-loop Stackelberg strategies can also be obtained, in the linear-quadratic case, by solving the corresponding coupled matrix Riccati equations.

It is also possible to obtain the coupled matrix Riccati equations the solution of which should provide both the Nash and the Stackelberg *feedback* equilibrium strategies. A description of these equations in the continuous-time framework and with reference to the feedback Nash solution can be found in Basar and Olsder (1982, appendix to chapter 6), while, with reference to the feedback Stackelberg solution, it can be found in Basar and Haurie (1984, section 5). However, given the existing software available today, it is not possible to obtain the numerical solution of these non-linear differential equations, which finite horizon differential games give rise to, when more than one state variable is considered. Computational difficulties are reduced in the infinite horizon case since, as we have seen in section 5.10, optimal feedback rules then become constant rules: the matrix Riccati equations are, in this case, static equations. However, the infinite horizon approach does not seem to provide a realistic description of the process of policy decision and, furthermore, other different problems arise in this case which need to be correctly addressed; as, for example, those concerning the stability of the controlled system and the finiteness of the objective functionals (see Basar, 1986).

8.5 Bargaining theory and cooperative solutions

A cooperative mode of play is suitable for describing

situations involving two individuals whose interests are neither completely opposed nor completely coincident. The word 'cooperative' is used because the two individuals are supposed to be able to discuss the situation and agree on a rational joint plan of action, an agreement that should be assumed to be enforceable. (Nash, 1953, p. 128)

This is the kind of situation that we intend to analyse in this section. We assume therefore that the players can communicate and reach agreements which are binding and enforceable by the rules of the game.

Evidently, when both players are willing to cooperate, many different agreements can in theory be reached; this is where the problem of bargaining arises.

Two main different approaches to bargaining have been proposed in the literature:

(i) *The strategic approach*, where a *dynamic* bargaining process is explicitly described and where the negotiation between the players takes place in the context of a non-cooperative game (Rubinstein, 1982; see also Binmore, Rubinstein and Wolinsky, 1985).

(ii) *The axiomatic approach*, which goes back to Nash (1950, 1953) and where, unlike the strategic approach, no bargaining process is considered. This approach is therefore static in nature and, as a matter of fact, describes a solution rather than a bargaining process (see Roth, 1979, for a survey of the axiomatic models).

This limitation, however, should not obscure the interest of this approach and of the solutions based on it. Furthermore, the explicit description of a bargaining process may be unnecessary if the existence of an arbitrator is assumed. This arbitrator, to whom the players submit their conflict, is supposed to propose a solution and to solve the bargaining problem. When this assumption is made, cooperative solutions based on the axiomatic approach are called 'arbitration schemes'.

An arbitration scheme can be defined as 'a function . . . which associates to each conflict . . . a unique payoff to the players. This payoff is interpreted as the arbitrated or compromised solution of the game' (Luce and Raiffa, 1957, p. 121). The axiomatic approach then consists in setting a precise set of axioms that any acceptable arbitration scheme may fulfil and in looking for those arbitration schemes which satisfy those axioms. The axioms should be based on assumptions of rationality and should restrict the domain of the arbitrating schemes, so that it is possible to end up with only one scheme which satisfies the given axioms.

Cooperative games were first introduced in the realm of *static* games, but the main concepts can easily be extended to the framework of *dynamic* games by considering the payoffs (or costs) of the players as those referring to the whole time horizon during which the game evolves. However, there is a problem that assumes greater importance in a dynamic context: the problem of 'cheating', that is, of unilateral deviation from the agreement. In general, each player can improve his situation (i.e. obtain a lower cost) by playing a different strategy while the other player sticks to the agreement. Consequently, a cooperative solution may not have the characteristics of an equilibrium, and, in that case, the only way to guarantee respect for the agreement over time is to make it binding. The assumption of a higher authority or arbitrator becomes thus fundamental in order to enforce the agreement.

An alternative to this assumption is to consider dynamic cooperative games with memory. It is then possible for each player to introduce *retaliation threats* into the formulation of their strategy, the strategies so defined being called *trigger strategies* (Radner, 1980). If the pair of threats is effective the players will never deviate from the agreement and the cooperative solution can thus be considered an equilibrium. This type of cooperative equilibria was first introduced by Friedman (1971, 1977) in the framework of supergames, and then developed by Rubinstein (1979) and Radner (1980). Cooperative equilibria in dynamic (differential and discrete) games have been studied in particular by Haurie and Tolwinski (1984, 1985, 1990) and by Tolwinski, Haurie and Leitmann (1986), to which we refer the reader.

Since a detailed description of the different approaches to bargaining is outside the scope of this chapter, the reader interested in this topic is referred to Friedman, 1986, where an exhaustive discussion of cooperative games can be found. For a discussion of cooperative equilibria in dynamic games, the reader is referred to Haurie and Tolwinski (1984, 1985, 1990).

In what follows we shall focus on two cooperative solutions which are the ones most often used in applied macroeconomics and are based on the axiomatic approach. We refer to the *Nash* and the *Kalai–Smorodinsky* bargaining solutions.

In the set of axioms on which these solutions are based, an important axiom that every cooperative solution must satisfy is *Pareto optimality*. Cooperative solutions that meet this requirement can be obtained by assuming that the two players minimize the weighted sum function

$$J(\gamma_1, \gamma_2) = \beta J_1(\gamma_1, \gamma_2) + (1 - \beta)J_2(\gamma_1, \gamma_2) \qquad (8.64)$$

with respect to $\gamma_1(t)$ and $\gamma_2(t)$, and for different values of β such that $0 < \beta < 1$. The solutions thus obtained are *Pareto optimal*, i.e.:

If for any pair of strategies (γ_1, γ_2)

$$J_i(\gamma_1, \gamma_2) \leqslant J_i(\gamma_1^*, \gamma_2^*) \quad \text{for} \quad i = 1, 2 \tag{8.65}$$

implies

$$J_i(\gamma_1, \gamma_2) = J_i(\gamma_1^*, \gamma_2^*) \quad i = 1, 2 \tag{8.66}$$

then (γ_1^*, γ_2^*) is *Pareto optimal*. This means that no solution exists which dominates the Pareto solution. A Pareto solution has also the property that no player can improve his outcome without worsening the situation of his opponent. In our case: no player can reduce his cost function without increasing the cost of the other player.

The Pareto optimal solutions obtained by minimizing (8.64) can also be derived within the dynamic setting considered in the previous sections simply by substituting J_1 and J_2 in (8.64) with the intertemporal objective functionals defined in (8.10), that is

$$J(\gamma_1, \gamma_2) = \beta \int_{t_0}^{t_f} I_1[x(t), \gamma_1(t), \gamma_2(t), t] \, dt$$

$$+ (1 - \beta) \int_{t_0}^{t_f} I_2[x(t), \gamma_1(t), \gamma_2(t), t] \, dt \tag{8.67}$$

and then by minimizing (8.67), given the state dynamics (8.9). The minimization of (8.67) can be solved simply by computing an optimal control solution for each β $(0 < \beta < 1)$.

Pareto optimality is also known in bargaining theory as *group rationality* since it would be irrational for the players (as a group) to cooperate on a non-Pareto optimal point. By moving to a Pareto solution the situation of at least one player can improve without damaging the situation of the other players.

However, by varying the value of β in (8.64), a *set* of Pareto optimal solutions may be obtained. Therefore, Pareto optimality is not sufficient to single out a unique cooperative solution. Other axioms should be considered that we shall briefly describe in the following two sub-sections, where the Nash (section 8.5.1) and the Kalai–Smorodinsky (section 8.5.2) bargaining models will be illustrated.

8.5.1 The Nash bargaining model

Before introducing the Nash bargaining model (Nash, 1953) it is important to define:

(a) the set $H \subset R^2$ of all attainable outcomes of the game called an *attainable set*. This set is assumed to be compact and convex in the (J_1, J_2) plane.

(b) the *status-quo* point $T \in H$, whose coordinates (J_1^T, J_2^T) represent the outcomes that the players would obtain in the case of no agreement. This point is also called the *threat point* since it represents the threat that each player can make to the other player if the latter does not accept the proposed agreement. T is obviously a result of non-co-operative behaviour and is a basic element in bargaining theory. It is assumed that both players know each other's threat.

Given these two elements, we can now proceed to the description of the Nash bargaining solution.

Besides satisfying Pareto optimality, the Nash bargaining solution must also satisfy the following four axioms[10] (see Luce and Raiffa, 1957, chapter 6, and Friedman, 1986, chapter 5, for details):

(i) individual rationality,
(ii) invariance with respect to utility (affine) transformations,
(iii) symmetry,
(iv) independence of irrelevant alternatives.

Axiom (i) states that, if a player behaved rationally, he would never accept an agreement the outcome of which would be worse than the one he could obtain by acting independently. As we shall see in figure 8.1, the axiom of *individual* rationality restricts the domain of the solutions that

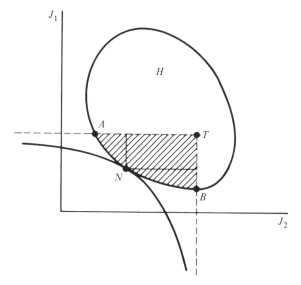

Figure 8.1 The Nash solution

satisfy the axiom of *group* rationality (Pareto optimality) to a smaller set called the *negotiation set*, but this still is not sufficient to single out a unique solution: there may be many Pareto efficient solutions the outcomes of which dominate the non-cooperative ones.

Axiom (ii) reflects the principle of non-comparability of utilities and imposes the condition that the solution of the bargaining game should be invariant to positive affine transformations of the objective functions, i.e. to changes in the scale and in the origin of these functions.

Axiom (iii) requires that, if initially the players have completely symmetric roles, the outcomes of the bargaining solution should also be symmetric; i.e., the players should obtain equal values of their payoff functions, the unit of measurement being the same as that which initially made the game symmetric.

Finally, axiom (iv) means that if the attainable set H is reduced to a new set H' that still contains the solution point of the original game, then this point will still be the solution of the new game, provided that the status quo remains unchanged.

The simultaneous verification of these axioms makes it possible to find a unique solution of the bargaining game, given the assumption that the attainable set H is compact and convex.

We can now see how the Nash bargaining solution is obtained. A figure will be useful for this purpose (see figure 8.1). Let H be the attainable set and $T(J_1^T, J_2^T)$ the status quo or threat point. The axiom of individual rationality reduces the domain of the solutions to the shaded area of H; Pareto optimality further reduces this domain to the *negotiation set S* defined by the segment AB. The Nash bargaining solution is a point N on the negotiation set, with coordinates (J_1^*, J_2^*), such that the product of the gains obtained from agreement (with reference to the threat point) is maximized, i.e.

$$(J_1^* - J_1^T)(J_2^* - J_2^T) = \max_{(J_1, J_2) \in S} (J_1 - J_1^T)(J_2 - J_2^T) \qquad (8.68)$$

Since the rectangular hyperbole which are asymptotic to the broken lines through T have the property that the product $(J_1 - J_1^T) \cdot (J_2 - J_2^T)$ is constant, the point of S at which this product is maximized must be the point of tangency of the set S with the lowest rectangular hyperbola that touches it. This point, indicated by N in figure 8.1, is the Nash bargaining solution.

It can be observed from figure 8.1, that, by connecting N with the broken lines TA and TB, a rectangle is obtained whose sides are precisely $(J_1^T - J_1^*)$ and $(J_2^T - J_2^*)$. The Nash solution can also be interpreted as that point on the AB segment which yields the largest rectangle from T.

The solution thus obtained simultaneously satisfies the set of axioms stated above (see Friedman, 1986, for a demonstration).

8.5.2. The Kalai–Smorodinsky bargaining model

Like the Nash bargaining model, the Kalai–Smorodinsky (KS) model (Kalai and Smorodinsky, 1975) is based on a set of axioms that an agreement between the players must satisfy. These axioms include those already defined for the Nash solution, except for axiom (iv) – independence of irrelevant alternatives[11] – which is not satisfied by the KS solution. Instead, a new axiom is introduced: (v) *Individual monotonicity*, which (roughly) states that, if the set of attainable outcomes H is increased in such a way that player i has the possibility to attain a better outcome while the situation of player j remains the same, the outcome of player i resulting from the solution of the new game should improve, provided that the status quo remains unchanged (see Kalai and Smorodinsky, 1975, and Kalai, 1977, for further details).

An important feature of the KS model is that it is based on two reference points: the *status quo* and another point, the *ideal point*, which represents the best outcome available for each player that is consistent with individual rationality. That is the best point that each player can reach without making the situation of the other player worse than in the status quo.

The coordinates (J_1^I, J_2^I) of the ideal point, I, are defined as

$$J_i^I = \min_{\gamma_1, \gamma_2} J_i(\gamma_1, \gamma_2) \tag{8.69}$$

such that

$$J_j(\gamma_1, \gamma_2) \leqslant J_j^T, \quad i, j = 1, 2, \quad i \neq j, \quad \gamma_1 \in \Gamma_1, \quad \gamma_2 \in \Gamma_2 \tag{8.70}$$

The KS solution is the one which satisfies Pareto optimality and axioms (i)–(ii)–(iii) and (v). This solution must also satisfy the following condition

$$\frac{J_2^* - J_2^T}{J_1^* - J_1^T} = \frac{J_2^I - J_2^T}{J_1^I - J_1^T} \tag{8.71}$$

where J_1^* and J_2^* are the outcomes of the KS solution.

Equation (8.71) simply means that the solution lies on the line which connects the ideal point I with the status quo T, and states that the gain that each player receives from the agreement (with reference to the status quo) is proportional to the gain that he would obtain from the ideal point, with the proportionality constant being the same for both players.

Geometrically the KS solution is defined by the point at which the line connecting the ideal point with the status quo intersects the negotiation set

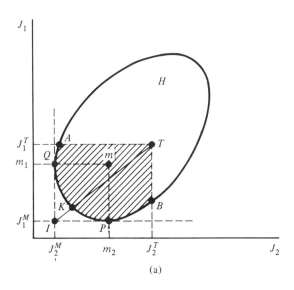

(a)

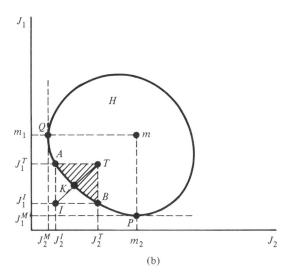

(b)

Figure 8.2   The Kalai–Smorodinsky solution

(see figure 8.2). The intuitive idea behind this solution can be deduced from
the work of Raiffa (1953), who had originally suggested it: the ideal point
represents that ideal situation which the players would like to reach, but
which is not simultaneously attainable by both of them. The two players

will therefore move from the status quo – which is considered as the initial point of the bargaining process – *towards* the ideal point. This process will lead the players to move along the line which goes from the status quo to the ideal point, until they reach the best attainable point on this line, i.e. the intersection with the negotiation set.

The KS solution concept will be clearer if we examine figures 8.2(a) and 8.2(b), which differ in the position of the status quo. Point T in figure 8.2(a) lies over point m – whose meaning we shall now explain – whereas it lies under m in figure 8.2(b). Therefore, point m dominates T in figure 8.2(a), while it is dominated by T in figure 8.2(b). This difference is important, as we shall see, for the determination of the ideal point.

Let us first consider figure 8.2(a). As before, H represents the attainable set and T the status quo or threat point. The shaded area represents the set of points which are individually rational. Point Q represents the best attainable point for player 2; in fact, J_2^M is the minimum attainable cost that he can get. Point P is analogously defined for player 1. Since both points Q and P are also individually rational (they belong to the shaded area under T), J_1^M and J_2^M represent the coordinates J_1^I, J_2^I of the ideal point I. This point is generally not attainable.

Once the ideal point has been determined, it only remains to draw a line from T to I. The intersection of this line with the segment QP provides the KS solution indicated by K in the diagram.

Let us now consider the meaning of point m which is called the point of *minimal expectations*. The coordinate m_1 of this point is the lowest cost that player 1 can obtain when player 2 gets J_2^M. An equivalent definition applies for m_2. The set of attainable points defined by the two coordinates of m on the frontier of set H (segment QP in both figures) is the set of attainable points which are also Pareto optimal. Segment PQ in figure 8.2(a) therefore represents the negotiable set, that is the set of points which satisfy both individual and group rationality. The KS solution must thus lie on this set.

Figure 8.2(b) is obviously similar. However, the point of minimal expectations m lies over the status quo and, therefore, the points on the PQ segment are Pareto optimal but *do not* satisfy the axiom of individual rationality. In fact P and Q lie outside the shaded area under T (which means that player 1 will be worse off in Q than in T and that player 2 will be worse off in P than in T). Therefore J_1^M and J_2^M cannot represent, as they did before, the coordinates of the ideal point. In this case, the best attainable point for player 1, which also satisfies individual rationality is point B, while point A is the best for player 2. The coordinates of the ideal point will therefore be given by J_1^I, J_2^I in figure 8.2(b). The negotiable set, in this case, is given by the segment AB, on which the KS solution must lie. Of course, mixed situations may occur in which one player is better off at m than at

T while the other is worse off. In those cases the determination of I is straightforward and we leave it as an exercise to the reader.

The solution that simultaneously satisfies the KS axioms defined above and condition (8.71) exists and is *unique* (see Kalai and Smorodinsky, 1975; Friedman, 1986, for a demonstration).

9 Applications of differential games*

9.1 Decentralized fiscal and monetary policies

In chapter 7 optimal control methods were applied to a continuous-time econometric model, alternative optimal policies were obtained and the outcomes of those policies compared. However, as we have already stressed in section 8.1, the optimal control approach to policy analysis implies the assumption that decision-making is centralized or that the political institutions charged with planning always act in complete harmony. This assumption may be appropriate in some particular situations or with reference to particular historical periods; it may also be justified as a simplifying assumption which makes it possible for policy-makers to obtain important insights as to the economic effects of alternative policies in a simpler way than with other, more sophisticated and complicated tools.

However, a common feature of most industrialized countries is the co-existence of different political institutions which separately participate in the decision-making process. A typical situation is that in which the Treasury (which, for simplicity, we shall call 'the Government') and the Central Bank manage fiscal and monetary policies independently.

Since both institutions can affect the performance of the economy through their own decision variables, it is essential for each policy-maker to take into account all possible interactions between his decisions and those of the other and this interdependence can only be analysed by the use of game theory methods. Furthermore, since we are here interested in intertemporal planning – i.e. we are concerned with the evolution of the economic system over time – the appropriate mathematical tools are those provided by dynamic game theory.

The aim of this chapter is to illustrate how differential game methods, like those examined in chapter 8, can be effectively applied in economic policy

*The results presented in this chapter have been taken from Petit (1989a) and Hughes Hallett and Petit (1988b).

analysis. For this purpose, we shall consider the same continuous-time econometric model of the Italian economy described in section 7.2, but we shall now assume that policy decisions are taken by two different political institutions: the Government and the Central Bank.

Some features of continuous-time models have already been illustrated in sections 1.4 and 7.1; we recall in particular the advantage of obtaining continuous-time paths for the control and state variables. The problems refer mainly to the continuous-time techniques available, that often involve tedious computations, even if the econometric model is not too large. As already stressed in section 7.1, most of the simplifying assumptions made in this chapter are due to computational problems. However, since we shall not be dealing with these topics again, we refer the reader to the above mentioned sections for further details.

We wish to stress that, unlike some recent work on decentralized policies in continuous time,[1] we here apply differential games to a macro-econometric model *estimated* in continuous time. We also note that the problems highlighted in sections 5.14–5.16 – referring to the economic implications of the use of optimal control techniques – also extend to the use of differential games in the case of decentralized policy-making.

The problem of decentralized policy design will be here examined in a linear-quadratic framework, that is, making use of the linearized version of the model and assuming quadratic objective functions for the policy-makers. We shall consider both the situation in which the two political institutions cooperate and that in which there is no cooperation between them. A comparison of the different solutions will be made and the gains from coordinating fiscal and monetary policies will be evaluated by considering not only the different values of the cost functions of the two policy-makers but also other indicators which are of particular importance where macroeconomic analysis is concerned.

9.2 The model and the institutional background

The econometric model that we shall use in this chapter is specified as a system of stochastic differential equations. A description of this model has already been provided in section 7.2 and its equations and estimates have been summarized in the Appendix to chapter 7. Further details can be found in Gandolfo and Padoan (1984). In what follows, we shall assume that both political institutions make use of the same econometric model.[2]

Since the dynamic-game exercises that we shall perform refer to the period 1977–81, it may be of interest first to have a look at the institutional situation in Italy during that period. This will help us to better understand the type of decision-making mechanism that characterized policy design in those years and the particular interconnections that existed between the two decision-making institutions.

Until 1981 the Bank of Italy was obliged to buy all the public bonds which the Italian Treasury was unable to sell elsewhere. Faced with very substantial budget deficits in the 1970s, this requirement severely restricted the ability of the Bank of Italy to follow any kind of independent monetary policy. The inflationary and trade deficit consequences made the undesirability of this arrangement all too obvious, but the Government bankruptcy which would have followed any refusal to fund the budget deficit was ruled out as unacceptable. The upshot of these policies was a series of speculative attacks on the Italian lira and increasing difficulty in maintaining this accommodating policy given the financial innovations of that period, the EMS, and increased capital mobility. The first change was to offer Treasury bills to the public in 1976. That gave the Bank of Italy the opportunity to try to control the growth in the monetary base by operating in the secondary debt market.

By 1977 the main holders of debt were the public rather than the banking system, and the Bank of Italy had managed to gain a limited degree of control over monetary growth through open market operations. However, monetary policy was still subordinate to the Government's fiscal policy, since the Bank of Italy was still obliged to buy any unsold bonds and the Treasury was still creating large fiscal deficits to be funded – particularly large at this stage since the Government had undertaken an aggressive policy of promoting growth and employment creation to counteract the world recession of 1979/81. The typical scenario was therefore one in which the Government created a large growth in the monetary base by issuing debt, underwritten by the Central Bank's obligation to fund the fiscal deficit, while the Central Bank then did what it could to destroy that monetary growth by open market operations in order to protect its targets of inflation and external balance.[3] Thus the 1977–81 period represents a classic case of non-cooperative policy-making driven by the need to attain different and conflicting objectives, although the Government dominated because it could force the Central Bank to accept any fiscal debt strategy.

However, all this changed with the 1981 'divorce', when the Bank of Italy was freed from its obligation to buy any unsold Treasury bonds. The non-cooperative policy mechanism described above was obviously inefficient, with the two policy-makers simply pushing against each other in a vain attempt to achieve their own targets. The consequences of the Government's unrestrained fiscal strategy were becoming increasingly obvious and unpopular, with inflation, frequent devaluations of the lira within the EMS, external trade deficits, high interest rates and capital controls. The 'divorce' was seen as a positive step for reducing these problems and for increasing the political authorities' sensitivity to some of the other targets of economic policy. In principle, the Bank of Italy and the Government could now choose between following a fully non-cooperative approach or they could agree to cooperate across the range of targets pursued by both institutions – but either way the Bank of Italy was able to create its own monetary policy (concentrating now on monetary control and interest rates) and the Government was obliged to adopt a more disciplined fiscal policy. In practice, however, the Government has retained something of a leading role in policy formation, since it is allowed to set – in accordance with the Bank of Italy – a minimum price for bonds in the public debt auctions.

This agreement clearly limits the Central Bank's freedom to operate an independent monetary policy and that leaves the Government with a stronger role in the policy process (which corresponds with the empirical results that we shall present in section 9.5). This is the case (to some degree) in many other countries, because of the need to fund and/control fiscal deficits. Indeed Pohjola (1986) argues that it has been found that the fiscal authorities have a leading role in most studies of decentralized policy-making.

9.3 The policy problem

Applications of dynamic game methods to *econometric* models for purposes of policy analysis are not yet very frequent[4] and they all concern discrete-time models; the techniques used are therefore those that characterize discrete-time optimization problems. Since we here consider a continuous-time econometric model, we shall use continuous-time optimization techniques, as we have already done in Chapter 7; therefore, Pontryagin's minimum principle will again be applied.

The use of this method in order to obtain the different equilibrium solutions of differential games has already been illustrated in chapter 8. Therefore, we need now only to apply those techniques to our policy problem. The computer program that we shall use is 'Continest' by C.R. Wymer.

In what follows we shall assume an open-loop information pattern so that, given the initial state, the equilibrium strategies are only functions of time. We have already stressed the limitations of this assumption in chapter 8. As we also saw in that chapter, our choice is due to the computational difficulties which make it impossible to obtain feedback strategies for continuous-time models of the dimension of the one we use here (see also Basar, 1986). However, in the specific policy problem that we are considering, an advantage of open-loop strategies should be emphasized:

since policy planning in Italy usually refers to short or medium-term periods, feedback rules could not be taken as stationary. Therefore, from the point of view of practical implementation, it may be easier for policy-makers to know in advance the time path of the policy variables rather than to deal with complicated (time-varying) rules.[5]

The general form that a continuous-time model may assume has already been illustrated in section 7.4 (equation 7.2), to which we refer the reader. As we have also seen in that section, linearization and transformation into state-space form makes it possible to deal with the following model

$$\dot{x}(t) = Ax(t) + B_1 u_1(t) + B_2 u_2(t) + Cz(t) \tag{9.1}$$

where $x(t)$ is the vector of state variables, $z(t)$ is the vector of non-control exogenous variables, $u_1(t)$ is the vector of control variables for policy-maker 1, $u_2(t)$ is the vector of control variables for policy-maker 2, and A, B and C are constant matrices of the required dimensions.

Each policy-maker chooses an optimal strategy for his own control variables over the given time period $[t_0, t_f]$ so as to minimize its own cost functional. Evidently, when policy decisions are decentralized, the objective functions of the policy-makers might differ. The targets, the priorities assigned to them, and the ideal paths that each policy-maker would like his targets to follow might be different. We shall therefore define two objective functions: the objective function of the Government and the objective function of the Central Bank.

We assume that the targets considered by the Government are output growth and inflation, with higher priority given to growth over inflation, whereas the main targets of the Central Bank are inflation and the balance of payments (in particular the level of international reserves), with higher priority given to inflation over reserves. For the sake of simplicity, we also assume that the ideal path of inflation (which is the only common target) is the same for both policy-makers.

As regards the control variables, we make the usual assumption that the Government is responsible for fiscal policy (public expenditure) and that the Central Bank is responsible for monetary policy (rate of growth of the money supply). The optimal control exercises carried out in chapter 7 by making use of the same econometric model have shown that these are the most effective policy instruments as regards the Italian economy (see, in particular, section 7.5).

The time horizon considered goes from the first quarter of 1977 to the last quarter of 1981. Our differential game exercises are 'in sample' exercises (1981 being the last year of the sample period considered in estimation) and might therefore be interpreted as 'what the Government and the Central Bank could have done'. The period 1977–81, as we have seen in section 9.2, covers the emerging decentralization of Italian policy making, and is therefore particularly suitable for examining policy problems under non-cooperation and cooperation.

We therefore assume that the objective function of the Government (player 1) is defined by the following quadratic cost functional

$$J_1 = \int_{1977}^{1981} \{w_{Y1}[\log Y(t) - \log Y^D(t)]^2 + w_{P1}[\log P(t) - \log P^D(t)]^2$$
$$+ w_{G1}[\log G(t) - \log G^D(t)]^2\} \, dt \qquad (9.2)$$

while the objective function of the Central Bank (player 2) is defined as

$$J_2 = \int_{1977}^{1981} \{w_{P2}[\log P(t) - \log P^D(t)]^2 + w_{R2}[\log R(t) - \log R^D(t)]^2$$
$$+ w_{m2}[m(t) - m^D(t)]^2\} \, dt \qquad (9.3)$$

The dynamic evolution of the economic system considered is described by a macroeconometric model of 20 differential equations which is represented by (9.1).

The ideal paths are defined as

$$\log Y^D(t) = \log Y(t_0) + 0.01t, \quad \log P^D(t) = \log P(t_0) + 0.02t,$$
$$\log R^D(t) = \log R(t_0) + 0.01t, \quad m^D(t) = 0.03$$
$$\log G^D(t) = \log G(t_0) + 0.01t,$$

$t_0 = 1976\text{–}I\hat{V}$, and the weights are

$$w_{Y1} = 2.0, \quad w_{P1} = 1.0, \quad w_{G1} = 1.0$$
$$w_{P2} = 2.0, \quad w_{R2} = 1.5, \quad w_{m2} = 1.0$$

The symbols have the following meanings:

P = domestic price level,
Y = real net domestic product and income,
R = nominal stock of international reserves,
m = proportional rate of change of money supply,
G = public expenditure in real terms.

Ideal paths correspond to EEC averages over the same period (see section 7.3 for details). As for the weights, they have simply been taken from those obtained in section 7.3 and slightly modified in a direction consistent with the actual relative priorities of the Government and the Central Bank during the period considered. It is important to note that the sensitivity of the results to changes in relative priorities is much higher in the cooperative than in the non-cooperative case, as shown in the exercises reported in section 9.9, where the sensitivity of the inflation-growth outcomes to changes in the corresponding priorities has been examined.

The objective functions described by (9.2) and (9.3) can be written in the more familiar form

$$
J_i = \int_{t_0}^{t_f} \{ [x(t) - x_i^P(t)]' Q_i [x(t) - x_i^P(t)]
$$

$$
+ [u_i(t) - u_i^P(t)]' R_{ii} [u_i(t) - u_i^P(t)] \} \, dt, \quad i = 1, 2 \tag{9.4}
$$

where the matrices Q_i are constant and diagonal, R_{ii} are, in this case, positive scalars, and the matrices R_{ij} defined in section 8.4 have been set equal to zero for simplicity. As specified above, $u_1(t) = \log G(t)$ and $u_2(t) = m(t)$.

Given the political situation prevailing in Italy during the period considered (see the previous section), the Stackelberg equilibrium solution with the Government as leader seems an appropriate solution concept to describe the non-cooperative case. The Nash non-cooperative solution and the cooperative solutions will also be computed in order to examine the consequences of a more independent monetary policy and of policy coordination respectively. The Nash non-cooperative solution has the advantage – over other symmetric solution concepts such as Consistent Conjectural Variations (CCV) – of computational tractability in continuous time (see chapter 8, footnote 6).

The cooperative case will be analysed by considering the Nash and the Kalai–Smorodinsky bargaining solutions described in section 8.5. The increased cost to each policy-maker, resulting from the non-cooperative mode of play, makes it possible to quantify the sub-optimality deriving from conflict. The non-cooperative Nash solution can be taken as a status-quo point from which the gains from cooperation may be measured. However, other indicators should be taken into account when comparing cooperative and non-cooperative situations. In particular we shall consider here the behaviour of targets and instruments (and of the economy taken as a whole) and the different speeds of convergence of the system towards equilibrium under the different (cooperative and non-cooperative) strategies. We shall also consider the modifications in the optimal inflation-output combinations which take place under non-cooperation.

9.4 The non-cooperative solutions

We assume, in this case, that there is no possibility of agreement between the two policy-makers considered, so that the problem that the Government has to solve is to minimize its objective function (9.2) with respect to its decision variable $G(t)$, while the problem that the Central Bank has to solve is to minimize its objective function (9.3) with respect to its decision variable $m(t)$, under the constraint of the dynamic model (9.1).

It is important to stress that each player makes his own policy decisions, taking into account current and *future* decisions of the other player (see Lucas and Sargent (1981), and chapter 10 of the present volume). Therefore, the Government decision regarding public expenditure at time t depends not only on monetary policy at time t, but also on monetary policy at time s $(t \leqslant s \leqslant t_f)$; on the other hand, the Central Bank decision regarding the rate of growth of money supply at time t depends not only on public expenditure at time t but also on public expenditure at time s $(t \leqslant s \leqslant t_f)$.

We shall first consider Nash equilibrium strategies. As we have seen in chapter 8, in this case the Government minimizes its objective function by taking the strategy of the Central Bank as independent of its own decisions, and vice versa. The open-loop Nash equilibrium solution therefore consists of the optimal paths $G^N(t)$ and $m^N(t)$, $t \in [t_0, t_f]$, such that $G^N(t)$ is optimal for the Government, given that the Central Bank follows $m^N(t)$, while $m^N(t)$ is optimal for the Central Bank, given that the Government follows $G^N(t)$, during the time interval considered. Assuming, as above, that the Government is player 1 and the Central Bank player 2, the optimal decisions $u_1^N(t), u_2^N(t)$ will satisfy $J^{(i)}[u_i^N(t), u_j^N(t)] \leqslant J^{(i)}[u_i(t), u_j^N(t)]$, $i = 1, 2$, and all feasible $u_i \neq u_i^N$.

To obtain this solution, we shall follow Pontryagin's minimum principle as described in section 8.4, point (i). We therefore define the two Hamiltonians corresponding to the Government and to the Central Bank. Considering the matrix form introduced in (9.4) we define the Government Hamiltonian

$$H^1 = \bar{x}_1'(t)Q_1\bar{x}_1(t) + R_{11}\bar{u}_1^2(t) + \lambda_1'(t)[Ax(t)$$
$$+ B_1 u_1(t) + B_2 u_2(t) + Cz(t)] \tag{9.5}$$

and the Central Bank Hamiltonian

$$H^2 = \bar{x}_2'(t)Q_2\bar{x}_2(t) + R_{22}\bar{u}_2^2(t) + \lambda_2'(t)[Ax(t)$$
$$+ B_1 u_1(t) + B_2 u_2(t) + Cx(t)] \tag{9.6}$$

where $\lambda_1(t)$ and $\lambda_2(t)$ are the costate vectors. The bars over the variables indicate, as usual, deviations from the ideal paths.

The Nash equilibrium solution can then be obtained by solving the following system of equations simultaneously

$$\dot{x}(t) = \frac{\partial H^i}{\partial \lambda_i} = Ax + B_1 u_1 + B_2 u_2 + Cz, \quad i = 1, 2 \tag{9.7}$$

$$\dot{\lambda}_1(t) = -\frac{\partial H^1}{\partial x} = -2Q_1 \bar{x}_1 - A' \lambda_1 \tag{9.8}$$

$$\dot{\lambda}_2(t) = -\frac{\partial H^2}{\partial x} = -2Q_2 \bar{x}_2 - A' \lambda_2 \tag{9.9}$$

$$\frac{\partial H^1}{\partial u_1} = 2R_{11} \bar{u}_1 + B'_1 \lambda_1 = 0 \tag{9.10}$$

$$\frac{\partial H^2}{\partial u_2} = 2R_{22} \bar{u}_2 + B'_2 \lambda_2 = 0 \tag{9.11}$$

$$x(t_0) = x_0 \tag{9.12}$$

$$\lambda_i(t_f) = 0, \quad (i = 1, 2)$$

Since our problem is a linear-quadratic one, equations (9.7) to (9.11) constitute a set of sufficient conditions for an open-loop Nash solution. Therefore, after substituting $u_1(t)$ and $u_2(t)$ obtained from (9.10) and (9.11) into (9.7), the problem is essentially that of solving a system of 60 differential equations (9.7)–(9.8)–(9.9) with the two-point boundary conditions (9.12). From the solution of this system we obtain the Nash equilibrium strategies for the two decision variables $G^N(t), m^N(t)$ and the corresponding target trajectories.

In order to calculate the Stackelberg equilibrium solution, we also follow Pontryagin's minimum principle as described in section 8.4, point (ii). We assume that the Government acts as leader and the Central Bank as follower; consequently, the Government is aware that the strategy of the Central Bank depends on its own strategy and knows the form of this dependence, that is, the reaction function of the Central Bank. The Government therefore minimizes its objective function by taking this reaction into account.

Since the Central Bank is the follower, we shall consider its Hamiltonian first, which is defined by

$$H^2 = \bar{x}'_2 Q_2 \bar{x}_2 + R_{22} \bar{u}_2^2 + \lambda'_2 (Ax + B_1 u_1 + B_2 u_2 + Cz) \tag{9.13}$$

The first-order conditions for the follower are

$$\dot{x}(t) = \frac{\partial H^2}{\partial \lambda_2} = Ax + B_1 u_1 + B_2 u_2 + Cz \tag{9.14}$$

$$\dot{\lambda}_2(t) = -\frac{\partial H^2}{\partial x} = -2Q_2\bar{x}_2 - A'\lambda_2 \tag{9.15}$$

$$\frac{\partial H^2}{\partial u_2} = 2R_{22}\bar{u}_2 + B'_2\lambda_2 = 0 \tag{9.16}$$

and, from (9.16), we obtain

$$u_2(t) = -2R_{22}^{-1}B'_2\lambda_2 + u^D \tag{9.17}$$

The leader's Hamiltonian is given by

$$H^1 = \bar{x}'_1 Q_1 \bar{x}_1 + R_{11}\bar{u}_1^2 + \lambda'_1(Ax + B_1 u_1 - 2B_2 R_{22}^{-1}B'_2\lambda_2$$
$$+ B_2 u_2^D + Cz) + \mu'(-2Q_2\bar{x}_2 - A'\lambda_2) \tag{9.18}$$

which reflects the fact that – as we have seen in section 8.3.2 – the leader's optimization problem is constrained, not only by system (9.1), but also by the optimality conditions of the follower, that is by (9.17) – which has been directly substituted into (9.18) – and by (9.15), which defines the dynamics of the costate vector of the follower.

The Stackelberg equilibrium solution for the leader can thus be obtained by solving the following system of equations

$$\dot{x}(t) = \frac{\partial H^1}{\partial \lambda_1} = Ax + B_1 u_1 - 2B_2 R_{22}^{-1}B'_2\lambda_2 + B_2 u_2^D + Cz \tag{9.19}$$

$$\dot{\lambda}_2(t) = \frac{\partial H^1}{\partial \mu} = -2Q_2\bar{x}_2 - A'\lambda_2 \tag{9.20}$$

$$\dot{\lambda}_1(t) = -\frac{\partial H^1}{\partial x} = -2Q_1\bar{x}_1 - A'\lambda_1 + 2Q_2\mu \tag{9.21}$$

$$\dot{\mu}(t) = -\frac{\partial H^1}{\partial \lambda_2} = B_2 R_{22}^{-1}B'_2\lambda_1 + A\mu \tag{9.22}$$

$$\frac{\partial H^1}{\partial u} = 2R_{11}\bar{u}_1 + B'_1\lambda_1 = 0 \tag{9.23}$$

$$x(t_0) = x_0$$
$$\mu(t_0) = 0 \tag{9.24}$$
$$\lambda_i(t_f) = 0, \quad (i = 1, 2)$$

Equations (9.19) to (9.23) constitute a set of sufficient conditions for an open-loop Stackelberg solution. Since, as we have seen, the econometric model is described by a set of 20 state equations, the problem now consists in solving a system of 80 differential equations (9.19)–(9.20)–(9.21) and (9.22) with two-point boundary conditions (9.24), after substituting $u_1(t)$ obtained from (9.23) into (9.19). From the solution of this system, we obtain the state and costate trajectories and the leader's equilibrium strategy $u_1^s(t), t \in [t_0, t_f]$. Then, to obtain the follower's equilibrium strategy $u_2^s(t)$ it is enough to substitute the solution obtained for $\lambda_2(t)$ into (9.17). The Stackelberg strategy for the leader $u_1^s(t)$ will satisfy $J_1[u_1^s(t), T^2 u_1^s(t)] \leqslant J_1[u_1(t), T^2 u_1(t)]$ for all feasible $u_1(t) \neq u_1^s(t)$, where $T^2 u_1^s(t)$ is the (unique) optimal response of the follower to the leader's strategy.

As we have seen in chapter 8 the equilibrium strategy of the leader is time inconsistent: the Government will be tempted to reoptimize in future moments of time. However, changing the announced strategy will give rise to problems of credibility (or reputation) *vis-à-vis* the Central Bank, which may act as a deterrent against the temptation to change policies (see, for example, Barro and Gordon, 1983; Rogoff, 1984, 1987). In what follows, we shall assume for simplicity that the Government pre-commits itself to the time-inconsistent strategy announced.

9.5 Fiscal and monetary policy coordination

In this section we analyse a situation in which the Government and the Central Bank wish to reach an agreement on economic planning so that future policy actions may be the result of cooperation between the two political institutions. It is therefore assumed, in this case, that the two players are able to communicate and to start a bargaining process until an agreement is reached.

Since the approach that we shall follow here is the axiomatic approach (see section 8.5), we shall not consider how the bargaining process evolves but we shall only focus on the type of solution finally reached by considering both the Nash and the Kalai–Smorodinsky (KS) bargaining models as described in sections 8.5.1 and 8.5.2 respectively.

Since, as we have seen in chapter 8, an axiom that both solutions must satisfy is Pareto optimality, the first step is to compute a set of cooperative solutions that satisfy this axiom. These solutions are the result of the minimization, with respect to the two control variables $u_1(t)$, $u_2(t)$, of the following function

$$J(u_1, u_2) = \beta J_1(u_1, u_2) + (1 - \beta)J_2(u_1, u_2), \quad (0 < \beta < 1) \tag{9.25}$$

where J_1 and J_2 are the objective functions of the Government and of the Central Bank respectively.

The minimization of (9.25) for all values of β $(0 < \beta < 1)$ under the constraint of the dynamic model (9.1) provides the set of Pareto-efficient solutions. We therefore simply need to substitute the two objective functions (9.2) and (9.3) into (9.25) and solve a standard optimal control problem for each value of β from 0.1 to 0.9. By then calculating the different values of the objective function of the two players for each value of β, we can plot them on a diagram in order to obtain the so-called Pareto-optimal frontier in the space of realized outcomes J_1, J_2, as shown by the line CC in figure 9.1.

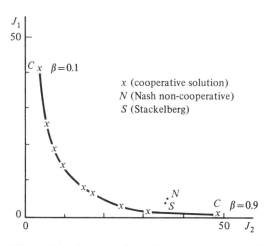

Figure 9.1   Cost frontier and non-cooperative solutions

Points N and S on the same diagram represent the outcomes obtained by the Nash and the Stackelberg non-cooperative equilibrium solutions respectively. The Nash non-cooperative equilibrium solution is taken as the status-quo or threat point. Each player can threaten to follow the non-cooperative strategy if the other player does not agree to cooperate.

As we have seen in sections 8.5.1 and 8.5.2, another axiom that both the Nash and the KS bargaining solutions must satisfy is that of individual rationality, i.e., the bargaining solution must dominate the non-cooperative one. The satisfaction of this axiom restricts the set of Pareto-efficient points to the *negotiation set* (segment AB on the CC line of figure 9.2). It appears clear that other points on the CC line outside this area represent a gain for one player (with respect to the non-cooperative outcome), but a loss for the other player. Neither policy-maker would agree to cooperate if the outcomes that he could obtain were worse than those he could obtain by acting in isolation. The position of the threat point reflects the relative power of each player in the negotiation, so that the stronger player may be able to influence the negotiation in his own interest (i.e. impose a relatively higher weight on his own objective function). The values of β which are obtained

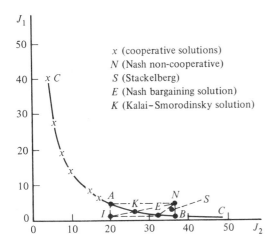

Figure 9.2   Nash and Kalai–Smorodinsky bargaining solutions

from the Nash and from the KS bargaining solutions depend, as we have seen in chapter 8, on the position of the threat point.

In our case – as can be seen from figures 9.1 and 9.2 – the Government is in a stronger position than the Central Bank; it can credibly threaten to follow the non-cooperative strategy, since by acting in isolation it still obtains a very low value for its objective function in relation to the outcomes that it can obtain with cooperation.[6] On the other hand, if the Central Bank follows the non-cooperative strategy, it obtains a very high relative value for its objective function and therefore it is not in a good position to make credible threats. The Government can therefore push the Central Bank into coordinating policies in a way which is clearly more advantageous to the former.

Evidently by coordinating monetary and fiscal policies both policy-makers may be better off (though the gains from cooperation are not very high), provided that they remain inside the AB segment. Therefore, if a bargaining process takes place between the Goverment and the Central Bank, they would both agree on a value of β between 0.74 and 0.83, which are the values of β which correspond to the cooperative outcomes represented by the points A and B respectively. It is obvious that the Government will prefer to agree to a value of β close to 0.83 while the Central Bank will prefer a value of β close to 0.74. All that remains therefore, at this stage, is to define the value of β.

By following the Nash axiomatic approach we obtain the Nash bargaining solution which corresponds to a value of β equal to 0.80 (point E in figure 9.2); this means that relative bargaining power is distributed 4 to 1 in favour of the Government.

A similar result is obtained by following the KS axiomatic approach (see section 8.5.2) since the KS bargaining solution corresponds to a value of β equal to 0.78, which confirms the stronger bargaining power of the Government with respect to the Central Bank. Figure 9.2 illustrates the construction of the KS solution, following the same procedure already described in section 8.5.2. Point I corresponds to the ideal point – which is obviously not attainable by both players simultaneously – while point K represents the KS bargaining solution (as can be easily seen, this case corresponds to figure 8.2(b) in chapter 8).

9.6 Macroeconomic policy implications

The results obtained call our attention to two main policy implications of the analysis. First, consider the values of the objective functions of the two policy-makers which are obtained with the different strategies. These values, already discussed in section 9.5 and represented graphically in figure 9.1, are also summarized in table 9.1. Only the values of J_1 and J_2 corresponding to $\beta = 0.2$, 0.5, 0.78 (Kalai–Smorodinsky) and 0.8 (Nash bargaining solution) are reported as representative of the cooperative solutions, together with the non-cooperative outcomes corresponding to the Nash and Stackelberg equilibrium solutions (points N and S respectively in figure 9.1).

An examination of both figure 9.1 and table 9.1 reveals the relatively low costs obtained by the Government with the Nash and Stackelberg non-cooperative solutions and the relatively high costs for the Central Bank. The Government loses from cooperation in all cases, except for $0.74 \leqslant \beta \leqslant 1$, while the Central Bank gains from cooperation in all cases, except for $0.83 \leqslant \beta \leqslant 1$ (see figure 9.2).

This result is not surprising: given the informational assumptions underlying the Nash and Stackelberg non-cooperative solutions, the Government knows the objective function of the Central Bank and knows that the latter is obliged to follow a restrictive monetary policy in order to achieve its two objectives on inflation and reserves. But inflation is also one of the two objectives of the Government and besides, in the framework of the Italian model considered here, a lower rate of inflation can give rise, through demand mechanisms, to higher output growth which is the Government's second objective. It should be remembered, by looking at the equations of the econometric model (Appendix to chapter 7, table A.7.1), that a restrictive monetary policy has favourable effects on inflation and

Table 9.1   *Values of the objective functions under different strategies*

	Policy institution	
Strategies	Government (J_1)	Central Bank (J_2)
Cooperative		
$\beta = 0.2$	24.98	5.57
$\beta = 0.5$	6.78	15.82
$\beta = 0.78$ (KS)	1.88	28.88
$\beta = 0.8$ (Nash)	1.18	32.01
Non-cooperative		
Nash	2.16	36.43
Stackelberg	2.09	35.69

that the lower rate of inflation has, in turn, a stimulating effect on demand and, through demand, on output (on this point, see section 7.5 and Hughes Hallett and Petit (1988a and c)).

The Government, therefore, is not particularly concerned to cooperate, since it knows that in any case the Central Bank will try to bring down inflation and this also coincides directly and indirectly with its own interests. By acting in isolation, the Government can thus focus on higher growth through an appropriate use of fiscal policy. The greater bargaining strength of the Government in this policy game therefore depends heavily on the economic mechanisms described by the econometric model and on the assumptions made as to the policy-maker's objectives. This stronger position of the Government with respect to the Central Bank leads to a situation in which the former will agree to coordinate policies only after imposing very unfavourable conditions on the latter (i.e. $\beta \simeq 0.8$).

However, non-cooperative solutions are not Pareto efficient, and therefore both political institutions may be better off by cooperating[7] on the set of non-dominated solutions defined in section 9.5. There will be an incentive to cooperate provided that this takes place on a point of the *AB* segment (figure 9.1). The gains obtained from policy coordination are however rather limited and their distribution undetermined: cooperating at point *E* (Nash bargaining solution) gives higher gains for the Government (45 per cent against 12 per cent) whereas gains are higher for the Central Bank (21 per cent against 13 per cent) if cooperation takes place at *K* (Kalai–Smorodinsky solution). Once cooperation has been established we assume that both players pre-commit themselves to the agreed-upon strategies. In any case the temptation to reoptimize and to 'cheat' the other player will be discouraged not only by a possible loss of reputation, but also by the threat of a return to non-cooperative strategies that would clearly put both players in a worse situation (see, for example, Haurie and Tolwinski, 1984, 1985).

A second kind of policy implication must now be highlighted. In macro-economic policy analysis it is not enough to derive the gains from coopera-tion simply by comparing the values of the pay-off functions of the players. Other elements should be considered: for example, the performance of the economy under the different (cooperative and non-cooperative) strategies.

This performance is represented graphically in figure 9.3. Only the trajectories of the target and control variables have been given. This does not mean that the overall behaviour of the model has not been considered, but only that is not described here for lack of space. The figures are expressed in logarithms, except for m which is the rate of growth of the money supply M ($m = D \log M$).

We have confined our attention to three representative solutions, the Nash and Stackelberg non-cooperative solutions and the cooperative solutions corresponding to $\beta = 0.8$, that is, the Nash bargaining solution.

By examining figure 9.3 it can be seen that it is not possible to single out the solution which gives rise to the 'best' target performances. The Nash (and Stackelberg) non-cooperative solutions give better results for output growth and inflation, while the best results for reserves are obtained in the case of cooperation. However, a negative feature of the non-cooperative solutions should be noted: the pronounced fluctuations in the behaviour of the targets, in particular of prices and international reserves.

It can also be observed that, in all cases considered, the results differ significantly from the solution of the model (base-run) in the same period. The base-run rate of inflation was 12.5 (average value), the base-run rate of growth of output was 3.2 per cent (average value) and the base-run rate of growth of reserves was 11.9 per cent (average value) in the period considered; the results obtained by assuming an optimizing behaviour of the two political institutions (both cooperative and non-cooperative) are much more satisfactory; they succeed in bringing inflation down to 7.8 per cent (average value) and in bringing the rate of growth of output and the rate of growth of reserves up to 8.4 per cent and to 18.6 per cent (average value), respectively (figures which correspond to the Nash bargaining solution, $\beta = 0.8$). The poor performance of the Italian economy in the period considered[8] cannot therefore be attributed to the lack of coordina-tion between the two political institutions; even in the non-cooperative cases the results obtained are in fact superior to those corresponding to the base-run. The unsatisfactory performance of the Italian economy must therefore be attributed to the use of non-optimal policies (see Gandolfo and

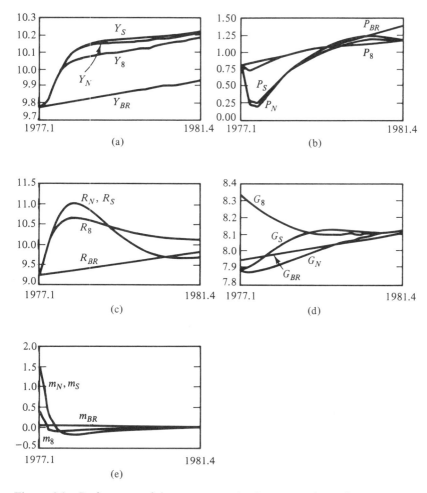

Figure 9.3 Performance of the economy under the cooperative and non-cooperative strategies
(a) Output
(b) Price level
(c) Reserves
(d) Public expenditure
(e) Rate of growth of the money supply
Note: The subscripts *BR* denotes the base run results. The subscript
8 denotes the cooperative solution for $\beta = 0.8$. The subscript
N denotes the non-cooperative Nash solution and the subscript
S denotes the non-cooperative Stackelberg solution (Government leader).

Petit, 1987). Optimal policies, even when decentralized and carried over in isolation, give rise to much better outcomes.

Let us now turn briefly to the trajectories of the policy instruments $G(t)$ and $m(t)$. It should be noted that the less expansionary fiscal policy is the one which corresponds to the non-cooperative solutions, in particular, the Nash non-cooperative strategy. It is this strategy that requires lower values of public expenditure. As regards monetary policy, only the non-cooperative solutions give rise to a decidedly worse situation when compared with the cooperative strategy, requiring sharp variations in m and, on the whole, a more restrictive monetary policy. Both fiscal and monetary policy are therefore more restrictive in the non-cooperative cases.

At this point the striking similarity between the non-cooperative Nash and Stackelberg solutions should be noted, both as regards the performance of the targets and the values of the cost functions. The only significant differences are those concerning fiscal policy, since lower values of public expenditure are required if the Government plays a Nash strategy. Therefore, the only element that might induce the Government to assume the leadership of the policy game is the opportunity of following a more expansionary policy, as was the case over the period considered.

Finally, a further element which should be taken into account when analysing the gains from cooperation is the speed of adjustment of the economic system to equilibrium. It is possible – once the stability conditions are satisfied, as is the case here – to examine the speed of convergence of the system simply by observing the lowest eigenvalues, since they correspond to the system's spectral radius which determines the rate of asymptotic convergence.

An examination of these eigenvalues shows a lower speed of adjustment to equilibrium when the policy-makers follow non-cooperative strategies, confirming Cooper's (1969a) argument that policy coordination attenuates the transitory effects of external shocks more rapidly. In the case of co-operative strategies, the speed of adjustment increases as the bargaining power of the Government increases and, therefore, as that of the Central Bank decreases (see table 9.2, where the minimum value of the eigenvalues is reported for each solution considered).

The greater strength of the Government to impose its own objectives seems therefore to give stability to the system, as shown by the speeds of convergence obtained in the different cooperative cases.

In conclusion, the inefficiency of the non-cooperative solutions with respect to the cooperative one shows itself not only in higher values of the cost functions of the players, but also in the fluctuating behaviour of the targets, in the more restrictive policies required and in the lower speed of convergence of the system. Therefore, even if the difference in the values of

Table 9.2 *Minimum negative eigenvalues*

	Cooperative solutions								
	$\beta=0.9$	$\beta=0.8$	$\beta=0.7$	$\beta=0.6$	$\beta=0.5$	$\beta=0.4$	$\beta=0.3$	$\beta=0.2$	$\beta=0.1$
Eigenvalue	-2.282	-1.763	-1.599	-1.537	-1.521	-1.494	-1.484	-1.478	-1.473

	Non-cooperative solutions	
	Nash	Stackelberg
Eigenvalue	-1.4703	-1.4704

the cost functions is not large enough to push the players towards cooperation, the other drawbacks of non-cooperative actions seem to be serious enough to induce the political institutions to coordinate their policies.

Needless to say, the results obtained should be interpreted with caution, since they are, as usual, strictly dependent on the macroeconometric model used and on the objective functions assumed to represent the preferences of the two political institutions. However, the analysis of the consequences of different policy strategies is important: as Neese and Pindyck (1984) rightly emphasized, even if one had the 'correct' model and knew exactly the objective functions of the country's political institutions, the possibility of such a wide spectrum of different 'optimal' policies, representing different equilibrium strategies, might give rise to serious problems for macroeconomic forecasting. The performance of the economy also depends on policy decisions and the possibility of a different strategic behaviour on the part of policy-makers should be taken into account.

9.7 Decentralized policies and efficient tradeoffs

We have seen in the previous section that there may be more reasons for coordinating fiscal and monetary policies than just efficiency gains. In this and in the following sections we shall discuss a further argument for policy coordination: the better outcomes obtained in relation to the efficient inflation-output tradeoff (see sections 7.8 and 7.9). By using the same continuous-time econometric model considered in the previous sections (see appendix to chapter 7), it is possible to show that non-cooperation imposes a policy conflict which would not otherwise be present and that the range of policy choices open to the policy-makers is also reduced under non-cooperation.

As we have shown in section 7.8, it is possible to identify the *best* inflation-output combinations available by using optimal control methods (Chow and Megdal, 1978. See also Chow, 1981; Henry *et al.*, 1982; Hughes Hallett and Petit, 1988a and c). However, these works on policy tradeoffs are all based on the assumption that policy decisions are centralized. This, however, is not the case in many countries where, as we have seen, two policy decision-making institutions, the Government and the Central Bank, can coexist and manage fiscal and monetary policy separately. Therefore, the efficient inflation-output combinations available in the case of decentralized policy-making should be identified.

As will be shown in the following section, lack of coordination may lead to a change in the optimal inflation-output tradeoff as calculated in the traditional way. In particular it may produce:

(a) a change in the position of the tradeoff curve itself, that is, a shift towards more inefficient target combinations; or

(b) a reversal in the slope of this tradeoff, converting a situation of no policy conflict into the familiar upward sloping inflation-output tradeoff (indicating instead a policy conflict) when non-cooperative policies are followed; or

(c) the collapse of the tradeoff between two targets to a single point, eliminating the policy-makers freedom to choose a preferred point on that tradeoff.

If (a) holds, the costs of non-cooperative behaviour are the usual efficiency losses. But if (b) or (c) holds, non-cooperation either imposes a policy conflict which would not otherwise be there or it restricts policy choice unnecessarily. Either of those situations constitutes an additional case for coordinating policies pursued by the two political institutions.

In what follows we shall use dynamic game theory to calculate the efficient tradeoff between output and inflation in the case of decentralization and to explore the differences in the policy possibility frontiers which arise as the result of cooperative and of non-cooperative policy-making.

In order to derive the output-inflation combinations for the case where decisions are taken by two separate policy-makers, the Government and the Central Bank, two different objective functions must be specified that we assume to be quadratic, i.e.

$$J_i = \int_{t_0}^{t_f} [\bar{x}_i'(t) Q_i \bar{x}_i(t) + \bar{u}_i'(t) R_{ii} \bar{u}_i(t)] \, \mathrm{d}t, \quad i = 1, 2 \tag{9.26}$$

where $\bar{x}_i(t)$ and $\bar{u}_i(t)$ represent, as usual, deviations from ideal trajectories. Q_i and R_{ii} are assumed to be constant symmetric matrices of the required dimensions ($Q_i \geqslant 0$; $R_{ii} > 0$).

The law of motion of the system is given by (see (9.1)).

$$\dot{x}(t) = Ax(t) + B_1 u_1(t) + B_2 u_2(t) + Cz(t) \qquad (9.27)$$

which is the model that describes the behaviour of the economy. Note that, although we are concerned with the tradeoff between inflation and output, these two variables may or may not be included in both objective functions.

Finally, if we assume that the Government and the Central Bank wish to reach an agreement on policy objectives, so that future policy actions benefit from explicit cooperation between the two policy-makers, the optimal inflation-output tradeoff can be derived by minimizing the 'collective' objective function (see (8.64)).

$$J = \beta J_1 + (1 - \beta)J_2, \quad (0 < \beta < 1) \qquad (9.28)$$

subject to (9.27). As in the case of centralized policy-making (see section 7.8), the coordinated inflation-output tradeoff can be obtained by changing the relative penalties assigned to the target failures in (9.28) over the interval $(0, \infty)$. This can be done for a range of different policy bargains, as defined by the bargaining coefficient.

Under non-cooperation, the optimal tradeoffs depend both on the solution concept taken to represent the non-cooperative situation and on the player whose policy options are represented in that tradeoff. If, for example, we assume that it is the Government which tries to derive the optimal tradeoff by changing the relative penalties assigned to its targets, then it seems reasonable to calculate this tradeoff on a 'ceteris paribus' hypothesis for the Central Bank, since there is no cooperation with the Central Bank. And the same holds in reverse for the case in which it is the Central Bank which tries to compute the optimal tradeoff. Moreover, since different equilibrium solutions can be calculated in each case, different tradeoffs will be obtained when the solution procedure is based on a Nash or a Stackelberg equilibrium.

9.8 The inflation-output tradeoff

The optimal tradeoff between output and inflation in the framework of a continuous-time model of the Italian economy has been derived and discussed in section 7.9 (see also Hughes Hallett and Petit, 1988a and c). It was shown that it would have been possible to bring down inflation while also increasing the rate of growth of output during the period 1977–81. These results presume centralized policies and show a tradeoff 'reversal', with no conflict arising between the output and inflation targets.

In this section, we consider the optimal inflation-growth combinations which can be obtained for the same period (1977–81), using the same model, but under the assumption of decentralized policy-making.

We therefore assume that the Italian Government and the Bank of Italy act as two different policy-makers who can decide either to cooperate or not to cooperate. We also assume that both political institutions make use of the same econometric model.[9] As above both the cooperative and the non-cooperative solutions are calculated on the assumption of an open-loop information structure and by applying Pontryagin's minimum principle. The objective functions that we consider are those described in section 9.3 (equation (9.2) and (9.3)).

In order to obtain the inflation-output tradeoffs under the different co-operative and non-cooperative solutions, the following exercises have been conducted:

(i) *The cooperative case*
The two policy-makers agree to minimize the 'collective' objective

$$J = \beta J_1 + (1 - \beta)J_2$$

where J_1 and J_2 are as defined in equation (9.2) and (9.3) and $\beta = 0.2, 0.5$ and 0.8. That is, the cases considered are those of a higher bargaining power on the part of the Central Bank ($\beta = 0.2$), the case of equal bargaining power ($\beta = 0.5$) and the case of a higher bargaining power on the part of the Government (which corresponds, as we have seen in section 9.5, to the Nash bargaining solution). To obtain the inflation-growth combinations attainable through cooperative policies, the weights assigned to prices ($w_{P1} + w_{P2}$) have been changed, while keeping the rest of (9.28) constant, and an optimal control problem has been solved for each value of ($w_{P1} + w_{P2}$).

(ii) *The non-cooperative case: the Nash equilibrium*
Two different assumptions can be made in this case: the assumption that it is the Government which tries to obtain the policy possibility frontier while assuming that the Central Bank will not modify its objective function. The Government therefore calculates its inflation-output tradeoff simply by varying the relative weights in its objective function (that is by varying w_{P1} while keeping w_{Y1} constant) and computing a Nash equilibrium solution for each value of w_{P1}. In the same way it might be assumed that it is the Central Bank which tries to obtain the policy tradeoff while assuming that the Government will not modify its objective function. The inflation-output frontier is therefore calculated by modifying w_{P2} while

keeping the rest of (9.2) and (9.3) constant and computing a Nash equilibrium solution for each w_{P2}.

(iii) The non-cooperative case: the Stackelberg equilibrium

We have considered only the case in which the Government acts as leader and the Central Bank as follower, since this seems to be the most realistic situation in the context of the Italian economy (see section 9.2). As for the Nash solution, two different assumptions can also be made in this case, according to whether it is the Government or the Central Bank which wishes to view the policy possibility frontier. A Stackelberg equilibrium solution with the Government as leader will therefore be computed for each value of w_{P1} while keeping the rest of (9.2) and (9.3) constant (Government tradeoff). In the same way, the tradeoff of the Central Bank (with the Government as leader) will be computed for each value of w_{P2}.

9.9 Numerical results

(i) The cooperative case

Table 9.3 and the curves in figure 9.4 present the output-inflation tradeoffs available to the Italian economy during the economic slow-down of 1977–81 calculated on the assumption of coordinating fiscal and monetary policies. The output-inflation conflict is presented in terms of (averaged) rates of growth over the period considered. The figures quoted correspond to a change in priority given to restraining inflation compared with raising output. It should be remembered that weights in (9.2) and (9.3) penalize percentage deviations from the ideal path equally, so that table 9.3 represents policies where proportional failures in the inflation target are treated as 3.33 times less important, through to 10 times more important, than the same failures in output.

The curve CC' represents the policy options under an 'equal shares' bargain with $\beta = 0.5$. Figure 9.4 and table 9.3 also present the results for the case where the Government assumes greater power ($\beta = 0.8$), and where the Central Bank has greater power ($\beta = 0.2$). These results clearly show a tradeoff 'reversal', with no conflict arising between the output and inflation targets. Indeed there is no question as to which policy package should be selected on this tradeoff; an increase in the weight on the inflation target $(0.5(w_{P1} + w_{P2}) \rightarrow 10)$ generates *higher* rates of output growth together with a *smaller* increase in prices than is the case with policies which give a lower priority to inflation.

Since the causes of this tradeoff 'reversal' have been thoroughly analysed in Hughes Hallett and Petit (1988a and c), we shall not pursue this argument

Table 9.3   *The average growth-inflation values for the Italian economy under cooperative policy-making, 1977–1981 (% growth pa)*

Bargaining power:	$\beta=0.2$		$\beta=0.5$		$\beta=0.8$	
w_p	$\dot{y}$	$\dot{p}$	$\dot{y}$	$\dot{p}$	$\dot{y}$	$\dot{p}$
0.3	6.48	14.60	7.14	10.36	6.82	8.58
0.5	7.70	11.57	7.41	9.08	7.44	7.98
1.0	8.10	9.01	7.59	8.20	7.74	7.49
3.0	9.51	8.05	8.63	7.71	8.51	7.52
5.0	9.70	7.82	8.68	7.71	8.51	7.63
10.0	9.87	7.77	8.79	7.71	8.57	7.71

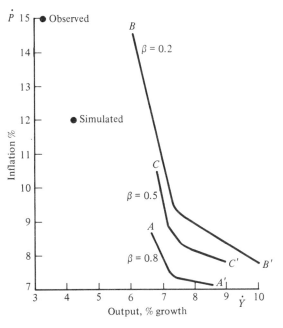

Figure 9.4   Cooperative policy tradeoffs (β: bargaining weight of the Government)

here, except to say that policy-makers appear not to have made use of their chance to start recovery by reducing inflation in the period 1977–81. As can be seen in figure 9.4, the observed (historical) output-inflation outcome, as well as the outcome obtained simply by simulating the base-run solution of the model, are clearly inferior to the majority of the points in the policy possibility frontier CC'. Better outcomes could always have been reached through optimal cooperative policies and by putting a higher weight on inflation than on output. That priority scheme would yield outcomes near point C' if $\beta = 0.5$, or the corresponding outcomes for other values. The interesting thing here is that giving the Government greater power to determine the optimal coordinated policies ($\beta = 0.8$) can produce better outcomes than if the Central Bank assumes greater power ($\beta = 0.2$). That is not to say any points on AA' dominate *all* points on BB', or indeed CC', in a Pareto sense – although some of them dominate most of BB' and CC'. More generally AA' dominates, in the sense that, for any given output growth rate, lower inflation can be achieved by giving the Government objectives greater weight. But, given an inflation rate, higher output would be achieved by allowing the Central Bank greater power (freedom). Moreover the range of policy choices is substantially restricted by allowing the Government greater power; AA' offers a much smaller range of choice than BB'.

These results illustrate the potential 'efficiency' costs incurred by forcing the Central Bank to accommodate the Government's fiscal plans as was done prior to 1981. Increasing Government power will ensure relatively good output and inflation results (compared to the corresponding position for lower β values, i.e. from shifts in the tradeoff curve itself). But increasing the role of the Central Bank opens up the opportunity for greater output at the same inflation level (i.e. shifts along the chosen tradeoff curve). In other words, by giving the Central Bank a free hand to combat inflation, the Government allows itself greater scope to pick policies which increase growth. So cooperation, with an independent role for the Central Bank, gives policy-makers a greater opportunity to exploit the favourable end of the inflation-output tradeoff. But the Government will still appear to play the leading role because, for most relative priority values, better outcomes emerge from higher β values and because, when β is reduced, better outcomes are obtained only in the form of extra output (which is the Government's, not the Central Bank's, main objective). This explains why, in section 9.5, we found that cooperation produces gains only when $0.7 < \beta < 0.9$. But these gains can be increased more by raising the priority on inflation and allowing the Central Bank independence, i.e. by allowing a greater role for 'independent' monetary policy.

(ii) Non-cooperative policies: the Government's tradeoff

The policy options under non-cooperative decision-making are completely different from and, as expected, inferior to, those of the cooperative case.

Table 9.4 and the small segment (which is almost a point) N in figure 9.5 present the output-inflation combinations (which cannot be called a trade-

Table 9.4   *Average growth-inflation values in the Government's tradeoff in a non-cooperative (Nash) solution, 1977–1981 (% growth pa)*

w_{p1}	$\dot{y}$	$\dot{p}$
0.6	9.06	8.30
1.0	9.05	8.31
2.0	9.05	8.33
6.0	9.07	8.16
10.0	9.07	8.17

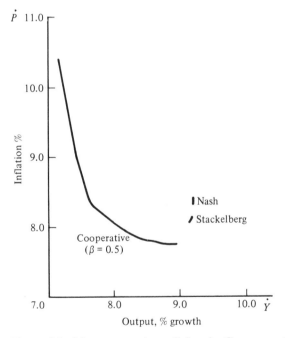

Figure 9.5   Non-cooperative policies: the Government's tradeoff

off) available to the Italian economy when the two political institutions play a Nash non-cooperative game, and it is the Government which wishes to identify the policy possibility frontier. The objective function of the Central Bank is therefore kept constant while the Government increases the priority assigned to inflation while keeping the other weights constant.

Table 9.5   *Average growth-inflation values in the Government's tradeoff in a Stackelberg game with Government as leader, 1977–1981 (% growth pa)*

w_{p1}	$\dot{y}$	$\dot{p}$
0.6	9.06	8.13
1.0	9.06	8.12
2.0	9.06	8.10
6.0	9.10	8.07
10.0	8.92	7.95
16.0	9.02	8.01

A Nash equilibrium solution computed for each value of w_{P1} gives the figures recorded in table 9.4.

Table 9.5 and the small segment S in figure 9.5 present the marginally better output-inflation combinations (which still cannot be called a tradeoff) available to the Italian economy on the assumption that the two policy-makers play a Stackelberg game with the Government as leader and that it is the Government that wishes to build an efficient policy frontier. A Stackelberg equilibrium solution, computed for each w_{P1}, all the rest constant, gives rise to table 9.5.

Thus in both cases the policy possibility frontier effectively disappears and, in so far as there is any tradeoff at all here, it is *not* reversed. Hence non-cooperative policy-making not only may impose a policy conflict which did not exist under cooperation, it also effectively removes the Government's freedom to choose its preferred policies for resolving that conflict. Any attempt by the Government to indulge in discretionary policy is therefore doomed to failure, since it cannot move the economy from N (if a Nash game is played) or S (if a Stackelberg game is played). Non-cooperation means that the Central Bank can, if it wishes, block any Government moves. Whether the Central Bank will actually wish to do that depends on whether it finds these outcomes satisfactory.

These results are therefore not unexpected. As we have seen above, lower inflation is obtained in the cooperative or centralized case through a greater use of (restrictive) monetary policy. Public expenditure is the main instrument for expanding output, together with the internal and external demand generated by reductions in the rate of inflation.[10] But public expenditure alone is not able to deal with inflation, and so the stimulating effects of lower inflation on output and aggregate demand do not materialize. The resulting situation will be characterized by higher inflation and the loss of extra output stimulus. Interestingly the situation is not much

Table 9.6   *Average growth-inflation values in the Central Bank's tradeoff in a non-cooperative (Nash) solution, 1977–1981 (% growth pa)*

w_{p2}	$\dot{y}$	$\dot{p}$
0.6	8.60	9.75
1.0	8.90	8.82
2.0	9.05	8.31
6.0	8.76	7.41
10.0	8.50	7.56

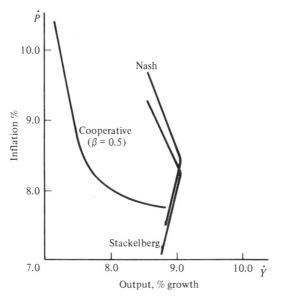

Figure 9.6   Non-cooperative policies: Central Bank's tradeoff

better in a Stackelberg game with the Government as leader. In this case lower inflation is possible for a given output, but there is still no effective tradeoff.

(iii) *Non-cooperative policies: the Central Bank's tradeoff*
    Table 9.6 and the 'Nash' line in figure 9.6 present the output-inflation combinations available to the Italian economy when the two policy-makers play a Nash non-cooperative game and it is the Central

Table 9.7 *Average growth-inflation values in the Central Bank's tradeoff in a Stackelberg game with Government as leader, 1977–1981 (% growth pa)*

w_{p2}	$\dot{y}$	$\dot{p}$
0.6	8.68	9.13
1.0	8.92	8.46
2.0	9.07	8.12
6.0	8.67	7.04
10.0	8.23	7.21

Bank which traces out its policy possibility frontier. The objective function of the Government is therefore kept constant in this case, while the Central Bank varies the priority assigned to inflation from 0.6 to 10, keeping the other weights constant. Table 9.6 thus presents the Nash equilibrium solution computed for each value of w_{p2}. Similarly table 9.7 and the 'Stackelberg' line present the output-inflation combinations available when the policy-makers play a Stackelberg game with the Government acting as leader and the Central Bank examines its policy possibility frontier.

It is not surprising that the policy possibility frontier reappears in this case – albeit with an unusual shape. Varying the priority on inflation in the Central Bank's objective function introduces varying strengths of monetary control, while public expenditure remains relatively fixed. That allows an independent monetary policy for reducing inflation and hence expanding output over and above what the fiscal programme is doing. Hence it is possible to go some way towards the better outcomes generated by the reversed tradeoff observed in the cooperative case – at least for some values of w_{p2}. However, since the Government is not cooperating in stimulating demand through public expenditure, the 'reversal' of the tradeoff does not last for very high values of w_{p2}. The restrictive monetary policy required by the increasing priorities in inflation has a restrictive effect on output that it is not compensated, in this case, by a sufficient fiscal expansion. The output-inflation tradeoff therefore turns, for $w_{p2} \geqslant 6$, to the familiar upward sloping form. The outcome for the Stackelberg solution is essentially the same, except that, as before, lower inflation is possible at any given rate of output growth.

One conclusion from these exercises is that monetary policy is not only important for controlling inflation but also indirectly for stimulating output. By acting non-cooperatively the Central Bank may have the effect of creating policy conflicts that would not otherwise be there and/or of substantially eliminating the Government's freedom of choice. Neither of these outcomes arises in the cooperative case. These two costs, additional policy conflicts and the loss of policy choice, may be more important than the efficiency losses which are traditionally cited as the reason for cooperating.

These results provide further confirmation of the argument that was already mentioned in section 9.6: that, as far as macroeconomic analysis is concerned, the drawbacks that emerge from non-cooperation are not only those depending on efficiency losses. Other features of non-cooperative solutions should also be considered (such as those examined in section 9.6 and the present section) which may constitute further reasons for cooperation and may therefore induce policy-makers to coordinate their policies.

10 Optimal policies and expectations

10.1 Expectations and economic modelling

Intertemporal economic policy decisions based on *quantitative* methods are usually the result either of simulations or of optimization procedures (optimal control methods) carried out – as we have seen in the preceding chapters – by making use of a dynamic econometric model which describes the working of the economy.

In both cases, it is fairly widespread practice to use macroeconometric models which, although dynamic, can be considered as passive models: passive in the sense that they describe the behaviour of the economy – and, in particular, of the private sector – on the assumption that the latter accepts policy actions passively, and reacts to them only during or after these actions have taken place. This was the case considered in chapters 7 and 9 where a specific dynamic econometric model was considered.

As we have seen, this type of macroeconometric model may be described by the familiar differential system

$$\dot{x}(t) = Ax(t) + Bu(t) + Cz(t) \tag{10.1}$$

where $x(t) \in R^n$ is a vector of endogenous (state) variables (including decision variables of the private sector), $u(t) \in R^r$ is a vector of control variables (policy instruments) and $z(t)$ is a vector of exogenous uncontrolled and uncertain variables. A, B and C are constant matrices of conformable dimensions.

Given an initial vector x_{t_0} (at $t = t_0$), the solution of system (10.1) is given by

$$x(t) = x(t_0)e^{At} + \int_{t_0}^{t} e^{A(t-\tau)}[Bu(\tau) + Cz(\tau)] \, d\tau \tag{10.2}$$

where, as can be easily seen, $x(t)$ is given by the solution of the corresponding homogeneous system $x(t_0)e^{At}$ (which represents the performance of the system when no exogenous effects are present) and by past policy actions (besides past exogenous effects). It can be observed from (10.2) that future policy actions *have no effect* on the performance of the endogenous variables.

However, a dynamic model in which no account is taken of the expectations of private agents about future policies seems rather limited; it therefore becomes important to consider the case in which the private sector becomes *active*, that is, forms expectations about Government policies and reacts to those expectations even *before* the policies are actually implemented. The assumption that the private sector forms expectations about future Government behaviour greatly complicates the economic policy problem and has significant implications as to how those policies should be selected. We are indebted to the new classical macroeconomics for having drawn attention to this problem, largely ignored before the seventies and only in recent years taken into account in the economic literature as a consequence of the introduction of the rational expectations (henceforth RE) hypothesis into economic modelling. The introduction of this hypothesis has made it possible to obtain interesting insights into the analysis of the interaction between the Government and the private sector when expectations are considered and also into the consequences of expectations on economic policy design.

Just to give an idea of the important outcome of this type of analysis, it should suffice to think of the burgeoning of literature on *policy neutrality* which followed the Lucas (1972) and Sargent and Wallace (1975) articles, the broad debate on the problem of *time inconsistency* of optimal policy decisions which followed Kydland and Prescott's (1977) paper, and the new line of research which produced the so-called *Lucas critique* of econometric policy evaluation (Lucas, 1976).

In this chapter we shall examine the implications of the assumption that the private sector forms expectations about future policies, and point out the problems which arise from this assumption and the solutions proposed to overcome them. We shall focus in particular on the time-inconsistency problem and on the Lucas critique of econometric policy evaluation, leaving aside the problem of policy neutrality. In fact, unlike the former two, policy neutrality refers only to some particular cases in which the rational expectations assumption is combined with the so-called 'Lucas supply equation' (see, on this point, Sargent and Wallace, 1975; Taylor, 1980; and, for a critical appraisal, Buiter, 1980, 1981a). Furthermore, both the Lucas and the time-inconsistency critique can be considered as two critical arguments about the use of optimal control techniques for policy analysis when expectations are present,[1] whereas the policy neutrality argument has nothing to do with policy selection techniques. That is why we prefer not to discuss this subject here, and refer the reader to Shiller (1978), Begg (1982), Minford and Peel (1983), where excellent surveys can be found.

We shall therefore consider, in sections 10.2 to 10.4, the case in which expectations (in particular, rational expectations) are explicitly considered in the economic model used. In this case, as we shall see, the application of optimal control methods may give rise to an important analytical problem: the time inconsistency of the optimal control solution.

The consequences of the introduction of the rational expectations hypothesis in economic modelling have mainly been studied in the literature by making use of discrete-time models.[2] When expectations are concerned this kind of dynamic models have an advantage over continuous-time ones, because expectations referring to any future date are more clearly formalized. For this reason we shall first introduce the problem of time inconsistency by considering a discrete-time model (sections 10.2–10.3), and then examine the same problem in the continuous-time framework (section 10.4).

We shall then consider in sections 10.6 to 10.10 the case in which econometric models that policy-makers use for policy evaluation and decision describe the behaviour of 'myopic' economic agents, that is of agents who do not take the future into account when formulating their own decisions. This is the case with most 'traditional' econometric models. As Lucas has stressed, the incorrect specification of this type of model can give rise to serious problems when these models are used for purposes of policy evaluation.

The Lucas critique and the time-inconsistency problem, as well as the suggestions put forward to deal with them, have highlighted a very interesting feature of policy design when the forward-looking behaviour of agents is considered: the interaction which takes place between the private sector – whose actions depend on current and future policy decisions – and the policy-makers – whose actions depend on the current and future behaviour of the private sector. This particular type of interaction has underlined the opportunity to determine policy decisions by making use of dynamic game methods, that is by analysing the policy problem as a dynamic game between two players: the Government and the private sector.

This new approach to the analysis of policy makes it possible to deal with the difficult problem of modelling expectations, without the need to introduce them explicitly into the economic model considered; expectations are implicitly incorporated into the dynamic game formalization of the policy problem (on this point, see Lucas and Sargent, 1981; Hughes Hallett, 1984a, Petit, 1985b, 1989b). However, although this approach is certainly promising from an analytical point of view and has already provided useful insights into the policy problem, it is difficult to apply in empirical work because of important and still unresolved technical problems.

10.2 The problem of time inconsistency

An important argument against the use of optimal control methods in macroeconomics has been raised by Kydland and Prescott (1977). The authors maintain that economic policy decisions obtained from optimal control techniques may be time inconsistent when the assumption is made that the private sector forms RE about future policies. This argument has been used to criticize the application of optimal control methods to policy decision problems (see also Prescott, 1977; Calvo, 1978).

We have already seen the meaning of time inconsistency in section 8.3, where we also examined the causes of the time inconsistency of the leader's global equilibrium strategy in a Stackelberg game. As a matter of fact the main features of an optimal control problem in a context in which the private sector forms RE about future policies are essentially similar to those of a Stackelberg game with the government acting as leader and the private sector as follower (see Buiter, 1981a; Miller and Salmon, 1985a; Petit, 1985b; see also section 10.3). It should therefore be clear by now that, if a policy is time consistent, the decision-maker will have no reason to revise his decisions at future moments of time, since the policy computed at the beginning of the planning horizon is still the best policy when reoptimizing at later dates.

The problem of time inconsistency is not new in economics. Strotz (1956) had already considered this problem in the framework of dynamic utility maximization. Strotz claimed that if a consumer is free to reconsider his plan of consumption at future dates he will generally not follow the plan originally calculated; consequently, the author argued that 'the individual's future behaviour will be inconsistent with his optimal plan' (Strotz, 1956, p. 165). However, the causes of time inconsistency considered by Strotz were completely different from those considered later by Kydland and Prescott (1977). An important feature of this difference is that Strotz examined a problem where the criteria according to which the consumption decisions were made at the initial time was subject to possible modifications at subsequent moments of the planning horizon. These possible modifications were related to the discount rates attached to utility at future dates: the discount rate referring to a future utility is likely to be different when the 'future' is closer. Therefore, in Strotz's problem, reoptimization at future dates may imply a modification in the original criteria.

It is important to make these differences in the causes of time inconsistency clear, because if

the criteria according to which a policy is chosen ... abruptly change at some point in the decision horizon, and the possibility of such a change has not been built into the original formulation, then one cannot expect an optimal policy to retain its optimality for the new problem and under new criteria. In other words, one cannot (and should not) expect (time) consistency of dynamic policies if the decision problem itself is not consistent over time (Basar, 1989, p. 2).

The reason for time inconsistency in the decision problem considered by Kydland and Prescott is, on the contrary, independent of changes in the criteria by which the policy is chosen: the *formulation* of the decision problem is *consistent* over time.

The problem raised by Kydland and Prescott can be summarized as follows: if it is assumed that the private sector forms RE about the Government policies, then policy decisions obtained by dynamic optimization methods are either *time inconsistent* or *sub-optimal*. In fact, two different cases can be considered: (a) if policy decisions obtained by dynamic optimization methods are optimal, these policies are time-inconsistent, and (b) if policy decisions obtained by dynamic optimization methods are time consistent, these policies are sub-optimal. Here and in the following sections we use the term *sub-optimal*, following the terminology introduced by Kydland and Prescott, to qualify those solutions which are dominated by the optimal time-inconsistent solution. We are aware that the use of this term may, in some cases, lead to misunderstandings.

As mentioned in chapter 8, an optimal policy is said to be time consistent if, when recomputed at a later date, we simply obtain a truncated version of the optimal policy calculated at the initial date, i.e. if it satisfies Bellman's principle of optimality. As is well known, this principle states that 'an optimal policy has the property that, whatever the initial state and decision (i.e. control) are, the remaining decisions must constitute an optimal policy with regard to the state resulting from the first decision' (Bellman, 1957). It is on this principle that the dynamic programming method of optimization, proposed by Bellman himself, is based.

In order to give a precise description of the argument for time inconsistency put forward by Kydland and Prescott and to understand its economic significance, we shall examine a deterministic dynamic decision problem specified in discrete time, as it was originally described by Kydland and Prescott (1977) in the framework of single-agent dynamic optimization. Assume therefore that the private sector forms RE about future policy and consider the following optimization problem

$$\min_{u \in U} J(u) = \min_{u_t \in U_t} \sum_{t=t_0}^{t_f} I(x_t, u_t) \tag{10.3}$$

subject to

$$x_{t+1} = \phi_t(x_t, u_t, u_{t+1/t}^e, u_{t+2/t}^e, \ldots, u_{t+p/t}^e) \qquad (10.4)$$

given x_{t_0}, where $x_t \in X_t$, $T = \{t_0, t_0 + 1, \ldots, t_f\}$ is the time horizon and $u = \{u_{t_0}, \ldots, u_{t_f}\}$ is the control sequence, with $u_t \in U_t$. For simplicity, we consider only one state and one control variable; therefore, x_t may represent a decision variable of the private sector such as consumption expenditure, while u_t may represent a policy variable of the Government such as public expenditure. Equation (10.3) describes the objective function of the Government (which we assume is stage decomposable and time invariant) whose optimization provides the optimal path for public expenditure. The variables $u_{t+1/t}^e, u_{t+2/t}^e, \ldots, u_{t+p/t}^e$, represent the expected values of the control variables $u_{t+1}, u_{t+2}, \ldots, u_{t+p}$ respectively, given the information available at time t.

Since we assume that expectations are rational and we consider a deterministic framework, we can set $u_{t+1/t}^e = u_{t+1}, \ldots, u_{t+p/t}^e = u_{t+p}$. Equation (10.4) thus becomes

$$x_{t+1} = \phi_t(x_t, u_t, u_{t+1}, u_{t+2}, \ldots, u_{t+p}) \qquad (10.5)$$

The optimization problem is therefore defined by (10.3) subject to (10.5), with $u_{t_f+1}, \ldots, u_{t_f+p} = 0$. If we solve this problem by means of dynamic programming, the solution will be time consistent, i.e. will satisfy Bellman's principle of optimality. This means that the optimal control sequence $\{u_t\}_{t=t_0}^{t_f}$ computed at $t = t_0$ (that we shall indicate as $u_{t(t_0)}^*$) and concerning the whole planning horizon T coincides (for *any* other sub-interval $\{s, \ldots, t_f\}$) with the optimal trajectory $u_{t(s)}^*$ computed at time s $(s > t_0)$ and concerning only the sub-interval $\{s, \ldots, t_f\}$, where the optimal trajectory $u_{t(s)}^*$ is computed with regard to the state resulting from the optimal state trajectory corresponding to the optimization problem starting at t_0 (see also the definition in section 8.3).

A policy decision based on this framework will therefore be time consistent and the Government will have no reason to revise its optimal decisions at future dates. However, as we shall see, the solution thus obtained will be *inferior* – in the sense that the value of the cost function of the Government will be higher – to another solution which can be obtained by a different optimization method. An intuitive explanation is that dynamic programming leaves aside some of the effects that future values of the policy variables have on current decisions of the private sector, effects that can instead be taken into account, as we shall see, by using other dynamic optimization methods (like Pontryagin's minimum principle or static optimization methods, which can be applied by stacking up the state and control variables).

Kydland and Prescott (1977) provide an alternative definition of time consistency for the case in which expectations about future policies are considered. This definition reads as follows: 'a policy u is *time-consistent* if, for each time period t, u_t minimizes (10.3), taking previous decisions, $x_1, \ldots, x_{t-1}$, as given, and that future policy decisions (u_s for $s > t$) are similarly selected' (Kydland and Prescott, 1977, p. 475).[3] As we shall see, dynamic programming is the only method through which the assumption that 'future policy decisions are similarly selected' is implicitly made.

10.2.1 The sub-optimality of the time-consistent policy

Let us now apply dynamic programming to a policy optimization problem with rational expectations, similar to the one considered by Kydland and Prescott (1977), in order to see how a time-consistent solution is obtained. Consider again the optimization problem described by equation (10.3) and (10.5) on the assumption that the planning horizon consists of two periods and that expectations at time 1 concern only policy at time 2.

Equations (10.3) and (10.5) can thus be written

$$\min_{u_t} \sum_{t=t_0}^{t_f} I(x_t, u_t) = \min_{u_1, u_2} W(x_1, x_2, u_1, u_2) \tag{10.6}$$

subject to

$$x_2 = \Phi_1(x_1, u_1, u_2) \tag{10.7}$$

$$x_1 = \Phi_0(u_1, u_2), \quad x_0 \text{ given.} \tag{10.8}$$

Assuming that a solution to this problem exists, we first solve the optimization problem at time $t = 1$ in order to obtain the control solution regarding periods 1 and 2 (which we indicate as $\tilde{u}_{1(1)}$ and $\tilde{u}_{2(1)}$), and then solve the optimization problem at time 2, to obtain the control solution for period 2 ($\tilde{u}_{2(2)}$). Since dynamic programming requires the optimization problem to be solved by backward recursion, we first solve for $\tilde{u}_{2(1)}$. Thus, by substituting the constraint (10.7) directly into (10.6) the optimization problem regarding period 2 becomes

$$\min_{u_2} W(x_2, u_2) = \min_{u_2} W[\Phi_1(x_1, u_1, u_2), u_2] \tag{10.9}$$

Assuming differentiability and an interior solution, we must have

$$\frac{\partial W}{\partial u_2} = \frac{\partial W}{\partial \phi_1} \frac{\partial \phi_1}{\partial u_2} + \frac{\partial W}{\partial u_2} = 0 \tag{10.10}$$

from which we can obtain

$$\tilde{u}_{2(1)} = g(x_1, u_1) \tag{10.11}$$

Going now back to period 1, the problem to be solved is

$$\min_{u_1} W(x_1, u_1) \tag{10.12}$$

subject to (10.8). By substituting $\tilde{u}_{2(1)}$ as defined by (10.11) into (10.8), the optimization problem becomes

$$\min_{u_1} W\{\phi_0[u_1, g(x_1, u_1)], u_1\} \tag{10.13}$$

where the constraint

$$x_1 = \phi_0[u_1, g(x_1, u_1)] \tag{10.14}$$

has been directly substituted into (10.12).

It should be observed at this point that by substituting $\tilde{u}_{2(1)}$ defined by (10.11) into (10.12), we are assuming that $\tilde{u}_{2(1)}$ has already been computed by the same method, i.e., that future policy decisions have been selected in the same way that current policy decisions are being selected[4] (see the definition of *time consistency* at the end of the previous section).

The necessary conditions require that

$$\frac{\partial W}{\partial u_1} = \frac{\partial W}{\partial \phi_0}\frac{\partial \phi_0}{\partial u_1} + \frac{\partial W}{\partial \phi_0}\frac{\partial \phi_0}{\partial g}\frac{\partial g}{\partial x_1}\frac{\partial x_1}{\partial u_1} +$$
$$+ \frac{\partial W}{\partial \phi_0}\frac{\partial \phi_0}{\partial g}\frac{\partial g}{\partial u_1} + \frac{\partial W}{\partial u_1} = 0 \tag{10.15}$$

From (10.15) we can obtain $\tilde{u}_{1(1)}$. Then, by substituting $\tilde{u}_{1(1)}$ into (10.14), we obtain $\tilde{x}_{1(1)}$. Finally, by substituting $\tilde{x}_{1(1)}$ and $\tilde{u}_{1(1)}$ into (10.11), we obtain $\tilde{u}_{2(1)}$.

In this way we have derived the control sequence $\tilde{u} = \{\tilde{u}_{1(1)}, \tilde{u}_{2(1)}\}$ computed at $t = 1$. This control sequence is time consistent since if we repeat the optimization process when time $t = 2$ effectively arrives – assuming that x_1 and u_1 take up the values $\tilde{x}_{1(1)}$ and $\tilde{u}_{1(1)}$ obtained from the optimization results at time 1 – we get the same result for $\tilde{u}_2$ as that previously obtained. The optimization problem to be solved when time 2 arrives is the following

$$\min_{u_2} W(x_2, u_2) = \min_{u_2} W[\phi_1(\tilde{x}_{1(1)}, \tilde{u}_{1(1)}, u_2), u_2] \tag{10.16}$$

and, from the necessary conditions, we have

$$\frac{\partial W}{\partial u_2} = \frac{\partial W}{\partial \phi_1}\frac{\partial \phi_1}{\partial u_2} + \frac{\partial W}{\partial u_2} = 0 \tag{10.17}$$

which, as can be seen, is equal to (10.10). We have therefore $\tilde{u}_{2(2)} = \tilde{u}_{2(1)}$, that is, *time consistency*.

However, the time-consistent policy $\tilde{u}_t, t = 1, 2$, thus obtained, is sub-optimal, in the sense specified above. The reason for sub-optimality is that, when computing $\tilde{u}_{2(1)}$ from (10.10), account is not taken of the effect of u_2 on x_1 (the term $\partial x_1 / \partial u_2$ is not considered).

With reference to the problem described by (10.3) and (10.5), we can express our results in more general terms: if a control trajectory $\tilde{u}_t, t \in T$, which is time consistent, is to be obtained, it is necessary to neglect the effects of $u_{t+1}, \ldots, u_{t+p}$ on x_t when $u_{t+1}, \ldots, u_{t+p}$ are determined, the effects of $u_t, u_{t+1}, \ldots, u_{t+p}$ on x_{t-1} when $u_t, u_{t+1}, \ldots, u_{t+p}$ are determined, and so on (the terms $\partial x_t / \partial u_{t+1}, \ldots, \partial x_t / \partial u_{t+p}$, and so on, are not considered). And, since the policy variable u_{t+1} depends in turn on x_t (through the feedback rule), the omission of the above effects also cancels the effects of $u_{t+2}, \ldots, u_{t+p}$ on u_{t+1} through x_t (that is, the terms $(\partial u_{t+1} / \partial x_t)(\partial x_t / \partial u_{t+2}), \ldots, (\partial u_{t+1} / \partial x_t)(\partial x_t / \partial u_{t+p})$, and so on, are not considered either). Therefore, the control sequence $\tilde{u}_t, t \in T$, obtained by ignoring all these intertemporal (non-causal) relations between the variables must necessarily be *sub-optimal*.

It follows from this discussion that a recursive method like dynamic programming, which neglects the above-mentioned interrelations between the variables, should be used only if we want to obtain a time-consistent policy; conversely, this method should not be used if our aim is to obtain an optimal control solution which incorporates all those effects of policy variables on the private sector's decision variables which arise as a consequence of the assumption of expectations (on this point, see Chow, 1981, chapter 15). Different optimization methods should be used in this latter case; however, as we shall see in the next section, the optimal solution thus obtained will be time inconsistent.

10.2.2 *The time inconsistency of the optimal policy*

Consider again the example of the previous section, that is the two-period optimization problem described by equation (10.6), (10.7) and (10.8). We shall again solve this problem here, but we shall now obtain the optimal control solution also by taking into account the influence, through expectations, of u_2 on x_1; this influence had been neglected in the optimization process examined in the previous section.

We shall follow a simple static optimization method which, in the case considered here of only one control and one state variable and two periods, can be very easily applied. As above, we shall first solve the optimization problem at time 1 to obtain the control sequence regarding periods 1 and 2, and then at time 2 to obtain the control solution for period 2.

Consider first the optimization problem at time $t = 1$. By substituting the constraints (10.7) and (10.8) directly into the objective function (10.6), the optimization problem reduces to

$$\min_{u_1, u_2} W\{\phi_0(u_1, u_2), \phi_1[\phi_0(u_1, u_2), u_1, u_2], u_1, u_2\} \qquad (10.18)$$

From the first-order conditions we get

$$\frac{\partial W}{\partial u_1} = \frac{\partial W}{\partial \phi_0}\frac{\partial \phi_0}{\partial u_1} + \frac{\partial W}{\partial \phi_1}\frac{\partial \phi_1}{\partial u_1} + \frac{\partial W}{\partial \phi_1}\frac{\partial \phi_1}{\partial \phi_0}\frac{\partial \phi_0}{\partial u_1} + \frac{\partial W}{\partial u_1} = 0 \qquad (10.19)$$

$$\frac{\partial W}{\partial u_2} = \frac{\partial W}{\partial \phi_0}\frac{\partial \phi_0}{\partial u_2} + \frac{\partial W}{\partial \phi_1}\frac{\partial \phi_1}{\partial u_2} + \frac{\partial W}{\partial \phi_1}\frac{\partial \phi_1}{\partial \phi_0}\frac{\partial \phi_0}{\partial u_2} + \frac{\partial W}{\partial u_2} = 0 \qquad (10.20)$$

which can be solved simultaneously for $u^*_{1(1)}$ and $u^*_{2(1)}$ (given x_0), that is for the optimal control sequence computed at time 1. It can be observed from (10.20) that in this case account has been taken of the effect of u_2 on x_1, through the term $\partial\phi_0/\partial u_2$.

Let us now see why the control solution thus calculated is time inconsistent. To this purpose we have again to solve the optimization problem when time 2 effectively arrives, on the assumption that x_1 and u_1 take on the values $x^*_{1(1)}$ and $u^*_{1(1)}$ obtained from the optimization process at time 1. The problem to be solved at time $t = 2$ is therefore equivalent to the one described by (10.16), that is

$$\min_{u_2} W(x_2, u_2) = \min_{u_2} W[\phi_1(x^*_{1(1)}, u^*_{1(1)}, u_2), u_2] \qquad (10.21)$$

From the necessary conditions we have

$$\frac{\partial W}{\partial u_2} = \frac{\partial W}{\partial \phi_1}\frac{\partial \phi_1}{\partial u_2} + \frac{\partial W}{\partial u_2} = 0 \qquad (10.22)$$

from which we can obtain $u^*_{2(2)}$.

It seems obvious that the solution $u^*_{2(2)}$ obtained in period $t = 2$ from (10.22) will be different from the corresponding solution $u^*_{2(1)}$ obtained in period $t = 1$ from system (10.19)–(10.20). We have therefore[5]

$$u^*_{2(2)} \neq u^*_{2(1)} \qquad (10.23)$$

which means that the optimal control sequence calculated at time 1 is no longer optimal when the optimization problem is solved again at time 2. The optimal policy $u^*_{t(1)}$, $t = 1, 2$, is time inconsistent.

At this point the reason why the presence of rational expectations produces time inconsistency should be clear. Since RE imply a forward looking behaviour of the private sector, when the Government computes the optimal control solution at the initial time t_0, account is taken of *all* the effects of current and *future* policy decisions on the decision (state) variables of the private sector at each $t \in T$. But when the optimal policy is again calculated at a subsequent stage s $(s > t_0)$ – by solving an optimization problem which is identical to the previous one, except for the length of the planning horizon – the effects of current and future policy, $u_s, u_{s+1}, \ldots, u_{t_f}$, on the state variables of the periods prior to s, x_t, $t \in [t_0, s)$, are no longer important and are therefore not considered; these effects are already incorporated in x_{s-1}, which is taken as given in the new optimization problem.

It is intuitively obvious that, if we solve a dynamic optimization problem at a given moment of time s, we are interested in the performance of the state variables, x_t, over the planning interval $\{s, s+1, \ldots, t_f\}$ but *not* in the performance of those variables during a previous time interval $\{t_0, \ldots, s-1\}$, as this performance already belongs to the past and is therefore a datum at time s.

It is this different way of tackling the optimization problem when it is solved at t_0 or when it is solved at a subsequent moment of time s $(s > t_0)$, which gives rise to the time-inconsistency problem. Of course *expectations* have a fundamental role in the generation of this problem since, as we have seen in section 10.1, the presence of expectations of the private sector about future Government policies assigns to the former an *active* role, allowing it to react to policy actions even *before* they are actually implemented. In fact, the above mentioned effects of future policies on current values of the endogenous variables would not manifest themselves if expectations were not considered.

However, expectations alone may not give rise to the time-inconsistency problem. As Calvo (1978) and Fischer (1980) correctly emphasize, another requirement is that policy instruments have a *distortionary effect* on the behaviour of private agents, that is, that policy instruments are a negative externality like, for example, inflation or distortionary taxes (see Sheffrin, 1983). A typical example of time inconsistency suggested by Prescott (1977) and developed by Fischer (1980) will be useful in order to clarify this point: a Government has to make a plan concerning direct taxation over a given number of periods, and has to decide whether to tax labour income or capital income. The assumption is made that, if the private sector had no expectations about future Government decisions, the optimal policy would be to tax capital income. However, since we assume that the private sector forms RE, the implementation of such a policy would produce a decline in capital accumulation, both present and future, and therefore a decrease in tax revenues. This is the distortionary effect of a capital income tax on capital accumulation. In a framework in which rational expectations are considered, the optimal policy at the beginning of the planning interval (t_0)

would therefore be to tax both capital and labour income over the whole time horizon $[t_0, t_f]$. However, once the last period t_f has effectively been reached, the optimal policy concerning that period will be to tax only capital, given that it has already been accumulated and that the policy-maker is not interested in the effects of the tax policy after t_f.

It is thus the distortionary effect of this type of taxation that, together with the assumption of RE, in this case produces the time inconsistency of the optimal policy. The example just considered might induce us to think that time inconsistency may also depend on the assumption of a finite time horizon. As a matter of fact, since the planning horizon is finite, it may be optimal, when the last period comes, to make a radical change in the policy followed in the preceding periods. In fact the policy-maker is not interested in the performance of the economy after the end of the planning interval.[6] The finiteness of the time horizon is not however a reason for time inconsistency. As has been demonstrated by Kydland and Prescott (1977, 1980), an optimal policy may be time inconsistent even when the time horizon considered is infinite.

Conversely, if the policy instrument used by the Government has no distortionary effects on the decisions of private agents, the problem of time inconsistency may not arise. An example is that in which the Government uses lump-sum (hence, non-distorting) taxes (see, for example, Lucas and Stokey, 1983; Hillier and Malcomson, 1984). Another obvious example would be a public policy which consists in an increase in public expenditure aimed at, say, the construction of new schools. In this case, even if the private sector is exactly informed as to the whole investment programme of the Government, this programme should have no distortionary effects on private-sector decisions and might thus be time consistent. This is a case in which expectations about future policies have not specific effect on the decisions of the private sector (a case in which $\partial\phi_0/\partial u_2 = 0$; see footnote 5).

10.3 Optimal policies, rational expectations and dynamic games

At this point the reader will have noted the similarities between the problem of the time inconsistency of optimal policies raised by the assumption of private agents' RE about future policies and the problem of the time inconsistency of the leader's equilibrium strategy in a Stackelberg game examined in section 8.3.2. Since it seems important to understand the reasons for these similarities, we shall try to identify them in the present section.

It is already common practice to describe optimal policy problems formulated on the assumption of RE as a dynamic game between two players: the Government and the private sector. RE however is a very specific assumption which goes beyond the simple interaction between economic agents. Therefore, even if dynamic games are clearly an appropriate analytical tool to describe the interaction between economic agents, two questions still need to be posed: (a) are dynamic games an appropriate method for describing the interaction between the Government and the private sector when the latter has RE? and, if so, (b) what is the most appropriate solution concept to describe this specific type of interaction? An answer to these questions can only be given after analysing the underlying assumptions of the optimal policy problem under RE, so that we can compare them with the assumptions underlying the different equilibrium solutions of dynamic games.

As above, the analysis will be conducted in a deterministic framework, since this allows us to obtain a clearer idea of the particular issues to be considered, while avoiding the greater complications that necessarily follow the introduction of uncertainty. On the other hand, the conclusions that we reach here would not be substantially different in a stochastic framework.

The assumptions that characterize *rational behaviour* can be seen as the main link between RE and dynamic game models. It is assumed in *both* cases that behavioural decisions are the result of the *optimization* of given preference functions of economic agents (or representative economic agents). This optimization is performed by taking into account not only the current economic situation but also the *expectations* about the economic situation in the future, expectations which are formed by using *all available information.*

An essential feature of dynamic games is that the equilibrium behaviour of each player depends on the time path of the state variables and on the equilibrium strategies of the other players, defined over the whole time horizon considered. It follows that the behavioural decision of each player depends also on his expectations about the other players' future decisions. Expectations are therefore a common feature of both RE and dynamic game models. But, since expectations are fundamentally based on the information available to each individual (player), it is important to examine the main assumptions about the information structure of an individual with RE and to compare them with those underlying the different information structures which characterize each type of equilibrium solution. Since the latter information structures have already been examined in chapter 8, we shall focus here on the information structure concerning the RE case.

The mechanism of RE formation is based on the assumption that the information set of an economic agent at time t_0, that is, at the moment when he formulates his expectations, is given by:[7]

(a) the current values[8] of all relevant variables,

(b) the structure of the economic model which describes the behaviour of these variables, and

(c) the structure of the policy rules.

It should however be noted that the assumptions about the exact composition of the information set of an economic agent with RE often is not very clearly defined in the literature, except for point (b), on which there seems to be general agreement. In any case, the information structure now defined is more or less implicit in most papers concerning policy problems in a RE framework (on this issue see also Wan, 1985). A point that is of particular importance is that the macroeconomic model upon which the private sector bases its own forecast and the model used by the Government to formulate current and future policy should be the same, so that expectations about future policy actions and policy actions themselves coincide (see Gale, 1982, chapter 1). Of course, it is assumed that the Government also has an information structure defined by the elements (a) − (b) − (c).

It follows from the above assumptions that, when the Government formulates an intertemporal optimal policy, this is correctly anticipated by the private sector, which can therefore react to current and future policy interventions. But, since the private sector's reaction is correctly anticipated by the Government, the latter takes this reaction into account when formulating its optimal policy.

Let us now see in more detail how this interaction between the Government and a RE private sector takes place. Consider again a dynamic model with RE of the type proposed by Kydland and Prescott (1977) (see equation (10.5))

$$z_{t+1} = \phi_t(z_t, u_t^2, u_{t+1}^2, \ldots, u_{t+p}^2) \tag{10.24}$$

but this time assume that $z_t' = [u_t^{1'}, x_t']$ is a vector of state variables formed by a sub-vector $u_t^1 \in U_t^1$ which represents the decision variables of the private sector, and a sub-vector $x_t \in X_t$ which represents other (non-decision) state variables; z_t is the state vector that usually characterizes macroeconometric models. $u_t^2 \in U_t^2$ is a vector of policy instruments, that is, of decision variables of the Government and u_{t+i}^2 $(i = 1, \ldots, p)$ are the expected values of these variables, as defined in (10.4).

The model described by (10.24) reflects the assumption that the private sector considers current and future policy variables as independent variables to which it can *react* (in the way described by system (10.24) itself), but upon which it cannot *act*: the private sector assumes that it is not able to influence the Government's decisions. The latter, which knows the economic model (10.24), therefore knows the reaction of the private sector to its own current and future policy actions, and optimizes its objective function with respect to its decision variables by taking into account this reaction.[9]

Assuming that the Government solves the following optimization problem (see (10.3))

$$\min_{u^2 \in U_2} J(u^2) = \min_{u_t^2 \in U_t^2} \sum_{t=t^0}^{t_f} I(z_t, u_t^2) \tag{10.25}$$

under the constraint of system (10.24), given z_{t_0}, an open-loop solution will be given by[10]

$$u_t^{2*} = \gamma_t^2(z_{t_0}), \qquad u_t^{2*} \in U_t^2, \quad t = t_0, \ldots, t_f \tag{10.26}$$

Once the Government has solved its optimization problem, and assuming for simplicity that the solution of this optimal control problem is unique, the optimal policy programme enters the private sector's information set. It seems obvious that the latter cannot know the optimal plan (10.26) until the Government has solved its optimal control problem.

The process of optimal policy formulation in a RE framework described above can therefore be seen as a process that unfolds in two different phases; this is due to the fact that the acquisition of information from the private sector takes place at two subsequent stages. There is an *initial stage* in which the private sector does not know the policy programme of the Government and, consequently, can only formulate a (generic) *optimal reaction* to the latter, a reaction described by (a part of) system (10.24). The private sector therefore has to wait until the Government computes its optimal plan, which will enter[11] the private sector's information set at a *second stage*.

On the other hand, it is clear that the Government cannot solve its optimal decision problem if it does not know the model which describes the economic system considered. And, since such a model contains, in general, the behavioural decisions of the private sector, this means that the latter has already formulated those decisions when the Government solves its own optimization problem, and that it has therefore formulated them *before* knowing the optimal policy that the Government will follow. The private sector will get to know this policy later, that is, when the Government has made its decisions: the information set of the private sector and that of the Government become equivalent, but only at this second stage. Initially, the information structure is clearly asymmetric, to the advantage of the Government.

This description of the problem of optimal policy selection under RE makes it clear that the type of interaction between the Government and the private sector is similar to the interaction between two players in a dynamic game. It should also be clear that, given the informational assumptions which underline the problem now described, the Stackelberg equilibrium solution, with the Government acting as leader, is the most appropriate solution for describing this policy problem. In particular, the global Stackelberg equilibrium solution, either open-loop or closed-loop, as defined in section 8.3.2, is based on the same assumptions that characterize the optimization problem just considered.

It is only this solution concept that makes it possible to take into account the initial informational asymmetry between the two players and the consequent sequentiality of their decisions. Furthermore, the fact that the leader announces his strategy at the beginning of the game, permits this strategy to enter the information set of the follower at a second stage of the game, in the same way that, as we have just seen, it enters the information set of the private sector in the RE framework now outlined.

The similarity of the two approaches is further confirmed by the fact that, in both cases (both when the policy problem with RE is described by a single-agent decision problem and when it is described by a Stackelberg game), there arises the problem of time inconsistency of the Government's equilibrium strategy. The causes of time inconsistency that we have analysed in the previous section and those considered in section 8.3.2 are the same. Moreover, as we also underlined in those two sections, in both cases the corresponding time-consistent solutions can be obtained by computing feedback solutions through dynamic programming methods. The sub-optimal time-consistent solution calculated in section 10.2.1 for the single-agent decision problem is comparable with the leader's feedback stagewise Stackelberg equilibrium strategy; in both cases the effects of future decisions of one of the agents (the leader) on current decisions of the other agent (the follower) are ignored. When these effects are introduced into the optimization problem, the time-inconsistent solution described in section 10.2.2 is obtained, which is again comparable with the leader's global open-loop Stackelberg equilibrium strategy.

10.4 Rational expectations in the continuous-time linear-quadratic case

The time inconsistency of optimal control decisions which arises when the private sector forms rational expectations can also be examined in continuous time. However, the reasons for time inconsistency in this framework do not appear so clearly as in the discrete-time case examined in previous sections. This is the reason why we have preferred to introduce the optimal control problem under rational expectations in the discrete-time framework first.

Consider now the differential system

$$\dot{x}_1(t) = A_{11}x_1(t) + A_{12}x_2(t) + B_1 u(t)$$
$$\dot{x}_2^e(t) = A_{21}x_1(t) + A_{22}x_2(t) + B_2 u(t)$$

(10.27)

where the state vector $x(t) \in R^n$ has been divided into two subvectors $x_1(t)$ and $x_2(t)$, i.e. $x'(t) = [x_1'(t), x_2'(t)]$. $x_1(t) \in R^p$ is a vector of so-called *predetermined* variables, that is variables whose initial values $x_1(t_0)$ are determined at time t_0. $x_2(t) \in R^{n-p}$ is a vector of so-called *non-predetermined* or *free* variables, that is variables that are free to adjust. According to the definition proposed by Buiter (1984) a variable $x(t)$ is predetermined if and only if its current value is not a function of expectations, formed at time t, of future endogenous and/or exogenous variables. Conversely, a variable $x(t)$ is non-predetermined or free if and only if its current value is a function of current expectations of future values of endogenous and/or exogenous variables (including policy instruments). Free variables can therefore respond instantaneously to changes in expectations due to 'news', and are free to take on any value and to make discrete jumps.

The economic interpretation of the distinction between predetermined and free variables is that there are some variables, such as the physical capital stock, which are predetermined, in the sense that their initial values are determined by history (i.e., by previous investment decisions), while there are other variables, such as the exchange rate or other asset prices, determined in markets dominated by speculators, which depend on the expected future evolution of the system.

As for the other symbols of (10.27), $\dot{x}_2^e(t) = x_2^e(t + dt, t)$ denotes the rational expectation about $x_2(t + dt)$ given the information available at time t, and $u(t) \in R^r$ is, as usual, the vector of policy instruments (control vector). The matrices which characterize the system are constant matrices of the required dimension. By the assumption of 'weak consistency' of expectations, $x_2^e(t, t) = x_2(t)$, and assuming further that the information set does not change over the period considered (see Buiter, 1984), $\dot{x}_2^e(t) = \dot{x}_2(t)$.

As is well known, macroeconomic models characterized by rational expectations agents posses a saddle-point dynamic structure (see, for example, Begg, 1982, chapter 3). Therefore, if there is a unique stable equilibrium, individuals can select a value for the free variables that places the economy on the stable path towards the (saddle-point) equilibrium of the system.

Assume now that the policy-maker's problem is to minimize

$$J(u) = \frac{1}{2} \int_{t_0}^{t_f} [\bar{x}_1'(t)Q_1\bar{x}_1(t) + \bar{x}_2'(t)Q_2\bar{x}_2(t) + \bar{u}'(t)R\bar{u}(t)]\, dt$$

(10.28)

under the constraint of system (10.27). As usual, the bars over the variables indicate deviations from the corresponding ideal values. We assume for simplicity that Q_1, Q_2 and R are weighting matrices of constant elements.

Applying Pontryagin's minimum principle, the solution of this linear-quadratic problem can be obtained by solving the following system of canonical equations:

$$\dot{x}_1(t) = \frac{\partial H}{\partial \lambda_1} = A_{11}x_1(t) + A_{12}x_2(t) + B_1 u(t) \tag{10.29}$$

$$\dot{x}_2(t) = \frac{\partial H}{\partial \lambda_2} = A_{21}x_1(t) + A_{22}x_2(t) + B_2 u(t) \tag{10.30}$$

$$\dot{\lambda}_1(t) = -\frac{\partial H}{\partial x_1} = -Q_1 \bar{x}_1(t) - A'_{11}\lambda_1(t) - A'_{21}\lambda_2(t) \tag{10.31}$$

$$\dot{\lambda}_2(t) = -\frac{\partial H}{\partial x_2} = -Q_2 \bar{x}_2(t) - A'_{12}\lambda_1(t) - A'_{22}\lambda_2(t) \tag{10.32}$$

$$\frac{\partial H}{\partial u} = R\bar{u}(t) + B'_1 \lambda_1(t) + B'_2 \lambda_2(t) = 0 \tag{10.33}$$

where $\lambda_1(t)$ and $\lambda_2(t)$ are the costate vectors corresponding to $x_1(t)$ and $x_2(t)$ respectively, and H represents the Hamiltonian function

$$\begin{aligned} H(x_1, x_2, \lambda_1, \lambda_2, u) = \tfrac{1}{2}[\bar{x}'_1 Q_1 \bar{x}_1 &+ \bar{x}'_2 Q_2 \bar{x}_2 + \bar{u}'R\bar{u}] \\ &+ \lambda'_1(A_{11}x_1 + A_{12}x_2 + B_1 u) \\ &+ \lambda'_2(A_{21}x_1 + A_{22}x_2 + B_2 u) \end{aligned} \tag{10.34}$$

From (10.33) we have

$$u(t) = -R^{-1}[B'_1\lambda_1(t) + B'_2\lambda_2(t)] + u^d(t) \tag{10.35}$$

Then, by substituting (10.35) into (10.29) and (10.30), and taking into account that $\bar{x}_i(t) = x_i(t) - x_i^d(t)$, $i = 1, 2$, we obtain a system of $2n$ differential equations:

$$\begin{aligned} \dot{x}_1(t) = A_{11}x_1(t) + A_{12}x_2(t) &- B_1 R^{-1}B'_1\lambda_1(t) \\ &- B_1 R^{-1}B'_2\lambda_2(t) + B_1 u^d \end{aligned} \tag{10.36}$$

$$\dot{\lambda}_2(t) = -Q_2 x_2(t) - A'_{12}\lambda_1(t) - A'_{22}\lambda_2(t) + Q_2 x_2^d(t) \tag{10.37}$$

$$\begin{aligned} \dot{x}_2(t) = A_{21}x_1(t) + A_{22}x_2(t) &- B_2 R^{-1}B'_1\lambda_1(t) \\ &- B_2 R^{-1}B'_2\lambda_2(t) + B_2 u^d \end{aligned} \tag{10.38}$$

$$\dot{\lambda}_1(t) = -Q_1 x_1(t) - A'_{11}\lambda_1(t) - A'_{21}\lambda_2(t) + Q_1 x_1^d(t) \tag{10.39}$$

This system has been written in the form of standard rational expectations models: with n predetermined variables, described by vectors $x_1(t)$ and $\lambda_2(t)$, and n non-predetermined variables, described by vectors $x_2(t)$ and $\lambda_1(t)$. The $2n$ boundary conditions – which represent the only difference with the standard optimal control problem examined in section 5.8 – are defined as follows (see Currie and Levine, 1987).

Since only the initial value of $x_1(t)$ is determined, p boundary conditions are given by

$$x_1(t_0) = x_0 \tag{10.40}$$

If the final state $x_1(t_f)$ is unspecified, then n boundary conditions are given by the transversality conditions

$$\lambda_1(t_f) = 0 \tag{10.41}$$

$$\lambda_2(t_f) = 0 \tag{10.42}$$

Furthermore, since $x_2(t)$ is a free vector, this requires that the initial value of the corresponding costate vector be defined (see Miller and Salmon, 1985a) by

$$\lambda_2(t_0) = 0 \tag{10.43}$$

which provides the remaining $n - p$ conditions.

Note that, similarly to the leader's optimization problem in the Stackelberg game examined in section 8.3.2, the costate vector $\lambda_1(t)$ associated with the predetermined state vector is free at the initial time, whereas the costate vector associated with the free state vector is predetermined at that time (i.e., $\lambda_2(t_0) = 0$). This particular feature of the optimal control problem is the mathematical reason for time inconsistency. As in the leader's case, if the optimization problem is again solved at a subsequent time s ($s > t_0$), the corresponding initial value of the costate vector $\lambda_2(s)$ should be set to zero in order to obtain the optimal trajectories for the state and control variables starting at s. However, since $\lambda_2(t)$ evolves according to (10.37), it is clearly improbable that the value of $\lambda_2(s)$ obtained from the previous optimization problem at t_0 is such that $\lambda_2(s) = 0$ (see also section 8.3).

It follows that the situation for a Government seeking to minimize its objective function, given the dynamics of a system of the type of system (10.27), is analogous to that of a leader in a Stackelberg game, as we have seen in the previous section. The optimal policies obtained in both cases will be time inconsistent.

10.5 A criticism of the use of optimal control methods and a way out of the time-inconsistency dilemma

The conclusion that intertemporal policy decisions obtained by means of dynamic optimization methods are either sub-optimal or time inconsistent has induced Kydland and Prescott to claim that optimal control methods are not appropriate for policy selection, and to suggest, as an alternative, the use of fixed policy rules. The argument put forward by these authors therefore strengthens the position of economists like Milton Friedman and the monetarist school who, for different reasons, advocated the preferability of fixed over flexible policy rules.

The criticism raised by Kydland and Prescott provides a further argument for preferring fixed to flexible (optimal) rules: time inconsistency puts a Government willing to follow an optimal policy on the horns of a dilemma since, as we have just seen, this Government will be continually tempted to revise its decisions at each stage of the planning horizon. But a Government that continually changes its own decision risks a loss of credibility *vis-à-vis* the private sector, and creates a situation of uncertainty and instability.[12] Therefore, having demonstrated that it is impossible to obtain a policy rule which is both optimal and time consistent, Kydland and Prescott come to the conclusion that it is more efficient to follow a fixed rule, which has at least the advantage of being more easily understood by the private sector.[13]

This argument has however been somehow attenuated in more recent years. Even new classical economists today accept the idea that the Government may choose policies by using optimization methods (see, for example, Lucas and Sargent, 1981; Lucas, 1987. See also section 10.10). The increasing applications of dynamic game theory to the analysis of the interaction between the Government and the private sector has also contributed to the rehabilitation of the assumption of an 'optimizing' Government.

A broad debate on the problem of time inconsistency of optimal policies has also taken place in the last decade and suggestions for the solution of this problem, or, more precisely, ways to obviate it, have been proposed. One suggestion is to consider the so-called 'reputational equilibria' (see Barro and Gordon, 1983; Barro, 1986; Levine and Currie, 1987; Rogoff, 1987). This type of equilibrium can be obtained by using policy models in which the Government has strong reasons for pre-commitment to the time-inconsistent strategy announced. The usual approach is to introduce some new elements such as 'reputation' or 'credibility' into the optimization problem of the Government, so that the risk of losing reputation and credibility in the future, as a consequence of too frequent changes in policy, may induce the Government to stick to the optimal policy calculated at the beginning of the planning horizon, even if this policy is time inconsistent.

When this type of approach is followed within the framework of dynamic games, the explicit introduction of memory strategies, as defined in section 8.2, is required. In this framework, a global time-consistent strategy for the Government (the leader) can also be obtained by assuming that it has the possibility to formulate threats or incentives so as to induce the private sector (the follower) to pursue the team-optimal solution to its own benefit (Basar and Selbuz, 1979; see also section 8.3.2 and the references therein).

When pre-commitment for the entire planning horizon is not feasible (or may seem too unrealistic in the specific policy problem under consideration), or when the Government has no means of formulating threats or incentives, dynamic game methods still provide an alternative approach for overcoming the time inconsistency dilemma. It is possible to consider those solutions that produce time-consistent equilibrium strategies. In this case, the equilibrium solution used to describe the interaction between the Government and the private sector can be a Nash equilibrium solution (either open loop or feedback), if the assumption is made that the two players have a symmetrical position in the policy game (see Buiter, 1983), or a feedback Stackelberg equilibrium solution (Basar and Haurie, 1984) if the leadership of the Government is to be retained. Another important advantage of feedback strategies (both Nash and Stackelberg),[14] is that, as we have already mentioned in chapter 8, they also have the property of subgame-perfectness in Selten's sense (1975).

As we shall see in section 10.10 dynamic games also constitute an important method for the solution of the problem raised by Lucas. However, the discussion of this point is postponed until after the exposition of the Lucas critique, which will be considered in the following sections.

10.6 Econometric policy evaluation and the Lucas critique

The use of econometric models for policy evaluation relies on the assumption that the relations which describe the behaviour of economic agents are not altered as a consequence of variations in the environment in which these agents operate. And, since a change in the policy rules constitutes a change in this environment, the above assumption implies that the behavioural relations of private agents (i.e. of the private sector) are invariant under policy changes. Lucas (1976) maintains that this assumption is false for most existing macroeconometric models and therefore criticizes the use of these models for purposes of *conditional* forecasting: that is, forecasting of the future behaviour of endogenous variables conditional on specific values of policy variables.

Methods of policy evaluation based on macroeconometric models can lead to serious errors since these models usually ignore the links between

Government actions and private sector behavioural decisions through expectations of private agents. 'To obtain the decisions ... we have to attribute to individuals some view of the behaviour of the *future* values of variables of concern to them' (Lucas, 1976, p. 263, emphasis added); and further, 'agents will have to form an opinion as to how future policy is to be made in order to decide how to react to current policies' (Lucas, 1987, p. 18). When these links are ignored the structure of the behavioural equations which characterize econometric models will vary systematically under the effects of alternative policy actions. Consequently, the results obtained from policy evaluation methods using this type of econometric model will be misleading and induce policy-makers to adopt the wrong policies.

As a consequence of the Lucas critique a new approach to the analysis of policy has been proposed by the new classical school. The analytical tools used by these economists are mainly dynamic optimization methods (in particular, optimal control and dynamic game theory), since these methods make it possible to take rigorously into account both the dynamic character of the problems considered and the interrelations between the optimal decisions of economic agents.

In the remaining sections of this chapter we shall show how the use of these mathematical methods makes it possible to deal correctly with the problem raised by Lucas. To this end, it will be useful to examine first how econometric models are generally used for policy evaluation; it will then be easier to understand the main features of the Lucas critique. Therefore, following Lucas (1976) let us consider a standard dynamic econometric model in implicit form

$$\dot{x}(t) = F[x(t), u(t), \theta, w(t)] \tag{10.44}$$

where $x(t)$ is a vector of state variables, $u(t)$ a vector of policy instruments and $w(t)$ a vector of random shocks. The form of F is determined a priori and θ is a vector of parameters estimated by using past values (observations) of $x(t)$ and $u(t)$. Reduced form models like (10.44) are usually obtained from structural equations describing behavioural relationships, identities or equilibrium conditions.

Let us now define a *policy* as a specification of actual and future values of $u(t)$. This means that we consider a change in policy not as a different single-act intervention, but as a *systematic* change in the way in which the policy variables are determined. A policy can therefore be described by a feedback rule of the form

$$u(t) = G[x(t), \psi, \mu(t)] \tag{10.45}$$

where the form of G is known, ψ is a vector of given parameters and $\mu(t)$ is a vector of disturbances. It is possible to represent alternative policy rules simply by modifying either the form of G or the values of the parameters ψ. Then, the usual practice is to evaluate the effects of these alternative policies upon the time behaviour of the endogenous variables $x(t)$. Thus, for example, consider the case of a change in ψ, from ψ to $\tilde{\psi}$, so that the new policy rule will be given by

$$\tilde{u}(t) = G[x(t), \tilde{\psi}, \mu(t)] \qquad (10.46)$$

The evaluation of the behaviour of the endogenous variables will then be obtained simply by substituting (10.46) into (10.44), that is

$$\dot{x}(t) = F[x(t), \tilde{u}(t), \theta, w(t)] \qquad (10.47)$$

The Lucas critique is addressed to this kind of policy evaluation since, as we have seen, no account is taken of the fact that the parameters of the model will not remain invariant under different policy rules. If a correct evaluation of the performance of the economic system is to be made, the effect of a change in ψ upon the behavioural vector θ must also be taken into account. Therefore, the time performance of $x(t)$ would be correctly written as

$$\dot{x}(t) = F[x(t), \tilde{u}(t), \theta(\tilde{\psi}), w(t)] \qquad (10.48)$$

This means that when simulations and forecasting are performed two different effects of a change in policy should be considered: (a) the effect on the time behaviour of $x(t)$ of a different time path of $u(t)$; and (b) the effect on the time behaviour of $x(t)$ of the induced change in θ. It follows that the evaluation of a change in policy by assuming vector θ unchanged will give rise to distorted policy indications.

An intuitive explanation of this induced change in θ is the following (Lucas, 1976; see also Shiller, 1978; Buiter, 1980 and McCallum, 1980, among others): the estimation of vector θ is obtained on the basis of a given time series of endogenous variables and policy instruments referring to the specific time interval considered. Vector θ therefore characterizes the (optimal) behaviour of private agents in a context in which policy variables have followed the time path described by the corresponding time series over the period. If we now assume, in the simulation exercise, that the policy variables follow a different path, the behaviour of private agents as indicated by the parameters θ will also be different, since a different policy rule will create different expectations about future policies. Furthermore, as Lucas (1976) asserts, changes in policy may not only give rise to slow and gradual changes in the estimated parameters θ, but can also be the cause of *immediate* changes in these parameters.

The fact that expectations are the cause of the structural changes in the decision rules of economic agents is underlined not only in Lucas' paper of

1976, but also in subsequent works such as, for example, Lucas and Sargent, 1981; Lucas 1981 and 1987. In these recent works, however, the emphasis has prevalently moved to the fact that *optimal* decision rules change as a consequence of changes in the environment. In fact, since private agents are supposed to follow an optimizing behaviour, the structural equations that form an econometric model will describe the optimal decisions of those agents. And since optimal decision rules vary systematically with changes in the decision rules of other agents (see the next section), it follows that a modification in the policy rules will alter the structure of the equations of an econometric model, that is the so-called 'structural' parameters.[15] However, the two explanations of the structural changes in decision rules can be reduced to one since, as we shall see, the optimal decision rules considered by Lucas are the result of *dynamic* optimization problems and are therefore obtained by taking into account current and future behaviour of all the relevant variables (see Lucas and Sargent, 1981). Dynamic optimization introduces *expectations* regarding future policy decisions into the decision problem of the private sector; this is a fundamental feature of the new approach to policy analysis.

10.7 The use of optimal control methods

Since the usual practice is to simulate econometric models under different policies, Lucas' 1976 paper mainly refers to this practice. However, his criticism covers all kinds of policy evaluation methods, including the more sophisticated techniques such as those based on controllability, optimal control and dynamic game theory, examined in the preceding chapters. The search for policies which either take the system along the desired path, or as close to it as possible, is carried out on the assumption that alternative policies leave the structure of the model equations unaltered. But if this assumption does not hold, it is possible that the control trajectories obtained might take the system away from the ideal path instead of leading it in its direction.

When, for example, optimal control or dynamic game analysis is performed, a policy rule like (10.45) is chosen from among all the admissible policy rules: an optimal rule is obtained as the result of the optimization of one (or more) objective function describing the preferences of policy-makers, under the constraint of an econometric model that describes the performance of the economy. However, an econometric model such as the one described by (10.44) is not a correct specification of the set of constraints since, as we have just seen, its parameters are not invariant to alternative policy rules.

The use of optimal control methods for policy evaluation has been further criticized by Sargent (1984) who provides an interesting interpretation of the Lucas critique. His argument is that the dynamic game played between the Government and the private sector during the estimation period is different from the dynamic game which is assumed to be played when the model is used for purposes of policy evaluation, and particularly, for optimal control analysis. Sargent argues that, when estimating an econometric model, it is usually assumed that the policy variables follow more or less *arbitrary* stochastic processes during the historical sample period, whereas private agents' decisions are the result of (stochastic) dynamic optimization problems. The estimates of the parameters of the econometric model are therefore obtained on the basis of these assumptions. However, when the model is subsequently used for optimal control applications, the assumption is made that the Government also optimizes, i.e. that policy instruments follow optimal time paths. The assumption of the asymmetrical behaviour[16] of the private sector and of the Government which characterized the estimation period is therefore substituted by the assumption of symmetrical behaviour, according to which both actors of the dynamic policy game optimize. Therefore, the structure of the estimated equations which describe the (optimal) behaviour of the private sector, given the first assumption, will not remain unchanged when a different assumption about the behaviour of the Government is made. It follows that the optimality of policy decisions obtained by using optimal control methods is questionable.

It should be noted at this point that, as we shall see in the following sections, some mathematical methods – in particular optimal control and dynamic games, whose use for policy evaluation is criticized by Lucas – become paradoxically the main mathematical tools of the new classical macroeconomics. It is these specific optimization methods which make it possible to build models that take into account the interrelations between economic policy rules and behavioural decisions of private agents, and thus overcome the problem raised by Lucas. Therefore the use of some specific analytical methods is not under discussion, but simply the *framework* in which those methods are normally utilized.

Finally, two points should be emphasized. First, it should be made clear that Lucas does not exclude the use of quantitative models for purposes of policy design:

useful policy discussions are ultimately based on *models*, not in the sense that policy decisions can be automated once and for all without the need for individual judgements, but in the sense that participants in the discussion must have, explicitly or implicitly, some way of making a quantitative connection between policies and their consequences. (Lucas, 1987, p. 6)

His point, therefore, is not to eliminate empirical models but to build different 'useful economic models' (ibid.) which take correctly into account the effects of alternative policy rules on the structure of the relations that describe the behaviour of private agents.

Another important point to be underlined is the fact that the critique raised by Lucas is independent of the assumption that private agents form expectations rationally, but simply requires that they take the future into account when making their behavioural decision. This evidently implies some assumption on the expectation-formation mechanism, but not necessarily that of rational expectations (see Buiter, 1980; Sims, 1982).

Of course, objections to the Lucas critique can be found in subsequent literature. They are however in general rather weak and simply set some (rather restrictive) limits to the 'area' of non-applicability of the critique (see, for example, Sims, 1982; Cooley, *et al.* 1984). It is possible to say that today the problem raised by Lucas is almost generally accepted.

The most constructive objections to the Lucas critique come from Sims (1982), who, on the one hand, accepts the theoretical implications of the critique – 'The rational expectations critique ... shows what serious errors can be made in econometric policy analysis if the response of expectation-formation mechanisms to policy is ignored'. (Sims, 1982, p. 112) – but, on the other hand, argues that the Lucas critique concerns only those changes in policy rules which are totally new, in the sense that historical data will never be able to catch the effects of similar policy actions. His main objection is that such 'permanent shifts in policy regime are by definition rare events' (ibid., p. 118) and he maintains that, in general, time series may correctly reflect the effects on private behaviour of changes in policy actions and also of expectations about future policies. His suggestion is to use reduced form models, based on vector autoregressions, for purposes of forecasting and policy evaluation. As is well known, this type of model (whose description lies outside the scope of this book; see Litterman, 1981; Sims 1980, 1982, for details) can be considered as atheoretical and the suggestion to use them is, evidently, not shared by Lucas. The following comment is fairly clear: 'for if the practical questions for which people look to economists for answers can be answered without recourse to economic theory, why do we need the theory?' (Lucas, 1981, p. 11).

10.8 Optimal behaviour of the private sector and the Lucas critique

The meaning of the Lucas critique becomes clearer when one directly considers behavioural decisions of private agents as the result of a dynamic optimization process, that is, obtained from the optimization of an intertemporal objective function which describes the preferences of these agents. For example, economic agents (or a representative economic agent) may be interested in maximizing expected utility and will therefore plan current and future consumption as the result of this maximization problem. Since maximization is carried out within a given framework – that is, the private-agent problem is solved given the constraints defined by a stochastic environment – the structure of private decisions will change when any element of these constraints changes. 'To imagine otherwise is to assume that the solution of a maximum problem does not vary with changes in the function being maximized' (Lucas, 1987, p. 11).

This problem can be analysed in a simple way by considering a dynamic linear-quadratic optimization problem (see Lucas and Sargent, 1981, Lucas, 1987, for the general case; and Chow, 1981, 1987 for the discrete-time case). Consider therefore the following linear differential system

$$\dot{x}(t) = Ax(t) + B_1 u_1(t) + B_2 u_2(t) + w(t) \tag{10.49}$$

which describes the law of motion of the state variables $x(t)$, such as, for example, the rate of inflation, income, and so on. These variables are under partial control of economic agents since, in this case, the control vector $u_1(t)$ represents the decision variables of the private sector, such as investment and consumption expenditure, whereas $u_2(t)$ represents policy instruments under the control of the Government, such as public expenditure, the rate of interest, and so on. $w(t)$ is a vector of independent and normally distributed random variables. A, B_1 and B_2 are constant matrices of conformable dimensions; this means that there are some fixed relations ('fixed techno-logy') which describe the dynamic performance of $x(t)$, given the actions of economic agents $u_1(t)$ and $u_2(t)$ and actions $w(t)$ by 'nature'. Note that the decision variables of the private sector are no longer a part of the state vector $x(t)$ as in system (10.44), but are given by the vector $u_1(t)$.

Let us assume that policy rules are described by

$$u_2(t) = G_2 x(t) + g_2 \tag{10.50}$$

where G_2 and g_2 are respectively a constant matrix and a constant vector. The stochastic process which determines $w(t)$ together with the policy rules described by (10.50) constitute the environment that private agents find themselves faced with.

By substituting (10.50) into (10.49), we obtain

$$\dot{x}(t) = \hat{A}x(t) + B_1 u_1(t) + B_2 g_2 + w(t) \tag{10.51}$$

where $\hat{A} = A + B_2 G_2$.

Now assume that the objective function of the private sector is defined by

$$J_1(u_1) = \int_{t_0}^{t_f} [\bar{x}(t)Q_1(t)\bar{x}(t) + \bar{u}'_1(t)R_1(t)\bar{u}_1(t)]\,dt \tag{10.52}$$

where $u_1 \in U_1$ represents the decisions $u_1(t)$ of the private sector for all $t \in [t_0, t_f]$ (see section 5.2); as usual the bar over the variables indicates deviations from ideal values and Q_1 and R_1 are symmetric matrices of appropriate dimensions $(Q_1 \geqslant 0;\ R_1 > 0)$. The optimal decision rule of private agents is obtained by minimizing the expectation of (10.52), given the constraint (10.51) (see chapter 5). This decision is given by

$$u_1(t) = G_1(t)x(t) + g_1(t), \quad t \in [t_0, t_f] \tag{10.53}$$

where $G_1(t)$ and $g_1(t)$ are defined by (see (5.158) and (5.159))

$$G_1(t) = -R_1^{-1}(t)B'_1K(t) \tag{10.54}$$

and

$$g_1(t) = R_1^{-1}(t)B'_1k(t) + u_1^D(t) \tag{10.55}$$

where $K(t)$ is the Riccati matrix obtained from the solution of (see (5.151))

$$\dot{K}(t) = -K(t)\hat{A} - \hat{A}'K(t) + K(t)B_1R_1^{-1}(t)B_1K(t) - Q_1(t) \tag{10.56}$$

and $k(t)$ is the solution of (see (5.152))

$$\dot{k}(t) = [K(t)B_1R_1^{-1}(t)B'_1 - \hat{A}']k(t) + K(t)B_1u_1^D(t)$$
$$- Q_1(t)x_1^D(t) + K(t)B_2g_2 \tag{10.57}$$

Since the optimization problem is a linear quadratic, multiperiod certainty equivalence holds (see Chow, 1975, chapter 7).

It can easily be seen from (10.56) and (10.57) that both $K(t)$ and $k(t)$ depend on the matrix $\hat{A}$ and, therefore, on the policy rule (10.50). Therefore, any change in G_2 will produce a change in $G_1(t)$; that is, if the policy rules change, the optimal behaviour of private agents will consequently change.

Note that, in this section, a time-invariant policy rule (10.50) and a time-invariant dynamic system (10.51) have been considered. It should however be emphasized that, when these equations are characterized by time-varying coefficients, the current optimal decisions of the private sector at time t will depend on current and future values of these coefficients, and therefore on the current and future structure of policy rules (see section 5.13). 'In other words, if we do not know the future exactly, then we cannot be expected to react now in a precise optimal manner' (Athans and Falb, 1966, p. 799). This point, which assumes great importance in the new approach to policy analysis, is also clearly underlined in Lucas and Sargent (1981).

To conclude, the dynamic optimization method just outlined serves to emphasize the fact that the so-called 'structural' behavioural equations of econometric models *cannot* be considered as structural in the sense of being invariant to alternative policy interventions. Furthermore, since this method makes it possible to take into account the effects of changes in policy rules on the behavioural equations of the private sector, it becomes the starting point of a different approach to policy evaluation which, as we shall see, allows us to overcome the Lucas critique.

10.9 Is there a response to the Lucas critique?

The problems discussed above have led both theoretical and applied research towards the formulation of economic models that might be correctly used for purposes of policy evaluation. These models should make it possible to take into account the effects of alternative policy decisions on the structure of the behavioural equations of the private sector.

Two different approaches along these lines can be singled out. The first consists in introducing explicit expectation terms into the econometric model considered. This has been done with particular reference to rational expectations. If we assume that agents form rational expectations, an econometric model in which these expectations are correctly specified can be used to evaluate alternative policies and to obtain optimal policy rules, since the assumption that agents anticipate the impact on the system of future Government policies is directly incorporated into the model. As Whiteman points out:

If agent's rational expectations, particularly of future values of policy variables, are the only potential source of reduced form parameter variation ... the parameters of the *expectational* difference equations *are* invariant to changes in policy rules. Thus, the policy problem can be viewed as one of maximizing the policy maker's objective function subject to a difference equation (or set of equations) which differ from ordinary equations (i.e., constraints), because of the presence of *expectations*. (1986, p. 1388, emphasis added)

This approach is discussed in Shiller (1978), Taylor (1979), Chow (1980a, 1981), Wallis (1980) and Whiteman (1986), among others. It clearly relies on the convinction that the Lucas critique can be considered substantially as a problem of incorrect specification of the model.

However, the above-mentioned approach involves a huge number of both theoretical and technical difficulties as far as applications are concerned. Besides the difficulty of a correct specification of expectations (see, for example, Taylor, 1980), further problems arise both from the estimation of RE models and from their use in policy simulations, forecasting and optimal control analysis.

Another approach to econometric policy evaluation has been put forward in order to deal with the Lucas critique. This approach, which has been decidely adopted by the new classical macroeconomics, is of great theoretical interest, but also presents many problems from a practical point of view. The starting point is the attempt to estimate *stable* economic relations, that is relations which are not sensitive to modifications in policy strategies or other external shocks. Then, from these stable relations, the (optimal) behaviour of economic agents should be obtained. The stable functions to be estimated are those which describe tastes and technology, since the structural parameters which characterize this type of relation should not be altered by changes in policies. 'It seems reasonable to hope that neither tastes nor technology vary systematically with variations in countercyclical policies' (Lucas, 1977, p. 12).

The theoretical basis of this approach was already laid down in Lucas (1976), though it has been proposed with greater emphasis and lucidity in Lucas and Sargent (1981). The line of research indicated by this approach seems today to be the most important issue in the new classical macroeconomics, as results from the recent books by Lucas (1987) and by Sargent (1987).

Econometric analysis should therefore focus on the estimation of the parameters of utility functions and production functions, that is, of agent's objective functions. Once these stable relations have been estimated, it is possible to derive from them economic agents' optimal decisions over the period considered. As we have seen in the previous section, the possibility of obtaining the behavioural decisions of private agents from the optimization of an intertemporal preference function makes it possible to evaluate the effects of alternative policy rules upon the structure of the behavioural equations and therefore to deal with the Lucas problem.

The main difficulty in this case lies in the estimation of the private agents objective function, from which optimal behavioural decisions must be derived. Kydland and Prescott (1980, 1982, 1988), who follow this approach, 'calibrate' their models by using parameter values obtained from prior estimates of other models (mostly 'micro' models). The parameters which cannot be determined in this way are obtained from a grid search, by selecting those values which best fit the actual data (see Kydland and Prescott, 1982, for details). A critical argument on the 'calibration' approach can be found in Singleton (1988).

Another line of research on the estimation problem derives from the works of Kennan (1979), Hansen and Sargent (1980, 1982), Sargent (1981) and Chow (1981, 1983). Although the method proposed by each of these authors is different, the approach that they follow is technically related to the so-called *inverse optimal problem* (Kurz, 1969; see also Chang, 1988); that is, the estimates of the parameters of the objective functions are obtained by making use of the optimality conditions. Thus Kennan (1979), Hansen and Sargent (1980, 1982) and Sargent (1981) obtain these estimates by means of the Euler equation, whereas Chow (1981, 1983), who considers only the case of quadratic functions, uses the matrix Riccati equation, as we saw in chapter 6 (section 6.7.1), when dealing with the estimation of the Government objective function.

With reference to the linear-quadratic case examined in the previous section, the problem consists in obtaining the parameters of function (10.52) through the estimation of systems (10.49) and (10.53), by considering the inverse of an optimal control problem. In other words, if we assume that (10.53) is the result of a linear-quadratic optimal control problem – and therefore directly related to the parameters of the objective function (10.52) – the parameters of the latter function can be obtained from the simultaneous estimation of systems (10.49) and (10.53).

Assume, as an example, that (10.53) describes consumption expenditure, that (10.49) defines the law of motion of the relevant state variables and that (10.52) is the utility function which represents consumer preferences. Since (10.53) is supposed to describe optimal behaviour of these consumers, its coefficients are directly related to those of the utility function (10.52) (see (10.54) to (10.57)). Taking these relations into account, the parameters of the utility function can be estimated through the estimation of (10.49) and (10.53). Further details can be found in the above-mentioned books by Chow. See also section 6.7.1 of this volume, where the limits of this method are discussed.

This new approach to policy evaluation presents considerable limitations as far as empirical analysis is concerned. These limitations depend on the one hand on the high number of a priori assumptions which are needed in order to solve the estimation problem,[17] and, on the other hand, on the considerable technical difficulties involved in the computations, especially when moving out of the linear-quadratic case (see Hansen and Singleton, 1982; Hotz *et al.*, 1988; Singleton, 1988). These difficulties restrict the applicability of these methods to models which are necessarily too simple.

The technical difficulties of this approach were clearly recognized by Sargent (1981, pp. 244–5): 'Remaking dynamic econometric practice so that it is consistent with the principle that agent's constraints influence their behaviour is a task that is far from finished'. Therefore, there is still a long way to go before arriving at a satisfactory procedure for estimating the parameters that characterize the so-called *stable* relations of the economy in order to be able then to evaluate, with this new type of model, alternative policy rules and so to deal correctly with the Lucas argument. However, considerable research effort in this direction is under way, as emerges from the recent articles by Hotz *et al.* (1988) and by Singleton (1988, see also the references therein).

10.10 From the Lucas critique to the dynamic game approach

In the preceeding sections we have considered the possibility of deriving (optimal) reaction functions of the private sector to alternative policy rules. No assumption has been made however as to how these policy rules were defined. In previous chapters of this book the assumption that the Government tries to stabilize the economic system by choosing optimal policies has been extensively considered. The approach followed here would be rather incomplete if account were not taken of the fact that *all* economic agents may choose their current and future actions by aiming to optimize some preference criteria. A deeper insight into the interaction between the Government and the private sector can be attained if we consider them as players in a dynamic game; this approach makes it possible to take rigorously into account the reciprocal effects of the two players' decisions.

The use of dynamic game theory as a method for analysing the mutual interaction between the Government and the private sector can be regarded as a consequence of the Lucas critique.[18] As we have seen in section 10.1, the assumption that private agents form expectations about future policies assigns an active role to the private sector, in contrast to the conventional analysis which had usually considered it as a passive player in the policy game. In this dynamic game between the Government and the private sector, each player takes into account the decisions of the other player when making his own decisions. And, since the game considered is dynamic, each player will take into account not only current but also future decisions of the other player. Expectations about future reciprocal behaviour are therefore implicitly introduced through the behavioural assumptions which characterize each equilibrium solution considered.

Lucas and Sargent (1981) provide an appealing presentation of this approach which is also reconsidered in Lucas (1987). Dynamic game methods make it possible not only to take into account the effects of policy rule modifications on the equations describing the behaviour of private agents (which is the point raised by the Lucas critique), but also to take into account the effects of modifications in the behaviour of private agents on the Government policy rules. We can therefore say that this approach not only makes it possible to overcome the Lucas critique but goes even a step further, setting Lucas' argument into a wider perspective that appears today as an important methodological basis of the new classical macroeconomics.

Let us now see what are the main assumptions and consequences of this approach. The interaction between the Government and the private sector can easily be described, if we again consider a linear-quadratic framework. Therefore assume, as above, that the law of motion of the state variables is given by

$$\dot{x}(t) = Ax(t) + B_1 u_1(t) + B_2 u_2(t) + w(t) \tag{10.58}$$

where $u_1(t)$ and $u_2(t)$ are the control vectors of the private sector and of the Government respectively.

Now assume that the objective function of the private sector (player 1) is given by

$$J_1(u_1, u_2) = \int_{t_0}^{t_f} [\bar{x}_1'(t)Q_1(t)\bar{x}_1(t) + \bar{u}_1'(t)R_{11}(t)\bar{u}_1(t)$$
$$+ \bar{u}_2'(t)R_{12}(t)\bar{u}_2(t)] \, dt \tag{10.59}$$

and the objective function of the Government by

$$J_2(u_1, u_2) = \int_{t_0}^{t_f} [\bar{x}_2'(t)Q_2(t)\bar{x}_2(t) + \bar{u}_2'(t)R_{22}(t)\bar{u}_2(t)$$
$$+ \bar{u}_1'(t)R_{21}(t)\bar{u}_1(t)] \, dt \tag{10.60}$$

where $Q_1(t)$, $Q_2(t)$, $R_{11}(t)$, $R_{12}(t)$, $R_{21}(t)$ and $R_{22}(t)$ are square matrices of the required dimensions and such that $Q_i \geqslant 0$, $R_{ii} > 0$ and $R_{ij} \geqslant 0$ ($i = 1, 2; i \neq j$); $u_i \in U_i$ ($i = 1, 2$) represents the control functions of player i defined over the whole time interval $[t_0, t_f]$ (see section 8.2).

Each player aims to minimize the expectation of his own objective function, given system (10.58) and the initial conditions $x(t_0)$. If, for example, we assume a feedback information pattern, feedback equilibrium strategies of the two players would be derived by solving the coupled matrix Riccati equations.[19] We would thus obtain

$$u_1(t) = G_1(t)x(t) + g_1(t), \qquad t \in [t_0, t_f] \tag{10.61}$$

and

$$u_2(t) = G_2(t)x(t) + g_2(t), \qquad t \in [t_0, t_f] \tag{10.62}$$

where the form of the matrices G_i and of the vectors g_i ($i = 1, 2$) will be different depending on the equilibrium solution computed. A Nash or a Stackelberg equilibrium solution can be obtained depending on the assumptions made as to the information structure and the dynamic behaviour of each player.

Since we have already discussed these different solution concepts in chapter 8, we shall not enter into details here. The important point to be emphasized is the fact that, in *all* cases, any modification in the behaviour of one player influences the structure of the relations which describe the behaviour of the other player. The matrices which characterize the structure of the decision rules of each player depend not only on the parameters of system (10.58) and on those of its own objective function, but also on the parameters of the objective function of the other player. Consequently the equilibrium strategy of the private sector (10.61) will change if the equilibrium strategy of the Government changes, and vice versa.

Furthermore, since each of the decision rules (10.61) and (10.62) at each t depends also on the parameters of the objective functions of both players regarding t and later, it follows that the equilibrium strategy of each player depends on current and *future* decisions of the other player. The equilibrium strategy of the private sector is therefore very closely linked – both through current actions and through expectations – to that of the Government, and vice versa, and will therefore change when the latter changes.

Let us now examine the practical implications of this approach in the context of economic policy analysis. If modelling of the interaction between the Government and the private sector is to be carried out along the above-mentioned lines, the objective functions of the two players must be estimated. As in the more simple case examined in the preceding section, the attention of the econometrician has to turn from the direct estimation of reduced form behavioural equations and policy-reaction functions to the estimation of preference functions both of the Government and of the private sector. Chow (1981, 1983) has extended the estimation techniques examined in the preceding section (see also section 6.7.1) to the more complex case of the estimation of the objective functions of two players. Of course, the computational complexities increase in this case while the limitations of the method remain.

The estimation method proposed by Chow for the linear-quadratic case is also based on the *inverse optimal problem* considered in section 10.9 for the case of a single decision-maker: the estimates of the parameters of the objective functions are obtained by making use of the relations that link optimal decision rules to those parameters. However, these relations are different for each different solution concept considered. This means that the relation which links, for example, the coefficients of the optimal feedback rule of the Government to the parameters of the objective functions will be different according to whether we consider a Nash or a Stackelberg equilibrium solution (and different again depending on which player takes the role of leader).

Therefore, an important consequence is that the numerical estimates of the objective functions of the Government and of the private sector will be *different*, depending on the assumptions made about the behaviour of the two players over the sample period, that is, about the type of game played over that period. Consequently, once a given assumption has been accepted (which it is presumed will be the one that best describes the effective behaviour of the players during the period considered), it should not be modified when subsequently using the model for purposes of policy evaluation. This means that, if the estimates of the objective functions of the Government and of the private sector have been obtained, for example, on the basis of a policy game described by a Nash equilibrium solution, the same functions *cannot* be used subsequently to simulate, say, a Stackelberg solution. Otherwise, the Lucas critique, which had been thrown out through the door, would come back in through the window, in a new form.

10.11 Concluding remarks

The issues discussed in this chapter show why the time-inconsistency problem and the Lucas critique can be considered as two arguments against the use of control methods for purposes of econometric policy selection. When the private sector is no longer considered purely as a passive player in the policy game, the 'traditional' methods of policy evaluation and decision may produce inappropriate policies.

However, are the two arguments mentioned above really relevant as far as policy analysis is concerned? To answer this question it is necessary to consider the two arguments separately since, in our opinion, the problem of time inconsistency is less serious and more easily avoidable, whereas the Lucas critique raises more important problems which, for the time being, are still difficult to solve.

As we have seen in section 10.5, the time-inconsistency dilemma can be obviated in many ways: by considering the reputation-credibility argument, by describing the policy problem as a symmetrical dynamic game, and so on. It is thus possible generally to compute some type of time-consistent strategy. It could still be argued, however, that the Government would be better off if it recomputed the optimal strategy at each successive stage of the planning horizon, rather than following the time-inconsistent strategy computed at the initial time or any other time-consistent strategy computed by using different equilibrium solutions, and that, therefore, it would always try to revise its decisions over time. Three different considerations can be made regarding this claim.

(i) First of all, it is worth asking to what extent the Government would really be pushed to modify its policy over time in order to improve its situation. Recent contributions[20] provide empirical evidence, in a RE framework, as to the difference between the values of the cost function of a Government that changes its optimal policy at each stage of the planning horizon and that of a Government which sticks to the policy calculated at the initial stage. The contributions show that these differences can be negligible. A Government's incentives to revise its policy may therefore be weaker than they are often assumed to be.

(ii) Even if we assume that the Government has important incentives to revise its policy over the planning period, the consequences of this revision should not be exaggerated. The revision of policies calculated at previous dates is something which has always been done by Governments of all countries at all times. The simple argument that new information is gained as time goes by would be a sufficient reason for revising the policies calculated at earlier dates. In a real and uncertain world, the private sector knows very well that there are many good reasons for the Government to reconsider its policy at each new date and therefore is unlikely to believe in any type of policy pre-commitment. Time inconsistency, therefore, seems no more than a further reason for a Government to revise its policy in a world where this revision is normally carried out.[21]

(iii) Most of the policy problems which give rise to the time inconsistency of optimal decisions are defined in a finite time horizon. This assumption increases the degree of the time inconsistency problem since, with a limited planning horizon, the Government will find it convenient to change its policy radically in the last period. As we have seen in section 10.2.2, when the Government recomputes its policy at the last stage of the planning interval, it does not need to take into account the effects of current policy either on past decisions of the private sector (which are by then a datum), or on its future decisions, since the future is no longer part of the Government's planning horizon.

The assumption of a fixed planning horizon is however rather unrealistic since, in general, no moment of time can actually be taken as *the last one*. Consider a Government which makes a policy programme for, say, three years ($t = 1, 2, 3$). It seems sensible to think that, when the third year effectively arrives and the Government revises its policy concerning this third year, it will extend its planning horizon for two more years, that is, it will recompute its policy programme for $t = 3, 4, 5$, and not just for $t = 3$, which is the assumption usually made in the literature. This simply means that Governments will always make programmes by considering the future, instead of looking, at certain given specific dates, only at the present.

If we consider optimal policies calculated according to this 'sliding plan' method, that is by overlapping the planning periods instead of considering them as limited and closed in themselves, the required modifications of optimal policies due to time-inconsistency would necessarily be attenuated and, if the economic situation has not undergone strong changes in the meantime, they might reduce to modifications of negligible magnitude.

An important point should be emphasized before concluding these comments on the time-inconsistency problem. We have seen above that this problem can be overcome by using different equilibrium solutions which give rise to time-consistent strategies. We want to stress here that these different approaches to the policy problem are not simply mathematical devices used with the sole purpose of obtaining time-consistent solutions. On the contrary, most of them reflect much more realistic assumptions about the behaviour of the private sector than those implicitly made in the RE literature. If the private sector behaves rationally, as the RE literature claims it behaves, there is no reason why it should blindly believe the announced (time-inconsistent) strategy of the Government and never realise that the latter might have incentives to renege at future dates. This would mean that the private sector does not correctly anticipate the behaviour of the Government, which in some way contradicts the assumption of RE. This assumption about the behaviour of the private sector implies that the latter can be systematically fooled by the Government even when previous experience teaches him that policy-makers will change their policies at future dates. This special behaviour of the private sector, which is fundamental for the existence of a time-inconsistency problem, can only be justified by some informational constraint which puts the private sector in an inferior position with respect to the Government, as described in section 10.3.

However, in the absence of any such constraint and in a framework in which the private sector is assumed to be an active player in the policy game and to behave rationally, there is no reason why its behaviour should be that of a follower in a Stackelberg game (see again section 10.3). Therefore, the solution of the policy problem by making use of reputational equilibria or of equilibrium solutions based on symmetrical information not only makes it possible to overcome the time-inconsistency dilemma from a mathematical point of view, but also provides a more realistic description of the policy problem in a rational world. In this type of world, in fact, the time-inconsistency problem will hardly arise.

The situation is different as far as the Lucas critique is concerned. This critique poses an important problem as regards the use of econometric models for policy evaluation and decision, and a problem which is of difficult solution. The importance of the critique still increases if we consider how the practice of econometric policy evaluation is widely spread throughout the world, both in academic research and in applied work.

Since the Lucas critique refers in particular to the use of empirical models, a response to this critique should consist in an alternative approach to the evaluation of policies from an *empirical* point of view. It is true that empirical economic analysis should be based on economic theory, as Lucas claims, and that therefore, a theoretical response to the Lucas critique was first needed. This response has arrived and has produced a new and interesting approach to macroeconomic analysis the implications of which, as we have seen, go beyond a simple answer to the Lucas critique. However, the second step – that is the use of this approach in empirical work – seems still far away. Although research has already been moving in this direction in recent years, as we have seen in section 10.9, computational barriers to the estimation of the models proposed by the new classical economics are still very high. This may explain why, notwithstanding the great diffusion of the new approach in books and specialized journals, 'traditional' macroeconometric models are still used for policy evaluation and decision throughout the world.

For the time being the lesson that applied economists can learn from the Lucas critique is to use econometric models with the awareness that the results obtained from them by the use of policy evaluation techniques may in some cases be distorted, and, therefore, that these models and techniques should be used with caution.

However, until new and alternative methods of analysis come on stream, the 'traditional' approach to policy analysis and decision – based on the 'traditional' methods of controllability, optimal control and dynamic game theory described in this book – is still likely to be used, since, as yet, it is the most rigorous approach available.

Notes

1 Introduction

1 In particular, in the realization of level regulators (see Isidori, 1979, 1986).
2 See the interesting survey by Schotter and Schwödiauer (1980). See also Rives (1975) for the early history of game theory.
3 Two important exceptions are Nyblén (1951) and Faxen (1957).
4 See, for example, the recent literature on non-linear control systems.
5 This approach was first used in economic applications by Theil (1958). See also sections 6.6 and 6.8.
6 See Goodwin (1948), Gandolfo (1981, 1988).
7 See among others Bergstrom and Wymer (1976), Knight and Wymer (1978), Kirkpatrick (1984), Sassanpour and Sheen (1984), Gandolfo and Padoan (1984, 1987), Jonson and Rankin (1986).
8 See section 1.3.

2 Mathematical preliminaries: the state space

1 The importance of state-space representations in economics has been recently stressed by Aoki (1983, 1987).
2 Let $f(t)$ be a function of time such that $f(t) = 0$ for $t < 0$, and let s be a complex variable. The *Laplace transform* of $f(t)$ that is indicated by $F(s)$, is given by

$$F(s) = \int_0^\infty e^{-st} f(t)\, dt \tag{I}$$

The Laplace transform of $f(t)$ exists if the integral (I) converges for some value s (see, for example, Ogata, 1970, chapter 2; Lepschy and Viaro, 1983, chapter 2). The role of the Laplace transform in continuous-time systems is played by the z transform in discrete-time systems.
3 See Ruberti and Isidori (1982, pp. 30–2). Here the reader will find an exhaustive analysis of the topics outlined in this section.
4 The same considerations hold in the case of time-varying systems. In this case

equation (2.1) will be given by

$$\overset{(n)}{y}(t) + a_1(t)\overset{(n-1)}{y}(t) + \cdots + a_{n-1}(t)\dot{y}(t) + a_n(t)y(t) = b_1(t)u(t)$$

which can be transformed into the state-space form as shown in the text.

3 Static and dynamic controllability

1 See Fox, Sengupta and Thorbecke (1966, p. 37), Preston and Pagan (1982, pp. 6–14), Hughes Hallett and Rees (1983, pp. 24–6). See also footnote 3.

2 The static controllability condition stated in the text remains the same if we consider a vector of constant terms (or of non-control exogenous variables) z. Equation (3.1) then becomes

$$\hat{A}y = \hat{B}u + z \tag{I}$$

which can also be written as

$$R = \hat{B}u \tag{II}$$

where $R = \hat{A}y - z$ is an m-dimensional vector. The problem of static controllability is then to show the existence of a vector u^* such that R assumes any pre-assigned value R^*.

3 When this is not the case, one or more columns of $\hat{B}$ can be expressed as a linear combination of the others. For example, let's assume that $\hat{B}$ is $m \times m$, that rank $\hat{B} = m - 1$ and that the first column of $\hat{B}$, $\hat{B}_1$, is a linear combination of the remaining $m - 1$ columns $\hat{B}_2, \ldots, \hat{B}_m$, that is $\hat{B}_1 = \alpha_2 \hat{B}_2 + \cdots + \alpha_m \hat{B}_m$. Then

$$\begin{aligned}
\hat{B}u &= \hat{B}_1 u_1 + \cdots + \hat{B}_m u_m = (\alpha_2 \hat{B}_2 + \cdots + \alpha_m \hat{B}_m)u_1 + \\
&\quad + \hat{B}_2 u_2 + \cdots + \hat{B}_m u_m = \\
&= \hat{B}_2(u_2 + \alpha_2 u_1) + \cdots + \hat{B}_m(u_m + \alpha_m u_1) = \\
&= \hat{B}_2 \hat{u}_2 + \cdots + \hat{B}_m \hat{u}_m = \\
&= [\hat{B}_2 \ \ldots \ \hat{B}_m] \begin{bmatrix} \hat{u}_2 \\ \vdots \\ \hat{u}_m \end{bmatrix}
\end{aligned}$$

Thus, even if the number of instruments is m, the fact that they are not linearly independent means that they can be reduced to an $(m-1)$ new instrument vector $\hat{u}$ whose elements are a linear combination of the elements of the instrument vector u (see Preston and Pagan, 1982, pp. 13–14).

4 Alternatively, we can say that a state x_{t_f} is *reachable*; such state can in fact be *reached* through adequate control actions.

5 The poles of the transfer function are also the eigenvalues of the matrix A (see, for example, Aoki, 1976a, chapter 2).

6 In order to make a comparison between the dynamic and the static systems, we must assume (though only in this section) that the dimension of matrix A is $m \times m$ and that of matrix B, $m \times r$.

7 The removal of this simplifying assumption would not change the substance of

the results. See, for example, Kalman, Ho and Narendra (1962), Ogata (1970, chapter 16).

8 In the case of multiple eigenvalues the Jordan canonical form of A has to be considered. See, for example, Ruberti and Isidori, 1982, chapter 4 and appendix C.

9 The removal of this simplifying assumption does not alter the substance of the analysis.

We recall that when $B_0 \overset{(n)}{u}(t) \neq 0$ the state-space form becomes

$$\dot{x} = Ax + Bu$$
$$y = Cx + Du$$

10 This assumption could be dropped if we consider the target vector $Y(s)$ as the difference between the same vector $Y(s)$ and the Laplace transform of the free response of the dynamic system (3.48) (i.e. the trajectory which is the solution of the corresponding homogeneous system). This is the approach followed by Brockett and Mesarovic (1965).

11 We refer the reader to Sain and Massey (1969), Silverman (1969), Silverman and Payne (1971), for further details of the invertibility property.

12 Notice that when state and output coincide

$$G = (sI - A)^{-1}B$$

and the N matrix becomes

$$N = \begin{bmatrix} B & AB\ldots\ldots & A^{2n-1}B \\ 0 & B & AB\ldots A^{2n-2}B \\ \ldots\ldots\ldots\ldots\ldots\ldots\ldots \\ 0 & 0\ldots B\ldots A^{n-1}B \end{bmatrix}$$

If the dimension of the state vector is n, the path controllability conditions (3.58) and (3.59) stated above become

$$\text{rank}[G_D(s)] = n$$

and

$$\text{rank}[N] = (n+1)n$$

respectively.

13 See, among others, Uebe (1977), Nyberg and Viotti (1978), Buiter and Gersovitz (1981, 1984), Wohltmann and Krömer (1983), Tondini (1984), Petit (1985a, 1987).

14 Since, we recall, $G_D(s) = G'(s)$, rank $[G_D(s)] = $ rank $[G(s)]$. Note also that, in the case in which the term $B_0 \overset{(n)}{u}(t) \neq 0$ in system (3.48), the transfer function matrix of that system is

$$G(s) = C(sI - A)^{-1}B + D$$

Therefore, the result just stated in the text is corroborated by the presence of the matrix D. In that case it is possible to have rank $[G(s)] = m$ even if rank $[C(sI - A)^{-1}B] < m$.

15 Notice that in this particular case it is as simple to verify the necessary and sufficient condition for path controllability (3.59) as it is to verify the sufficient conditions stated in section 3.6.3. As a matter of fact the first two of those conditions, which are the easiest to check, are not satisfied.

16 Another case in which dynamic point controllability will be a sufficient criterion is the case in which the final time t_f is an election date. Governments may wish to bring the economy to a given point just before an election and may attach little importance to what will happen to the economic system thereafter (see, for example, Buiter and Gersovitz, 1981; Hughes Hallet and Rees, 1983).

17 In this and in the next section we report some mathematical results, well known in the control literature, which are used exclusively in the derivation of the path controllability and stabilizability conditions (section 3.6.1 and 4.3 respectively). They can therefore be skipped on a first reading.

18 For simplicity's sake, we remove the term $Du(t)$ in (3.119). Its introduction does not alter the substance of the analysis.

19 Phase-variable canonical forms can also be obtained for systems of multiple inputs, though the procedure is more complicated. We refer the reader to Ruberti and Isidori (1982, chapter 5).

4 Different approaches to dynamic policy analysis

1 The idea of considering stabilizing control rules had also been considered by Simon (1952) in the context of production theory.

2 Doubtful cases may however arise as, for example: is a slower but monotonic convergence better than a quicker but oscillatory one? Or, is it more efficient to have a quicker convergence with oscillations of higher amplitude rather than a slower convergence with more damped oscillations? (see on this point Lange, 1970, chapter 4).

3 The reader is referred to Phillips' (1954, 1957) articles for a more complete description of his model. We focus here only on the essential elements required for a general view of his approach.

4 See Aoki (1981, chapter 10), where the concept of stabilizability is applied to an economic model.

5 System (4.6) is obtained by defining the transformed state vector

$$z(t) = T^{-1} x(t)$$

where $T = [T_1, T_2]$ is a non-singular $n \times n$ matrix such that the columns of T_1 form a basis for the q-dimensional controllable sub-space and the columns of T_2 together with those of T_1 form a basis for the whole n-dimensional space.

6 An indication of the proof of condition (ii) is the following: if the characteristic equation of a given matrix KB

$$\lambda^n + p_1 \lambda^{n-1} + \cdots + p_{n-1} \lambda + p_n = 0$$

is stable, all the coefficients $p_1, p_2, \ldots, p_n$, are strictly positive; and since

$$p_1 = -(k_1 A_1 + k_2 B_1 + k_3 C_1 + \cdots)$$
$$p_2 = +(k_1 k_2 A_2 + k_1 k_3 B_2 + \cdots)$$
$$\cdots\cdots\cdots\cdots\cdots\cdots\cdots\cdots\cdots\cdots$$
$$p_n = (-1)^n k_1 k_2 k_3 \ldots k_n A_n$$

where $k_1, k_2, \ldots, k_n$, are the elements of the main diagonal of K and A_j, B_j, C_j, ... are the j-th order principal minors of B, it follows that, if all the principal minors vanish for some j, it is no longer possible to obtain a stable characteristic equation of KB by simply choosing the values of $k_1, k_2, \ldots, k_n$.

7 Notice that, in this case, only one of the $\tilde{K}^i$ matrices ($i = 1, 2, \ldots, n!$) would be diagonal.

5 Optimal control

1 Theil (1954, 1956, 1958), Frisch (1956, 1957).

2 However, contrary to engineering applications of optimal control methods, in economics the point of arrival of the system may, in some cases, be unimportant. This is the case, for example, in the literature on optimal growth, which goes back to Ramsey (1928), where the problem is to maximize a given utility function over time and the point (or set) that the system has to reach at the end of the optimization process is of no particular concern.

3 Since this topic will not be treated here, we refer the reader to Athans and Falb, 1966, chapters 5 and 10, or to Kamien and Schwartz, 1987, sections 10, 11 and 12.

4 We may also have a different control problem when the final time t_f is not fixed in advance but is free. The *minimum time* (or *brachistochrone*) problem is an example and consists in taking the system from the initial position x_0 at time t_0 to the given final position x_f in the minimum time interval. Since we shall not deal with this problem here, we refer the reader, for example, to Athans and Falb, 1966, chapter 6, or to Intriligator, 1971, chapter 11.

5 This special problem in which a fixed-objective is attained through optimization methods is typical of the dynamic approach and could not be posed in a static context.

6 There are also some, though very few, applications of Pontryagin's principle to discrete-time macromodels. See, for example, Pindyck (1973, 1975).

7 See, just to mention some of the existing volumes, Athans and Falb (1966) and Kwakernaak and Sivan (1972) for engineering applications; and Intriligator (1971), Feichtinger and Hartl (1986), Kamien and Schwartz (1987) and Seierstad and Sydsaeter (1987) for applications to economic problems.

8 If the optimal control problem is a maximum problem, condition (5.32) becomes $\max_u H[\ldots]$ and therefore the matrix defined in condition (5.34) must be negative definite. The other conditions remain unaltered.

9 A 'smooth' hypersurface has one and only one tangent hyperplane at every point.

10 See Athans and Falb (1966, pp. 300 and ff).

11 Provided that the feasible set satisfies the required conditions. See section 6.4.

12 When the optimal control problem consists in taking the dynamic system to a given fixed-end point $x(t_f) = x_f$, the boundary conditions will be given by

$$x(t_0) = x_0, \quad x(t_f) = x_f$$

and the optimal control solution can also be obtained simply by solving the canonical system.

13 The matrix $C'Q(t)C$ is a positive semidefinite matrix since $Q(t) \geqslant 0$ and the system is observable by hypothesis.

14 See Chow, 1975, for other methods. These other methods are, however, equally cumbersome to apply to large econometric models.

15 See, for example, Karakitsos and Rustem, 1984; Currie and Levine, 1985a and b; Ghosh *et al.*, 1987, chapter 7; Rustem, 1989. We also note that, under some specific assumptions, simple macropolicy rules may coincide with the control rules obtained from the corresponding infinite horizon problem (see Levine and Currie, 1985).

16 For example, Karakitsos and Rustem, 1984, use the exchange rate and the money supply (on which daily and weekly information respectively is available) as indicators; and inflation, unemployment and current account as ultimate targets.

17 See, for example, Karakitsos and Rustem, 1984; Christodoulakis and Van der Ploeg, 1987; Holtham and Hughes Hallett, 1987; Rustem, 1988.

18 If the economic model is not linear and/or the objective function is not quadratic, adequate approximations can be performed. See, for example, Garbade (1975) and Kendrick (1980).

19 Though the name 'adaptive' control is also used sometimes to indicate a passive learning procedure.

20 See Mitchell, 1979; Stöppler, 1979.

21 See Laughton, 1964; for applications of sensitivity analysis to empirical models, see Gandolfo, 1981, chapter 6; Hughes Hallett and Rees, 1983, chapter 9.

22 An exception is Christodoulakis, 1989, where an appropriate measure that indicates the degree of robustness is derived.

23 See Chow, 1977; Becker *et al.*, 1986; Rustem, 1988. The techniques used to solve this problem require the model to be written in stacked-up form, so that static optimization algorithms can be used. This limits the applicability of these techniques to discrete-time models.

6 The objective function

1 We refer in particular to Frisch (1956, 1957) and Theil (1954, 1964) simply to indicate some of their most important contributions on the subject. Tinbergen (1952, 1954) also refers, though very briefly, to the optimization approach, but his analysis – as we have seen in chapter 3 – focusses mainly on the controllability approach.

2 This is why Frisch called this function the 'preference' function.

3 Frisch adopts other terms like 'econometrician', 'technician', 'analytical technician', 'expert' and so on. Here we shall use the term 'economist'.
4 Since Frisch considers static models, the problem of the distinction between state and output variables does not arise.
5 See section 6.4 (i) for an exception to this argument.
6 This method, described by Frisch in various articles, was described in detail in his 1969 Nobel Price lecture. See also Johansen (1974) for an excellent review.
7 Assuming, for simplicity, that matrix Q is diagonal, (6.31) can be written as

$$J(x) = \sum_{i=1}^{n} q_{ii}(x_i - x_i^D)^2$$

and, if the operations indicated are developed, as

$$J(x) = \sum_i q_{ii}(x_i^D)^2 - 2\sum_i q_{ii}x_i^D x_i + \sum_i q_{ii}x_i^2$$

which is a quadratic function of the general form of (6.13).
8 See also Hughes Hallett and Rees, 1983, chapter 10.
9 Time inseparability can be a cause of time inconsistency of optimal decisions (see Hughes Hallett and Rees, 1983, chapter 11).
10 See, for example, Cochrane and Zenely (1973) and, for a selection of more recent papers, Gruber (1983).
11 The estimation of an objective function in general decision problems can also be performed by making use of cross-section data obtained from interviews, enquiries, and so on. See, for example, Merkies and Nijman (1983).
12 The possibility of applying this method also to non-linear models is discussed in Chow (1980b, 1981).
13 An alternative is to set $Q_t = \beta^t Q$, $R_t = \beta^t R$ and $z_t^D = \phi^t z^D$ (β, ϕ constants). See Carraro 1988, 1989, for an application of Chow's approach to the estimation both of the objective function of a single policy-maker and of the objective functions of several policy-makers.
14 Wallenius (1975) observes that policy-makers find it difficult to specify their own preferences at each iteration when the number of variables in each combination is greater than seven. Notwithstanding these difficulties, a few applications of multicriteria decision methods to dynamic policy problems have been carried out (see, for example, Geoffrion and Dyer, 1972; Deissenberg, 1983).
15 This and sections 6.9 and 6.12 rely very heavily on chapter 10 of Hughes Hallett and Rees (1983), on previous papers by Ancot et al. (1982) and by Hughes Hallett and Ancot (1982). Many details and proofs have been omitted which can be found in these references.
16 In this latter case dynamic interactive methods could be extended to the continuous-time framework.
17 Stochastic terms could also be considered within vector s. See Theil (1964, chapter 4), Hughes Hallett and Rees (1983, chapter 7).
18 See Friedman (1975) for a solution algorithm and for its application to an econometric model.

19 Interaction between policy-makers will then lead to the choice of a vector $z^{(p)}$ which will represent a negotiated solution among the individual (best) choices. See Hughes Hallett and Rees (1983, chapter 10) for details.

7 Applications of optimal control

1 See Gandolfo, 1981, 1988, and section 1.4 of the present volume for a discussion on other aspects of continuous-time modelling.
2 In a continuous-time framework, the reciprocal of the speed of adjustment $(1/\alpha)$ is the mean time lag, i.e. the time necessary for about 63 per cent of the discrepancy between the actual and desired values of the variable to be eliminated. See, for example, Gandolfo 1981, chapter 1.
3 A longer horizon, 1974–81, has also been considered. The results are available on request.
4 It should suffice to consider the Lucas critique (Lucas, 1976; see also chapter 10).
5 A continuous-time model can also be stacked by calculating dynamic multipliers, but this choice would have cancelled all the advantages of working in a continuous-time framework.
6 The model considered here can be described as a system of twenty (differential) state equations and eighteen output equations.
7 The historical values over the same period were worse than the base-run results. We also note that the strong initial jump that most of the optimal paths present (of both the target and control variables) is due to the initial values given to the endogenous variables. These values are the observed (historical) values and not those corresponding to the solution of the model in that period. It follows that a certain interval of time is required for the model to adjust, after the initial jump.
8 This special result might be due to an incompatibility between the ideal rate of growth of reserves and the ideal rate of revaluation of the exchange rate, which was not present when only monetary policy was considered.
9 See Hughes Hallett and Petit (1988a, c) for an analysis of the causes of a tradeoff 'reversal'.

8 Decentralized decisions and differential games

1 Since we assume that the elements of U_i are infinite, the policy game cannot be described in matrix form or by means of a tree structure. The use of a tree structure is also ruled out by the continuous-time definition of the game which, as we have seen, implies a continuum of levels of play.
2 As we have seen in chapter 5, when the macroeconomic model considered is described by a system of differential equations of a higher order than the first, it can be reformulated in terms of the state-space form (8.1) (see also chapter 2).
3 Our choice of focussing on open-loop strategies may also be interpreted as accepting the possibility of policy commitments for the whole planning period (see Reinganum and Stokey, 1985).
4 See Starr and Ho (1969a) and Cruz (1975).

5 Also open-loop strategies can be subgame perfect in all those cases in which they coincide with feedback strategies (see above).

6 This limit may be overcome by considering the Consistent Conjectural Variations (CCV) solution concept which is simply an extension of the ideas suggested by Bowley (1924) and by Frisch (1933) within the framework of oligopoly theory (see Friedman, 1983, chapter 5; Kamien and Schwartz, 1983). The extension of the CCV solution concept to the realm of dynamic games is however quite recent (see Fershtman and Kamien, 1985; Basar, 1986), and its computation in applied work has been exclusively concerned up to now with games specified in discrete time (see, for example, Hughes Hallett, 1984a, 1986; Basar, Turnovsky and d'Orey, 1986). The CCV solution in the continuous-time case still presents unresolved problems.

7 Cohen and Michel (1984, 1988) propose the computation of a time-consistent equilibrium strategy for the leader by using Pontryagin's principle and by imposing a specific static constraint on the optimal dynamics of the follower. This solution concept, however, has been considered only in relation to infinite-horizon problems. See Miller and Salmon 1985a and b, for an application; see also Dockner and Neck, 1988 for a clarifying discussion.

8 In some cases this solution can also be subgame perfect (Tolwinski 1981).

9 In order to simplify the exposition, a terminal cost is not considered here. We refer the reader to chapter 5, since the implications of introducing a terminal cost are similar to those already examined for optimal control problems. See also Basar and Olsder, 1982, chapters 6 and 7.

10 It can be shown (Roth, 1979) that Pareto optimality is implied by the simultaneous verification of axioms (i) to (iv) stated in the text.

11 See Luce and Raiffa (1957, chapter 6) and Kalai and Smorodinsky (1975) for a criticism to this axiom.

9 Applications of differential games

1 See Balducci (1985), Neck (1985) and Dockner and Neck (1986). See also Currie and Levine (1985a) and Miller and Salmon (1985b) for applications of differential games to a problem of international policy coordination.

2 Though this assumption appears realistic, it should be noted that, whenever the monetary and fiscal authorities use different models, the outcomes obtained from cooperation may, in some cases, be worse then those derived from non-cooperation (Frankel, 1987; see also Frankel and Rockett, 1986; Holtham and Hughes Hallett, 1987).

3 See Tabellini, 1988, for further details.

4 Some exceptions are Neese and Pindyck (1984); Hughes Hallett (1986); Holtham and Hughes Hallett (1987).

5 See section 5.14.

6 We assume that each policy-maker is using the same multiplicity scale for the cost function. Thus, a loss of one unit for policy-maker i in one game is just as significant for him as a loss of one unit in a different game (see Kalai, 1977).

7 It should be noted that, when interaction with the private sector is considered

and rational expectations are assumed, cooperation between policy-makers could be counter productive as Rogoff (1985) points out for a case of international policy coordination.

8 The historical values over the period were worse than the base-run results.

9 See footnote 2.

10 See also section 7.5 and Gandolfo and Petit (1987).

10 Optimal policies and expectations

1 As we shall see in the following sections, the time-inconsistency argument is a specific critique of the use of optimal control methods in policy analysis, while Lucas' criticism, though it covers more general quantitative methods (like simulations), refers to optimal control applications also, as a particular case.

2 A few exceptions are Miller and Salmon (1985a and b), Currie and Levine (1985a and b).

3 Note that the symbols have been changed solely to bring them into line with the ones used in this book.

4 This problem does not arise in the case without expectations since x_1 does not depend on u_2. It is therefore possible to compute $\tilde{u}_{1(1)}$ at $t = 1$ without any need to consider how $\tilde{u}_{2(1)}$ has been computed.

5 The two solutions may coincide if $\partial\phi_0/\partial u_2 = 0$ or if W is independent of x_1, that is if $\partial W/\partial\phi_0 + (\partial W/\partial\phi_1)(\partial\phi_1/\partial\phi_0) = 0$ (Kydland and Prescott, 1977), two cases of scant interest.

6 It may seem unrealistic that a Government does not care about the performance of the economy after the end of the planning horizon (unless new elections or a change in Government is assumed). On the other hand, it is difficult to avoid putting a temporal upper limit to a policy programme. On this topic see section 10.11 (iii).

7 We deliberately ignore here the process of learning, that is, the process by which economic agents come to know the elements that enter their information sets. The reader is addressed, for example, to Cyert and De Groot (1974), Towsend (1978), De Canio (1979) and the articles collected in the Frydman and Phelps volume (1983).

8 It is sometimes assumed that the information set also contains past values of the relevant variables (see, for example, Begg, 1982, chapter 3). However, in our case, this point can be ignored.

9 This assumed asymmetry is usually explained by the fact that the private sector is formed by a great number of small agents which, being small, behave non-cooperatively and can only optimize for given policy (Prescott, 1977; see also section 10.11 for a critical argument).

10 The same conclusions hold if the solution is of the feedback type: in this last case, once the private sector knows the optimal feedback rule, system (10.24) can be solved for the optimal state trajectory z_t^*, and subsequently for that of u_t^{2*}, $t = t_0, \ldots, t_f$, given the initial vector z_{t_0}.

11 As we have already stressed in footnote (7) we are not here interested in how the private sector 'learns' the policy rule. However, it could be assumed, for example, that the Government announces its policy (see, for example, Hillier and Malcomson, 1984).

12 On this point see section 10.11 (ii). We also note that, by using a two period optimization model with rational expectations Fischer (1980) shows that in the case in which the Government optimizes the private sector's objective function (the so-called 'benevolent' Government) the position of the private sector will also improve if the Government reoptimizes (i.e. changes strategy) at each t. This is however a special case. We observe incidentally that time inconsistency may arise even in the case of a 'benevolent' Government (see Calvo, 1978; Turnovsky and Brock, 1980).

13 We note however that the same type of problem may arise with a fixed rule since a rational Government will want to renege and change the fixed rule at later dates if there is any incentive to do so. Furthermore, as Buiter (1981a) has shown, in an uncertain world the optimal time-inconsistent flexible rule (global closed loop) dominates the optimal time-inconsistent fixed rule (open loop), in the sense that it produces a lower value of the cost function of the Government.

14 The two equilibrium solutions, feedback Nash and feedback Stackelberg, may coincide in some specific cases (see Dockner and Neck, 1988). However, this equivalence does not hold in general, as demonstrated in Basar and Haurie, 1984.

15 Evidently the same problem arises for the reduced form parameters which, as is well known, are given by (more or less) complicated relations between the structural parameters: 'A change in policy necessarily alters some of the structural parameters ... and therefore affects the reduced form parameters in a highly complex way' (Lucas and Sargent, 1979, p. 298).

16 Sims (1980) does not agree about this assumed asymmetry, arguing that, on the contrary, Governments can also be assumed to behave optimally and that, therefore, time series concerning policy variables may reflect this optimal behaviour. There would not therefore be any change in the underlying assumptions when the model is subsequently used for policy optimization analysis (see Sargent, 1984, for a discussion on this point).

17 An alternative approach to the direct estimation of the objective function is the revealed preference method proposed by Hughes Hallett and Ancot (1982, 1983) and described in section 6.9. As we have seen there, this method makes possible the numerical determination of a local (quadratic) approximation of the matrix of the parameters in the objective function. However, the iterative process which characterizes the method is itself based on policy evaluation techniques and will therefore provide estimates of the parameters which will be invalidated by subsequent changes in policy, that is by Lucas' own argument.

18 It should be noted that a substantial boost to the use of dynamic games in policy analysis is also due to Kydland and Prescott (1977).

19 See Basar and Olsder, 1982, chapter 6; Basar and Haurie, 1984.

20 See Buiter, 1981b; Holly and Zarrop, 1983; Currie and Levine, 1987; Ghosh *et al.*, 1987, chapter 12.

21 See, on this point, Holly and Hughes Hallett, 1989, chapter 4; Westaway, 1989.

References

Allen, R.G.D., 1956, *Mathematical Economics*, London: Macmillan.

1967, *Macro-economic Theory: A Mathematical Treatment*, London: Macmillan.

Amoroso, L., 1921, *Lezioni di Economia Matematica*, Bologna: Zuffi.

Ancot, J.P. and A.J. Hughes Hallett, 1982, Consensus decisions and individual preferences in economic planning: an empirical study, *Greek Economic Review*, 4: 3–35.

Ancot, J.P., A.J. Hughes Hallett and J.H.P. Paelinck, 1982, The determination of implicit preferences: two possible approaches compared, *European Economic Review*, 18: 267–89.

Aoki, M., 1967, *Optimization of Stochastic Systems*, New York: Academic Press.

1974, Non-interacting control of macroeconomic variables, *Journal of Econometrics*, 2: 261–81.

1975, On a generalization of Tinbergen's condition in the theory of policy to dynamic models, *Review of Economic Studies*, 42: 293–6.

1976a, *Optimal Control and System Theory in Dynamic Economic Analysis*, Amsterdam: North Holland.

1976b, On decentralized stabilization policies and dynamic assignment problems, *Journal of International Economics*, 6: 143–73.

1981, *Dynamic Analysis of Open Economies*, New York: Academic Press.

1983, *Notes on Economic Time Series Analysis: System Theoretic Perspectives*, Berlin and New York: Springer–Verlag.

1987, *State Space Modelling of Time Series*, Berlin and New York: Springer–Verlag.

Aoki, M. and A. Leijonhufvud, 1976, Cybernetics and macroeconomics: a comment, *Economic Inquiry*, 24: 251–8.

Aoki, M. and M. Canzoneri, 1979, Sufficient conditions for control of target variables and assignment of instruments in dynamic macroeconomic models, *International Economic Review*, 3: 605–16.

Apostol, T.M., 1969, *Calculus*, 2nd edn New York: John Wiley & Sons.

Athans, M. and P.L. Falb, 1966, *Optimal Control*, New York: McGraw Hill.

Bacharach, M., 1976, *Economics and the Theory of Games*, London: Macmillan.

Balducci, R., 1985, È efficiente decentrare le decisioni di politica economica?, *Politica Economica*, 3: 399–428.

Barro, R.J., 1986, Recent developments in the theory of rules versus discretion, *Economic Journal*, Supplement, 36: 23–37.

Barro, R.J. and D.B. Gordon, 1983, Rules, discretion and reputation in a model of monetary policy, *Journal of Monetary Economics*, 12: 101–21.

Basar, T., 1980, Stackelberg strategies in continuous time, unpublished notes.

1986, A tutorial on dynamic and differential games, in T. Basar, ed., *Dynamic Games and Applications in Economics*, Berlin and New York: Springer-Verlag.

1989, 'Time consistency and robustness of equilibria in noncooperative dynamic games', in F. van der Ploeg and A.J. de Zeeu, eds., *Dynamic Policy Games in Economics*, Amsterdam: North-Holland.

Basar, T. and H. Selbuz, 1979, Closed-loop Stackelberg strategies with applications in the optimal control of multi-level systems, *IEEE Transactions on Automatic Control*, AC-24: 166–78.

Basar, T. and G.J. Olsder, 1982, *Dynamic Noncooperative Game Theory*, New York: Academic Press.

Basar, T. and A. Haurie, 1984, Feedback equilibria in Stackelberg games with structural and model uncertainties, in J.B. Cruz, ed., *Advances in Large Scale Systems*, vol. 1, Connecticut: JAI Press, 163–201.

Basar, T., S.J. Turnovsky and V. d'Orey, 1986, Optimal strategic monetary policies in dynamic interdependent economies, in T. Basar, ed., *Dynamic Games and Applications in Economics*, Berlin and New York: Springer-Verlag.

Basile, G. and G. Marro, 1971, On the perfect output controllability of linear dynamic systems, *Ricerche di Automatica*, 2: 1–10.

Becker, R., B. Dwolatzky, E. Karakitsos and B. Rustem, 1986, Rival models in policy optimization, *Journal of Economic Dynamics and Control*, 10: 75–81.

Begg, D.K., 1982, *The Rational Expectations Revolution in Macroeconomics*, Oxford: Philip Allan.

Bellman, R., 1957, *Dynamic Programming*, Princeton, N.J.: Princeton University Press.

Bergstrom, A.R., 1984, Continuous time stochastic models and issues of aggregation over time, in Z. Griliches and M.D. Intriligator eds., *Handbook of Econometrics*, vol. 2, chapter 20, Amsterdam: North-Holland.

1988, The history of continuous time econometric models, *Econometric Theory*, 4: 365–83.

Bergstrom, A.R. ed., 1976, *Statistical Inference in Continuous Time Economic Models*, Amsterdam: North-Holland.

Bergstrom, A.R. and C.R. Wymer, 1976, A model of disequilibrium neoclassical growth and its application to the United Kingdom, in A.R. Bergstrom, ed., *Statistical Inference in Continuous Time Economic Models*, Amsterdam: North-Holland.

Bertsekas, D.P., 1976, *Dynamic Programming and Stochastic Control*, New York: Academic Press.

1978, *Stochastic Optimal Control. The Discrete Time Case*, New York: Academic Press.

1987, *Dynamic Programming: Deterministic and Stochastic Models*, Englewood Cliffs, N.J.: Prentice Hall.

Binmore, K., A. Rubinstein and A. Wolinsky, 1985, The Nash bargaining solution in economic modelling, *LSEPS Discussion Paper* n. 112.

Borel, E., 1953, The theory of play and integral equations with skew symmetrical kernels. On games that involve chance and skill of the players. On systems of linear forms of skew symmetric determinants and the general theory of play (translated by L.J. Savage), *Econometrica*, 21: 97–117.

Bowley, A.L., 1924, *The Mathematical Groundwork of Economics*, Oxford: Clarendon Press.

Brockett, R.W. and M.D. Mesarovic, 1965, The reproducibility of multivariable systems, *Journal of Mathematical Analysis and Applications*, 11: 548–63.

Bruno, S., 1986, La scelta del decisore come processo culturalmente connotato, in Lorenzo Sacconi, ed., *La Decisione*, Milano: Franco Angeli.

Buiter, W.H., 1980, The macroeconomics of Dr. Panglos. A critical survey of the new classical macroeconomics, *The Economic Journal*, 90: 35–40.

1981a, The superiority of contingent rules over fixed rules in models with rational expectations, *The Economic Journal*, 91: 647–70.

1981b, The role of economic policy after the new classical macro-economics, in D. Currie, R. Nobay and D. Peel, eds., *Macroeconomic Analysis*, London: Groom Helm.

1983, Optimal and time-consistent policies in continuous-time rational expectations models, NBER Technical Working Paper, no. 29, Cambridge, Mass.

1984, Saddlepoint problems in continuous time rational expectations models: a general method and some macroeconomic examples, *Econometrica*, 52: 665–80.

Buiter, W.H. and M. Gersovitz, 1981, Issues in controllability and the theory of economic policy, *Journal of Public Economics*, 15: 33–43.

1984, Controllability and the theory of economic policy. A further note, *Journal of Public Economics*, 24: 127–9.

Calvo, G.A., 1978, On the time consistency of optimal policy in a monetary economy, *Econometrica*, 46: 1411–28.

Caravani, P., 1987, Modelling economic policy with non-symmetric lossess and risk aversion, *Journal of Economic Behaviour and Organization*, 8: 1–15.

Carlson, D.A. and A. Haurie, 1987, *Infinite Horizon Optimal Control*, Berlin: Springer-Verlag.

Carraro, C., 1988, The implicit objective function of Italian macroeconomic policy: 1963:1–1980:4, *Economic Modelling*, 3: 261–77.

1989, The tastes of European Central Bankers, in M. De Cecco and A. Giovannini, eds., *Monetary Regimes and Monetary Institutions: Issues and Perspectives in Europe*, Cambridge University Press.

Chang, F.R., 1988, The inverse optimal control problem: a dynamic programming approach, *Econometrica*, 56: 147–72.

Chipman, J.S., 1965, A survey of the theory of international trade: Part 2, *Econometrica*, 33: 477–519.

Chow, G.C., 1975, *Analysis and Control of Dynamic Systems*, New York: John Wiley & Sons.

1977, Usefulness of imperfect models for the formulation of stabilization policies, *Annals of Economic and Social Measurement*, 6: 175–88.

1980a, Econometric policy evaluation and optimization under rational expectations, *Journal of Economic Dynamics and Control*, 2: 1–13.

1980b, Estimation of rational expectations models, *Journal of Economic Dynamics and Control*, 2: 241–56.

1981, *Econometric Analysis by Control Methods*, New York: John Wiley & Sons.

1983, *Econometrics*, New York: McGraw-Hill.

1987, Developments of control theory in macroeconomics, in C. Carraro and D. Sartore, eds., *Developments of Control Theory for Economic Analysis*, Dordrecht: Kluwer Academic.

Chow, G.C. and S.B. Megdal, 1978, The control of large scale econometric systems, *IEEE Transaction on Automatic Control*, 2: 344–9.

Christodoulakis, N.M., 1989, Robust policy formulation using models with structural uncertainty, *Proceedings of the 6th IFAC Symposium on Dynamic Modelling and Control of National Economies*, Edinburgh.

Christodoulakis, N. and F. Van der Ploeg, 1987, Macrodynamic policy formulation with conflicting view of the economy, *International Journal of System Science*, 18: 449–76.

Cochrane, J.L. and M. Zenely, 1973, *Multiple Criteria Decision Making*, University of South Carolina Press.

Cochrane, J.L. and J.A. Graham, 1976, Cybernetics and macroeconomics, *Economic Inquiry*, 24: 241–50.

Cohen, D. and P. Michel, 1984, Towards a theory of optimal precommitment I: an analysis of the time consistent equilibria, *CEPREMAP Discussion Paper*, no. 8412.

1988, How should control theory be used to calculate a time-consistent government policy?, *Review of Economic Studies*, 55: 263–74.

Cooley, T.F., S.F. Le Roy and N. Raymon, 1984, Econometric policy evaluation: a note. *American Economic Review*, 74: 467–70.

Cooper, R.N., 1969a, Macroeconomic policy adjustment in interdependent economies, *Quarterly Journal of Economics*, 83: 1–24.

1969b, The assignment problem, in R. Mundell and A. Swoboda, eds., *Monetary problems of the international economy*.

Cournot, A.A., 1838, *Recherches sur les Principes Mathematiques de la Theorie des Richesses*, Hachette, Paris (English edition, 1960, *Researches into the Mathematical Principles of the Theory of Wealth*, New York: Kelley).

Cruz, J.B., 1975, Survey of Nash and Stackelberg equilibrium strategies in dynamic games, *Annals of Economic and Social Measurement*, 4/2: 339–45.

Culbertson, J.M., 1968, *Macroeconomic Theory and Stabilization Policy*, New York: McGraw-Hill.

Currie, D. and P. Levine, 1985a, Macroeconomic policy design in an interdependent world, in W.H. Buiter and R.C. Marston, eds. *International Economic Policy Coordination*, Cambridge University Press.

1985b, Simple macropolicy rules for the open economy, *Economic Journal* (Supplement), 95, 60–70.

1987, Credibility and time inconsistency in a stochastic world, *Journal of Economics*, 47: 225–52.

Cyert, R.M. and M.H. De Groot, 1974, Rational expectations and Bayesian analysis, *Journal of Political Economy*, 82: 521–36.

De Canio, S.J., 1979, Rational expectations and learning from experience, *Quarterly Journal of Economics*, 92: 47–57.

Deissenberg, C., 1983, Interactive solution of multiple objective, dynamic, macro-economic stabilization problems: a comparative study, in J. Gruber, ed., *Econometric Decision Models*, Berlin: Springer-Verlag.

1985, Robustifying macroeconomic policies, in G. Feichtinger, ed., *Optimal Control Theory and Economic Analysis*, 2, Amsterdam: North-Holland.

Dewald, W.G. and H.G. Johnson, 1963, An objective analysis of the objectives of American monetary policy, 1952–61, in D. Carson, ed., *Banking and Monetary Studies*, Homewood, Illinois: R.D. Irwin, Inc.

Dockner, E. and R. Neck, 1986, Cooperative and non-cooperative solutions for a linear quadratic differential game model of stabilization policies, in A. Bensoussan and J.L. Lions, eds., *Analysis and Optimization of Systems*, Berlin and New York: Springer-Verlag.

1988, Time-consistency, subgame-perfectness, solution concepts and information patterns in dynamic models of stabilization policies, mimeo, University of Vienna.

Dockner, E., G. Feichtinger and S. Jorgensen, 1985, Tractable classes of nonzero-sum open-loop Nash differential games: theory and examples, *Journal of Optimization Theory and Applications*, 45: 179–97.

Edgeworth, F., 1925, *Papers relating to Political Economy*, London: Macmillan.

Ehtamo, H. and R.P. Hämäläinen, 1986, On affine incentives for dynamic decision problems, in T. Basar, ed., *Dynamic Games and Application in Economics*, Berlin and New York: Springer-Verlag.

van Eijk, C.J. and J. Sandee, 1959, Quantitative determination of an optimum economic policy, *Econometrica*, 27: 1–9.

Falb, P.L. and W.A. Wolovich, 1967, Decoupling in the design and synthesis of multivariable control, *IEEE Transactions on Automatic Control* AC-12: 651–9.

Faxen, K.O., 1957, *Monetary and Fiscal Policy under Uncertainty*, Stocholm: Almqvist & Wicksell.

Feichtinger, G. and R.F. Hartl, 1986, *Optimal Kontrolle Okonomischer Prozesse: Anwendungen des Maximumprincips in den Wirtschaftswissenschaften*, Berlin, de Gruyter.

Fershtman, C. and M.I. Kamien, 1985, Conjectural equilibrium and strategy spaces in differential games, in G. Feichtinger, ed., *Optimal Control Theory and Economic Analysis*, 2, Amsterdam: North-Holland.

Fischer, S., 1980, Dynamic inconsistency, cooperation and the benevolent dissembling government, *Journal of Economic Dynamics and Control*, 2: 93–109.

Fisher, I., 1898, Cournot and mathematical economics, *Quarterly Journal of Economics*, 12: 119–32.

Fisher, M.E. and A.T. Fuller, 1958. On the stabilization of matrices and the convergence of linear iterative processes, *Proceedings of the Cambridge Philosophical Society*, 54: 417–25.

Fox, K.A., Sengupta, J.K. and E. Thorbecke, 1966, *The Theory of Quantitative Economic Policy with Applications to Economic Growth and Stabilization*, Amsterdam: North-Holland.

Frank, P.M., 1978, *Introduction to System Sensitivity Theory*, London: Academic Press.

Frankel, J.A., 1987, Obstacles to international macroeconomic policy coordination, *International Monetary Fund WP*, 87/29.

Frankel, J.A. and K. Rockett, 1986, International macroeconomic policy coordination when policy-makers disagree on the model, *NBER Working Paper*, no. 2059.

Friedlander, A., 1973, Macropolicy goals in the postwar period: a study in revealed preference, *Quarterly Journal of Economics*, 87: 25–43.

Friedman, A., 1971, *Differential Games*, New York: Wiley-Interscience.

Friedman, B.M., 1972, Optimal economic stabilization policy: an extended framework, *Journal of Political Economy*, 80: 1002–23.

1975, *Economic Stabilization Policy: Methods in Optimization*, Amsterdam: North-Holland.

Friedman, J.W., 1971, A non-cooperative equilibrium for super-games, *Review of Economic Studies*, 38: 1–12.

1977, *Oligopoly and the Theory of Games*, Amsterdam: North Holland.

1983, *Oligopoly Theory*, New York: Cambridge University Press.

1986, *Game Theory with Applications in Economics*, Oxford University Press.

Friedman, M., 1953, The effects of a full-employment policy on economic stability: a formal analysis, in *Essays in Positive Economics*, Chicago: University of Chicago Press.

Frisch, R., 1933, Monopole, Polypole. La notion de force dans l'economie, *Nationaleconomisk Tidsskrift*. Reprinted in *International Economic Papers*, 1 (1951): 23–36.

1949, A memorandum on price-wage-tax subsidy policies as instruments in maintaining optimal employment, UN Document E (CN1/Sub 2), New York. Reprinted as *Memorandum from Universitets Socialokonomiske Institutt*, Oslo, 1953.

1956, Macroeconomics and linear programming, in *Twentyfive Economic Essays in Honour of Eric Lindahl*, Stockholm: Ekonomisk Tidskrift.

1957, Numerical determination of a quadratic preference function for use in macroeconomic programming, *Memorandum from the Institute of Economics at the University of Oslo*, no. 14. Reprinted in Studies in honour of Gustavo del Vecchio, *Giornale degli Economisti e Annali di Economia*, 1961, 1: 43–83.

1969, From utopian theory to practical applications: the case of econometrics, Nobel Prize Lecture. Reprinted in *American Economic Review*, 1981, 71: 1–16.

Frydman, R. and E.S. Phelps, 1983, *Individual Forecasting and Aggregate Outcomes*, Cambridge University Press.

Gale, D., 1982, *Money: In Equilibrium*, Cambridge University Press.

Galperin, E.A. and N.N. Krasovskii, 1963, On the stabilization of stationary motions in nonlinear control systems, *Journal of Applied Mathematical Mechanics*, 27: 1521–46.

Gandolfo, G., 1970, La scelta degli strumenti di politica economica in regime di cambi flessibili, *Rivista di Politica Economica*, 9: 1195–208.

1974, Political monetaria e fiscale in regime di cambi fissi: il problema del coordinamento, *Rassegna Economica*, 38: 613–34.

1980, *Economic Dynamics: Methods and Models* (2nd edn), Amsterdam: North-Holland.

1981, *Qualitative analysis and Econometric Estimation of Continuous Time Dynamic Models*, Amsterdam: North-Holland.

1986, *International Economics*, Berlin and New York: Springer-Verlag.

1988, A propos de la construction des modelles macroéconomètrics: l'approche en temps continu, in J. Demongeot and P. Malgrange eds., *Biologie et Economie: les Apports de la Modelisation*, Dijon: Librairie de l'Université.

Gandolfo, G. and P.C. Padoan, 1984, *A Disequilibrium Model of Real and Financial Accumulation in an Open Economy*, Berlin and New York: Springer-Verlag.

1987, The Mark V version of the Italian continuous time model, *Quaderni dell'Istituto di Economia* n. 70, Siena.

Gandolfo, G. and M.L. Petit, 1987, Dynamic optimization in continuous time and optimal policy design in the Italian economy. *Annales d'Economie et de Statistique*, 6/7: 311–33.

1988, The optimal degree of wage-indexation in the Italian economy; rerunning history by dynamic optimization, in G. Ricci and K. Velupillai eds., *Growth Cycles and Multisectoral Economics: the Goodwin Tradition*, Berlin: Springer-Verlag.

Garbade, K.D., 1975, *Discretionary control of aggregate economic activity*, Lexington, Mass.: Lexington.

Geoffrion, A. and M. Dyer, 1972, An interactive approach for multicriterion optimization, with an application to the operation of an academic department, *Management Science* 19: 357–63.

Ghosh, S., C.L. Gilbert and A.J. Hughes Hallett, 1987, *Stabilizing Commodity Markets*, Oxford University Press.

Goodwin, R.M., 1948, Secular and cyclical aspects of the multiplier and the accelerator, in *Income, Employment and Public Policy: Essays in Honor of A.H. Hansen*, New York: Norton.

Gruber, J., 1983, Towards observed preferences in econometric decision models, Introduction to J. Gruber, ed., *Econometric Decision Models*, Berlin: Springer-Verlag.

Hansen, B., 1958, *The Economic Theory of Fiscal Policy*, London: Allen & Unwin.

Hansen, L.P. and T.J. Sargent, 1980, Formulating and estimating dynamic linear rational expectations model, *Journal of Economic Dynamics and Control*, 2: 7–46.

1982, Instrumental variable procedures for estimating linear rational expectations models, *Journal of Monetary Economics*, 9: 263–97.

Hansen, L.P. and K.J. Singleton, 1982, Generalized instrumental variable estimation of nonlinear rational expectations models, *Econometrica*, 50.

Haurie, A. and B. Tolwinski, 1984, Acceptable equilibria in dynamic bargaining games, *Large Scale Systems*, 6: 73–89.

1985, Definition and properties of cooperative equilibria in a two-player game of infinite duration, *Journal of Optimization Theory and Applications*, 46: 525–33.

1990, Cooperative equilibria in discounted stochastic sequential games, *Journal of Optimization Theory and Applications*, 64.

Henry, S.G.B., E. Karakitsos and D. Savage, 1982, On the Derivation of the 'Efficient' Philips Curve, *Manchester School*, 50: 151–77.

Heymann, M., 1968, Comments on pole assignment in multi-input controllable linear systems, *IEEE Transactions on Automatic Control*, AC-13: 748–9.

Hillier, B. and J.M. Malcomson, 1984, Dynamic inconsistency, rational expectations and optimal government policy, *Econometrica*, 52: 1437–51.

HMSO, 1978, *Committee on Policy Optimisation Report*, Cmnd 7148, London.

Holly, S. and M.B. Zarrop, 1983, On optimality and time consistency when expectations are rational, *European Economic Review*, 20: 23–40.

Holly, S. and A.J. Hughes Hallett, 1989, *Optimal Control, Expectations and Uncertainty*, Cambridge University Press.

Holtham, G. and A.J. Hughes Hallett, 1987, International policy coordination and model uncertainty, in R. Bryant and R. Portes, eds., *Global Macroeconomics: Policy Conflict and Cooperation*, London: MacMillan.

Horowitz, A.R., 1987, Loss functions and public policy, *Journal of Macroeconomics*, 4: 489–504.

Hotz, V.J., E. Kydland and G.L. Sedlacek, 1988, Intertemporal preferences and labor supply, *Econometrica*, 56: 335–61.

Hughes Hallett, A.J., 1979, Computing revealed preferences and limits to the validity of quadratic objective functions for policy optimization, *Economics Letters*, 2: 27–32.

1984a, Noncooperative strategies for dynamic policy games and the problem of time inconsistency, *Oxford Economic Papers*, 36: 381–99.

1984b, The stochastic inseparability of dynamic risk sensitive decisions, *International Journal of System Sciences*, 15: 1301–10.

1984c, Optimal stockpiling in a high-risk commodity market: the case of copper, *Journal of Economic Dynamics and Control*, 8: 211–38.

1986, Autonomy and the choice of policy in asymmetrically dependent economies, *Oxford Economic Papers*, 38: 516–44.

1989, Econometrics and the theory of economic policy: the Tinbergen-Theil contributions 40 years on, *Oxford Economic Papers*, 41: 189–214.

Hughes Hallett, A.J. and J.P. Ancot, 1982, Estimating revealed preferences in models of planning behaviour, in J.H.P. Paelinck, ed., *Qualitative and Quantitative Mathematical Economics*, Dordrecht: Martinus Nijhoff.

1983, The determination of collective preferences in economic decision models: an application to Soviet economic policy, in J. Gruber, ed., *Econometric Decision Models*, Berlin and New York: Springer Verlag.

Hughes Hallett, A.J. and H. Rees, 1983, *Quantitative Economic Policies and Interactive Planning*, Cambridge University Press.

Hughes Hallett, A.J. and M.L. Petit, 1988a, Trade-off reversals in macroeconomic policy, *Journal of Economic Dynamics and Control*, 12: 85–91.

1988b, Decentralized policies and efficient trade-offs: the costs of uncoordinated fiscal and monetary policies, *CEPR Discussion paper*, no. 251.

1988c, The reversed trade-off problem in optimal economic policy selection, in G. Feichtinger, ed., *Optimal Control Theory and Economic Analysis* 3, Amsterdam: North-Holland.

Intriligator, M.D., 1971, *Mathematical Optimization and Economic Theory*, Englewood Cliffs N.J.: Prentice-Hall.

Isidori, A., 1979, *Sistemi di Controllo*, Roma: Siderea.

1986, *I Robot Industriali*, Scienza e Dossier No. 6.

Johansen, L., 1974, Establishing preference functions for macroeconomic decision models, *European Economic Review*, 5: 41–66.

1978, *Lectures on macroeconomic planning*, Amsterdam: North Holland.

1980, Parametric certainty equivalent procedures in decision making under uncertainty, *Zeitschrift für Nationalökonomie*, 40: 257–79.

1983, On the status of the Nash type of noncooperative equilibrium in economic theory, *Scandinavian Journal of Economics*, 84, 421–41.

Jonson, P.D. and R.W. Rankin, 1986, Continuous time modelling. A report from down under, in G. Gandolfo and F. Marzano, eds., *Essays in memory of Vittorio Marrama*, Milano: Giuffrè.

Kalai, E., 1977, Proportional solutions to bargaining situations: interpersonal utility comparisons, *Econometrica*, 45: 1623–30.

Kalai, E. and M. Smorodinsky, 1975, Other solutions to Nash bargaining problem, *Econometrica*, 43: 513–18.

Kalman, R.E., 1960, Contributions to the theory of optimal control, *Boletin de la Sociedad Matematica Mexicana*, 5: 102–19.

Kalman, R.E., Y.C. Ho and K.S. Narendra, 1962, Controllability of linear dynamical systems, in *Contributions to Differential Equations*, vol. I, New York: Interscience.

Kamien, M.I. and N.L. Schwartz, 1981, *Dynamic Optimization*, Amsterdam: North Holland.

1983, Conjectural variations, *Canadian Journal of Economics*, 16: 191–211.

Karakitsos, E. and B. Rustem, 1984, Optimally derived fixed rules and indicators, *Journal of Economic Dynamics and Control*, 8: 33–64.

Karakitsos, E., B. Rustem and M. Zarrop, 1980, Robust economic policy formulation under uncertainty, PROPE DP. no. 38, Imperial College.

Kendrick, D., 1976, Applications of control theory to macroeconomics, *Annals of Economic and Social Measurement*, 5: 171–90.

1980, Control theory with applications to economics, in K.J. Arrow and M.D. Intriligator, eds., *Handbook of Mathematical Economics*, Amsterdam: North Holland.

1981, *Stochastic Control for Economic Models*, New York: McGraw Hill.

Kennan, J., 1979, The estimation of partial adjustment models with rational expectations, *Econometrica*, 47: 1441–56.

Kirkpatrick, G., 1984, Estimation, simulation and analysis of a GLOBUS prototype OECD model: preliminary results for Germany, Institut für Weltwirtschaft, Kiel.

Knight, M.D. and C.R. Wymer, 1978, A macroeconomic model of the United Kingdom, *IMF Staff Papers*, 25: 742–78.

Kunstman, A., 1984, Controlling a linear dynamic system according to asymmetric preferences, *Journal of Economic Dynamics and Control*, 7: 261–81.

Kurz, M., 1969, On the inverse optimal problem, in H.W. Kuhn e G.P. Szego, eds., *Mathematical System Theory and Economics I*, Berlin and New York: Springer-Verlag.

Kwakernaak, H. and R. Sivan, 1972, *Linear Optimal Control Systems*, New York: Wiley-Interscience.

Kydland, F., 1975, Noncooperative and dominant player solutions in discrete dynamic games, *International Economic Review*, 16: 321–35.

1976, Decentralized stabilization policies: optimization and assignment problems, *Annals of Economic and Social Measurement*, 5: 249–61.

Kydland, F.E. and E.C. Prescott, 1977, Rules rather than discretion: the inconsistency of optimal plans, *Journal of Political Economy*, 85: 473–91.

1980, A competitive theory of fluctuations and the feasibility and desirability of stabilization policy, in S. Fischer, ed., *Rational Expectations and Economic Policy*, NBER, Chicago: University of Chicago Press.

1982, Time to build and aggregate fluctuations, *Econometrica*, 50: 1345–70.

1988, The workweek of capital and its cyclical implication *Journal of Monetary Economics*, 21: 343–60.

Lange, O., 1970, *Introduction to Economic Cybernetics*, Oxford: Pergamon Press (Polish edition, Warsaw: PWN, 1965).

Laughton, M.A., 1964, Sensitivity in Dynamical System Analysis, *Journal of Electronics and Control*, 1: 577–91.

Lee, E.B., 1963, A sufficient condition in the theory of optimal control, *SIAM Journal of Control*, sez, A, 1: 241–5.

Lepschy, A. and U. Viaro, 1983, *Guida allo Studio dei Controlli Automatici*, Bologna: Patron.

Levine, P. and D. Currie, 1985, Optimal feedback rules in an open economy macromodel with rational expectations, *European Economic Review*, 27: 141–63.

1987a, Does international macroeconomic policy coordination pay and is it sustainable?: a two country analysis, *Oxford Economic Papers*, 39: 38–74.

1987b, The design of feedback rules in linear stochastic rational expectations models, *Journal of Economic Dynamics and Control*, 11: 1–29.

Litterman, R., 1981, A Bayesian procedure for forecasting with vector auto-regressions, *MIT Working Paper*.

Lucas, R.E., 1972, Expectations and the neutrality of money, *Journal of Economic Theory*, 4: 103–24.

1976, Econometric policy evaluation: a critique, *Journal of Monetary Economics*, Supplement, *Carnegie-Rochester Conference Series on Public Policy*, 1: 19–46.

1977, Understanding business cycles, *Journal of Monetary Economics*, Supplement, *Carnegie-Rochester Conference Series on Public Policy*, 5: 7–29. Reprinted in Lucas, 1981: 215–39.

1981, *Studies in Business-Cycle theory*, Cambridge, Mass.: MIT Press.

1987, *Models of Business Cycles*, Oxford: Basil Blackwell.

Lucas, R.E. and T.J. Sargent, 1979, After Keynesian macroeconomics, *Federal Reserve Bank of Minneapolis Quarterly Review*, 3. Reprinted in Lucas and Sargent, 1981: 295–321.

1981, *Rational Expectations and Econometric Practice*, London: Allen & Unwin.

Lucas, R.E. and N. Stokey, 1983, Optimal fiscal and monetary policy in an economy without capital, *Journal of Monetary Economics*, 12: 55–93.

Luce, R.D. and H. Raiffa, 1957, *Games and Decisions*, New York: John Wiley & Sons.

Makin, J.H., 1976, Constraints on formulation of models for measuring revealed preferences of policy makers, *Kyklos*, 29: 709–32.

McCallum, B., 1980, The significance of rational expectations theory, *Challenge*, 22: 37–43.

McFadden, D., 1969, On the controllability of decentralized macroeconomic systems: the assignment problem, in H.W. Kuhn and C.P. Szego, eds., *Mathematical Systems Theory and Economics I*, Berlin, New York: Springer-Verlag, 221–40.

Merkies, A.H. and T.E. Nijman, 1983, The measurement of quadratic preference functions with small samples, J. Gruber, ed., *Econometric Decision Models*, Berlin: Springer-Verlag.

Miller, M. and M. Salmon, 1985a, Dynamic games and the time inconsistency of optimal policy in open economies, *Economic Journal*, Supplement.

1985b, Policy coordination and dynamic games, in W.H. Buiter and R.C. Marston, eds., *International Economic Policy Coordination*, Cambridge University Press.

Minford, A.P.L. and D. Peel, 1983, *Rational Expectations and the New Macroeconomics*, Oxford: Montin Robertson.

Mitchell, D.W., 1979, Risk aversion and macro policy, *The Economic Journal*, 89: 913–18.

Mundell, R.A., 1960, The monetary dynamics of international adjustment under fixed and flexible exchange rates, *Quarterly Journal of Economics*, 74: 249–50.

1962, The appropriate use of monetary and fiscal policy for internal and external stability, *IMF Staff Papers*, 9: 70–9.

1968, *International Economics*, New York: McMillan.

Murata, Y., 1982, *Optimal Control Methods for Linear Discrete Time Economic Systems*, Berlin and New York: Springer-Verlag.

Nash, J.F., 1950, The bargaining problem, *Econometrica*, 18: 155–62.

1951, Non-cooperative games, *Annals of Mathematics*, 54: 286–95.

1953, Two-person cooperative games, *Econometrica*, 21: 128–40.

Neck, R., 1985, A differential game model of macroeconomic policies, in G. Feichtinger, ed., *Optimal Control and Economic Analysis 2*, Amsterdam: North-Holland, 607–32.

Neese, J.W. and R.S. Pindyck, 1984, Behavioural assumptions in decentralized stabilization policies, in Hughes Hallett, ed., *Applied Decision Analysis and Economic Behaviour*, Dordrecht: Martinus Nijhoff.

von Neumann, J., 1928, Zur theorie der Gesselschaftspiele, *Mathematische Annalen*, 100: 295, 320.

1937, Uber ein ökonomisches gleichungs-system und eine verallgemeinerung des Brouwerschen fixpunktsatzes, *Ergebnisse eines Mathematic Kolloquiums*, 8: 73–83.

von Neumann, J. and O. Morgenstern, 1944, *Theory of Games and Economic Behaviour*, 3rd edn, 1967, London: John Wiley & Sons.

Nyberg, L. and S. Viotti, 1978, Controllability and the theory of economic policy. A critical view, *Journal of Public Economics*, 9: 73–81.

Nyblén, G., 1951, *The Problem of Summation in Economic Science*, Lund: C.W.K. Cleerup.

Ogata, K., 1970, *Modern Control Engineering*, Englewood Cliffs, N.J.: Prentice Hall.

Papavassilopoulos, G.P. and J.B. Cruz, 1980, Stackelberg and Nash strategies with memory, *Journal of Optimization Theory and Applications*, 31: 253–60.

Patel R.V., M. Toda and R. Sridhar, 1977, Robustness of linear quadratic state feedback designs in the presence of uncertainty, *IEEE Transactions on Automatic Control*, AC-22: 945–7.

Patrick, J.D., 1968, The Optimum policy mix: convergence and consistency, in P.B. Kenen and R. Lawrence, eds., *The Open Economy*, New York: Columbia University Press.

1973, Establishing convergent decentralized policy assignment, *Journal of International Economics*, 3: 37–52.

Perkins, J.O.N., 1985, *The Macroeconomic Mix in the Industrialised World*, London: Macmillan.

Petit, M.L., 1984, Sulla teoria dinamica della politica economica: due approcci alternativi, *Note Economiche*, 3: 24–42.

1985a, Path controllability of dynamic economic systems, *Economic Notes*, 14: 26–42.

1985b, Aspettative razionali e giochi dinamici, *Note Economiche*, 3/4: 28–50.

1987, A system theoretic approach to the theory of economic policy, in C. Carraro and D. Sartore, eds., *Developments of Control theory for Economic Analysis*, Dordrecht: Martinus Nijhoff (Kluwer).

1989a, Fiscal and monetary policy coordination: a differential game approach, *Journal of Applied Econometrics*, 4/2.

1989b, Dalla critica di Lucas ai giochi dinamici, in L. Spaventa ed., *La Teoria dei Giochi e la Politica Economica*, Bologna: Il Mulino.

Petkovski, Dj., 1987, Time-domain robustness criteria for large-scale economic systems, *Journal of Economic Dynamics and Control*, 11: 249–54.

1989, Robustness of discrete time systems: tutorial, *Proceedings of the 6th IFAC Symposium on Dynamic Modelling and Control of National Economies*, Edinburgh.

Phillips, A.W., 1954, Stabilization policy in a closed economy, *Economic Journal*, 64, 290–323.

1957, Stabilization policy and the time form of the lagged response, *Economic Journal*, 67, 265–277.

Pindyck, R.S., 1973, Optimal policies for economic stabilization, *Econometrica*, 41: 529–60.

1975, *Optimal Planning of Economic Stabilization*, 2nd ed., Amsterdam: North Holland.

1976, The cost of conflicting objectives in policy formulation, *Annals of Economic and Social Measurement*, 5: 239–48.

1977, Optimal economic stabilization policies under decentralized control and conflicting objectives. *IEEE Transactions on Automatic Control*, AC-22: 517–30.

Pissarides, C.A., 1972, A model of British macroeconomic policy, 1955–1969, *The Manchester School*, 5: 245–56.

Pohjola, M., 1986, Applications of dynamic game theory to macroeconomics, in T. Basar ed., *Dynamic Games and Applications in Economics*, Berlin and New York: Springer-Verlag.

Pollak, R.A., 1971, Additive utility functions and linear Engel curves, *Review of Economic Studies*, 38: 401–14.

Pontryagin, L.S., V. Boltyanskii, R. Gamkrelidze and E. Mishchenko, 1962, *The Mathematical Theory of Optimal Processes*, New York: Interscience.

Pratt, J.W., 1964, Risk aversion in the small and in the large, *Econometrica*, 32: 122–36.

Prescott, E.C., 1977, Should control theory be used for economic stabilization?, in K. Brunner and A. Metzler, eds., *Optimal policies, control theory and technology exports*, Amsterdam: North Holland.

Preston, A.J., 1974, A dynamic generalization of Tinbergen's theory of policy, *Review of Economic Studies*, 41: 65–74.

Preston, A.J. and A.R. Pagan, 1982, *The Theory of Economic Policy*, Cambridge University Press.

Radner, R., 1980, Collusive behavior in noncooperative epsilon equilibria of oligopolies with long but finite lives, *Journal of Economic Theory*, 22: 136–54.

Raiffa, H., 1953, Arbitration schemes for generalized two-person games, in H.W. Kuhn and A.W. Tucker eds. *Contributions to the theory of games*, II, Annals of Mathematical Studies, 28, Princeton: Princeton University Press.

Ramsey, F., 1928, A mathematical theory of saving, *Economic Journal*, 38: 543–59.

Reinganum, J.F. and N.L. Stokey, 1985, Oligopoly extraction of a common property natural resource: the importance of the period of commitment in dynamic games, *International Economic Review*, 26: 161–73.

Reuber, G.L., 1964, The objectives of Canadian monetary policy, 1949–61. Empirical trade-offs and the reaction functions of the authorities, *The Journal of Political Economy*, 72: 109–731.

Rives, N.W., 1975, On the history of the mathematical theory of games, *History of Political Economy*, 7: 549–65.

Rogoff, K., 1984, The optimal degree of commitment to an intermediate monetary target, *Board of Governors of the Federal Reserve System*.

1985, Can international monetary policy cooperation be counterproductive? *Journal of International Economics*, 18: 199–217.

1987, Reputational constraints on monetary policy, in K. Bruner and A. Meltzer, eds., *Bubbles and other Essays*, Carnegie-Rochester Conference Series on Public Policy, vol. 26, Amsterdam: North-Holland.

Roth, A.E., 1979, *Axiomatic Models of Bargaining*, Berlin and New York: Springer-Verlag.

Ruberti, A. and A. Isidori, 1982, *Teoria dei Sistemi*, 2nd edn, Boringhieri Torino.

Rubinstein, A., 1979, Equilibrium in super games with the overtaking criterion, *Journal of Economic Theory*, 21: 1–9.

1982, Perfect equilibrium in a bargaining model, *Econometrica*, 50: 97–109.

Rustem, B., 1988, A constrained min–max algorithm for rival models, *Journal of Economic Dynamics and Control*, 12: 101–7.

1989, Optimal time consistent robust feedback rules under parameter, forecast and behavioural uncertainty, *Proceedings of the 6th IFAC Symposium on Dynamic Modelling and Control of National Economies*, Edinburgh.

Rustem, B. and K. Velupillai, 1983, On the formalization of political preferences: a contribution to the Frischian Scheme, *EUI Working Paper*, no. 69.

1984, Cooperation between politicians and econometricians and the search for optimal economic policy, *Journal of Policy Modelling*, 6: 341–50.

Rustem, B., K. Velupillai and J.H. Wescott, 1978, Respecifying the weighting matrix of a quadratic objective function, *Automatica*, 14: 567–82.

Sain, M.K. and J.L. Massey, 1969, Invertibility of linear time-invariant dynamical systems, *IEEE Transactions on Automatic Control*, 2: 141–9.

Samuelson, P.A., 1971, Turnpike theorems although tastes are intertemporally dependent, *Western Economic Journal*, 9: 21–5.

Sargent, T.J., 1979, *Macroeconomic Theory*, New York: Academic Press (2nd edn, 1986).

1981, Interpreting economic time series, *Journal of Political Economy*, 89: 213–48.

1984, Autoregressions, expectations and advice, *American Economic Review*, 74: 408–15.

1987, *Dynamic Macroeconomic Theory*, Cambridge, Mass.: Harvard University Press.

Sargent, T.J. and N. Wallace, 1975, 'Rational' expectations, the optimal monetary instrument and the optimal money supply rule, *Journal of Political Economy*, 83. Reprinted in Lucas and Sargent, 1981: 215–28.

Sassanpour, C. and J. Sheen, 1984, An empirical analysis of the effects of monetary disequilibrium in open economies, *Journal of Monetary Economics*, 13: 127–63.

Schotter, A. and G. Schwödiauer, 1980, Economics and the theory of games: a survey, *Journal of Economic Literature*, 18: 479–527.

Seierstad, A. and K. Sydsaeter, 1987, *Optimal Control Theory with Economic Applications*, Amsterdam: North-Holland.

Selten, R., 1975, Reexamination of the perfectness concept for equilibrium points in extensive games, *International Journal of Game Theory*, 4: 25–55.

Sheffrin, S.M., 1983, *Rational Expectations*, Cambridge University Press.

Shiller, R.J., 1978, Rational expectations and the dynamic structure of macro-economic models; a critical view, *Journal of Monetary Economics*, 4: 1–44.

Shubik, M., 1959, Edgeworth market games, in A.W. Tucker and R.D. Luce, eds., *Contributions to the Theory of Games*, Annals of Mathematic Studies, no. 40, Princeton: Princeton University Press.

1982, *Game Theory in the Social Sciences: Concepts and Solutions*, Boston: MIT Press.

Silverman, L.M., 1969, Inversion of multivariable linear systems, *IEEE Transactions on Automatic Control*, 3: 270–6.

Silverman, L.M. and H.J. Payne, 1971, 'Input–output structure of linear systems with applications to the decoupling problem', *SIAM Journal of Control*, 9: 199–233.

Simaan, M. and J.B. Cruz, 1973a, On the Stackelberg strategy in nonzero-sum games, *Journal of Optimization Theory and Applications*, 11: 533–55.

1973b, Additional aspects of the Stackelberg strategy in nonzero-sum games, *Journal of Optimization Theory and Applications*, 11: 613–26.

Simon, H.A., 1952, On the application of servomechanism theory in the study of production control, *Econometrica*, 247–68.

1956, Dynamic programming under uncertainty with a quadratic criterion function, *Econometrica*, 24: 74–81.

Sims, C.A., 1980, Macroeconomics and reality, *Econometrica*, 48: 1–48.

1982, Policy analysis with econometric models, *Brookings Papers on Economic Activity*, 1: 107–51.

Singleton, K.J., 1988, Econometric issues in the analysis of equilibrium business cycle models, *Journal of Monetary Economics*, 21: 361–86.

von Stackelberg, H., 1934, *Marktform und Gleichge-wicht*, Springer, Vienna. English Trans. *The Theory of the Market Economy*, 1952, Oxford University Press.

Starr, A.W. and Y.C. Ho, 1969a, Nonzero-sum differential games, *Journal of Optimization Theory and Applications*, 3: 184–206.

1969b, Further properties of nonzero-sum differential games, *Journal of Optimization Theory and Applications*, 3: 207–19.

Stöppler, S., 1979, Risk minimization by linear feedback, *Kybernetes*, 8: 171–84.

Streuff, H. and J. Gruber, 1983, The interactive multiobjective optimization method by E. Rosinger, in J. Gruber, ed., *Econometric Decision Models*, Berlin: Springer-Verlag.

Strotz, R.H., 1956, Myopia and inconsistency in dynamic utility maximization, *Review of Economic Studies*, 23: 165–80.

Tabellini, G., 1988, Monetary and fiscal policy coordination with a high public debt, in F. Giavazzi and L. Spavanta, eds., *High Public Debt: the Italian Experience*, Cambridge University Press.

Taylor, J.B., 1979, Estimation and control of a macroeconomic model with rational expectations, *Econometrica*, 47: 1267–87.

1980, Foreword, *Journal of Economic Dynamics and Control*, 2: 1–5.

Theil, H., 1954, Econometric models and welfare maximization, *Weltwirtschaftliches Archiv*, 72: 60–83.

1956, On the theory of economic policy, *American Economic Review*, 46: 360–6.

1957, A Note on certainty equivalence in dynamic programming, *Econometrica*, 25: 346–9.

1958, *Economic Forecasts and Policy*, Amsterdam: North Holland.

1964, *Optimal Decision Rules for Government and Industry*, Amsterdam: North-Holland.

Tinbergen, J., 1952, *On the Theory of Economic Policy*, Amsterdam: North Holland.

1954, *Centralization and Decentralization in Economic Policy*, Amsterdam: North-Holland.

1966, *Economic Policy: Principles and Design*, Amsterdam: North-Holland.

Tolwinski, B., 1981, Closed-loop Stackelberg solution to a multistage linear-quadratic game, *Journal of Optimization Theory and Applications*, 2: 485–501.

Tolwinski, B., A. Haurie and G. Leitmann, 1986, Cooperative equilibria in differential games, *Journal of Mathematical Analysis and Applications*, 119: 182–202.

Tondini, G., 1984, Further discussion on controllability and the theory of economic policy, *Journal of Public Economics*, 24: 123–5.

Towsend, R.M., 1978, Market anticipations, rational expectations, and Bayesian analysis, *International Economic Review*, 19: 481–94.

Turnovsky, S.J. and W.A. Brock, 1980, Time consistency and optimal government policies in perfect foresight equilibrium, *Journal of Public Economics*, 13: 183–212.

Tustin, A., 1953, *The Mechanism of economic systems*, Cambridge, Mass.: Harvard University Press.

Uebe, G., 1977, A note on Aoki's perfect controllability of a linear macro-economic model, *Review of Economic Studies*, 46: 191–2.

Vines, D., J.M. Maciejowski and J.E. Meade, 1983, *Demand Management*, London: Allen & Unwin.

Wallenius, J., 1975, Comparative evaluation of some interactive approaches to multicriterion optimization, *Management Science*, 21: 1387–96.

Wallis, K.F., 1980, Econometric implications of the rational expectations hypothesis, *Econometrica*, 48: 49–73.

Wan, H.Y. Jr., 1985, The new-classical economics. A game theoretic critique, in G.R. Feiwel, ed., *Issues in Contemporary Macroeconomics and Distribution*, London: MacMillan.

Waud, R.N., 1976, Asymmetric policy maker utility functions and optimal policy under uncertainty, *Econometrica*, 44: 53–66.

Westaway, P.F., 1989, Does time-inconsistency really matter?, *Proceedings of the 6th IFAC Symposium on Dynamic Modelling and Control of National Economies*, Edinburgh.

Whiteman, C.H., 1986, Analytical policy design under rational expectations, *Econometrica*, 54: 1387–405.

Whittle, B., 1983, *Optimization over Time: Dynamic Programming and Stochastic Control*, New York: Wiley.

Wohltmann, H.W., 1984, A note on Aoki's conditions for path controllability of continuous-time dynamic economic systems. *Review of Economic Studies*, 51: 343–9.

Wohltmann, H.W. and W. Krömer, 1983, A note of Buiter's sufficient condition for perfect output controllability of a rational expectations model, *Journal of Economic Dynamics and Control*, 6: 201–5.

1984, Sufficient conditions for dynamic path controllability of economic systems, *Journal of Economic Dynamics and Control*, 7: 315–30.

Wonham, W.M., 1967, On pole assignment in multi-input controllable linear systems, *IEEE Transactions on Automatic Control*, 12: 660–5.

1974, *Linear Multivariate Control: A Geometric Approach*, Berlin: Springer Verlag.

Wymer, C.R., 1972, Econometric estimation of stochastic differential equation systems, *Econometrica*, 40: 565–77.

1976, Continuous-time models in macro-economics: specification and estimation, paper presented at the SSRC-Ford Foundation Conference, Ware, England.

various dates, Continest Programme.

Zheng, Y.P., T. Basar and J.B. Cruz, 1984, Incentive Stackelberg strategies for deterministic multi-stage decision processes, *IEEE Transactions on Systems, Man and Cybernetics*, SMC-14: 10–20.

Author Index

Subject Index

Heterick Memorial Library
Ohio Northern University

DUE	RETURNED	DUE	RETURNED
1.		13.	
2.		14.	
3.		15.	
4.		16.	
5.		17.	
6.		18.	
7.		19.	
8.		20.	
9.		21.	
10.		22.	
11.		23.	
12.		24.	

Heterick Memorial Library
Ohio Northern University
Ada, Ohio 45810